THE BETRAYAL

THE
BETRAYAL

THE 1919 WORLD SERIES AND THE BIRTH
OF MODERN BASEBALL

CHARLES FOUNTAIN

OXFORD
UNIVERSITY PRESS

OXFORD

UNIVERSITY PRESS

Oxford University Press is a department of the
University of Oxford. It furthers the University's objective
of excellence in research, scholarship, and education
by publishing worldwide.

Oxford   New York

Auckland   Cape Town   Dar es Salaam   Hong Kong   Karachi
Kuala Lumpur   Madrid   Melbourne   Mexico City   Nairobi
New Delhi   Shanghai   Taipei   Toronto

With offices in

Argentina   Austria   Brazil   Chile   Czech Republic   France   Greece
Guatemala   Hungary   Italy   Japan   Poland   Portugal   Singapore
South Korea   Switzerland   Thailand   Turkey   Ukraine   Vietnam

Oxford is a registered trade mark of Oxford University Press
in the UK and in certain other countries.

Published in the United States of America by
Oxford University Press
198 Madison Avenue, New York, NY 10016

Library of Congress Cataloging-in-Publication Data
Fountain, Charles.
The betrayal : the 1919 World Series and the birth of modern
baseball / Charles Fountain.
pages   cm
Includes bibliographical references and index.
ISBN 978-0-19-979513-0
1. Chicago White Sox (Baseball team)—History.
2. World Series (Baseball) (1919)
3. Baseball—Corrupt practices—United States—History.
4. Baseball—United States—History.   I. Title.
GV875.C58F68   2015
796.35709773'1109041—dc23   2015010575

5 7 9 8 6 4

Printed in the United States of America
on acid-free paper

IN LOVING MEMORY OF

William Francis Fountain

Contents

THE BETRAYAL

Introduction

1919 and Its Legacies

We will never know precisely how the fixing of the 1919 World Series began. White Sox first baseman Chick Gandil claimed that it was in Boston, with ten days left in the 1919 regular season. Gandil had a visit from old friend Sport Sullivan while the first-place White Sox were in town to play the Red Sox. The two men met in the Hotel Buckminster in Kenmore Square, just a few yards beyond the left-field fence—there was no Green Monster as yet—of Fenway Park. The two men talked of fixing the World Series; Gandil told the Boston gambler he could deliver the fixers; the gambler told the ballplayer he could get the money; and a dark piece of American history had its genesis. That's what Gandil said in a *Sports Illustrated* article in 1956. And author Eliot Asinof put it into the popular legend in the opening of *Eight Men Out*, which remains the best known if also the least-reliable book on the subject. For years, before they remodeled the place in the early twenty-first century, the Buckminster displayed a brass plaque in the lobby, claiming it as the birthplace. And what bespeaks history more authoritatively than a brass plaque?

Or perhaps its first moment came on September 18, the week before that Gandil-Sullivan meeting in Boston, when the White Sox were in New York, and ex-big-league pitcher Sleepy Bill Burns met with Gandil and Eddie Cicotte in the lobby of the Hotel Ansonia on Broadway and 73rd Street and told them he thought he could get the flamboyant gangster Arnold Rothstein to finance a fix. That was what Burns testified to under oath in 1921.

It also could have started in the Ansonia the day before that, when Gandil and Fred McMullin asked Eddie Cicotte what it would take to get him on board in a plot to throw the Series, and the Sox star pitcher told them he wouldn't do it for anything less than $10,000. That was what Cicotte told a Chicago grand jury when he confessed in September of 1920, on the day that eight White Sox became forever known as the "Black Sox."

It could also have all begun a week and a half before that Ansonia meeting, on September 8, when the White Sox were on the train to Washington to begin their final eastern swing of the season, and a group of them got to talking about the rumors they had heard around Chicago that summer about the Cubs taking money to tank the 1918 World Series against the Red Sox. One player said he had heard some of the Cubs had gotten $10,000 each. Another one said: maybe we could get some of that money this year. That was how Cicotte, once again, remembered it all beginning when he came clean to his boss Charles Comiskey, before he went before the grand jury on that September day it all came undone.

Or maybe Eddie Cicotte was misremembering what really happened when he talked to Comiskey and the grand jury. Maybe he had not been a last-minute conspirator after all, but instead one of the instigators, and had been thinking fix as early as the beginning of August, two full months before the Series even began. That was third baseman Buck Weaver's story; he told an investigator working for Comiskey that the first he had heard that anyone on the team was thinking of throwing the 1919 World Series was when Cicotte approached him during the team's second trip to Boston in early August.

Maybe it didn't all start with Cicotte or Gandil or Sullivan, but with Arnold Rothstein. According to one-time Cubs owner Charlie Weegham, testifying before that 1920 grand jury, Rothstein not only financed the fix; he conceived it, and controlled it from the very beginning, before it was certain the White Sox would even play in the Series. Weegham had heard that in Saratoga Springs, New York, where he spent the month of August, along with Rothstein—who ran a high-end gambling house called The Brook—and much of the rest of America's gambling elite. Weegham had heard this from Mont Tennes, the doyen of Chicago gambling and believed to control the horseracing wire nationwide. Tennes told Weegham that it was all set—the Series was going to be fixed. Tennes, Weegham testified, had heard it from Rothstein himself.

Maybe it wasn't Rothstein, but one of the other gamblers who started it all, like Carl Zork of St. Louis or David Zelcer of Des Moines. They were the gamblers indicted in the case, the ones who eventually stood trial with the White Sox players.

Another theory is that the notion to throw the Series got going in mid-July, when the White Sox nearly went on strike after their owner refused to consider their request to bump up their deflated 1919 salaries in light of the unexpectedly high attendance the Sox were enjoying that year.

Others argue that its seeds are somewhere in the 1918 season, when the government shut down horse racing for the duration of the war, and the gamblers—the big ones, the ones who ran the pools, marshaling up several hundred to several thousand dollars and then taking bets from all comers—shifted their base of operations from the race track to the ballpark. The baseball magnates—the team owners—happy to just be in business after having been declared a "non-essential industry" by the War Department, effectively ignored the gamblers, who became a little more brazen around the ballparks.

The whole thing could have had its roots in 1917, two years before the series, right after the White Sox had won the World Championship by beating the Giants four games to two, when the entire White Sox team, together with the entire Giants team, had to petition the National Commission, the organization running Major League Baseball, for the release of their full World Series' shares. The commission had been withholding $1,000 of each winning and losing share, to ensure that the White Sox and Giants players did not violate a ban on post-season exhibitions by the World Series clubs, an edict that had been frustrating World Series participants for years and, not surprisingly, was quite regularly violated.

Maybe it was something or somebody else entirely that made it happen, persons or events that eluded the notice of ballplayers and investigators in 1919 and 1920, and have eluded the notice of historians ever since.

We really don't know. The Black Sox story is like a puzzle with a thousand pieces. Any five hundred pieces come together nicely and make a clear picture. That leaves a lot of pieces left on the side. Fit some of the extra pieces in and those too make a clear picture, but now some of the pieces in the first picture have come out. Try to force them all in and you're breaking off the edges, or layering the pictures on top of one another to the point where all sense of order and clarity is blurred.

We don't even know whether the Series was even fixed—whether the White Sox lost because they were trying to lose or because the Reds simply beat 'em. The Black Sox scandal is baseball's eternal mystery. It has villains and victims—some innocent and some not so innocent. It has betrayal, double-crosses, and a few—surprisingly few, really—people of principle and conscience who tried to do the right thing, despite the odds against them. It poses questions large and small, many of which remain unanswered nearly a century later and likely always will.

But just as there is much that remains unknown about the Black Sox story, there is much that is known and yet has been ignored or underappreciated. The story of the Black Sox scandal isn't merely the story of a few players who tried to play crooked and got caught. It is also the story of vain and powerful men who refused to see beyond their own self-interest, even when it actually hurt their self-interest. Behind the Black Sox story stretches a long history of organizational dysfunction and incorporated hypocrisy. The scandal resulted in the hiring of a strong commissioner, though he was brought in less to clean up baseball than as a tool of revenge in a bitter personal rivalry.

And it is a story with many legacies. Governance of Major League Baseball today may be less dysfunctional than in the pre-Babe Ruth, dead-ball era, but vain and powerful men still rule it, disagreeing among themselves as to how to best divide the billions of dollars in revenue baseball generates. And modern players still fall prey to temptation. In the Black Sox' day, the reserve clause and depressed salaries left players vulnerable to the temptation of gambling and game fixing. In the twenty-first century, free agency and hundred-million-dollar contracts leave players vulnerable to the temptation of performance-enhancing drugs.

So we revisit the Black Sox story because settled history is never fully settled, and because it holds a mirror up to the game as it is played today.

Ultimately the Black Sox scandal is the story of the loss of a sport's collective innocence, and the coming of a collective pain that has lingered for much of a century. Whether one comes to believe the accused players guilty or innocent, the perception remains that they betrayed baseball and the many millions who believed in the game's sanctity, and the virtue and principle of the men who played it. But the Black Sox players were also among the betrayed—first by the gamblers, and later by their boss and his lawyers, and by others in a criminal justice system in which they had placed their trust.

And, as the decades have passed, there has been the growing sense that some of the players who were banished—mainly Buck Weaver and Joe Jackson, but to some degree Eddie Cicotte, Lefty Williams, Happy Felsch as well—have been betrayed by the judgment of history. Damning these men for what they did is much more convenient than understanding their reasons.

However it all began, and whatever it all means, here are the things we do know beyond a certain measure of doubt: eight members of the American League champion Chicago White Sox discussed throwing the 1919 World Series, and seven of them agreed to do it, in return for the promise of somewhere between

$5,000 and $50,000 per man from gamblers or groups of different gamblers, who stood to reap many times that number by betting against the heavily favored White Sox in their series against the National League champion Cincinnati Reds. The players received only a fraction of the money they were promised. Some of the gamblers in the loop won big; others supposedly in the loop lost everything.

It has never been satisfactorily determined what any of the conspirator players may have done to lose any of the games. There are uncharacteristic plays and some suspicious moments, but over the course of nearly a century there has been no confirmation that any of the plays, however carefully dissected, were indeed deliberate errors. Most of the conspirator players—those who said anything at all—later claimed they played their best throughout. There were a few admissions about "laying down," but these were general mea culpas; no specific, deliberate failures were ever cited.

Rumors of something crooked swirled about the Series in 1919 but were not given serious credence until nearly a full year later, when an unrelated allegation of game fixing by the Chicago Cubs and a newspaper story in Philadelphia prompted Eddie Cicotte, Joe Jackson, and Lefty Williams—victims of their own lack of guile and some ethically questionable legal advice—to confess their supposed sins to a Chicago grand jury. The confessions led to indictments, though not for throwing baseball games; there was nothing illegal about throwing a baseball game in 1919. The players were indicted on an array of arcane charges, the most comprehensible of which was conspiring to injure the business and reputation of the Chicago White Sox and the team's owner, Charles A. Comiskey. The players stood trial in 1921 and were swiftly acquitted of all charges, to the joyous shouts of a courtroom crowded with baseball fans, and smiles from the jurors and the judge alike.

And we know as certainly as we know anything in baseball history that the day after their acquittal, the eight players, "regardless of the verdicts of juries," were banned from the game for life by Judge Kenesaw Mountain Landis, baseball's new commissioner, brought into the game precisely because of the intrigue and speculation surrounding the 1919 World Series.

While there will forever be much that is in doubt about the 1919 World Series, what is beyond any measure of uncertainty is that it changed baseball and American sport. However accidentally the scandal came to light, however clumsily the whole process unfolded, however callously the players involved may have been treated, however much it may have exposed the workings of organized baseball as inept and corrupt, the Black Sox scandal was a cleansing moment for baseball. The 1919 World Series is baseball's tipping point, maybe its most significant pivotal moment.

Baseball and crooked baseball had grown up together, good twin and evil twin; gambling and throwing games were as much a part of early baseball as spitballs, bunts, and doubleheaders. The 1919 World Series is the moment that finally forced baseball to stop condoning the impropriety. The banished White Sox players paid not only for their own sins but for those of generations of crooked ballplayers and their enablers in the front office and the press box. Had the moment arrived less dramatically, it may not have arrived at all, and over time baseball might have devolved into little more than a vehicle for the betting men, a sort of American jai alai, the final score a far less important stat than the day's handle.

What made the 1919 scandal erupt was that it involved the sport's best team and some of its best players. Celebrity and talent offered no protection. If Joe Jackson, arguably the game's biggest star at the time, could be cast aside and banned for life, along with Buck Weaver, who didn't take any money, didn't throw any games, didn't do anything wrong except refuse to rat out his team-mates, this signified a marked change. After 1919, it was no longer a guessing game as to what would happen to players if they got caught gambling or trying to fix a game. Baseball rule 21 (a) and (d)—posted prominently on the walls of major league clubhouses to this day—left no uncertainty about the magnitude of the crime:

> 21 (a) MISCONDUCT IN PLAYING BASEBALL. Any player or person connected with a club who shall promise or agree to lose, or to attempt to lose, or to fail to give his best efforts towards the winning of any baseball game with which he is or may be in any way concerned; or who shall intentionally fail to give his best efforts towards the winning of any such baseball game, or who shall solicit or attempt to induce any player or person connected with a club to lose, or attempt to lose, or to fail to give his best efforts towards the winning of any baseball game with which such other player or person is or may be in any way connected; or who, being solicited by any person, shall fail to inform his Major League President and the Commissioner....
>
> (d) BETTING ON BALL GAMES. Any player, umpire, or club official or employee, who shall bet any sum whatsoever upon any baseball game in connection with which the bettor has no duty to perform shall be declared ineligible for one year. Any player,

umpire, or club or league official or employee, who shall bet any sum whatsoever upon any baseball game in connection with which the bettor has a duty to perform shall be declared permanently ineligible.

Few twentieth century players, walking past that notice every day, have dared test just how serious Major League Baseball was about prosecuting violations. Pete Rose—every bit as iconic a figure in his day as Shoeless Joe Jackson was in his—was one who did; and he found that A. Bartlett Giamatti and his successors did a good job channeling Judge Landis when it came to meting out the punishment for gambling.

Pivotal social moments rarely have a tidy beginning, whether the event is the American Revolution or the 1919 World Series. It starts with a whisper, a rumor, a sense of disbelief that it can even be done. Gradually, however, the lights and the volume get turned up, the conversation circle expands ever outward, and what once seemed fantastically impossible eventually seems not only possible but inevitable. Understanding how the Black Sox scandal happened begins with understanding how baseball was governed in the early twentieth century.

"Organized baseball" was rather slow to become organized over its first four decades. Indeed, for much of the nineteenth century, baseball was a loose confederation of independent teams operating as independent businesses. Early teams in the 1860s and 1870s belonged to what was known as the National Association of Baseball Players, in the same way different business might join the Chamber of Commerce. The National Association was a support group, not a governing body.

The formation of the National League in 1876, the first fully professional league, brought with it a certain measure of organization and governance. The National League, known in its day simply as the "League," had an assertive president—William Hulbert, also the owner of the League franchise in Chicago—who had the power to set a schedule, determine territorial rights for franchises, and, as we will see, discipline players who cheated or threw games. National League membership was limited—it was determined that schedule making was impractical for more than eight teams; moreover, League owners believed there was not enough baseball talent for more than eight highest-level teams, and to add others would damage competitiveness and dilute the on-field product to the detriment of ticket sales and the bottom line. Lesser professional leagues sprouted in the smaller cities, and while the terms "major league" and "minor league" were slow to evolve, the class system was quickly established. These lesser leagues were mostly regional endeavors, where team owners made a good percentage of their money not from ticket sales but from selling the contracts of their best players to League teams.

The National League's most dramatic contribution to the game's stability was the establishment of the reserve clause in 1878. Owners realized that competition for the best players was driving up player salaries to the point where it was threatening the profitability of all but the most successful franchises. This threatened to create a caste system, where the teams with the most money would buy up all the best players and dominate play on the field, further threatening the bottom line of the lesser franchises and thus the overall business model of the League. So the owners agreed to add a provision to the standard player contract, which would hold the player "in reserve," meaning that after the contract period was over the player would be prohibited from negotiating or signing with any other League team so long as his original team held him in reserve.

The reserve clause would be the core of the professional baseball business model for the next century.

While the National League was establishing a solid internal structure, it faced challenges from without. The game's growing popularity in the late nineteenth century, and the National League's limited geographical footprint, ensured that others would soon stake a claim to playing "major league" baseball. The most important of these challenges came from the American Association, which thrived in the 1880s. The quality and success of the American Association prompted a swift recognition that it would be in everyone's interests to broker a peace. Détente with the National League led to what became known as the "National Agreement," a pact between the National League, the American Association, and a number of minor leagues to respect the territorial rights of the franchises in other National Agreement leagues, and most significantly to honor the reserve-clause contracts of all teams party to the National Agreement. The coming of the National Agreement in 1883 marked the beginning of what we know today as "organized baseball."

The National Agreement did not end the challenges to National League hegemony. The growing unpopularity of the reserve clause among players led to the Brotherhood League in 1890. A number of the best players in the National League and the American Association jumped to the Brotherhood League on the promise that players would be partners in the new endeavor, sharing in the team's profits, and free to move from team to team when contracts expired. The Brotherhood teams never caught on with fans, however, and the experiment lasted but one season.

Finally came the American League. The American League had existed for years as the Western League, but moved into some new cities and changed its name in 1900 and, in 1901, announced that it would henceforth be a second major league, no longer a party to the National Agreement, and ready to sign away National League stars, which it did by the wagonload. The American League, with its former National League stars, gained instant parity at the box office, and after two years of war the National League sued for peace. In 1903, the American League once again became a part of the National Agreement, and, as part of the American-National league peace accord, a governing tribunal called the National Commission was established. It was comprised of the two league presidents and a chairman, chosen from among the ranks of the owners.

But baseball peace did not mean baseball tranquility. The two leagues remained as much rivals as partners, and personal enmity, suspicion, self-interest, and argument dominated the boardrooms of organized baseball under the National Commission.

Organized baseball under the National Commission faced little threat from without—the short-lived, underfunded Federal League in 1914–15 was the only external challenge to its hegemony. But under the National Commission organized baseball had to contend instead with threats from within. The men in charge of baseball were so busy guarding the gates of their garden—from outsiders, but mostly from each other—they had no time to notice and tend to the weeds—gambling and game fixing chief among them—that were sprouting and threatening to overwhelm the garden.

Those looking for the headwaters of the Black Sox scandal can look to 1903, the first year of peace between the American and National leagues, when the White Sox were actually the beneficiaries of some thrown games in their intercity series with the Cubs. In that first year of peace, in addition to the series between league champions Boston and Pittsburgh, the cities with teams in each league—Philadelphia, St. Louis, and Chicago—staged wildly popular intercity series. There was quite a bit of league pride, as well as city bragging rights, at stake in these series. But what was mostly at stake was a pile of extra money for everyone involved; the exhibition games drew some of the biggest crowds of the season.

The Cubs–White Sox games in question were hardly baseball's first fixed ball games; fix scandals dated to the Civil War. But baseball seemed to have beaten back the tide of game fixing by the 1880s, and the previous twenty years had been mostly scandal free. So the Cubs–White Sox games marked a disquieting return of a problem baseball's magnates had thought solved. But more importantly, it marked the first time game fixing came before the National Commission.

The awkward, ineffectual governing structure was still in place in 1919, though the events of 1919 would prove its final undoing. Had they more decisively handled things in 1903, the National Commission might have survived the Black Sox. More importantly, there might never have been a Black Sox scandal.

The White Sox and Cubs played fourteen games in that 1903 series, and each team won seven. But Cubs owner James Hart was convinced it was only because pitcher Jack Taylor—who had won twenty-one games for the Cubs during the regular season but lost three in the city series—had been bought. He shipped Taylor off to the Cardinals during the off-season, and when the Cardinals came to Chicago for the first time in 1904, Cubs fans berated their former ace for his performance against the White Sox, and Hart told the Chicago sportswriters why he had traded the pitcher. The writers naturally asked Taylor about it.

"Why should I have won?" Taylor brazenly told reporters. "I got $100 from Hart for winning, and I got $500 for losing."

The National Commission investigated. The tribunal comprised National League president Harry Pulliam, American League president Ban Johnson, and Cincinnati Reds president August A. (Garry) Herrmann. They initially ignored Hart's charges against Taylor, but the pitcher quickly found himself in more trouble, almost immediately accused of throwing a July game against the Pirates. Both the National League board of directors and the National Commission held hearings on the matter in the 1904–05 off-season.

Taylor's defense was classic. He admitted to committing most every sin a man could commit, except throwing baseball games. He had been roaring drunk the night before the game in Pittsburgh, he said, and gambling heavily; and he got up the next morning and drank some more in the hours before the game against the Pirates, hoping his manager wouldn't pitch him. He had also once used loaded dice in a crap game against some teammates, he confessed, but only because they had earlier cheated him with a deck of marked cards. "I am not a saint," he told the hearing. "I have generally kept myself in shape during the playing season, but at times have dissipated. I have shot craps, and have played poker. But that doesn't show that I am a baseball crook, and I challenge anyone to prove that I ever made a dishonest dollar on the diamond."

The Taylor case demonstrated the timidity and feebleness of the men who ran organized baseball, particularly the men of the National Commission. The National League exonerated Taylor of the game-throwing charge, but fined him $300 for conduct prejudicial to the game off the strength of his confession to all his other transgressions. The National Commission did even less than that. They issued a terse report saying that Taylor's own statements could not be held against him because they were hearsay. "The evidence submitted, alleging that the player made certain remarks relative to the post season games of 1903, is insufficient to find him guilty of conduct detrimental to the welfare and good repute of the game," read their report. American League owners, still eager to seize any chance to embarrass the long-entrenched National League, laid the blame for whole kerfuffle at the feet of Cubs owner Hart, arguing that it was his embarrassment at having lost to the White Sox that led him to make the charges. Charles Comiskey went even further. He claimed that Hart's allegations had besmirched baseball and requested the National Commission rewrite its report on the Taylor case to include a censure of Hart.

The baseball public, meanwhile, cried whitewash. The *Chicago Tribune*'s I. E. Sanborn called the report of the National Commission "the weakest effort ever produced." Pittsburgh Pirates club secretary W. H. Locke, in a prescient letter to Commission chairman Garry Herrmann, acknowledged that the Taylor storm would soon blow over, because "the newspapers are willing to drop the case and allow the people to forget it as they surely will if the baseball men refuse to talk about it." But the price of refusing to talk about it and sweeping the Taylor case aside was likely to be high, he warned.

"If Taylor escapes punishment the crusade will be a difficult one, as gamblers will be convinced that the league is only bluffing."

That is exactly what happened. Four decades of hard work by organized baseball to rid the game of gambling and fixes all came undone in the National Commission's see-no-evil, hear-no-evil, speak-no-evil approach to the Jack Taylor case. The timidity loosened the shackles on would-be fixers and crooked ballplayers, and proclaimed open season once again for illicit baseball. Game fixing, there from the game's very beginning and never fully eliminated, flourished afresh, and—abetted by the denial of organized baseball, a too-cautious press, and a largely indifferent paying public—built inevitability toward 1919, when professional baseball's moment of reckoning arrived.

ONE

"Honorable Joes"

Gamblers and ballplayers sat comfortably in one another's company over the first half-century of the game. They were something of a like kind, the "ballists" and the "sporting men"—misfits of a sort, intriguing yet slightly ignoble men whom decent, churchgoing America consigned to the edges of proper society, even as it devoured stories about their lives in the newspapers. "Players often bet," remembered Chick Gandil. "After the games, they would sit in lobbies and bars with gamblers, gabbing away. Most of the gamblers we knew were honorable Joes who would never think of fixing a game. They were happy just to be booking and betting." Believing that most gamblers were "honorable Joes"—particularly those gamblers who sought out the company of ballplayers and traveled the baseball circuit—might require a bit more faith in the goodness of man than most people innately possess. So numerous were the gamblers drawn into baseball's orbit in the first years of the game that even if most were indeed honorable, that still left plenty who were not content to be just "booking and betting," but were instead looking to work some angle. And what gambler, honorable or not, isn't forever looking to improve the odds—to be a part of the sure thing?

The Civil War had been over but five months when baseball had its first game-fixing scandal. In September of 1865, one William Wansley, catcher for the New York Mutuals, was paid $100 by a gambler named Kane McLaughlin to make sure that the Mutuals lost their game that week to the Brooklyn Eckfords. Wansley obliged, sharing the money with two teammates he had recruited to help. He more than did his part in losing the game, going hitless in five at-bats and allowing six passed balls in fewer than five innings behind the plate, as the Eckfords prevailed 23–11. Fans in the crowd of 3,500 at Hoboken's Elysian Fields cried fix; the Mutuals players met following the game and charged Wansley with "willful and designed inattention." He confessed to his complicity and gave up his accomplices, and all three were banned from the National Association of Base Ball Players, the rules and practices organization that was the closest thing the game had to a governing body in those early, ostensibly amateur days. The punishment was short-lived; all three banished players were playing again for other teams within a year, and formally reinstated within three.

During its short existence, the National Association, which officially became the National Association of Professional Base Ball players in 1871, was a cesspool of gambling and game fixing. Few Americans alive today have ever encountered the word "hippodroming"—an arcane and archaic term that most modern dictionaries have dropped. But it was a familiar word to nineteenth-century baseball fans. They would have seen it in the newspaper several times a season, and known that it meant "conducting or engaging in a contest, the results of which have been prearranged." And readers would have known that the word's appearance in a newspaper story meant the writer either knew or suspected—and newspaper reporters in the 1870s often made no distinction between suspicion and evidence—that yet another baseball game had been crooked.

The New York Mutuals, the team that apparently inaugurated game fixing, was controlled by Tammany Hall kingpin William Marcy "Boss" Tweed and implicated in so many early game-fixing allegations that when shortstop Tom Carey had a particularly frightful defensive day in a New York *win* over Boston, the newspapers suspected the worst. "Carey could not apparently throw the game all by himself," reported one journalist.

These early fixes were hardly subtle affairs; the wanton ineptitude of the fixers on the field hardly escaped the notice of fans, writers, and teammates. Player after player was thrown off his team, only to be invariably picked up by another club, in violation of the agreement that banishment from one National Association club for gambling or game fixing meant banishment from all. The fixers even began to acquire a certain celebrity. In 1875 the *Brooklyn Eagle* named a "rogue all star" team, a position-by-position rundown of those most skillful and incorrigible of the suspected hippodromers. Early sports journalist Henry Chadwick, a strident crusader against gambling and game fixing, whose contributions to baseball would earn him a spot in Cooperstown, warned that the game would collapse under the weight of these relentless scandals. "It cannot be denied that hippodroming has prevailed," he wrote in 1872, "or that rum drinking as well as pool selling and gambling has prevailed on some prominent ball grounds of the country during the past two years."

The game did not collapse, as Chadwick predicted, but the National Association did, in 1875, under the weight of the hippodroming and the National Association's impotence against it. At the start of 1876, it was replaced by the beginnings of the modern National League, in the hopes of turning baseball into "a respectable, honorable and profitable business." Nonetheless the new organization welcomed into its ranks of players most of the hippodromers from the National Association, and it took just a year before it too was rocked by a game-fixing scandal. The difference between the new National League and the old National Association came in the National League's treatment of the guilty.

The scandal involved the Louisville Grays, which had led the league for most of the 1877 season before a late-season swoon left them in second place behind perennial champion Boston. The Grays had also suffered a late-season swoon in the business office. The debt-ridden team had not paid its players since the month of August; fans had taken to passing the hat to help the players pay their rent.

It was a newspaper reporter who first sniffed something foul. John Haldeman of the *Louisville Courier-Journal*, who had traveled all season with the team (he had even played second base one day when the team was shorthanded), was a particularly privileged and well-connected reporter. His father, William Haldeman, owned both the newspaper John worked for and the team he covered. Haldeman began noticing a lot of late-season miscues, and further noticed that the men committing those miscues suddenly began sporting diamond stickpins and flashy rings. He also noticed that a substitute by the name of Al Nichols was receiving an inordinate number of telegrams, sometimes several a day. Haldeman went to Grays team president Charles Chase, who had been receiving some telegrams himself, most of them warning him to watch his team. Chase confronted Nichols, demanding so see the telegrams he had been getting. Nichols refused; Chase told him that a refusal was tantamount to an admission of guilt. Haldeman printed the story. Nichols ultimately confessed to being the go-between between a New York gambler and three of the Grays regulars—Jim Devlin, who had pitched every inning of every one of the team's sixty-one games that season; left fielder George Hall, a lifetime .345 hitter; and shortstop Bill Craver, a member of that *Brooklyn Eagle* "all-rogue team," whose National Association career included a dismissal from the Chicago White Stockings in 1870 for fixing games and suspicion in game-fixing incidents during his time with the Troy Haymakers and the New York Mutuals.

Devlin and Hall also confessed to their part in a scheme to throw seven games during the season, including two nonleague exhibitions, which was where the fixing started. Craver maintained his innocence. Nonetheless he was expelled from the club together with the others. Conveniently, the expulsions also gave the bankrupt team cause to announce that the back pay they owed the four players was "hereby declared forfeited."

For the first time in the dozen-odd years that the game had been combating the crookedness, the expulsions stood. In December of 1877, the National League reviewed the actions taken by the Louisville club and made the expulsions league-wide, "for conduct in contravention of the objects of this League." And the players swiftly discovered that, contrary to baseball history to that point, the league meant what it said. The players could not find work. In the immediate aftermath of their suspensions from Louisville, Devlin and Hall signed with St. Louis for the 1878 season, but never got to play there. St. Louis, together with the Louisville franchise, went out business shortly thereafter; but the contracts would have been voided anyway by the league action in December. Devlin and Hall next tried to find work in the minor leagues, signing contracts with Utica for the 1878 season, but they found the reach of the National League now extended throughout all of baseball. Pressure from the National League, and newspaper pressure from the influential Henry Chadwick, caused Utica to rescind their offers to the erstwhile Louisville fixers. The banishment was complete.

And it was permanent. The players repeatedly appealed for reinstatement to the game, but league officials were intractable. Devlin's life swiftly descended into one of destitution and ill health. He wrote a number of pathetic letters to people throughout the game. "I am living from hand to mouth all winter," he wrote in one; "I have not got a Stitch of Clothing or has my wife and Child. . . . The Louisville People have made me what I am today a Beggar."

Particularly steadfast in keeping Devlin and the others out of the game was league president William Hulbert, the owner of the Chicago White Stockings who had been the principal figure in the formation of the the National League.

When Devlin came before Hulbert personally, begging to be reinstated, if only as a groundskeeper, so that he might feed his starving family, Hulbert managed to find a compromise between humanity and principle and gave him fifty dollars. "Devlin, that is what I think of you personally," he said, "but damn you, you have sold a game, you are dishonest, and this National League will not stand for it."

Hulbert's fifty bucks did little to arrest Devlin's sad decline. He died of consumption in 1883, six years after being bounced from the game. He was thirty-four.

The conspicuous absence of four onetime stalwarts did not elude the attention of the other players in the game. As the National League grew gradually and steadily into fiscal, geographical, and competitive stability over the next quarter century, the game remained remarkably free of scandals. By 1881, four years after the Louisville Grays scandal, Henry Chadwick could write, with certitude and evident satisfaction, that "the [National L]eague has been death to crooked play, and has made crookedness so costly to players prone to indulge in it that what used to be a general thing in professional baseball has become quite a rare exception."

Things were never fully quiescent on the hippodroming front. An umpire was dismissed in 1882 for betting on games and then making calls to ensure his bets were winners. There were grumbles during the 1886 World Series between Cap Anson's Chicago Nationals and the American Association St. Louis Browns, managed at the time by their young first baseman, Charles Comiskey. Some fans and reporters thought that the heavily favored Chicago team had tanked an early game in order to prolong the series and increase the winner-take-all gate. If true, it was an ill-advised stratagem; St. Louis won the series in six. Two years later, in 1888, the Browns' flamboyant owner, Chris Von der Ahe, made headlines by accusing the umpires of favoring the Giants because they had bet on the New Yorkers. But these allegations were never proven, nor was anything ever proven on the rumors that popped up from time to time during the 1880s and 1890s. Baseball was riding a wave of public approbation regarding the game's integrity. Fans were back—they'd briefly stayed away in the wake of the Louisville scandal— and no longer reflexively perceived nefarious, game-fixing motives in every costly error or ill-timed strikeout. This perception of propriety was essential to the game's well-being. "Americans might tolerate corruption in government and business and indeed take a certain amount of it for granted," claimed historians Harold and Dorothy Seymour, "but baseball to them occupied a loftier sphere."

The memory of the Louisville banishments, the vigilance of owners who might look the other way when hippodroming hurt their place in the standings but not when it affected the bottom line—all that began to fade from baseball's collective consciousness by the turn of the new century. And the financial dynamic reverted back to one in which the owners held all the cards and the players were forced into accepting a take-it-or-leave-it workplace, instilling resentment and an inclination to temptation on the players' part.

A ballplayer's financial lot had improved a bit during the years following the Louisville scandal, and that had helped quell the cheating urges. The formation of the American Association in the 1880s, the short-lived Players League in 1890, and finally the American League in 1901 gave players an open marketplace in which to sell their skills, and salaries rose as a result, particularly for the established players. But the coming of peace between the American and National leagues in 1903 meant the end of bidding wars for player contracts. The key provision of that 1903 accord was an agreement to honor the contracts—and the reserve clauses—of teams in the other league. Owners had always held the advantage in contract negotiations with players. Now that advantage was, once again, unassailable. Wages stagnated. Players started looking again for other ways to pick up a buck. These were first and foremost *professional* ball players who played the game for money, and who were always looking to ways to bring in a little extra beyond their salaries. They were skilled tradesmen, who put food on the table and a roof over their heads by dint of their ability with a ball, a glove, and a bat. And just as a tradesman is not averse to a bit of moonlighting, ballplayers moonlighted.

Generally a tradesman's moonlighting involves his time off, and probably comes with his boss's full knowledge and consent. So it was with ballplayers; they played games on Sundays and other off days, and after the close of the season, with local nines and picked-up sides of fellow professionals. The owners knew about it, and felt no need to intervene. Every dollar a player made on the side was a dollar they wouldn't have to pay him. But it was only a matter of time before some ballplayers once again threw in with the gamblers. It was chance to make a little money, that was all. Who was getting hurt? Not the owner—he still had the gate, which was unaffected by the outcome of any one game. Not the players on either team—pay envelopes were no fatter during the week the team went 3–3 than they were when the record was 2–4. And the fans? How would they ever know, and thus how could it matter? They paid their fifty cents to see nine innings; those nine innings came with no guarantee beyond the rain check. "Victimless crime" was not yet a phrase, but if the hippodromers ever thought deeply enough to see game fixing as a crime, they would certainly have seen it as one without victims.

The years between the agreement between the American and National leagues in 1903 and the Black Sox scandal in 1919 became the second golden age of game fixing, years that were every bit as rife with rumor and suspicion as the rough-and-tumble 1860s and 1870s.

If game fixing had faded from the headlines since the 1870s, gambling had not. Through the entire period between 1870 and 1919, nearly every saloon, billiard hall, smoke shop, and corner candy store in every big city and small town in

America had a bookie that took bets on the weekly major league run pools. Newspapers carried a running tally of the run-pool totals, and fans checked the numbers against their bets daily, just as elsewhere in the paper wealthier men followed the up-and-down numbers of the stock market. Baseball pools were the lottery tickets of early twentieth century America; ten cents bought a fellow a dream. Weekly prizes on many of the bigger pools could be $1,000, enough to buy a house in a lot of places. Those pools that were paying out $1,000, meanwhile, were taking in $30,000–$50,000 per week; they were controlled by organized crime and protected by city officials and police officers on the take. Fans could follow the games in those preradio days via the Western Union wire brought in to those establishments that catered to the sporting trade. At one point early in the century, after a public report charged that the telegraph wire facilitated illegal gambling, Western Union cut off service to pool halls and saloons. Immediately after the press conference announcing the cancellation, however, Western Union quietly reinstated the severed service.

In addition to the pools, sporting men and fans could wager on individual games. There was always someone to take those bets too—in the pool hall, in the lobbies of hotels where the visiting teams stayed, even in the ballparks themselves; nearly every big league park had one particular section known as the "gamblers reservation," where there was action of any size and kind, the odds shouted out like the cries of the vendors, money changing hands openly. A house directly across the street from Shibe Park in Philadelphia bore a large sign reading "MAKE YOUR BETS."

Everybody bet on baseball—fans, players, managers, owners, clubhouse boys and scorecard salesmen, even members of the National Commission. Most of the betting was mano a mano, between owner and owner, manager and manager, pitcher and pitcher, White Sox fan and Tigers fan. The more money bet on a game, the greater the buzz, the greater the interest. Fans saw it as a mark of confidence when a player or manager wagered a bit of his own money on the outcome; the fan, in turn, considered it a mark of loyalty to put his money where his mouth was. But every wager has a loser, and not many losers are willing to fully accept fate or their own flawed judgment for the loss. Losers went looking for people to blame, and rumors of game fixing again became rife after 1903.

The bigger the game, the louder the rumors. No games were bigger than those in the World Series. By 1919 writers, and even the baseball people themselves, were reluctant to pursue these fix rumors or dignify them with a mention. Their skepticism was born of the fact that they had all been there before; there were precious few World Series that hadn't had fix rumors lurking in the shadows and gambling stories in the headlines.

They dated back to the very beginning, the first modern World Series, between Pittsburgh and Boston in 1903. In their stories on the opening game, Boston newspapers took notice of Boston's most noted sporting man, one Joseph Sullivan, known as "Sport" among the patrons. According to the papers, "Sport" had bet $2,500 on the Bostons to win. Again, gambling was no scandal. It was a validation of an event's significance. If the sporting men were there, then here, surely, was an event deserving of public notice. The pre-Series stories in the Boston papers were less about the strengths and weaknesses of the two teams than about the money that was being wagered. "The amount of money wagered yesterday will easily amount to $25,000," reported the *Boston Post* on September 29, two days before the Series began. At the Vendome Hotel in Kenmore Square, home to the Pittsburgh team and its supporters, money was changing hands in the lobby like at a back-alley crap game. Pittsburgh owner Barney Dreyfuss was betting heavily on his team, promising to share his winnings with the players if they prevailed. On the day before the Series began, the *Post* delicately brought up the matter of a fix. "Baseball is too open to be crooked," the writer claimed, but then felt compelled to urge the players to play it straight up. "There is too much at stake to risk having the series prolonged [by fixed games]."

According to at least some historians, however, the admonitions of the newspapers did not stop Boston and Pittsburgh players from fixing the first two games of the Series. "The very first game of the very first 'world's series,' was, in all likelihood, thrown by Boston," Glenn Stout and Richard Johnson write in *Red Sox Century.* They cite some uncharacteristic wildness by Boston ace Cy Young, four first-inning errors of commission and omission by catcher Lou Criger, and four poorly timed errors in the field by others. "The likelihood of all this happening at the same time by coincidence is remote," they write, then argue that Pittsburgh returned the favor by throwing the second game the next day. Player-manager Fred Clarke pulled his starter in the second inning, ostensibly because of a sore arm, and went to the back of his bullpen for the replacement. Boston won the game 3–0 to tie the Series at one game apiece. Supposedly the reason for the tit-for-tat throwing of these first two games was strictly financial; the players were due to earn quite a bit more if the best-of-nine series went eight or nine games than if it ended in five or six. Where was the harm is starting the series off at 1–1, with some extra cash in the till?

When the Series moved to Pittsburgh for games four through seven, some Pittsburgh sporting men approached Boston catcher Criger in the lobby of the Monongahela Hotel before game four and offered him $12,000 to throw the Series to Pittsburgh. He took this information to American League president Ban Johnson, and would later be awarded a lifetime pension by Johnson for his honesty. It was a peculiar sort of ethic—it was fine to fix a couple of games in order to extract extra money from the paying fans, but wrong to take a gambler's money to do the same thing.

And so it began. Gambling news rivaled baseball news in every season that followed, particularly at World Series time, and the accompanying fix rumors floated in the air like so much ambient ballpark chatter. It was two years before there would be a second World Series, in 1904; winning National League manager John McGraw refused to play the American League champion Bostons because he was in a snit about the upstart American League invading his National League turf in New York that year. But the championship series in 1905 was no longer simply a postseason exhibition left to the discretion of the two winning teams. It was now the official major league championship series, or world series (the capital letters wouldn't come until decades later), and much anticipated because of that fact. And much like 1903, gambling news made the headlines, and again fix rumors fluttered in the breeze.

Giants manager John McGraw was baseball's preeminent sporting man. Ball games in those days generally began in the late afternoon, 3:30 or 4:00, and McGraw would customarily start his day at the track, getting in a few wagers before he had to report to the ballpark. Later in his career he would own a pool hall in partnership with Arnold Rothstein, the city's best-known gangster, who would later play a central role in the 1919 story. And John McGraw would bet on any game where there was someone willing to take the other side. For the 1905 Series, which pitted the Giants against the Athletics, it was reported that McGraw had bet $400 on the Giants and encouraged his players to bet their money as well. When word leaked out that some Giants players had partnered up with Athletics players and agreed to split their share of their player's shares fifty-fifty, McGraw was livid—not necessarily at the collusion, which was not regarded as inappropriate, but because he could not understand a player who refused to back his ballplaying skill with a wager. "I was disgusted at their unwillingness to take a chance," he said.

A Philadelphia newspaper took the whispers public during that 1905 series. The allegation involved Athletics lefthander Rube Waddell, the guy the newspapers called "the sousepaw," a happy, affable, storied inebriate, who nonetheless ranked with Cy Young, Christy Mathewson, and Walter Johnson as one of the very best pitchers of the dead-ball era. When he was sober and not hungover—which was not often—he might have been the best of them all. Waddell led the American League with twenty-six wins and a 1.48 ERA in 1905, but he missed the Series after suffering a late-season shoulder injury. A Philadelphia sports-writer named Horace Fogel accused Waddell of taking a payoff from gamblers in return for faking the severity of his injury and sitting out the Series, won easily by the Giants. There's no proof of this, of course. Nor is there any proof against it. Later in the decade, interestingly, Fogel, as the figurehead president of the Philadelphia Phillies, would make other allegations of bribery and game fixing. His allegations did not gain much traction in their day, but they did un-nerve the other owners in the National League, who drummed him out of the game in 1912 for violating "league rules" and lacking the "high principles" the league's charter demanded. The short of it was that Fogel was simply too much of a pot stirrer and general nuisance, and since he was only a minority owner of the Phillies despite his title of president, the game's owners found it easiest to be rid of him and his uncomfortable allegations. Kept in the shadows, gambling and game fixing may or may not have been a threat to their business; openly talking about gambling and game fixing, however, was definitely a threat to business.

The next swirl of rumors surrounding a postseason championship game did not affect the World Series itself, but might have affected who got to play in it. In 1908 the National League pennant came down to a season-ending makeup game between the Cubs and the Giants, a game made necessary by the famous "boneheaded" base-running blunder by the Giants' Fred Merkle in a game against the Cubs in early September. Merkle, running on first base, failed to touch second on an apparent game-winning, walk-off single; he was called out on a force play at second, and the game was declared a tie, necessitating the game that would determine the National League pennant.

Before the game, a physician by the name of Joseph Creamer—a personal friend of John McGraw, and recently added to the Giants payroll as a masseur—approached legendary umpire Bill Klem under the stands before the game, flashed a large wad of bills and said: "Here's $2,500. It's yours if you'll give all the close decisions to the Giants and see that they win sure." Klem declined the bribe and then reported it; Creamer's identity came out only later, and he vehemently denied the charge. The National Commission investigated, and "timid" would be a kind description of their actions in the case. To begin with, they put John Brush, the owner of the Giants, in charge of the investigation, despite the fact that it was the Giants being investigated. "While the individual mentioned is unquestionably a S.O.B. it would be hazardous for any one financially responsible...to publicly charge him with having committed the offense," wrote Brush in his report to National Commission chairman Garry Hermann. "Lack of evidence," a familiar determination in National Commission investigations, was publicly given as the reason for the Commission taking no action against Creamer.

There were other game-fixing rumors and allegations involving the Giants during that 1908 season, involving a critical late-season series against the Phillies. Still more rumors dogged the Giants, involving a series with the Cardinals in 1912 and a final-week, pennant-deciding series with Brooklyn in 1916. Yet John McGraw, "the Little Napoleon," as he was dubbed in the press, in charge of the Giants all these years—always a source of irritation to, and never a favorite of, league presidents and National Commission members Ban Johnson and John Tener—was never once called before the National Commission to answer to the rumors.

The Commission would preside over the game until the Black Sox scandal and a bitter power struggle between American League president Ban Johnson and a group of American League owners headed by White Sox owner Charles Comiskey would force the owners to instead turn to a single, independent commissioner and cede control of the game to Judge Kenesaw Landis. Two men were members of the National Commission for its entire seventeen-year existence—American League president Ban Johnson and Cincinnati Reds president Garry Herrmann. Four different men served terms on the Commission as president of the National League. Regardless of its makeup, regardless of the nature of the hippodroming case that came before it, the National Commission's actions were always the same. While vocally against gambling whenever the conversation came up in the press, the National Commission was far less aggressive and confrontational when the matter actually came before them. A half dozen times prior to the Black Sox scandal the Commission sat in judgment in cases alleging game fixing. Not once would they find evidence sufficient to take action. The timorousness of baseball's hierarchy was never more in evidence than just a few months before the 1919 troubles, when the men who ruled the game were finally forced to confront the man who may have been the greatest hippodromer of them all—the graceful, elegant, charming, incorrigible, and thoroughly corrupt Hal Chase.

T W O

The Prince of Fixers

Hal Chase is the Babe Ruth of ball-game fixers, a mythic figure whose exploits so transcended those of the players around him that he's become that larger-than-life legend about whom there is no argument. Argue about his skills or the extent of his corruption, perhaps, but about legacy there can be no argument: the game never had anybody else quite like Hal Chase. He was, by common consent, the greatest fixer in history; yet was never found guilty of having fixed even a single game.

Nobody knows how many games Hal Chase fixed, or tried to fix, or intentionally did not play his best in, though a reasonable guess might put the number in the hundreds. He played fifteen years in the big leagues, from 1905 to 1919, and the first rumblings that perhaps he wasn't always trying his hardest surfaced in his third season. They were ever present ever after. He threw games for money, he threw games for spite, he threw games as favors for friends, he threw games apparently for no reason at all other than to stay in practice. Playing crooked was a part of his baseball DNA. Long after he was finally drummed out of organized baseball in 1919, Chase played for several years in an outlaw sagebrush league covering the southwest from West Texas to Arizona. A columnist for the *El Paso Herald* witnessed such wantonly bad play by Chase one day that he confronted him after the game.

"You tried to throw that one," said the writer.

"Sure," replied Chase.

"Why?"

"You know that Chinaman from Lordsburg?" Chase asked the writer, referring to one of the local sporting men. "Well, he came up to me before the game and asked if I wouldn't boot a few and try to help [the other team]. He's a nice fellow, and I said sure, but I didn't have any money on the game, and he wasn't paying me."

Ultimately, there is nothing remotely redeeming about Hal Chase or his legacy. He was a bitter, brooding, and cynical misanthrope, who cast perhaps the darkest shadow on baseball in the dead-ball era. "Chase was completely and congenitally amoral," said one writer who knew him for more than twenty-five years. "The man was born without any sense of right and wrong."

When he first came east from California to join the New York Highlanders in 1905, however, he was a most appealing figure, and an irresistible story. On the playing field he had the transcendent grace of the natural athlete; not only did he do things that others could not; he did them with fluidity and balletic élan, did them "so well that he made all other men appear mechanically imperfect by comparison," as one reporter wrote. Off the field, the sportswriters found him—or at least painted him—to be a man with an intelligence and personality that perfectly complemented his athletic gifts. "I found him without any tinge of affectation or egotism," wrote *Baseball Magazine* editor F. C. Lane, a man whose voice had considerable reach and influence in its day. "[Chase has] the easy disingenuous air of the man who is perfectly at peace with his surroundings and with life in general, the attitude of the happy-go-lucky individual who takes things as he finds them and can find gilded linings to every cloud." By 1912, when Lane wrote those words, there was already considerable evidence that none of it was true. But Lane was hardly the only one to fall under Chase's spell, to wish that he were actually the player and man he might have been.

When Chase joined the Highlanders in 1905, the team that would become the New York Yankees ran a hopeless second to John McGraw's Giants in the hearts and minds of New Yorkers. The Highlanders—and the writers who covered them—were more than a bit defensive of this second-class status. The team and its writers saw the arrival of Hal Chase as the coming of the franchise's first real star. Before he played a single game, sportswriters were comparing him to Christy Mathewson, presumptuous hyperbole certainly, but telling of the first impression Chase made on those who saw him in his early days.

Writers noted the marked physical resemblance to the sainted Mathewson. Both men had blond hair and blue eyes and stood six feet tall, a full head higher than most of their peers in early-twentieth-century America. Reporters took notice of an increase in female fans at Hilltop Park after Chase joined the team, just as they seldom failed to notice the higher percentage of women at the Polo Grounds on the days when Mathewson pitched. Both, the writers noted, were college men. That was technically true, though only technically. Mathewson spent three years at Bucknell, leaving just a few credits shy of a degree; Chase starred for the University of Santa Clara baseball team in 1903–04, but he was apparently on campus only during baseball season, and only, it would seem, for baseball games and practice. Chase later told writers he had studied civil engineering at Santa Clara, but the university has no record of his ever having been enrolled in a single class.

The New York writers needed a nickname for Chase, who promised to be a central part of their stories for the next decade or more. They quickly settled on "Prince Hal," which suited perfectly. The term could be used in praise or derisively, or both at the same time. He was the future king—the victor at Agincourt—but also the rapscallion who whored and drank with Falstaff. The good Prince Hal was that creature touched by destiny—handsome, virile, quick-witted, erudite, physically graceful and possessed of a magnetic personality, "a player equipped by nature to be one of the game's immortals." There was an incandescence to Hal Chase, on the field and off, that was evident to all.

But the bad Prince Hal was evident to everybody too. He had a spoiled child's sense of entitlement, a petulant expectation of getting his own way, a crass and cruel condescension toward the less blessed. "I could make plays like that every day, only I am afraid to turn the ball loose," he once told a sportswriter who'd complimented him on a particularly good play, "because I am afraid I might hit one of those dopes in the head."

Chase was the Highlanders' first superstar, and by the middle of his second year, *Sporting Life*, throwing all restraint to the wind, claimed that "a more brilliant ball player never broke into base ball.... Pretty big talk this... but you can throw it back at us if the future does not prove Hal Chase the most valuable man in the game." He was steady enough at the plate, batting .249, .323, and .287 in his first three years in the big leagues; on the base paths, he pioneered the head-first slide. But it was in the field where he really set himself apart. He was fluid, fearless, and intuitive. His range was home plate to medium-depth right field, the grandstand's edge to the area that normally belonged to the second baseman. In an era when every third or fourth batter would attempt to lay down a bunt, Chase would creep in from first base, move past the pitcher's mound, and snatch the ball as it came off the bat, catching it sometimes before it hit the ground, thwarting sacrifices and turning potential hits into double plays. It was this play that cemented his early legend.

"The first time he tries that with me," sniffed Napoleon Lajoie of Cleveland, "I'll hit the ball back at him and knock his brains out," thereby ensuring that Chase would indeed try that with him. When Cleveland and New York next met, Lajoie came up with a runner on second and feigned a bunt. Chase sprinted in and was no more than ten feet away when Lajoie pulled back and smashed a line drive directly at Chase, who caught it before it could kill him, then nonchalantly threw to second, doubling off the base runner. As the seasons passed and Chase's reputation was stripped of all its virtue, the memory of his brilliance afield burned bright. Thirty years after his playing career had ended, men who had in later years seen George Sisler, Bill Terry, Lou Gehrig, Jimmie Foxx, Hank Greenberg, and Stan Musial still did not hesitate to name Hal Chase the best. "Just as at shortstop there was only one Wagner, so at first base there was only one Chase," wrote Frank Graham, "greater than Gehrig or Terry or Sisler or anyone you care to name."

"You wouldn't believe a man could do all the things on the ball field Chase could do," said Clark Griffith, his first manager, and later the longtime owner of the Senators. "There wasn't a modern first baseman who could come close to him. There wasn't ever any 'second Hal Chase.' He was in a class by himself."

But Hal Chase was a limit tester. And because he was one of the game's brightest stars, he got away with testing limits, again and again. So he kept testing them, ever more significant limits, ever more brazenly. In his second year with the Highlanders, Chase flaunted a rule against playing with any semipro team in an exhibition that took place within five miles of any game involving a team in organized baseball. The rule was meant to protect minor league teams from having their fans co-opted by moonlighting major leaguers. Chase played with two different semipro teams on a single Sunday in September of 1906, both within the five-mile protected zone of the Newark club. Newark filed a complaint with the National Commission, but there is nothing in the Commission's records to indicate that it took any action.

Had the Commission chosen to enforce that rule, the punishment would have likely been minimal. In 1907 and 1908, however, Chase took a chance that could have ended his major league career just as it was beginning. At the close of his first two seasons with the Highlanders, in 1905–06, Chase returned home to California and played for another couple of months with the San Jose Prune Pickers of the California State League. The California weather permitted the extended season, and major leaguers flocked to the state, mostly for the extra money, partly for the extra seasoning their games would get, and partly for the simple, childlike joy of being able to still play the game after the big league ball fields of the northeast and Midwest shut down.

But in the fall of 1907, the major leagues put the California State League off-limits, declaring it an "outlaw league" for its failure to sign the National Agreement, that provision of the American–National League merger, which organized the minor leagues into classifications and established procedures and prices for the drafting of players by major league clubs. The edict came down after the close of the major league season in 1907; Chase and a handful of others were already playing in the California State League. The players were told they would face a $100 fine for a first violation of the cease-and-desist order and permanent banishment for a second. Chase played the rest of the season, some thirty games, under the name "Schultz," though, when sportswriters inquired, he rakishly admitted that he was indeed "Schultz." When the season was over he applied for reinstatement in organized baseball, claiming his month's worth of games after the order to stop was continuous play and thus all a "first offense." The National Commission, lobbied hard by Highlanders owner Frank Farrell, fined Chase the $100 and reinstated him for the 1908 season.

A year later, Chase went back to the California State League, and this time he didn't even wait for the close of the major league season. At odds with new Highlander manager Kid Elberfeld, in part because he felt that *he* should have been named manager when Clark Griffith left the team in midseason, and upset at an August newspaper article that criticized his attitude, Chase packed his bags in early September and returned to California, signing a contract with California State League Stockton Millers. He claimed to be through with big league ball and the Highlanders, and happy to be home in California, prepared to finish his career in independent baseball.

Yet once again, in 1909, the Highlanders welcomed their prodigal son home. American League president Ban Johnson, whose interests in this were the competitive and fiscal health of the New York ball club, ruled that Chase warranted special consideration in his request for reinstatement, because his defection had been prompted by "ill health."

"How could anyone say that Hal Chase caused trouble in a ball club?" asked his new manager George Stallings, welcoming him back. "He is the greatest ballplayer I have seen." Little wonder Hal Chase would come to believe that the rules did not apply to him.

The first hint that Chase might not be giving his all on the field had come in 1907. The Highlanders were in a midseason funk that would see them lose eighteen out of twenty-four games; there was dissension on the club and considerable dissatisfaction with manager Clark Griffith. In one 10–4 loss to the Tigers the team committed an almost unthinkable eleven errors. The *New York Times* tentatively raised the specter of game fixing. "In years gone by there have been instances in baseball of games having been 'thrown,'" the *Times* story on the game read. "Such things, of course, have passed away. But the old-time enthusiast, unacquainted with modern baseball, who happened to drop in at American League Park yesterday, might have suspected that he was witnessing a revival of the old customs." The article went on to point out that there were a number of unnamed players, the "leaders of the malcontents," who "have been particularly unfortunate in making mistakes at critical times, and have committed errors of omission that were very costly." Chase wasn't named—nobody was—but readers would remember a Chase play two games earlier during which he thought he had an inning-ending out at first base. Rolling the ball back to the mound, he started for the dugout before turning to realize that the umpire had called the runner safe. It was an "error of omission" that cost the Highlanders a run.

Over the next season and a half, readers still needed to read between the lines of stories for suggestions of any Chase duplicity, but the between-the-lines suggestions of impropriety would become more common. When Chase left New York for the Cal State League before the end of the 1908 season, Joe Vila of the *New York Sun* wrote, "Chase and a gang of cowardly knockers...have done all sorts of things to ruin the American League in this town....There is no longer any reason to hide the fact that Chase was a disturbing element."

By the close of the 1910 season, readers didn't have to read between the lines for hints that Chase was tanking plays and games. It was right there in the headlines. His accuser was Highlander manager George Stallings, who had named Chase team captain at the start of the season. Any good feelings the manager and his star may have had for one another in spring training, however, had vanished by August. The team tumbled from the first division ever deeper into the second as the season moved along. Owner Frank Farrell summarily dismissed one player for showing up drunk once too often. A number of players chafed under Stallings's bullying and autocracy, Chase chief among them. In August Chase simply left the team during a road trip in Detroit, not even bothering to tell his manager or anyone else where he was going or why. He would later variously claim both illness and injury, but it would emerge that he had returned to New York to lobby Frank Farrell for the dismissal of Stallings, suggesting at the same time that Farrell name him as Stallings's successor. In September, Stallings met with Farrell to air his grievances. He told Farrell, and Farrell told the newspapers, that Chase had cost the team a number of games in 1910, "either through carelessness or willful indifference." But as Farrell spoke to the press, it seemed clear that Hal Chase was again going to get the benefit of the doubt.

"To my surprise, Mr. Stallings made grave accusations against Hal Chase," reported Farrell. "Mr. Stallings charges that Chase has not been giving his best services to the club, and that he has been guilty, in baseball parlance, of 'laying down.' No ball player can afford to have his reputation and the reputation of his club smirched by such charges....If I find they are true I shall lay the entire matter before the National Commission and ask that Chase be punished.

"If Mr. Stallings fails to prove his charges against Chase," he added a little ominously, "it is up to me to deal with Stallings as I see fit as Chase is too great a ball player to have his reputation blackened by such charges."

There was no question which way Farrell, league president Ban Johnson, and the rest of the major league owners wanted this investigation to turn out. Substantiate the charges against Chase and the game would be rocked to its core. Not only would it almost certainly mean the dismissal of the Highlanders' biggest star; it would require a top-to-bottom, game-wide investigation, and who knew what might slither out when officials started turning over rocks. Conversely, if they failed to prove the charges against Chase, all Farrell had to do was dismiss a manager who had lost control of his team anyway.

The investigation consisted of conversations conducted the next day with the Highlander players. While these teammates had no great love for Chase, they hated Stallings more, and took Chase's side in their talks with Farrell. Stallings was gone by day's end. Ban Johnson, whose hatred of Stallings was well known and went back more than a decade to when Stallings owned a piece of the Detroit club, took an evident satisfaction in finding in Chase's favor. The Johnson-Stallings dispute dated to the pre–American League days, when Detroit was a Western League club and Johnson believed Stallings deliberately tried to sabotage his plans to transform the Western League from a minor league to a second major league. Stallings, Johnson believed, passed information on to National League officials and conspired to have Detroit join the older league. Johnson drummed Stallings out of Detroit then, and had worked to keep him out of the American League ever since. It was hardly surprising that Johnson's formal statement in the case is less an exoneration of Chase than a condemnation of Stallings. "Stallings has utterly failed in his accusations against Chase," said Johnson in his statement to the press. "He tried to besmirch the character of a sterling player. Anybody who knows Hal Chase knows that he is not guilty of the accusations made against him, and I am happy to say that the evidence of New York players...this morning showed Stallings up."

Stallings would go on to manage the Boston Braves to a World Series championship in 1914. Hal Chase replaced him as the Highlander manager, but his tenure was brief and undistinguished. Still, his triumph in his scuffle with Stallings confirmed yet again that the rules did not apply to him. He was almost certainly guilty of all that Stallings alleged. Yet not only was he not punished; he was promoted.

Over the next eight years, Chase's name was seldom out of the headlines, but their range was bewildering. Readers would have been hard-pressed to decide whether Chase was one of the game's brightest stars, one of its most star-crossed victims of ill luck, or one of its most intransigent delinquents. The on-field headlines continued to chronicle a career that most feel would have made him a cinch for Cooperstown, had baseball playing been his only legacy. "CHASE TO THE FRONT WITH NEEDED HIT"; "CHASE BLAZES WAY TO VICTORY"; "I wouldn't trade Chase for Ty Cobb," gushed one of his managers. And there were headlines about off-field opportunities that came only to the game's brightest stars, Chase spurning an offer to do an off-season vaudeville tour, or Chase playing himself in a 1911 film called *Hal Chase's Home Run*, a silent one-reeler in which the hero's marriage plans hinge upon the Highlanders winning the pennant.

But there was a big scrapbook full of negative headlines as well, though not all were of Chase's own making. He missed the start of the 1909 season when he was stricken with a mild case of smallpox; he missed a month in 1912 when he suffered a nervous breakdown following the breakup of his marriage. Any sympathy that may have come his way as a result of his illness, however, quickly evaporated during the divorce-trial testimony, which showed him to be a serial adulterer.

Following his dismissal as manager at the end of the 1911 season—forever putting the best spin on things, the newspapers quoted Chase as saying he had asked to be relieved of the managerial reins and quoted Frank Farrell saying he would have not have replaced Chase had he not been asked—Chase had one quiet season under replacement Harry Wolverton, though Wolverton led the team to a last-place finish. But Chase couldn't get along with Frank Chance, after the former Cubs first baseman and manager was named manager of the Yankees for the 1913 season.*

* The Yankees name originated with the New York sportswriters somewhere around 1909–10. After two or three seasons of the writers using Highlanders and Yankees interchangeably in their stories, the team officially changed its name to Yankees for the 1913 season.

Still thinking he should be managing the team, Chase quickly came to resent Chance, and seized on the new manager's tendency for histrionics to mock him behind his back. For his part, Chance looked from the start of the season for an opportunity to trade Chase. Chance hoped to get something approaching equivalent value in return, but by the end of June he just wanted to be rid of Chase.

By July the depth of animosity was apparent. Chance stormed into the press box after one game, where Fred Lieb of the *Press* and Heywood Broun of the *Tribune* were finishing their stories. "I want to tell you fellows what's going on," he told them. "Did you see some of the balls that got away from Chase today? They weren't wild throws; they were only made to look that way. He's been doing that right along. He's throwing games on me!" The two writers brooded about what to do with the story. Lieb's editor chased him off the story completely; Broun wrote a tepid piece that suggested Chase's loose play at first—with no suggestion that it was deliberate—was hurting the team. Two days later Chase was traded to the White Sox for a "bunion and an onion," in the words of New York writer Mark Roth, meaning that the Yankees hadn't gotten much in the two players they had traded for Chase. The "bunion" was a player best noted for the time he'd missed through the years due to foot problems; the second player was simply an "onion," pre–World War I slang for a player of no impact or consequence.

With the White Sox, Chase played alongside future Black Sox Buck Weaver and Eddie Cicotte, though there's no record that they were particularly close to their notorious teammate, nor any suggestion that they might have come by any later game-fixing notions through their association with Chase. Chase's biggest headlines with the White Sox came in the way he left them to jump to the Federal League Buffalo team in the middle of the 1914 season. The standard major league contract at that time had a clause that allowed termination of a contract for any reason, simply by giving ten days' notice. Chase invoked the ten-day clause in notifying the White Sox that he would be leaving them. The White Sox quite naturally fought back; the ten-day clause was a tool for the teams, not the players. Chase was served with court papers on the field, as he walked back to the dugout following his first Federal League at-bat. The Feds prevailed in court, and Chase spent a season and a half with Buffalo before the negotiated peace that brought an end to the Federal League following the 1915 season. One of the terms of the peace was that the Fed League teams retained the rights to the players they had signed away from organized baseball, and could sell those players back to any team in organized baseball that wanted them.

It seemed for a while that nobody wanted Hal Chase. Owners denied that Chase had been blacklisted. But newspapers published a litany of the dark prince's behavior, and speculated that owners had finally, independently, determined that the risks far outweighed the rewards. Chase should have been the prize of the Federal League, which mainly consisted of players who were either very young or well past their prime. Chase was thirty-three, and productive; he hit .347 and .291 in two seasons with Buffalo. But his reputation for inviting trouble was finally a problem. In late March 1916, with teams deep into spring training and Chase still unsigned, Hugh Jennings, then the manager of the Tigers, said out loud, on the record, what players, managers, and writers had been muttering about in private for more than a decade.

"For all his ability, I would not have him on my club, and I do not believe any other major league manager will take a chance with him," said Jennings. "He will not heed training rules and has a demoralizing influence on the younger players." Jennings described Chase as a "tunnel worker," meaning someone who stirred up trouble. "One of his favorite stunts is to go around telling one man what another is supposed to have said about him, with the result that in a very short time he has the fellows pulling in all directions instead of working together. He is apt to take a dislike to the manager and work against him with the players until the whole squad is sore and will not give the sort of work that it is paid for." Although, Jennings added, having a player of Chase's caliber on the team would help them win the pennant "beyond question," it wasn't worth taking on Chase. "I have a very well-behaved, earnest lot of boys under my charge now and I do not want them to be spoiled by a chronic trouble-maker."

It appeared that the other fifteen big league managers, and their owners, agreed with Hugh Jennings. As the opening of the season crept ever closer with Chase still unsigned, Harry Sinclair, the oilman and erstwhile owner of the Newark Federal League franchise—who bought up most the Federal League contracts, with the hopes of recouping some of his investment by selling the contracts back to organized baseball—admitted that nobody was interested in Chase, and that he might be legally bound personally to pay him the terms of his Federal League contract, an $8,000-per-year contract with two years to run.*

---

* Sinclair is best known to history as a central figure in the Teapot Dome Scandal during the presidency of Warren Harding. He is the man to whom Interior Secretary Albert Fall granted exclusive rights to the lucrative oil reserves in the Teapot Dome oil fields near Casper, Wyoming, in return (it was later charged) for substantial cash gifts and interest-free loans from Sinclair. Sinclair was acquitted of bribery charges, but did spend six months in prison on contempt-of-court and contempt-of-Congress charges in the case.

But then, in early April, with opening day less than a week away, the Cincinnati Reds signed Chase. And in his first year as a Red, with no spring training, and after having come perilously close to seeing his major league career come to a close, all Chase did was lead the National League in hitting, with a career-high .339. But it would be in Cincinnati that he would cross the line of public perception, going from gifted-but-star-crossed ballplayer to "archetype of all crooked ballplayers."

Long after Chase was out of the game, men who played with him throughout his career admitted that they had known he had bet on the games he played in, sometimes for his team to win, other times for his own team to lose. These same teammates suspected that he hadn't always played his hardest in the games on which he had bet his team to lose, but said nothing at the time, and very little even later. It's a line from a thousand television cop-and-lawyer shows: knowing and proving are two different things. What proof exists of Chase trying to fix games comes from very late in his career.

It was Christy Mathewson who finally brought him to the dock. On August 7, 1918, Mathewson, now Chase's manager with the Reds, suspended him indefinitely for "indifferent playing." The Reds, who had had designs on a National League pennant when the season opened, were kicking around the middle of the league standings all year, and Chase had raised the ire of his teammates with that "indifferent" play. At least three players, third baseman Heinie Groh, left fielder Greasy Neale, and utility man Sherry Magee, had gone to Mathewson and begged him to suspend Chase for throwing games. Later, Reds players went back through the season and counted up Chase's suspicious plays and came up with the mind-boggling allegation that during 1918 he had deliberately cost the team twenty-seven games, or nearly one half of the sixty games the team lost in the 148-game season. His teammates weren't alone in their suspicions about Chase. In the week leading up to his suspension in August, opponents had taken to shouting out "Hey Hal, what are the odds today?" Three days after suspending him indefinitely, Mathewson met with Chase and told him that the suspension would be for the balance of the season. Mathewson would not elaborate on the reasons for his actions when talking to reporters, saying only that he could not stand "indifferent or careless playing on the part of a man of such great natural ability as Hal possesses." His remarks made it seem that Chase was guilty of little more than failing to hustle down to first on a ground ball.

The writers, meanwhile, a largely docile bunch, whose dispatches generally reflected the interest of the teams that picked up their traveling expenses, wrote stories that were only slightly less oblique. "It is not a pleasant thing to say about so fine a natural player as Chase, but the other players on the team have all expressed themselves as glad he is out of the lineup," reported the *Cincinnati Enquirer*. "Every now and then, he has been letting easy rollers hit right at him, go past," added the *Sporting News*. "On several occasions these mishaps have hurt the team's chances, and caused more or less friction between Chase and the pitchers." The writers never pressed for an articulation of the charges against Chase, and the team continued to hint at grave misdeeds without detailing what they were. "I must say, the evidence against him looks damaging," said team president Garry Herrmann; "there is a great deal of it, and it seems accurate and straightforward."

But Herrmann, and later the National League and the National Commission, were anything but straightforward in their assessment of Chase. Their reluctance to come right out and accuse him of being crooked was wholly consistent with the way baseball had so often treated earlier game-fixing cases. There is little doubt here that Chase was guilty, and that this time officials had the goods to prove it. Yet by getting rid of Chase the baseball hierarchy had created another more damaging problem—proving to the public that baseball truly was no longer beset by the gambling woes of the past. They had to prove somehow that the trouble began and ended with Chase.

Or, was it possible to convict the criminal, yet keep the crime a secret? As the baseball hierarchy girded for the crisis shortly after the formal charges against Chase were filed, Garry Herrmann, now wearing his National Commission chairman's hat, indicated in a letter to National League president John Heydler that secrecy would be the route to take. "In discussing this matter in a confidential way with Mr. Johnson last Sunday night," Herrmann wrote, "he was strongly of the opinion that if that testimony warrants [Chase's] expulsion, that the reason for it should not be made public. The evidence is so damaging that he believes, and I agree with him, that it would be a severe 'black eye' for the game if the details became fully known."

Chase himself approached the issue more squarely. In an interview with the *Sporting News*, he said: "Let's not dodge around the bush. I'm accused of betting on games and trying to get a pitcher to throw a game for money." While he admitted that he hung out in pool rooms and made bets on horse races, he categorically denied that he had made any bets on baseball and had "never thrown the team." The pitcher Chase referenced was Pol Perritt of the Giants, who told manager John McGraw that Chase had approached him before a mid-July game in Cincinnati and offered him $800 to throw his next start against the Reds.

McGraw dismissed the charges, saying that Chase was "a practical joker and says many things he doesn't mean."

But Perritt's claim was part of the dossier of allegations and evidence that Mathewson and Herrmann prepared for the case against Chase that they presented to National League president John Heydler. Also included were the allegations by Mathewson and those of Chase's teammates—more of whom had come forward after Mathewson leveled his charges—and affidavits from six Cincinnati police officers, claiming that Chase had bet against the Reds as often as he had bet on them.

The most damning piece of evidence in the dossier sent to National League headquarters in late August was an affidavit from Cincinnati pitcher Jimmy Ring, who claimed that during a 1917 game in Philadelphia Chase was waiting for him on the pitcher's mound when he had come into the game in relief and offered him money if he threw the game. Ring refused the bribe, he claimed, but gave up two hits and the game-winning run anyway, and the next morning Chase dropped a roll of bills in his lap.

This was far and away the most serious fix that Chase had been in during his career; indeed, it would be the incident that ultimately ended his major league days. But not immediately. Once again, the game's reluctance to shine a light into this particular dark corner, coupled with the fact that the nation was then preoccupied by World War 1, gave Chase another lease on his baseball life. As the 1918 season ended and Chase headed for his day in court, Christy Mathewson was headed for France.

At just about the point in the season where he had suspended Chase, Mathewson had applied for a commission in the army's Chemical Warfare Service.* Whether stirred by the sense of duty that had moved many men to serve or frustrated by his dealings with Hal Chase and a team that had slipped below .500, Mathewson had offered, and the army accepted. He left the Reds with ten games left in the season and didn't return to the United States until after the war was over, and after Chase's hearing was over.

That hearing took place on January 30, 1919, in Heydler's office in New York, closed to the press and public. In keeping with their fear of their sport being tainted as rife with gambling and game fixing, baseball officials had still not publicly outlined the charges against Chase. Chase, for his part, had leaked most of the details to the many New York newspapermen who had always liked him,

---

* For some reason, the Chemical Warfare Service was the Army branch for future baseball hall of famers. In addition to Mathewson, Branch Rickey, Ty Cobb, and George Sisler also served in the CWS.

most notably Sid Mercer of the *Globe*, who seldom wrote anything but praise for Chase, going back to the Highlander days, and would appear at the hearing as a character witness on Chase's behalf.

Chase showed up with an entourage of three lawyers, a stenographer, and three character witnesses. Heydler had the assistance of a single lawyer; the Reds sent only the three players who were appearing as witnesses against Chase. On the witness list but absent from the hearing were Mathewson, still in France, and Giants pitcher Pol Perritt, who sent word from his Louisiana farm that he would be unable to make it. Also testifying, ostensibly against Chase, was Giants manager John McGraw, who reiterated his view that Chase was a prankster when asked about the charges Perritt had leveled against the first baseman. McGraw's credibility as a witness was not challenged by the League. This was somewhat surprising, given the fact that he had been quoted frequently in the newspapers as saying that, were Chase exonerated in his hearing, he, McGraw, would be very interested in having him play for the Giants in 1919.

The only direct evidence came from Jimmy Ring, and he proved a "poor witness," according to Heydler. Ring, said Heydler, "made statements differing from what he has stated in his affidavit, so much so that I brought him back here on Monday for further testimony." The other evidence against Chase was either hearsay or could not be corroborated by Mathewson and Perritt, neither of whom was present. Chase, meanwhile, was masterful in his own defense, claiming that Greasy Neale—who had testified to a whole laundry list of betting and game-fixing admissions Chase had made to him and others on the Reds—was the head of a "clique that had it in" for him. Chase did admit to giving money to Ring, but called it a loan. All the other allegations he either denied or dismissed as misunderstandings or misinterpretations of things he had said. He was poised, articulate, and earnest on the stand.

Heydler found in his favor. In his formal statement, the National League president finally acknowledged that the hearing had indeed been about betting against his team. "In justice to Chase," Heydler wrote, "I feel bound to state that the evidence and the records of the games to which reference was made, fully refute this accusation." In his cover letter sending the text of the decision to Garry Herrmann, Heydler was both apologetic about not having been able to ban Chase from the game and irritated at the Cincinnati club for not doing a better job of marshaling its evidence.

"There was no evidence whatsoever produced at the trial to show that Chase had made a bet, and the only direct evidence of his crookedness was made by Player Ring," he wrote. "To have found Chase guilty on this man's unsupported testimony would have been impossible." In Heydler's view, the Reds had done a lousy job of policing their ranks. "I feel that it is unfortunate indeed that the Cincinnati club could not, in any manner, furnish me with evidence that Chase had placed a bet against his team." Should any player's honesty again be doubted, he said, the club should investigate the matter more carefully before any charges are "made to the president of the League and publicity given to same." Doing otherwise, he said, would "do the game irreparable harm."

Do the game irreparable harm. Sparing the game "irreparable harm" had always been at the fore of the thinking of the men who ran the game. Mostly that had meant finding ways to look the other way, as they had done once again with Chase. Rumors weren't good. The only thing that might be worse was proof.

True to his word, McGraw worked a trade with the Reds and signed Chase to a Giants contract for 1919. Nobody made much of a fuss about it in the newspapers, most writers playing some variation of the theme that of all the managers in organized baseball, the Giants manager was the one best equipped to handle Chase. When he realized that Christy Mathewson would be mustered out of the army too late to resume his managerial duties with the Reds, McGraw offered Mathewson a job coaching with the Giants. What could you be thinking, wondered the reporters, bringing Mathewson and Chase together like this? McGraw told the reporters that he would have never done that had he not had assurances from both men, Chase and Mathewson, that coexistence would not be a problem.

That was almost certainly just so much John McGraw bullshit. Chase and Mathewson spoke not a word to one another during the 1919 season, during which the thirty-six-year-old Chase hit .284 for his new team, as the Giants battled the Reds throughout the summer for the National League lead. Chase mostly stayed out of the headlines, though every error and ill-timed failure at the plate brought the inevitable mutterings, both in the press box and in the Giants dugout.

And then on September 11, 1919, with the Giants losing touch with the Reds in the race for the National League pennant, McGraw suddenly suspended third baseman Heinie Zimmerman, ostensibly for staying out late on the nights before games and making no attempt to stay in shape—both violations of club rules. What the newspapers didn't report was that pitcher Fred Toney had gone to McGraw and told him that Zimmerman had offered him $200 to throw the previous day's game against the Cubs. Other Giants players later claimed that Zimmerman's offer to Toney was hardly an isolated incident, and he was not working alone, but rather in partnership with Hal Chase, and that the bribe offers had been coming all season.

As to what happened next, there are many accounts, all viable, none corroborated. McGraw's biographer argues when the manager returned to New York, he and team owner Charles Stoneham questioned Zimmerman, and exacted not only a confession, but an admission that Chase was in on the deal as well. Fred Lieb of the *New York Press*, meanwhile, reported that National League president John Heydler now went to the Giants with proof that Chase had indeed been guilty in the Cincinnati case and that Heydler wanted him out of the game, now. "I was never satisfied with my earlier acquittal of Chase," Lieb quoted Heydler as telling him. "I was unconvinced. Eventually I got a signed affidavit from a Boston gambler and a photographic copy of Chase's canceled check for $500 given him by a gambler as pay for throwing a game in 1918." According to Lieb, Heydler took the evidence to Charles Stoneham, the owner of the Giants, and essentially told him that Chase's career was over.

Chase was nonetheless not suspended from the team, though his playing time after the Zimmerman decision was limited to a single pinch-hitting appearance. When he didn't turn up on the season's final day, writers wanted to know why. McGraw merely said that Chase was sick and that hadn't "been feeling well for a long time."

And thus did Hal Chase's major league career come to a close: neither in celebration and triumph, as the promise of his very first days might have suggested, nor in a headline-making scandal, as most who played with him through the years might have guessed, but with a manager's lame excuse. When Chase wasn't at the Giants camp in 1920, McGraw told reporters that he was finished with the Giants, suggesting that more than illness was the reason. No other team in baseball inquired about acquiring Chase. He spent the 1920 baseball season playing on Sundays only with a San Jose team in the independent Mission League in California.

By the end of 1920, Chase was swept up in the Black Sox scandal. When news of the World Series fix began to percolate during September of 1919 and many both inside and outside the game began wondering whether the Series really could be successfully manipulated, they came to Hal Chase for counsel. When the indictments were handed down a year later, in addition to the eight White Sox players and a small circle of gamblers, the indicted also included Hal Chase. Rumors swirled that he had masterminded the fix. Others said that he had been the go-between between the players and the gamblers. The indictment claimed only that Chase had guilty knowledge of the plan to throw the series and failed to report it. He was never tried in the case, never convicted of anything, never even officially thrown out of the game. His indictment in the Black Sox case stands rather like one of those Lifetime Achievement Oscars—a recognition that somehow, in the normal circumstance of events, someone very, very deserving had been inexplicably and too long overlooked.

THREE

Baseball at War

Just as the 1919 World Series scandal has its seeds in the 1903 Major League merger and the Hal Chase story, so too is it connected to the cataclysmic events going on in Europe. The First World War intruded upon Organized Baseball as no other outside event either before or since—even World War II brought less disruption and uncertainty to the game. The war took away a sizable percentage of the game's players; of the 531 players on the active rosters or held in reserve by Major League teams at the close of the 1917 season, 154, or 29 percent, were in the military by midseason 1918. The war caused others to scramble to avoid the draft through a loophole in the Selective Service "work or fight" order, and a number of the game's brightest stars, including Joe Jackson of the White Sox, left their teams to play for teams representing the shipyards and factories doing work for the War Department. The "shipyard ballplayers" found themselves the subject of immediate—and lingering—criticism and scorn, both inside and outside the game, and when the war was over their perceived "slacker" status complicated their reentry into the game. Moreover, the war brought big-time gamblers back to the ballparks, and in greater numbers after the government shut down horseracing and closed the tracks.

For a time it seemed certain that the ballparks themselves would shut their gates in the middle of the 1918 season, and the season was eventually shortened by one month. When the parks did go dark in September of 1918, no one knew when baseball might return; most felt certain that it was unlikely to come back anytime in 1919. Even after the armistice on November 11, 1918, the fate of the 1919 season seemed problematic. All of this created a nervous uncertainty and a suspicion on all sides when baseball did finally convene for the 1919 season. And a nervous, uncertain, suspicious community is a vulnerable community.

Most significantly, World War I proved the beginning of the end for the National Commission. A series of political and public relations missteps by the Commission in trying to stave off closure of the game heightened the festering frustration that many of the game's owners had with the Commission, and particularly with Ban Johnson, whose strong voice through the years had made him very much the group's primus inter pares. Most prominent among Johnson's critics was Charles Comiskey, who didn't just dislike that Johnson was president of the American League and the dominant voice and de facto ruler of the National Commission; he didn't like Ban Johnson, period; the two men hated one another and had for years. While intermediaries had in the past always been able to broker a truce between the two, in the best interests of the game, the events of the war years widened and deepened the rift to the point where reconciliation was no longer possible. And while the Comiskey-Johnson enmity played no direct role in precipitating the events of 1919, it was central to the way the investigation into the allegations unfolded a year later. Had Comiskey and Johnson not hated one another, it is highly unlikely that there would have been a Black Sox Scandal to begin with, for whatever might have come out after the fact would have come with a healthy dose of plausible deniability.

When Congress declared war a few days before the opening of the baseball season in April of 1917, the country was seized with a simultaneous anxiety and patriotic fervor. Ban Johnson, driven by anxiety and recognizing that the short-term survival of baseball would be well served by wrapping the game in the American flag, handed down some directives to Major League teams that he hoped would demonstrate both baseball's patriotic fervor and its essential place in daily American culture. Most were minor gestures—pregame announcements urging enlistments, collections at the gate on designated days for the Red Cross, the purchase of Liberty Bonds by players and front-office personnel. At Johnson's insistence, Major League teams were also instructed to conduct one hour of military training each day. Soldiers were recruited to lead the drills, which consisted of players in full baseball uniform, with bats on their shoulders to simulate rifles parading in close-order drill on the outfield grass before the games. The spectacle may have sold an extra ticket or two, and it was very popular with the newspaper photographers, but less so with the players. Johnson even offered a $500 prize to the best-drilled team. The St. Louis Browns won it, which was the first time the hapless Browns had won anything since the 1880s, and the last time they'd win anything until the war-ravaged rosters of 1944 gave them their only twentieth-century pennant.

Nobody knew what would happen to baseball in those early months of the war. Would the government permit the game to continue? Would the draft leave enough players to field competitive teams? Braves catcher Hank Gowdy became the first to enlist in June of 1917; only a trickle of players followed his lead, but the draft, instituted in midseason, hung like a sword over the game and its players. And not having enough players was not the owners' only fear. Even if the gates did remain open, would fans be too distracted by the war to come?

For all of the owners' concern, professional baseball faced no real threat in 1917; President Wilson indicated that it was his wish that sports would continue "as usual." Once it became apparent that baseball was safe, at least for the immediate future, the National Commission could turn to the other issues threatening the game. One was the increased visibility of gamblers in some major league parks, particularly the two parks in Boston. Here again, it was Ban Johnson driving policy, and while he may have been motivated by the best interests of the game, his handling of the Boston situation left some bad feelings between the two leagues.

Reacting to articles in the Boston newspapers on the increase in ballpark gambling, Johnson, on behalf of the National Commission, hired the Pinkerton National Detective Agency to investigate and to prod law enforcement authorities to see if something might be done. A team of Pinkertons descended on Braves Field and Fenway Park, beginning with a Braves-Reds series in early July. They reported open betting going on in the Braves Field pavilion along the first base line. Men were betting on everything—the outcome of the game, of course, but also on whether individual batters would reach first base, or second base, or whether men on base would score. Police officers present in the section weren't exactly condoning the activity, but were apparently not actively discouraging it either. All the detectives—there were at least three different men filing reports—identified the center of the gambling activity as Joseph "Sport" Sullivan, nearing fifty now, but a fixture at Boston ballparks for the better part of two decades; the first mentions of his name in the Boston papers date to at least 1901. "Wait until Sullivan arrives and see what he has to say," one Pinkerton reported overhearing as the early arrivals discussed the odds on that day's game. Sullivan arrived and fixed the odds for that day at even money; they would change, growing ever longer in

Cincinnati's favor as the Reds took an early lead and held it into the late innings. Bets were made with every change in odds. Sullivan was the only man whose full name was given, but the detectives reported bets being made by Joe, Doc, Sharkey, Tim, Happy, Sporty, Ben, K. Joel, Murphy, Ika, Morris, Jackie, Jake, Bruce, Max Lax, and Greece. Reports over the next month all fixed Sport Sullivan as the center of betting activity. They also characterized him as a very careful man, attempting to "hush the noisier gamblers," as the report put it. He never exchanged any money inside the park and seldom exchanged any words that might be overheard; instead he sometimes showed a notepad to the others, and sometimes pantomimed odds and bets, "in deaf-and-dumb form, fingers and lips," particularly after the Pinkertons began attending the games in the company of Boston police officers.

After the detectives established to Ban Johnson's satisfaction that gamblers were indeed operating at the ballparks, he next engaged the services of a Boston attorney to represent the interests of the National Commission. The attorney he secured was Thomas Lavelle, who also happened to be an assistant district attorney. It was after Johnson had engaged Lavelle that the police began accompanying the Pinkertons to the games. Less than a week later, police arrested seven people at Braves Field, Sport Sullivan notably not among them. In court, Lavelle asked that the maximum $20 fine be levied on the defendants, and said that he was asking for the maximum punishment "at the personal solicitation of President Johnson, who is determined to stamp out gambling in connection with the various ball parks of the country." The newspapers dutifully reported it. "To be obliged to pay out $20 for the pleasure of gambling at the ball parks is expensive," noted the Boston Post. "It discourages the pastime to a considerable extent." But Johnson knew perfectly well that a $20 fine was not going to dissuade men from gambling the $50–$100 a pop that was commonly bet at the ballparks. "The Commission must determine upon a better course of procedure," he wrote to Garry Herrmann.

The "better course" that Johnson decided upon was to compile a list of known gamblers and prohibit them from entering either Boston ballpark. The list had twenty-two names on it. The name at the top was Sport Sullivan. With the cooperation of Assistant District Attorney Lavelle, on Monday, August 27, the Pinkertons, Boston Police, and officials of the Boston Braves began stopping those on the list from entering the ballpark, refunding their money and sending them away. This continued for three days, the balance of the Braves' home stand. When the Red Sox returned home from a two-week road trip the following day, the newspapers took note of the fact that no similar effort to bar the gamblers had been made at Fenway Park. "No individual who had the price was denied admission to the grounds," noted the Journal. "Many of those who were turned away from [Braves Field] passed placidly through the gates of [Fenway Park] and seated themselves in their favorite seats as usual....A suspicion has been entertained that the astute Ban Johnson slipped something over on the Boston National club when he timed the anti-betting crusade of the National Commission to coincide with a home sojourn of the Braves."

The Braves management was entertaining that same suspicion. Business manager Walter Hapgood, writing on behalf of team president Percy Haughton,* told the National Commission that "unless the same vigilance is shown at the other park in this city, the crusade we have started may act unfavorably...against this club, not so much because of any revenue lost at the gate, but because of the very general feeling in Boston that, if the crusade is confined to Braves Field alone, discrimination is being shown against this club." Johnson did nothing to placate the growing frustration of the National League. In fact, he seemed to go out of his way to antagonize them. "Since this work [identifying the gamblers] was started, there has been no evidence of cooperation or a sense of duty on the party [sic] of the National League," he wrote to Herrmann in August. "This is an amazing condition." A month later, he reiterated his irritation with the National League, in another letter to Herrmann. "It seems to me you require something to wake up the dormant and indifferent attitude of the National League to a re-alization of the great danger that confronts baseball from this quarter."

Of course, Johnson did not depend upon National League owners for his job as president of the American League, nor for his seat on the National Commission. He believed he could afford to take an imperial attitude with the National League and its owners because he always had. And the National League people were getting sick of it. "I am surprised to note that Mr. Johnson had detectives at Braves Field, and that he endeavored to give great prominence to the fact that gambling existed at our park," wrote National League president John Tener to Herrmann in September.

"In a general way this is not his affair, and he should have been content to stamp out this abuse at Fenway Park....I have no doubt that if I were to place detectives on Comiskey's grounds, or any other American League Park in the circuit, I could find some betting, and it would be just as sensible for me to do so as what Mr. Johnson has done."

In the grand scheme of Ban Johnson's relations with National League owners and executives, the issue of policing the park was perhaps a small one. But over fourteen years there had been a lot of small issues, and inevitably they were all

* Haughton is best known to sports history for compiling a 72–7–5 record as coach of the Harvard football team from 1908 to 1916. The Harvard record under Haughton included five undefeated seasons.

adding up to one very big issue, and Johnson's high-handedness with the National League would ultimately backfire. Two years later, in the summer and fall of 1920, before the lid blew off on the Black Sox scandal, when Charles Comiskey and his confederates began angling to replace the National Commission with a single commissioner, effectively wresting control of the game from Johnson, his bitter enemy, he was able to do so by building a coalition comprised of but three American League owners. But Comiskey's disaffected three would be joined by all eight National League owners.

The campaign to eradicate gambling in the Boston ballparks, meanwhile, played out as so many other similar campaigns had over the past decade. It made headlines for a few weeks, after which everything returned to normal, and the sporting men again had no trouble passing unfettered through the turnstiles and laying off their wagers at the ballparks.

Ban Johnson's next misstep came in November 1917, after the draft board did a reset and declared that all of the previous five months' deferments—handed out rather liberally—were now null and void, and that anyone with a case for deferment must re-present that case to his local draft board. Moreover, the standards for deferment were now going to be much higher. It meant that any man between twenty-one and thirty was likely to be drafted, and that demographic included fully 90 percent of Major League ballplayers. A reporter from the *Pittsburgh Post* went through the National League rosters and determined that no more than three or four players would be left on any one team. Giving the impression he was speaking in his role as a member of the National Commission, which was not the case, Johnson announced that he would petition the government to exempt 288 players—eighteen per team—from the draft in order that the game might continue in 1918. "The high standard of the game would be destroyed if the players were indiscriminately drafted for military service," he argued. Johnson's words were shocking in their insensitivity, particularly so when it came to those half dozen players on each team who would not be among the chosen eighteen. "The rest of the players now under contract or reservation to the Major Leagues we would gladly donate to the nation if it wants them," he said. "And an unknown bench warmer might be a better soldier in the trenches than a star pitcher or champion batsman."

Reaction to Johnson's comments was visceral and immediate, both within and beyond the game. Johnson was called everything short of traitor for seeking further privilege for those perceived as already being privileged. While he gained the public support of his longtime National Commission ally Garry Herrmann, nearly everyone else in professional baseball rejected his position and sought to distance themselves from it. The first and most resonant of his critics was John Tener, the National League president. "Let Ban Johnson confine his remarks to his own league. We are fully competent to take care of our own affairs," said Tener.

"I would not go one inch toward Washington to ask President Wilson or the Secretary of War for special favors for baseball." Tener added that if any of his club owners made a request like Johnson's, he would "walk out of this office and never return." He called Johnson's suggestion "unpatriotic" and "selfish," saying "nothing could be further from the purposes of baseball." He also ridiculed Johnson's whole idea of players marching around in close-order drill with wooden bats.

A number of club owners in both leagues lined up to echo Tener. The National League owners who spoke out were, like Tener, quick to emphasize that Johnson was an American League guy and shouldn't presume to speak for them. "It is the misfortune of the National League that it must bear part of the stigma of this thing," said Phillies president W. F. Baker. Even some American League owners took public issue with Johnson's remarks. Yankees owner Colonel Jacob Ruppert, whose title came by way of eight years of service in the National Guard, took particular umbrage, reminding everyone that his co-owner, Captain Tillinghast Huston, was then on active duty. "My partner...is now in France dodging German shells and helping his country to win the war. I certainly am not in favor of asking exemption for a ball player, while my partner is risking his life in the service."

Public reaction was likewise roundly critical. A few of Johnson's longtime friends in the press, most notably Joe Vila of the *New York Sun*, tried to spin the story to Johnson's benefit, but otherwise the president of the American League was "panned to a crisp in the leading Eastern and Southern papers," noted Fred Lieb, who then proceeded to pan Johnson to a crisp himself. "The more one analyzes Johnson's plan," wrote Lieb, "the more audacious it appears. The audacity of an amusement promoter putting 'the high standards' of his particular amusement above the welfare of a country at war is shocking to the sensibilities of the average American.

"Another brazen part of Johnson's suggestion is the manner in which he offers his bench warmers and extra pitchers to the government, saying 'we would willingly sacrifice these men....' The idea of turning his least competent players over to the government strikes at the heart of the democratic idea behind the selective draft, whose primary aim was to put the millionaire's son on the same plane with the son of the village shoemaker and the $15,000-a-year Tris Speaker with $1500-a-year colt pitcher. Were such a plan adopted it would be favoritism of the rankest sort."

Johnson was forced to retract. He maintained he hadn't been seeking any favors from the government. "My suggestion that eighteen men on each of the Major League teams be exempted was merely that—a suggestion." He insisted he had simply been offering his thoughts about how baseball might still be played in wartime.

The criticism of Johnson's pronouncement was mainly focused on style rather than substance. Johnson had made the game look petty and selfish at a time when it needed all the sympathy and goodwill it could get. But the truth of the matter is that Johnson had said what everybody in baseball was thinking; when the sixteen owners convened in December, the only item on the docket was how they might persuade the government to keep their players out of the draft and playing during the 1918 season.

Early signs from local draft boards were encouraging. Most of the men who had had deferments—anyone with dependents mostly—retained those deferments. And in their planning for 1918, the owners were cautious. Attendance had been down in 1917 from the record-breaking 1916 season—not dramatically, but measurably. They feared a greater drop-off in 1918. They also agreed to limit 1918 rosters to eighteen players, not because Ban Johnson had suggested it but because an eighteen-man payroll was going to be less expensive than a twenty-five-man payroll. Further, they cut the season from 154 to 140 games, and cut salaries proportionately, and sometimes a bit more than proportionately. Spring training was shortened, but the 1918 season began on time with largely recognizable rosters.

The first genuine crisis for organized baseball came on May 23, 1918, when the provost marshal of the United States, General Enoch Crowder, issued the government's work-or-fight order. The edict read that on July 1, anyone of draft age who was either unemployed or employed in a "non-useful" occupation must either find a job that somehow supported the war effort—in farms, shipyards, munition factories, and the like—or face induction into the military. Previous deferments were no longer valid. Of the 309 men on the active rosters and reserve lists of Major League baseball, 258 would be forced to leave the game in six weeks and either enlist or find work in the war industry.

Baseball's task now was to persuade the government—Provost Marshal Crowder, Secretary of War Newton Baker, and President Wilson—that baseball was effectively an "essential industry," and that baseball players should be exempt from the draft because they were already in effective compliance with the work-or-fight order. "The game offers a field for relaxation, diversion and recreation unequaled by any amusement throughout the country," read a portion of baseball's formal presentation to Provost Marshal Crowder, and that was true not only for fans on the home front but for the troops in uniform, the Commission claimed. Giving the game up would be "a serious detriment to the morale of our forces," read the report.

If the morale of the country wasn't reason enough to keep the turnstiles open, baseball owners also suggested the government consider the contribution that the game was making to the war effort financially. Club owners and officials had purchased $8.5 million worth of Liberty Bonds, and players another quarter of a million dollars worth. Twenty-two thousand dollars had been collected for the Red Cross, and despite a rainy spring throughout the game, baseball had already collected more than $88,000 in the government's new war tax on tickets.

The argument for exemption for organized baseball—which was in effect an amicus curiae brief in the case of Washington Senators catcher Eddie Ainsworth, who had had his draft status reclassified and was appealing to the War Department—had been prepared by Garry Herrmann, and baseball's emissary in presenting it to the government was Herrmann's personal friend Senator Warren Harding of Ohio. Harding presented the game's case personally to Provost Marshal Crowder on Monday June 17, and reported back to the National Commission that while Crowder was inclined to look favorably on baseball's petition, Secretary of War Baker was not. Harding urged Herrmann and the Commission to approach President Wilson directly.

This Garry Herrmann did not do, a decision that angered Ban Johnson, and one Herrmann himself had cause to regret when Secretary Baker ruled that baseball was not an exempt industry and that players must comply with the work-or-fight ruling. Baker did, however, make one significant concession; he granted a two-month extension, ruling that players did not have to comply with work-or-fight until September 1. Baseball could very nearly play out its full season.

The immediate question was what this would mean for the World Series. Would the regular season have to end on August 20 or thereabouts, in order to complete the Series before September 1? Would the government give an extension to the two pennant winners and allow them to play past the September 1 deadline? The magnates of the game were of several minds on what the best course might be. John Tener was adamant that no World Series be played. So intransigent was he on this point that National League owners named Pittsburgh owner Barney Dreyfuss to replace Tener as the league's representative to the National Commission meeting to discuss the matter.

That meeting was held in Cleveland on August 3, and while it resulted in a determination to petition the government to hold the Series in early September—a petition the War Department swiftly and happily granted—its greater legacy was that it probably marked the beginning of the end for the National Commission.

John Tener wasn't there; after being replaced at the meeting, he had resigned. He had been restless in the job for several months, frustrated at his lack of power relative to that of his colleague Johnson, as well as with having to deal with Johnson, whom he had grown to dislike. His disagreement with the owners over their eagerness to hold the World Series was the final straw.

But the bigger loser in the meetings was Johnson, and, again, it was a combination of hubris and his own big mouth that got him in trouble. Before the Cleveland meetings began, for the third time in a year, Johnson wandered off the reservation in his remarks and aroused the ire of the men who paid his salary. Without consulting his owners, Johnson announced that the American League season would end on August 20, and that the World Series would conclude before the War Department's September 1 deadline. Going into a meeting of American League owners in Cleveland on August 3, he reiterated to reporters that August 20 would be the end of the regular season. When the meeting in Cleveland convened, however, the owners let Johnson know that this was not the case. Their interests were at stake here, they informed him, not his, and they fully intended to play out the schedule until Labor Day. The owners were in effect unwilling to forego ten days of ticket sales, particularly when it wasn't at all certain when they might be able to sell tickets again. Johnson was contrite after the meeting when he announced officially that the season would continue until Labor Day. But he was contrite only to a point. "If the club owners wish to take a chance on acting contrary to the ruling of the war department, that is their business," he said.

The scolding tone of Johnson's comment rankled at least three American League owners, including Charles Comiskey, who didn't need much to set him off. The three American League owners—Comiskey, Harry Frazee of the Red Sox, and Clark Griffith of the Senators—drafted a statement that was effectively a call for Johnson's ouster as president.

"Just why President Johnson should take the stand he did in this matter is beyond our comprehension," the statement read; "he has bungled the affairs of his league in this particular case. . . .

"His 'rule or ruin' policy is shelved. . . . He has tried to close our gates several times this season, but he is through spending our money. From now on the club owners are to run the American League. If anyone is to close our gates it will be the government or club owners, not a salaried official."

A salaried official. In his two decades at the helm of the American League, nobody had so demeaned Ban Johnson or his place in the game. Nonetheless, he survived this crisis, for Comiskey backed down from the criticism a week later; he'd no doubt counted the votes and realized that the criticism of the disaffected troika had little traction with the other owners. Johnson retained a solid five-vote majority in the American League. Comiskey would have to wait to see Johnson stripped of his power. But the events of 1918 had at least stripped the American League president of his aura. For perhaps the first time, owners, writers, players saw him differently. He was now "a salaried official," not the supreme ruler he had been.

In July, when the War Department's work-or-fight order took effect, players began leaving their teams to comply, the short-term exemption given to the game notwithstanding. Many of those who left early did so because they found some pretty sweet deals. Some joined the army and navy and were assigned to baseball teams that would play charity games for the troops or sell Liberty Bonds. Others found work in the shipyards and steel plants, ostensibly as welders, painters, and general laborers, but in truth their sole job in the defense industry was playing ball for the factory and shipyard teams.

Babe Ruth signed a contract to play for a Chester, Pennsylvania, shipyard team in July, but changed his mind within twenty-four hours and stayed with the Red Sox. Stars like Ruth were presented with multiple options, for the shipyard, steel-plant, and munitions-factory teams were actively recruiting. The Remington Arms Company in Bridgeport, Connecticut, for example, sent a letter to all sixteen teams, offering work to virtually any and all major league players. "There is no more vitally essential work in the United States than that which is being done by the Remington Bridgeport Works and it is more than likely we can provide opportunities for a majority of your men should any of them wish to come to Bridgeport." This kind of entreaty from the employment manager at Remington, and others like it, sent shock waves through Major League front offices. For the owners—already nervous about the suddenly uncertain state of the game—grew even more alarmed at what they perceived as a threat not only to the 1918 season but to the very foundation of their business.

Of the hundreds upon hundreds of amateur and semipro baseball leagues playing in virtually every American city and town in 1918, the big factory teams played a pretty high level of baseball, even before the war. They could offer year-round employment, and many retired major leaguers, as well as many minor leaguers shrewd enough to understand that full-time professional baseball provided an uncertain future, found a comfortable sinecure playing for teams representing big factories.

Major League Baseball in 1918 was not the dominant and all-powerful cartel it would become soon after the war. It was run essentially by sixteen men of varying degrees of wealth, all competing for America's entertainment dollar as best they could. Their control of professional baseball was still tenuous. While they had successfully fought off the Federal League incursion less than half a decade earlier, the Federal League, like the American and National leagues, was set up along the same lines, and therefore not a challenge to the business model. Like the American and National Leagues, the Federal League was run by a collection of owners of the same varying degrees of wealth and depended for its revenue on ticket sales, and maybe a little ballpark advertising. Factory baseball was another creature entirely. Factories had potentially millions of dollars in profits with which to subsidize its baseball teams, if they so chose. In a day when nearly every major leaguer was in need of off-season work to pay the off-season bills, the factories could put as many ballplayers as they wished on their winter payroll. They were already offering salaries equal to and sometimes greater than those the Major League teams offered players. It was not difficult to imagine corporate baseball on a national level after the war, a level that would prove a very real threat to organized baseball.

Despite the fact that the players going to the defense-industry teams did nothing illegal or immoral, the baseball owners set out to discredit the shipyard ballplayers in the surest, and cruelest, way they could—denigrating the players as selfish, cowardly slackers. They found willing accomplices in their slander campaign in the generally pliant baseball press.

Nobody was more eviscerated by the game and its fourth estate than Joe Jackson, who left the White Sox in mid-May to join the Harlan and Hollingsworth Shipbuilding Company, a subsidiary of Bethlehem Steel in Wilmington, Delaware. His departure took place before the work-or-fight order was to be enforced, but immediately after his South Carolina draft board had reclassified him 1-A. Jackson was by far the biggest star to play defense-industry baseball, and that earned him a disproportionate share of the scorn. The *Chicago Tribune* editorialized that while Jackson was "man of unusual physical development" who would make "an excellent fighting man," he seemed to prefer to avoid the war. This, the editorial concluded ominously, would have repercussions when he tried to return to the game. "Good Americans will not be very enthusiastic over seeing him play baseball after the war is over." Another Chicago paper compared Jackson unfavorably to Stonewall Jackson and Andrew Jackson, who had "fighting blood." The *New York Herald*, meanwhile, claimed Jackson had "conscientious objections to getting hurt in the service of his country and associating with patriots."

Charles Comiskey insinuated that he might not even let Jackson return to the game. In remarks carefully crafted and certainly aimed less at Jackson than at those among his teammates who might have the notion of following him to the shipyard, Comiskey said there would be "no room for the jumpers" on the White Sox. "I don't consider them fit to play for my club. I hate to see players, particularly my own, go to the shipyards to escape service." The phrase that jumps out there is "particularly my own." The owners' concern was not that the players were exhibiting cowardice but that they were exercising independence. Baseball's reserve clause protected an owner's rights to the services of his players only within the fabric of the American and National leagues, along with the minor leagues that were a party to the National Agreement; it was completely without standing when it came to third-party baseball.

Editorial after editorial, article after article, particularly in the baseball press— the *Sporting News*, *Sporting Life*, and *Baseball Magazine*—decried the practice. So alarmed were the owners over the threat to their business that the industry teams might pose that they implored the government to put a stop to it. "Attention has already been called to the *desertion* [emphasis added] of their teams by players to accept employment in ship-building, munition and other plants," read part of a letter from the National Commission to Secretary of War Baker in early August, "ostensibly as expert employees in these respective lines, but as a matter of fact, their principal purpose was to escape active service under the work-or-fight order and draw salaries for ball playing on teams representing such plants." They asked that the government investigate the matter, suggesting it would "cause great dissatisfaction and discord among bona fide employees of such industries," and that the government should for that reason put a stop to it. In the end, the government didn't intervene, but the owners' bluster and threats served their purpose. Fewer major leaguers than might have been expected succumbed to the lure of the shipyards, and those who did had their supposed lack of patriotism held against them during 1919 contract negotiations.

Some ninety years after it was played, the notion that the 1918 World Series between the Red Sox and the Cubs had been fixed had a Warholian fifteen minutes of fame when Eddie Cicotte's confession surfaced in 2008. Cicotte's confession, stolen from the Cook County Courthouse along with other Black Sox documents in 1920, was part of a trove of papers acquired by the Chicago Museum of History in 2008. The papers were bought at auction from an anonymous seller, though they were at one time part of the files of Charles Comiskey's attorney, Alfred Austrian. Cicotte's offhand mention that the 1918 World Series between the Cubs and the Red Sox might have been fixed made headlines. A spate of newspaper stories and a book came out of it. But the evidence to support the argument of a 1918 fix is frightfully thin and wholly speculative.

The line that created such a twenty-first-century buzz came from Cicotte's deposition given before Comiskey and Austrian in Austrian's office the morning the whole White Sox cover-up came undone in September 1920. Cicotte said:

> The way it started, we were going east on the train. The ball players were talking about somebody trying to fix the National League ball players or something like that in the World Series of 1918. Well anyway there was some talk about them offering $10,000 or something to throw the Cubs in the Boston series. There was talk that somebody offered this player $10,000 or anyway the bunch of players were offered $10,000 to throw this series.

That was it. *Talking about. Something like that. Talk that somebody offered this player. Or anyway the bunch of players were offered.* Cicotte's assertions don't exactly provide the foundations for either airtight prosecution or library-worthy history. The grand jury did not pursue it in 1920; whether this was for lack of evidence or lack of interest is not clear. The only other contemporaneous suggestion that there was anything untoward about the 1918 Series came in the diary of Harry Grabiner, Comiskey's secretary, who was intimately involved in the Black Sox investigation and in the 1920 movement to replace the National Commission with Judge Landis as commissioner. Bill Veeck, who bought the White Sox in the late 1950s, discovered the diary in the 1960s and wrote about it in his 1965 book, *The Hustler's Handbook*, after which the diary disappeared again. In a notation involving a meeting with Judge Landis, sometime after the Black Sox scandal, Grabiner recorded that Landis had asked him for a list of people to whom even the suggestion of game fixing was attached. Grabiner turned over twenty-seven names he had earlier listed in the diary. The list, Veeck reported, included Eugene Milo Packard, a career 86–67 pitcher, who played for the Cubs in 1916 and part of 1917, and for the Cardinals in 1917–1918. In the margin next to Packard's name, Grabiner had written "1918 Series fixer."

A deposition in which the witness recalled "something like that" happening and a notation in the margins of a diary nobody but Bill Veeck has ever seen about a player nobody born after 1910 had ever heard of. Weak evidence, but so powerful is the orbit of the Black Sox story that conspiracy theories get built upon such sawdust-filled foundations.

Even without speculation about a fix, the 1918 World Series had problems aplenty. This was a star-crossed series from the very beginning, born in part from disagreement whether it should even be played.

By the time it began, it was clear that the paying public had lost much of its interest in the game. Attendance across Major League baseball in 1918 came in at just over three million people, a drop of more than two million, or more than 40 percent, from 1917 figures, which had themselves represented a drop from 1916. The attendance number was the lowest in the modern era. Wary that this disinterest would carry over to the Series, the National Commission decreed that the tickets be sold at regular-season prices, rather than with the usual World Series premium. Still, ticket sales were slow. Moreover, 1918 was the first year of a plan to share some of the players' shares of the Series money with the second-, third-, and fourth-place finishers in each league. At some point during the first three games in Chicago, the National Commission told the players the winning and losing shares would be $1,200 and $800, the lowest ever, and much lower than the $2,000 and $1,400 the Commission had earlier told the players they could expect.

On the train ride from Chicago to Boston after game three of the Series, the two teams appointed a delegation of six players, three from each team, to petition the Commission to reinstate the $2,000 and $1,400. At ten o'clock on the morning of the fifth game, the full three-man Commission told the player delegation they could not change the amount of the Series share without a vote of the owners. Garry Herrmann urged the players to play out the Series, and promised things would be made right afterward. The players weren't buying it. At game time on the afternoon of game five, with the Fenway Park stands filled with wounded war veterans, the Cubs and Red Sox players sat in their locker rooms in their street clothes, refusing to take the field in a dispute over the size of their World Series shares. Negotiating with them was a drunken Ban Johnson.

Johnson had gone straight from the morning meeting with the players to a liquid lunch at the Copley Plaza Hotel, and from there to Fenway Park, where he arrived at game time and found the stands full, the field empty, and his colleagues on the Commission in frustrated conversation with the player delegation in the umpires' room beneath the stands. He swept into the room and took charge, his impaired state evident to everyone present. He either cajoled or bellowed, or both. According to John Heydler, who would soon become National League president, Johnson put his arm around Red Sox outfielder Harry Hooper, the lead Boston negotiator, and appealed to his loyalty to "the Great American League," to the game in general, and to the wounded soldiers in the stands. According to the memory of Red Sox manager Ed Barrow, Johnson screamed at the room: "With a war going on and fellows fighting in France, what do you think the public will think of you ballplayers striking for more money?"

Hooper and Les Mann, the lead negotiator for the Cubs, recognizing both the merits of Johnson's argument and the futility of dealing with a man who was both uncompromising by nature and quite compromised at the present moment, agreed to play "for the sake of the public and the wounded soldiers in the stands," first exacting a promise from the Commission that there would be no retaliation against the players for the strike, which ended up lasting an hour. Johnson had saved the day, and had he not been so evidently drunk, it might have been one of his finest hours. News of his condition was widely talked about within the game, however, and it took him down a notch in the estimation of both players and his colleagues—yet another 1918 nail in his professional coffin.

When the Series was over, with the Red Sox winning it four games to two, the Commission immediately reneged on its promises. They did not revisit the matter of the share size. The Red Sox winner's share was $1,102, the smallest ever. The losing share was only $671. The National Commission also retaliated against the players, deciding to forego awarding the traditional World Series medals to each player. "The Commission has unanimously decided that the mutinous and mercenary action of the contest players in the recent Series demonstrates that the members of the championship team are unworthy of a World Series emblem," read a letter sent to each player in early November, "and none will be presented to them."

When baseball shut its gates on Labor Day, owners, players, writers, and fans were resigned to seeing the ballparks remain dark throughout the 1919 season. There were some newspaper discussions about reorganizing the two leagues along geographical lines—the eight eastern teams would comprise one league, the eight western teams the other—with games played exclusively on weekends, with maybe a midweek twilight game here and there. That, proponents claimed, would ease the logistics and cost of travel, all the while keeping the game in front of the nation's fans. It didn't address who the players might be, and the plan never went beyond the pages of the newspapers. One wag noted that the idea of keeping the game alive was motivated purely by self-interest on the part of sports writers—no baseball meant no baseball writers. The owners were not discussing anything, so abstract did the return of the game seem.

And then suddenly there was peace in Europe. The armistice on November 11 effectively cancelled the draft, which nullified the work-or-fight rule, seemingly clearing baseball to play in 1919. But it wasn't that simple. The players currently working in civilian essential-industry jobs would presumably be able to play, but how about the five hundred or so major and minor leaguers then in the service? Would they be mustered out in time to play baseball in 1919? "The AEF takes its own time about asking for waivers," noted sportswriter Grantland Rice. One question was whether the factories that had recruited professional ballplayers to their teams would make a financial pitch to keep them, and whether the players would be enticed. And there were other issues. There was no schedule in place, no travel plans made. There was even a question as to whether there was enough equipment to play a full season of professional baseball, the manufacture of bats and ball having been suspended during the months of the war. And then there were the fans. A great many of them had shown they could live without major league baseball during 1918. Would they continue to live without it going forward?

Although opening day was still more than five months away, these were all issues that would require cooperation, and after the fractious events of 1918, with the coffers across the game depleted, cooperation in organized baseball was in short supply. "[The war] has acted like the acid test in distinguishing the twenty-four-caret gold from the dross in the matter of patriotism and loyalty," wrote I. E. Sanborn of the *Chicago Tribune*, who went on to note that most of the games figures—owners and players—"displayed a desire to put self-interest ahead of the nation's ultimate triumph that has done professional baseball no good."

Following the armistice, John Heydler, soon to be appointed to replace John Tener as National League president and National Commission member, understood that peace in Europe did not mean peace in baseball, and that the path to the 1919 season would not be an easy one. "There is altogether too much aloofness, suspicion and lack of confidence between the club owners of the two great leagues," he said in late November. "It is all right to fight each other on the ball field during the playing season, but at all other times there should be at least the ordinary business cooperation that exists in other competitive lines.

"To attempt to carry on a so-called reconstruction program in baseball without the sincere aid of the sixteen club owners...would result in absolute failure."

Heydler's broadside was followed by an announcement that the owners had agreed to a joint American–National League meeting in December. Individual owners began to speak hopefully of playing baseball in 1919. Ban Johnson wrote to the War Department, asking for permission for the game to resume, a letter that was aimed more at garnering headlines than permission, given that the government had never ruled that the game must be stopped, only that its players were not exempt from work-or-fight. The response, from War Department chief of staff General Peyton March, not only gave baseball the government's blessing to continue, but suggested that when the game did resume, all would again be right with the world: "The wholesome effect of a clean and honest game like baseball is very marked."

FOUR

Brothers and Enemies

As he neared his sixtieth birthday in the summer of 1919, Charles Comiskey was the very epitome of American prosperity, success, rectitude, and standing, a man secure in the love of family, the affection of his public, and the respect and admiration of his peers.

A bit above six feet in height, he was a head taller than most of his contemporaries, and somewhat heavier than the 180 pounds he had been when he played first base for the Saint Louis Browns more than thirty years earlier. But a paunch was not a source of embarrassment, nor was it perceived as a sign of sloth in his day, but rather as a sign of status—proof of prosperity, evidence that a man had earned the right to make his living sitting and thinking, and not by the sweat of his brow and the strength of his back. And if by 1919 he had lost some of the athlete's physique, he still cut a rakish figure. His dusky hair was flecked with silver now, but had thinned only little, and his face still bore the chiseled features that had invited comparisons to actor Edwin Booth when Comiskey was a younger man.

Friends and his team's fans called him Commy. The newspaper writers, who never encountered a nickname they couldn't type into a cliché, called him the Old Roman, a name that had been with him since at least his playing days with the Browns back in the 1880s, though its origins have been lost. He must have liked it though, because his hold over the newspapermen who covered him was such that they seldom wrote anything he didn't like. Few public men were as kindly covered in the newspapers as Charles A. Comiskey. He was particularly solicitous of newspapermen, picking up all the expenses for those who traveled with the White Sox, of course; all teams carried the beat writers on the dole, a small investment measured against the column after column of free publicity the newspapers gave their businesses. But Comiskey treated the writers better than most of his brethren did. The pressroom food was just a little more plentiful at Comiskey Park, the liquor just a little better than at the other ballparks. Comiskey also brought a personal touch to his dealings with reporters. He was a backslapper, skilled at making a working-stiff newspaperman believe he was a part of the Comiskey inner circle. He was also very good at conveying the impression that he did not play favorites. No Chicago paper had ever been seen as the house organ, no single writer ever perceived as Comiskey's guy—well, maybe Gus Axelson of the old *Record-Herald*, who was writing a very flattering biography of Comiskey that summer of 1919. But Comiskey had any number of go-to writers when he wanted to see something reported, or refuted, or his side of something spelled out in his way. When something in the newspapers displeased him, he might call it to the reporter's attention, but he would do it in an off-handed, nonthreatening way. He had long ago absorbed the old maxim of never picking a fight with those who buy ink by the barrel. As a result, he was seen by the public less as a tycoon and more as a down-to-earth baseball guy, the benevolent owner who put the interests of fan and player ahead of his own. "One way or another," wrote Damon Runyon, "Charles Comiskey has probably spent more money on his Chicago White Sox than has been spent by any other baseball magnate in the country." Gus Axelson said that when it came to owners, Comiskey was simply "the King of them all."

Comiskey was unquestionably the best-known nonplayer in all of baseball. He had been the sole owner of the Chicago White Sox since their inception back in 1900, and there was no more successful franchise, on or off the field. Since he helped to start the American League in 1900—more than help start it actually; he was a driving force—the White Sox had won pennants in 1900, 1901, 1906, and 1917, winning the World Series in the latter two. That was one pennant short of the Red Sox and Cubs and two short of the Athletics, but none of those teams could match Comiskey's success at the gate.

The ballpark that bore his name at the corner of 35th and Shields on Chicago's South Side opened in 1910. The five millionth fan came through the gates of Comiskey Park during the summer of 1919. That led all of Major League Baseball over the past decade; only John McGraw's New York Giants came even close to that number, and popular teams like the Red Sox and Cubs were more than a million fans behind. Most of the rest of the Major League teams fell short of White Sox attendance by two to three million fans. And the 1919 White Sox were almost surely the best team Comiskey had ever put together. A lot of people were saying they may just be the best team *anyone* had ever put together.

Charles Comiskey had been a Chicagoan his entire life, born on August 15, 1859, at the corner of Union Avenue and Maxwell Street, on the Irish West Side, the third of the eight children of "Honest John" Comiskey. Honest John was one of the most popular men in the city, for eleven years an alderman from the West Side Irish wards and one-time president of the Chicago city council. But he was a difficult man to have as a father if your passions ran to baseball, as young Charley's did. Baseball was a pursuit the hard-working immigrant father deemed "frivolous," and it was a source of friction between father and son from an early age.

Honest John was insistent that his children have an education and that they also learn a trade. Accordingly, his son spent a year at Saint Ignatius College in Chicago, and another at Saint Mary's in Kansas, and Honest John also apprenticed young Charles to a plumber when the boy was sixteen. But Charley's passions for baseball ran deeper than those of the other boys; he was miserable as a plumber and stole away at every opportunity. Eventually Honest John gave up on trying to make his son a plumber and instead used political connections to find him work as a teamster, driving a brick wagon from a South Side brickyard to the downtown site where a new city hall was rising from the ruins of Great Fire of 1871. When on a summer's day in 1876 one of Charley's wagonloads of brick was long overdue, Honest John went searching for his son and his bricks. He found the dray and its team parked by the side of a ball field and his son on the mound, pitching. Alderman Comiskey drove the bricks to city hall himself, and that evening he and his son had a set-to at the dinner table. Charley's teamster days were over; his baseball odyssey begun. And his relationship with his father, while never exactly estrangement—Charley would return to his father's home at Union and Maxwell most winters during his early baseball apprenticeship—would be notably strained for much of the next decade.

Before he returned home to Chicago for good in 1900, Comiskey would build perhaps the most singular résumé in baseball history—player, manager, innovator, team owner, visionary behind the American League. He started in minor league ball as a pitcher, but he had played all the positions growing up, and in minor league seasons in Milwaukee and Dubuque, he pitched and played second and the outfield, before settling in at first base, where he remained for the rest of his playing career. He broke into the big leagues with the St. Louis Browns of the American Association in 1882, and put his mark on the game's history almost immediately. The responsibility of an 1880s first baseman was to catch any ball thrown his way by the others on the field; it was thus his responsibility to be where the others wanted him—glued to the bag. Comiskey, the story goes—and, as with most nineteenth-century baseball innovations, the truth is in some dispute—realized he could be of greater value to the defense playing off the bag. An umpire in Pittsburgh once delayed the start of play because he thought the Browns were short a player; nobody was standing on the first base bag. As Comiskey sometimes moved even further from the bag, he began encouraging his pitcher to cover first base on balls hit to the right side of the infield. Moreover, he started the practice of moving the infielders in to the edge of the grass when there was a runner on third base and fewer than two outs. Soon all of baseball had adopted Comiskey's innovations.

Comiskey wasn't much at the plate. A lifetime .260 hitter, he batted .300 only once in thirteen big league seasons. But he had a knack for being in the center of things; included among his 1,531 career hits were an unusually high number of game winners and rally starters, and this, combined with his play in the field and his sense of the game, made the Browns' colorful owner, saloon proprietor Chris Von der Ahe, recognize in his young first baseman a limber and creative baseball mind. "Der Boss" Von der Ahe named the twenty-four-year-old Comiskey player-manager in 1884. Beginning in 1885, Comiskey led the Browns to four consecutive American Association pennants and an 1886 world championship series win over the National League champions, Cap Anson's Chicago White Stockings.

Autocratic, eccentric, and egocentric, Von der Ahe was a difficult man to work for—"I am der boss president of der St. Louis Browns," he reminded all who worked for him. By the end of the Browns pennant run, he was having financial troubles, which he addressed by selling off his players to other teams. The Browns slipped to second in 1889, and after the season ended Comiskey took his leave, jumping to become player-manager of his hometown Chicago team in the brand new Brotherhood League. The Brotherhood League was an ambitious and idealistic experiment. The players and the owners—they were called "backers," not owners—were to share in the governance and profits of the game. Despite having attracted many of the game's top stars, however, the Brotherhood League had no profits to share, and folded after a single season. Comiskey returned to the Browns, but Von der Ahe's financial woes had only worsened in the year Comiskey had been away, as had the financial woes of the American

Association in general, and at the end of the 1891 season the American Association closed its doors. Comiskey left St. Louis for Cincinnati and the National League. No stop along Charles Comiskey's baseball odyssey would be as important to his life—or to the game of baseball—as Cincinnati, for it was in Cincinnati that Charles Comiskey met Ban Johnson.

At the time he met Comiskey, Johnson was the sports editor of the *Cincinnati Commercial-Gazette*. He had been drawn to sportswriting perhaps because he knew it was likely the last career his rigid father would have wanted for him. Johnson had been groomed for a life in the church or the law, but these were always his father's dreams, never his, and he never went far down either path. By 1892, he had been at the *Commercial-Gazette* for six years and had built a reputation as a feisty, confrontational, slightly imperious yet altogether able newspaperman. He was twenty-nine years old, four years younger than Comiskey and nearly identical in size and frame—five foot eleven, and an athletic 180 pounds. Johnson was a lifelong Cincinnatian, born and raised in Avondale—then a suburb of the city, now a part of the city proper—where his father was superintendent of schools. He grew up in a family for whom the twin pillars of life were education and religion. He chafed against both; his interests ran to good times and baseball; and at Oberlin Preparatory School in Cincinnati and later for a single year at Marietta College, he excelled at both. At Marietta he was summoned to a professor's office one day and told he had been seen coming out of a saloon. "Well what should I have done?" he was said to have replied. "Stayed in it?" A fellow student, later writing about Johnson's college days, reported: "In the study of botany, he could collect and classify fine specimens of mint, hops and rye."

At Oberlin Johnson had been a good enough catcher as a preparatory (high school) student to play for the college varsity team, and it was later reported that he was impressive enough in an Oberlin exhibition against the Cleveland National League team to attract the attention of the Cleveland scouts, though early-twentieth-century newspapermen frequently wrote that sort of thing about successful men who had played the game as boys. Whether or not Johnson was good enough for a chance at the pros, he was certainly the anchor of his prep school and college teams, a steady hitter and fielder, and above all a student of the game, which made him a team leader at both Oberlin and Marietta. Following his single year at Marietta—he had been suspended for a time as a freshman, and his biographer speculates that it may not have been entirely his decision not to return—Johnson spent a year and a half at the University of Cincinnati law school. But he found the study of law wanting, and left for the sports editor's job at the *Commercial-Gazette* in early 1886, his entire life to this point a disappointment to his parents.

Johnson would prove himself an imaginative editor, mixing analysis, gossip, and commentary with game reportage, and instituting baseball-related reader contests that boosted circulation. He was a fluid writer, a practitioner of the jargon- and argot-filled style of the day, certainly, but his prose was also clear, lively, and readable. He was not shy about calling a stupid play "stupid," and regularly upbraided players and fans alike for a lack of ballpark decorum. He was critical of players for being greedy when it came to their contract demands, and also critical of owners for being so parsimonious in their business dealings with the players. The criticism could extend to how the game was played. When Comiskey was manager of the Browns, Johnson would routinely take the team to task for an aggressive style of play that he felt crossed the line into thuggery.

Still, he generally liked the new Reds manager and hailed him as one the "great leaders in baseball" when he arrived in town in 1892. The two men had already crossed paths several times over the years, to their mutual benefit. Johnson's reporting on the game had never been confined to the playing field; he was equally interested in the business workings and the management structure of the game, and became close to front-office personnel, not just in Cincinnati but throughout the game. The Brotherhood war of 1889–90 provided the basis for a reporting tour-de-force by the young editor of the *Commercial-Gazette*, one that brought him ever closer to Comiskey, who, in his role as player-manager of the Brotherhood team in Chicago, became one of Johnson's most reliable sources. The two would speak on an almost daily basis during Comiskey's three years as Reds manager, the subjects covering everything baseball, from hit-and-run strategy to the reserve clause, from the merits of players on the Cincinnati team to the umpires, and how shamefully the men in blue were treated by players, fans, and owners alike. Johnson and Comiskey became regulars at a Vine Street saloon known as the "Ten Minute Club," because house rules required that someone at every table order a drink every ten minutes or leave. Commy took to calling Johnson "Beebee," a play on the way Johnson formally signed his name, "B. B. [Byron Bancroft] Johnson."

While on a scouting trip after the 1893 season, Comiskey ran into the owners of the Toledo and Kansas City clubs of the moribund Western League, a historically unstable, on-again, off-again league that had been dark in 1893. Team owners were planning to give it another shot in 1894 and looking for someone to handle the administrative details. Comiskey told them about Ban Johnson.

Beginning in November 1893, Johnson added the presidency of the Western League to his duties at the *Commercial-Gazette*. "I was president, secretary and treasurer of nothing," Johnson recalled of the moment he had been hired, at a salary of $2,500 per year. He would be effectively building a league from scratch. The Western League had ownership groups in eight cities when Johnson became president. There was no schedule, no player rosters, no ballpark leases. Yet somehow the league managed to have a successful first season under Johnson. All eight franchises finished the season and met all their payrolls—no small feat in nineteenth-century minor league baseball. Seven of the eight even made money. The one that didn't was league champion Sioux City, a town soon judged too small to compete financially in the revitalized league. So the league took over the franchise and agreed to move it to St. Paul. They awarded ownership of the new franchise to Charles Comiskey, who hung up his uniform, surrendered his managerial obligations, and devoted his full energies to being an owner.

Over the next six seasons, the Western League would prosper and grow, sometimes fitfully—with franchises switching cities with some regularity—but always steadily. Comiskey and Johnson were the league's two constants, Johnson the steady hand on the tiller, Comiskey in sync with his friend's vision and with considerable influence over his fellow owners. Not only were they alike in their thoughts; they were alike in their ambitions. Comiskey was restless in St. Paul; Johnson restless with his increasingly fractious dealings with the National League; both men were restless as minor leaguers. At the close of the 1899, they took the first steps to do something about that restlessness.

St. Paul had been a middle-of-the-pack team under Comiskey, and it was beginning to see its attendance numbers slip. Comiskey wanted to come home to Chicago; Johnson helped him get there. Over drinks, Johnson talked about the matter with Cubs owner James Hart, who was not at all interested in sharing his city with another ball club, least of all a team—minor league or not—operated by a well-known and popular hometown boy like Comiskey. But Johnson kept pouring and kept talking. Comiskey could open a ball field down by the stockyards, Johnson told Hart, far away from the Cubs West Side Park and the city's Gold Coast fans. Hart agreed to that. He also agreed to let Comiskey call the new team the White Sox, a new-century version of the historic name of Cap Anson's White Stockings, the National League predecessors of Hart's Cubs. The one concession Hart won from Johnson was that Comiskey would not use "Chicago" as part of the team name. Johnson and Comiskey agreed, knowing that whatever the official name of the franchise, Hart could not stop newspapers from identifying it by its home city.

When Johnson and Comiskey arrived in Chicago, they took an office together on the twelfth floor of the Fisher Building in the downtown Loop area, and remained business roommates for seven years. For the 1900 season, Johnson changed the league name from the Western League to the American League. The new name was less regional and had more of a big league cachet to it, and big league was exactly what Johnson was thinking. With Comiskey, the acknowledged leader among the new league's owners, having held his own in attendance and newspaper space against the long-established Cubs, Johnson began planning to take on the National League on more of their own turf in 1901. Over the 1900–01 off-season, Johnson dissolved the American League franchises in Indianapolis, Minneapolis, and Kansas City and established new franchises in Washington, Baltimore, and Philadelphia. Johnson also shifted the Buffalo franchise to Boston, giving the league an eastern core of Boston, Philadelphia, Baltimore, and Washington and a western grouping of Cleveland, Detroit, Milwaukee, and Chicago. Moreover, he said his reconstituted league would no longer be party to the National Agreement, which bound members to honor the reserve clauses of players under contract to other teams.

At this same time, the players in the National League, who had formed a "Players' Protective Association" in midseason, were petitioning the owners for some concessions in the basic contract, almost all of which would have given the players some control over where they played. The owners naturally rejected the players' demands, and the disgruntled players and the player-starved owners from the American League began eyeing one another across the smoky bar floor. In a swift, stunning, and coordinated raid, the American League signed away more than three dozen established National League stars, including future Hall of Famers Cy Young, Jimmy Collins, and Nap Lajoie. This gave the self-declared new major league instant parity at the box office during the 1901 season. Over the next two years the American League signed away more National League stars, moved the Milwaukee franchise to St. Louis to directly challenge the National League there, and began making plans to move the Baltimore franchise into New York. The National League swiftly lost its imperious attitude toward the upstarts, and prior to the 1903 season the two sides brokered a truce. There would be no more raids and no more lawsuits; all sides signed off on once again honoring reserve clauses. In the process, however, the players' brief moment of leverage in contract negotiations was gone, not to return for three-quarters of a century.

To govern the new structure, owners established the National Commission to oversee the game. It would be a three-member body, comprised of the presidents of both leagues along with third man chosen by the league presidents from the ranks of team owners. The owner representative would serve as commission chairman. Each member would have one vote. But voting equality did not necessarily go hand in hand with power equality. From its first moments, the National Commission was Ban Johnson's fiefdom. Three years after coming into Major League Baseball by picking the lock on a side door, Ban Johnson was effectively ruling the game.

The man whom Johnson and National League president Harry Pulliam chose as the Commission's third member was August Herrmann of the Reds. Herrmann—who went by Garry, a shortening of his childhood nickname, Garibaldi—was a Cincinnati native, born in 1859, given to wearing checkered suits and pinkie rings. He always traveled with a supply of the Cincinnati sausage he favored, and out on the town, whether in Cincinnati or elsewhere, he welcomed everyone to his table, invariably picking up the check. Herrmann had lost his father as a boy and started his working life as a printer's devil. That led to his starting a small newsletter that became the official newspaper of the Cincinnati courts, which led to his appointment as clerk of courts, which led to several other political appointments in Cincinnati. This in turn made him a part of the Cincinnati political power structure, which led to his being invited by Republican Party boss George Cox to join a group headed by Cox and brothers Max and Julius Fleischmann (heirs to the Fleischmann gin and yeast companies) when they were making an offer to buy the Cincinnati Reds in 1902. Herrmann didn't have much money to contribute, but he had something the group needed more—an agreeable, outgoing personality and a remarkable lack of ego, which had given him a proven ability to broker compromises and get things done.

Herrmann played host to the talks that had brought about the National Agreement in January of 1903, and his fellow owners gave him credit for getting the deal done. Ban Johnson was the first to suggest Herrmann as Commission chairman; the two men had known each other casually during Johnson's Cincinnati newspaper days. Pulliam quickly endorsed Herrmann, and across baseball everyone was in agreement; Herrmann was very popular among the owners of both leagues. National League owners were happy to have one of their own in that seat of power; American League owners trusted him to be fair and not automatically side with his own league in matters under dispute.

Herrmann's go-along-to-get-along way resulted in a Commission that the aggressive Johnson was able to bend to his will. While the caricature of Herrmann as Johnson's lapdog is a distortion, historians of the National Commission do agree that whenever Johnson felt strongly on an issue, Herrmann was inclined to vote his way. Johnson's biographer Eugene Murdock can cite only a handful of times when major decisions went against Johnson's wishes. But in truth the National Commission had relatively limited power; its principal responsibilities were resolving disputes concerning minor league player assignments and, after 1905, organizing and running the World Series.

The real power in baseball still resided in the leagues, and it was here that Ban Johnson marshaled and wielded power in such a way that he came to be known, respectfully by his many admirers, mockingly by his critics (few in number at the beginning but growing steadily through the years), as the "Czar of Baseball." Johnson's vision of the American League was that it would be the gentleman's league, as opposed to the earthier, rowdier National League. He discouraged umpire baiting, and fined and disciplined offenders. He wanted his managers to be men of the utmost rectitude, and thus was destined to clash repeatedly with John McGraw, whom he had brought in as the owner-manager of Baltimore Orioles because of the manager's star power. McGraw was the all-time umpire baiter, of course, and when it became evident that he would never change, Johnson found a buyer for McGraw's Baltimore stock and facilitated his shift from the American League Orioles to the National League Giants.

Johnson's vision was that the American League was at its strongest when there was competitive balance in the league, so he would frequently resolve disputes over minor league contract ownership in favor of the American League's weaker teams. But he was also committed to having strong franchises in Chicago, St. Louis, Philadelphia, Boston, and especially in New York, all cities where the American League went head to head with the National. Johnson handpicked most of the original team owners, and no American League team changed hands without Johnson having a say in who would be the new owner. There was unsurprisingly an incestuous quality to the early American League. Cleveland industrialist Charles Somers owned the Indians, but at Johnson's behest also put money into the Boston, Philadelphia, and Chicago franchises. It was said that Ban Johnson founded the American League, but that he did so with Charles Somers's money.

It all added up to a nice tidy fraternity of baseball brethren, and no two men in the fraternity were closer than Johnson and Comiskey. The two men were inseparable in those early years of the American League, whether in the workaday world of their shared office, in the boardroom deciding league matters, or vacationing together—sometimes stag, sometimes with their wives, some three or four times a year, before the season began and again right after it ended. In the winter months the two men would head south, to Excelsior Springs, Missouri, and Hot Springs, Arkansas, for golf—though neither played with any regularity or skill—and relaxation with their wives. They would sail the Mississippi on Comiskey's houseboat, the *White Sox*, or go on hunting trips, either with friends or by themselves.

Indeed, their postseason trips became legend, particularly when others joined in. Comiskey was the host of a group that numbered upward of two dozen. There were club owners like Herrmann of the Reds, Jimmy McAleer of the Red Sox, Tom Loftus of Washington, Frank Navin of Detroit, George Stallings of the Braves, and, in later years, the two colonels from the Yankees—Tillinghast Huston and Jake Ruppert; sportswriters like Hugh Fullerton of the *Herald*, Cy Sanborn of the *Tribune* and Charles Spink of the *Sporting News*; and politicians and civic officials of every stripe, from a half dozen different major league cities, including, at least one year, Chicago judge Charles A. McDonald, who some years later would oversee the grand jury looking into the Black Sox.

The group occasionally traveled to Dover Hall, a 2,400-acre estate near Brunswick, Georgia, owned jointly by a number of baseball men, but they would most often—every year for more than two decades, in fact—repair to northern Wisconsin, first to the remote wilderness of Springstead and later to Camp Jerome, on Trude Lake in Mercer, which Comiskey bought in 1907. The trip would began with a four-hundred-mile, private-car train ride from Chicago to Fifield, Wisconsin, followed by a day-long ride in horse-drawn carriages over rough and rutted logging roads. (The move from Springstead to Camp Jerome in 1907 shortened the wagon-ride portion of the trip from thirty-five to twelve miles.) A cook and a maid were sent ahead the week before to ready the two cabins the men used, one for sleeping, one for dining, drinking, and talk.

It was on these trips to the northern Wisconsin woods that the so-called Woodland Bards were born. After a day of hunting, fishing, hiking, and card playing and an evening's repast that more often than not included venison, partridge, and fish from the day's kill, the final hours of the day were given over to liquid-fueled verse writing, creating doggerel that marked the day's adventures or mocked one of their own. Chicago songwriter, press agent, and longtime Comiskey friend Joseph Farrell began calling the group the Woodland Bards somewhere around 1910. Comiskey was so taken with the term that he built a Woodland Bards room in his new ballpark, decorated it with trophies from the hunts, and welcomed the group's members to drink and dine there during White Sox games. Anyone who had attended a Wisconsin trip was automatically a member; first-timers would undergo an initiation rite on the trips, and the group would eventually number 250 and become a visible and admired presence in their special room at Comiskey Park and when the White Sox played in the World Series in 1917 and 1919.

The Comiskey-Johnson rift—which grew into a hatred that might have consumed the game—may have begun over nothing more than the simple fact that proximity often breeds irritation. The two men saw one another in their shared office in the Fisher Building on a daily basis for more than seven years. The camaraderie of the early years inevitably began to wane as the years passed, and each man tended to his separate interests.

The origins of the falling-out are murky, and were perhaps murky even to the principals, but it seems to have started, as such feuds often do, with little things. Johnson took umbrage at being the victim of some Woodland Bards pranksterism in the early days of the trip—some accounts put it in 1902, others in 1904, others as late as 1912. Johnson had had custom-made a new Parker shotgun and a natty suede hunting vest to go with it He was quite proud of each, showing them to one and all on the overnight train ride to the trailhead. His days as the group's worst hunter were over, he assured his friends. In the morning, while Johnson and most of the group were having breakfast at the train station, two of the Bards replaced the pellets in Johnson's shotgun shells with paper wadding.

On the carriage ride through the forest, Johnson was given the prized spot, in the front seat next to the driver, so that he might test his new weapon upon the partridge that were sure to present themselves on the daylong ride to the cabin. In the target-rich environment, Johnson blasted away to no avail, to his great frustration and the increasing amusement of his fellow Bards, who laughed and teased and passed the flask. Now the one fundamental decorum of bird hunting is that the target must be taken on the wing, but Johnson, champion of fair play and the civil treatment of umpires in baseball, grew so exasperated that at one point he climbed down from the wagon, crept up on a sitting bird, and fired point-blank. The bird survived and flew off. Finally Johnson nailed a paper target to a tree, fired from a foot away, and realized he'd been had. All of the Bards laughed, but Johnson blamed only Comiskey for his humiliation—"I can't believe Commy would do this to me," he said. He pouted uncharacteristically, and was a frosty companion for a couple of days before arranging to leave the forest early.

Sometime thereafter Johnson sent Comiskey a string of freshly caught bass. It may have been intended as an olive branch, Johnson sensing perhaps his pique in the Wisconsin forest may have been excessive. That was certainly how the gesture was received when the ice-packed bass arrived. "Look what Beebee sent me," Comiskey beamed to visitors as he showed off the fish, and he hung them in a place of honor in his office. But within hours of the arrival of the bass came another communication from Johnson that immediately spoiled Comiskey's good mood and left him feeling that Johnson and his fish were mocking him. White Sox outfielder Ducky Holmes had been thrown out of a game the day before for using abusive language in an argument with an umpire. The matter had come before Johnson to determine whether there should be any additional discipline. Johnson ruled a three-game suspension was in order. Comiskey had little issue with Johnson's ruling; it was consistent with his decisions in similar cases. But Comiskey took great issue with the way it was carried out. Rather than drop his ruling in the mails, as he usually did in such matters, Johnson had the decision hand-messengered to Comiskey, so that it took effect a day earlier than it otherwise would. Johnson knew that the White Sox were already short-handed due to another suspension. "What's that fat so-and-so expect me to do? Play the fish in the outfield?" Comiskey bellowed and unceremoniously threw the fish out the window and left them to rot on the sidewalk. Comiskey may not have had to play the fish in left field, but the White Sox were forced to play a pitcher there that day, and they lost.

Shortly after this that Comiskey moved out of the office he shared with Johnson in the Fisher Building. Johnson, for his part, stopped coming to White Sox games. Their vacations together with their wives stopped, though Johnson remained a regular on the Woodland Bards' trips for several more years. Yet if the two men were no longer friends beyond 1910 or so, they were also not yet foes. The enmity would take another decade to fester and grow. Throughout the 1910s the two men shared the dais at big events, one generally honoring the other, as in 1914 when Johnson was among a thousand people who gathered at the Congress Hotel to celebrate the White Sox's triumphant return from the Comiskey-organized and paid-for world tour, where players representing the White Sox and Giants played before sometimes enthusiastic (and sometimes per-plexed) crowds in Japan, China, the Philippines, Australia, and India, and in the shadow of the Sphinx in Egypt. The touring ballplayers were blessed by Pope Pius X in Rome, rained out in Paris, and played extra innings in front of King George V of England. However he may have felt about Comiskey personally, Johnson knew that what he had done was good for the game. Charles Comiskey likewise showed a consistent professional respect for Ban Johnson during those years, voting to renew his contract as president whenever it came up, support-ing, and oftentimes proposing, handsome pay raises.

In rendering his decisions as league president, Johnson never showed Comiskey any special favors, even when the two men were as close as brothers; he also never discriminated against him after their falling-out. Johnson was instrumental in Comiskey's securing the services of both Eddie Collins and Joe Jackson, two men who would loom very large in the White Sox world championship in 1917, and of course, in the pennant and subsequent events in 1919. Connie Mack had come to Johnson following the 1914 World Series—the fourth time the Athletics had played in the Series in five years—and told him he was broke and was going to have to break up his championship contingent in order to pay the bills. The biggest prize, as well the recipient of the biggest salary in the group, was Eddie Collins. Johnson called the second baseman in and appealed to his vanity and his American League patriotism. The Chicago Whales of the Federal League had just signed Walter Johnson to a big contract (Johnson never actually played for the Feds), and Johnson told Collins that it was imperative the White Sox make some headlines and have a man on their team who could rival Johnson's star power. If American League loyalty weren't enough, Johnson assured Collins that Comiskey would honor and perhaps even sweeten the lucrative contract Collins had just signed with Philadelphia. Collins agreed to play for the White Sox. A year later, Johnson gave his blessing to the deal that sent Joe Jackson from the Indians to the White Sox.

However, through the years the men grew apart on matters of baseball's governance. They disagreed on who the owners should be. Johnson was partial to men of great wealth, like Charles Somers of Cleveland or Frank Navin of Detroit. Comiskey felt that owners should be men like himself, or Clark Griffith or Connie Mack, baseball lifers who'd grown up in the game and derived 100 percent of their livelihood from it. Johnson knew that it often took more than ticket revenue and concessions to pay the bills of a major league team. Comiskey's success at the gate kept the wolf from his door, but Griffith's Senators and Mack's Athletics were perennially two of the game's most threadbare franchises.

Johnson's open criticism of some owners for the way they were handling gambling in the ballpark, and the high-handed way he treated most owners in general, came to irritate Comiskey. So too did Johnson's wartime management—not only the decisions he made, but the fact that he made so many of them without seeking approval, or even the counsel of the owners for whom he worked. Also, Comiskey wanted the shipyard ballplayers who had jumped their White Sox contracts in 1918 punished, and seethed when Johnson decided on amnesty for the returning players.

The Comiskey-Johnson relationship reached its final breaking point before the start of the 1919 season. Jack Quinn would win 247 games over a twenty-three-year big league career, but was at the time a journeyman whose contract Comiskey had purchased from Vernon of the Pacific Coast League midway through the 1918 season. Vernon, and the entire Pacific Coast League, had been forced to suspend operations midway through 1918, and the players were declared free agents for the balance of the 1918 season, with the understanding that their contracts would revert back to their original teams when those teams resumed operations. Comiskey inquired of the National Commission before signing Quinn and received the go ahead. Quinn went 5–1 in his time with the White Sox, and Comiskey wanted him back in 1919. But while Quinn was playing for the White Sox, he was still technically the property of the Vernon club, and Vernon reached a separate agreement to sell his contract to the Yankees for the 1919 season. It was a contractual nightmare: two arguably valid claims to the services of the player. Whatever decision the National Commission reached on the matter was going to anger someone.

The National Commission ruling favored the Yankees, but acknowledged its own lack of thoroughness in the matter during the 1918 signing by Comiskey. "The advice given to Mr. Comiskey in the matter of the Commission was in line with the thought that was in its mind at the time," read the statement, "yet at the same time the advice probably would have been qualified had the Commission known that another club was negotiating for the player's release." The report went on to say that by following the Commission's advice Comiskey had unfortunately not been able to deal with Vernon directly and secure Quinn for the White Sox.

The Commission called the whole thing "unfortunate." Comiskey called it spite. While the decision carried the signature of Commission chairman Garry Herrmann, Comiskey saw Ban Johnson's hand in it, and he was convinced it was done only to hurt Comiskey and the White Sox. The two men never again exchanged a warm word; the Quinn decision marked the end of any pretense of civility and respect between Comiskey and Johnson. Each man's enmity for the other, each man's steely conviction that his vision was best for all of baseball was the backdrop in front of which the game-changing events of 1919–21 played out.

Each would come to use the Black Sox moment to plot the other's ruin. And when Comiskey was in declining health in his last years, one friend noted that he "remained alive only that he might enjoy hating Ban Johnson."

FIVE

The Conversations

On the last day of May 1919, in the top of the eighth inning of a Saturday game at Comiskey Park, Cleveland outfielder Tris Speaker slid hard into White Sox first baseman Chick Gandil, and the two men came up swinging wildly. "An old-time fist fight such as this probably hasn't occurred in the last fifteen years or more," wrote James Crusinberry in the *Tribune*. The ferocity of the fight suggests it was rooted in something more than a hard slide. No reason was ever given for the enmity between the two men. But they had played together on the Indians in 1916, and to play with Gandil for more than a short time was to generally develop a dislike for the man.

"It started as a fist fight," continued Crusinberry, "but it was a rough-and-tumble tiger battle with claws, spikes, fists, feet and possibly even teeth before the two finally were dragged apart."

The dugouts emptied and players formed a circle around the fighters. None of the White Sox players came to Gandil's aid, and some were even reported to be openly rooting for Speaker.

"When are you going to break it up?" somebody eventually inquired of umpire Tommy Connolly.

"Who is getting the best of it?" asked Connolly, who was on the outside of the circle and had his view blocked.

"Speaker has Gandil down," he was told.

"Well," replied Connolly, "let them go for another minute. Gandil has it coming to him."

Nobody much liked Chick Gandil. Still, he had standing among his fellow players, born of equal parts fear, awe, and respect. His pummeling at the hands of Tris Speaker notwithstanding, he was a tough, ornery, contrary, largely friendless misanthrope, who gave no quarter on or off the field and asked for none in return.

He maintained that he had left his home on a freight train when he was sixteen years old, never to return. The biography of his playing days, such as it is, begins with that boxcar ride to Amarillo, Texas, where he was hoping to catch on with a semipro ball club. He never offered up details about his boyhood, but the occasional oblique inferences suggested that it hadn't been a very happy one. Gandil had been born in St. Paul but grew up in Berkeley, California. He was apparently a hellion as a child and did leave home as a teenager, whether by boxcar or otherwise, to pursue a baseball career, playing on semipro teams in Los Angeles, Fresno, and Amarillo before catching on for a couple of years with a team in Cananea, Mexico, a hardscrabble, wide-open border town, "which suited me just fine." He did some prizefighting during his off time in Mexico— earning as much as $150 a bout, he claimed—and did a lot of bar fighting to stay in shape for his fights in the ring. He signed his first professional contract with Shreveport in 1908, and married that same year. He claimed that marriage calmed his wild ways, but apparently it did not eliminate them. Playing for Sacramento in the Pacific Coast League in 1909, he was arrested and charged with stealing $225 from the Fresno team cashbox.

Still, the White Sox bought his contract at the end of that year, and he played seventy-seven games with Comiskey's club in 1910, batting a miserable .193 and earning himself a trip back to the minors in 1911. The Washington Senators bought his contract early in the 1912 season and didn't regret it; he was seen as the catalyst for the seventeen-game winning streak the Senators enjoyed after his arrival. He batted .305 that season and led American League first basemen in fielding. But inevitably he quarreled with Senators owner Clark Griffith. Gandil was a chain-smoker, and Griffith was said to hate cigarettes more than umpires, and he would repeatedly catch Gandil stealing a smoke in the dugout. Persuasion didn't work, threats didn't work, fines didn't work; so after the 1915 season Griffith sold Gandil off to Cleveland. Gandil had a mediocre year in Cleveland, batting a career-low .259, but when Charles Comiskey bought his contract and brought him to the White Sox during spring training, the *Tribune* was sufficiently excited to announce the deal with the headline: "Get Your Seat for '17 Series! White

Sox Purchase Gandil." Newspaper hyperbole became newspaper prophecy when the White Sox won one hundred games, beating out the Red Sox by nine games for the pennant and then dispatching John McGraw and the Giants in the World Series.

Gandil hit .273 that season, hitting over .300 for the second half of the season after a slow start, and showing, as he had through his career, a knack for run-delivering hits in key moments. But his biggest contribution to the White Sox championship probably came off the field.

Gandil was the guy who collected $45 per man from the White Sox players in September of 1917, some $1,100 in all, and gave it to the Detroit Tigers pitcher Bill James. According to Gandil, the money was a payoff to Tigers pitchers for "sloughing off" during a four-game Labor Day–weekend series against the White Sox, during which the Sox took all four games. According to James, it was a reward for the Tigers sweeping a three-game series against second-place Boston in late September. That the money was collected and paid was not in dispute; White Sox players freely admitted contributing and Tigers players freely admitted accepting the money. The details came out in a hearing in front of Commissioner Landis in 1927; both Gandil and James testified. James's story is bolstered by the fact that the money was not collected and paid until September 28, after the Tigers' series with Boston, and by the fact that most of Gandil's teammates who admitted contributing to the pot insisted it was for beating Boston. Bolstering Gandil's story is the fact that after a mid-September swoon, the Red Sox had fallen eight games behind the White Sox at the time of the Detroit series and were already out of it. Gandil said he had met James under the grandstand at Comiskey before the first game of the Labor Day–weekend series. "These are going to be some pretty soft games," he reported James saying to him. "Well, Bill, if it goes all right I will see that you are fixed up for it," Gandil said he had replied. Further bolstering Gandil's side of things is the fact that the fourth-place Tigers were particularly miserable in that series; the pitchers that the White Sox players were passing the hat to reward had given up thirty-four runs over the four games.

Whatever the truth of the 1917 story, Gandil had, in his own peculiar way, emerged as one of the White Sox leaders, even if no one in the locker room fully trusted him. The man who would become the hub in the scandal's wheel made his White Sox teammates nervous. He had no real friends on the team. Even the guys he hung out with—Eddie Cicotte, Swede Risberg, Fred McMullin—later admitted they never felt at ease in his presence. Others on the team, like Eddie Collins, Ray Schalk, openly despised him, and he them. Gandil and Collins, the first and second basemen, played next to one another every day for three years and said not a single word to one another during that time, off the field or on. And these were his teammates. As for the guys he played against, one contemporary observer noted simply, "Gandil is none too popular with players of other teams." Had anyone familiar with the White Sox of 1919 been asked to vote for the player most likely to be at the center of a conspiracy to betray his teammates and the game, Chick Gandil would have gotten the most votes.

While 1920s court testimony and retrospective remembrances disagree on the genesis and the particulars of the 1919 World Series fix, everyone with any knowledge agrees on one point: Chick Gandil was at the center of whatever happened. He was there at the beginning; he was the central figure in every remembrance, every piece of testimony. He was the only player who ever spoke with the gamblers involved, the player who collected and dispersed the money. "He was the whole works of it, the instigator of it," Joe Jackson told the grand jury in 1920.

Gandil's story was that it was Sport Sullivan, the Boston gambler who had built himself quite a high profile in the game, who initiated the idea of a fix. Sullivan had been the heart of baseball gambling in Boston beginning at the turn of the century, and by 1919 he was something of a legend, both in his native city and beyond. He was the central figure in the Pinkerton investigation conducted at Ban Johnson's behest in 1917. When he had been arrested for gambling at the South End Grounds, home of the National League Braves, in 1907, he told the judge that he was a broker in the curb market, which may have had some truth to it; a clipping in the *Boston Globe* from the year before identifies him as a man accused of bribing state legislators to defeat a bill that would have banned "bucket shops"—shadowy stock businesses that were somewhere between a bookie parlor and a primitive derivatives market—in Massachusetts. (The allegation that he had bribed legislators never gained any traction, and the judge threw out the gambling charge for "lack of evidence.")

In the newspaper mentions in the years before the Black Sox, Sullivan comes off as the very embodiment of his nickname, a rakish, mischievous rogue. He knew everyone worth knowing in the gambling world, and was plugged into the baseball world as well. He had long made a habit of befriending ballplayers who came to Boston. He and Gandil had known one another since Gandil's first season with Washington in 1912. Gandil would share information with Sullivan on starting pitchers and the like while the two men played pool together. It was during one of these regular conversations, Gandil would later assert, that Sullivan first talked to him about a fix.

Sullivan himself didn't have an explanation for how the fix got started; he never publicly talked to anyone about 1919. Despite being indicted, he was never tried, never called before the grand jury, and aside from one angry denial after he was indicted, never talked to a newspaper reporter. Other gamblers, however—Abe Attell, Bill Burns, Billy Maharg—insisted that the idea of a fix came from the players (Gandil and Eddie Cicotte are the two most commonly named) who approached them at various points during September, saying that a fix could be had for the right price, and the price generally mentioned, according to these gamblers, was $100,000.

When and however the conversations began, they were certainly taking place before Chick Gandil and Sport Sullivan spoke in Boston in mid-September. The Black Sox record includes Eddie Cicotte testifying that it had first come up on a train ride east in early September, Bill Burns and Abe Attell both telling of a meeting at the Ansonia Hotel in New York the week before Boston, and Buck Weaver telling one of Charles Comiskey's private detectives that Cicotte was talking about it as early as June.

The ballplayers had surely talked about a fix among themselves before they had coalesced into their group of eight, before they had met with any gamblers promising to provide the money. The plot matured from theory to a tentative action throughout mid- and late September. But it finally came together remarkably late; the conspirators did not commit until Friday night, the 26th of September, in a meeting in Eddie Cicotte's room at the Warner Hotel. Cicotte was not only the host; he was one of the principal talkers, there to allay the doubts of the uncommitted. Eddie Cicotte was in this as deeply as Chick Gandil.

Eddie Cicotte is far and away the most complicated of the Black Sox; he is certainly the most fascinating, the key to the whole thing, really, from beginning to end. He was clearly deeply involved, and he had to have been for the whole thing to work. So dominating a pitcher was Cicotte in 1919 that everyone else on the team could have been playing crooked baseball and still not offset Eddie Cicotte at his best. His mere involvement was enough to convince the conspirators the fix was possible; his absence would have convinced them of just the opposite. He was 29–7 in 1919, with a 1.82 ERA and thirty complete games. Even when he was supposedly not trying in two of the three games he pitched during the World Series, he still had an ERA under 3.00.

Cicotte is also the key to the whole thing coming undone. All the rumors, charges, allegations, and news stories might have easily remained just so much newspaper noise without Cicotte's confession in September 1920. The guilt of shaming himself and his game would weigh more heavily on Cicotte than it did on any of his brother conspirators. A normally pleasant if taciturn man, he grew sullen and withdrawn during the 1920 season; it would later be reported that he'd spent much of that season following the fix talking with his priest about what he had done.

Cicotte was Ring Lardner's favorite ballplayer; had there been nothing else on Cicotte's resume, this alone would make him deserving of historical attention. Lardner, perhaps the best of all baseball writers, whose journalism, sketches, and fiction provided maybe the clearest window into the baseball world of his own or any other era, had made a lot of ballplayer friends as a young beat writer between 1908 and 1912. Lardner enjoyed the antic and affable camaraderie of the ball club, and not only because he pulled material from the clubhouses, hotel lobbies, and Pullman cars that would provide the backbone of some of his most famous and enduring work, but because he genuinely did like the boys on the team and made friends with them easily. But most of those were strictly workplace friendships, and lasted little longer than the train rides that spawned them. But Lardner's friendship with Eddie Cicotte was different. The two men went back to Boston in 1911, when Cicotte was pitching for the Red Sox and Lardner was a baseball writer for the *Boston American*. They came to Chicago within a few months of one another in 1912, and remained friends after Lardner left the baseball beat to write a general-interest column beginning in 1913. The two men would dine and drink together. Lardner found the pitcher an introspective and intelligent conversationalist. When he put Cicotte on his all-time, all-star team in 1915, together with Christy Mathewson, Walter Johnson, and Grover Cleveland Alexander, it was Cicotte's intelligence as well as his physical acumen that he noted. "They ain't a smarter pitcher in baseball," he wrote, "and they's nobody that's a better all-around ball player, no pitcher, I mean."

Lardner's son, Ring Jr., sees a sign of his father's affection for Cicotte in the way he treats him in the "Busher" stories, the *Saturday Evening Post* articles that appeared between 1914 and 1919 and made Lardner a writer of national renown. The Busher stories, collected in *You Know Me Al* and two later volumes, combine the story of the vainglorious protagonist, the fictional White Sox pitcher Jack Keefe, with several real-life White Sox from the era. Cicotte makes a number of appearances in the series, most notably in the final four stories, written and published during the 1919 season. "It is clear from these final four Jack Keefe stories that my father had a genuine affection for Cicotte," wrote Ring Lardner Jr., "to whom he assigns the best jokes and sagest counsel."

In September of 1919, at thirty-five years old, Eddie Cicotte was pitching better than he had in his life. A solid, steady performer through his first eleven seasons in the big leagues—he had a 119–100 record from 1905 to 1916—he'd blossomed into an elite major league pitcher in 1917, going 28–12, with a 1.53 ERA for the White Sox world championship team. In 1919 he was putting together an even better season. His twenty-nine wins would lead the league, as would his .806 winning percentage, thirty complete games and 306 innings pitched—all in a 140-game season. But in between these two stellar seasons, 1917 and 1919, he had a down year, maybe his worst in the majors, going 12 and 19 in 1918, albeit with a respectable 2.77 ERA. Ring Lardner's thinking ballplayer was smart enough to know that it could slip away again, as it had in 1918; and at age thirty-five, one of the next times it slipped away it might likely be forever. Cicotte knew that he was living on borrowed baseball time. He had a farm in Michigan, where he planned to retire and live out his life. That farm had a mortgage. He had a wife, two daughters, and a baby son. He thought often about how he was going to pay that mortgage and support that family when the baseball checks suddenly stopped.

It is possible Gandil conceived of the plot and recruited Cicotte; it's also possible that the two men, pool-shooting companions, would have had conversations about it through the summer and would have thus been privy to one another's thoughts and feelings. It is also quite certain that Swede Risberg and Fred McMullin, Gandil's running mates, were involved from the beginning. Nobody until Eliot Asinof in *Eight Men Out* ever talked about recruiting Risberg and McMullin; they were an indigenous part of the fix, just like Gandil. Cicotte testified that his commitment to the fix came in New York on September 16, in a meeting at the Ansonia with Gandil and Fred McMullin, on an off day before the Sox began a three-game series against the Yankees. "Either Gandil or McMullin started by saying that we were not getting a devil of a lot of money, and it looked as if we could make a good thing if we threw the series to Cincinnati," remembered Cicotte before the grand jury. "Either Gandil or McMullin asked me what I would take to throw the series and I said I would not do anything like that for less than $10,000. And they said, well, we can get together and fix it up.

"That was all there was to that conference."

With Cicotte committed, together with Gandil, Risberg, and McMullin, the plot was now viable. But it was hardly a sure thing. The plotters needed more players. Another starting pitcher would be the most valuable addition, and Lefty Williams was the only real candidate. Thirteen-game-winner Dickie Kerr was a rookie, and his sentiments on something like this thus largely unknown to the conspirators. Red Faber, an eleven-game winner in 1919, was hurt and didn't figure to see much action in the postseason. Besides, Faber was part of the Eddie Collins clique. Collins's participation was out of the question; even had he been inclined, he wouldn't throw in with Gandil if the first baseman were proposing a fund to help war widows and orphans. Collins's other friends on the team, Ray Schalk and Nemo Leibold, were likewise unapproachable. That left Joe Jackson and Buck Weaver.

Gandil handled the recruiting. Williams was apparently first; Gandil approached him on the sidewalk outside the Ansonia Hotel in New York, probably right after getting Cicotte to commit. Had anyone talked to him about the World Series?

"Just what do you mean?" asked Williams.

"Of being fixed," said Gandil.

"Not yet," replied Williams, almost as if he had been waiting for someone to ask.

"What do you think of it?" asked Gandil. "If it was fixed, would you be willing to get in on it and go through with anything?"

"I'm in no position to say right now," replied Williams. "I'll give you my answer later, after thinking it over."

Gandil took Williams's response as a yes. He included Williams as one of the involved in talking to Joe Jackson and Hap Felsch. Gandil approached Jackson in Boston and asked if he would consider taking $10,000 to frame something up. Jackson asked what. When Gandil told him the World Series, Jackson said no. That ended the Boston conversation, but a week later in Chicago, Gandil caught up to Jackson on the bridge leading into the White Sox clubhouse at Comiskey and told him he could pay him $20,000 for being a part of the fix. Jackson again said no. This time Gandil didn't leave it alone. He pressed Jackson, telling him that he "could either take it or let it alone, they were going through." In between the Boston and Chicago meetings with Gandil, Jackson had also had conversations with his roommate Lefty Williams. While Jackson denied he and Williams ever directly discussed their own involvement with one another at that early date, he did concede that over the final two weeks of the regular season, the two men talked of all the conversations being held about the possibility of fixing the Series.

Though he was Cicotte's roommate on the road, Happy Felsch was apparently approached rather late. His first thought was that he would be betraying Charles Comiskey, a boss he'd always felt had treated him well. But Felsch was very much a go-along-to-get-along sort, and he eventually figured, What the hell? "When they let me in on the idea too many men were involved," he told a reporter a year later. "I didn't like to be a squealer and I knew that if I stayed out of the deal and said nothing about it they would go ahead without me and I'd be that much money out without accomplishing anything."

Who it was who first talked to Buck Weaver remains unknown. Weaver's remarks to Comiskey's detective that Cicotte had told him fix was a possibility as early as June were the only words he ever spoke on the subject. When he decided he would not be a party to any game fixing is also unknown. But the other seven considered Weaver a part of the scheme. He was present at two meetings where the fix was discussed—the critical Warner Hotel meeting on the twenty-sixth and a meeting in Chick Gandil's room after the first World Series game in Cincinnati.

Over the final days of the 1919 season, the men who would become the Black Sox "would meet one or two at a time" and would begin to agree "that for a piece of the money [they] would throw the World Series."

Where the money came from has been argued about as much as anything in the Black Sox story, but the only plausible source is Arnold Rothstein. The other purported fixers were poseurs, or entered the conversation either too early or too late to have played a part. What little money made it into the hands of the ballplayers came from two Rothstein associates. Moreover, everyone mentioned in connection with the fix—gamblers from other cities mostly—had a direct and proven connection with Arnold Rothstein. And none of these men or groups of men had a connection with each other, except through Rothstein.

Rothstein himself would always deny involvement. Those who charged that it was him, he pointed out, were up to their own necks in the scandal and looking to save them. When asked about the 1919 World Series, Rothstein always said his only involvement was betting on the White Sox and losing money. He made the case for his innocence under oath before the grand jury in 1920, and did it so convincingly that he was never indicted in the case. That was the way it was with Rothstein. In a criminal life that spanned more than a quarter century, he was never convicted of any crime. He had connections and charm and the best lawyers, and nothing ever stuck to him.

Escaping culpability for his role in the 1919 Series fix may have been Rothstein's most famous dodge, but it wasn't his most remarkable. Earlier in 1919, he had shot three policemen in front of nineteen witnesses—and gotten away scot-free. He was overseeing a crap game in a West 57th Street apartment when, at two in the morning, there came a heavy rapping on the door and voices demanding to be let in. Rothstein had been robbed twice during private gambling evenings in the previous year and wasn't taking any chances this time. He responded to the knock by firing three shots through the closed door. Each one struck a New York City police detective. Three shots, three officers, three wounds. The officers weren't hurt badly, a shoulder wound and two flesh wounds in the arm. Rothstein was as solicitous as he could be. His limousine took the officers to the hospital. Knowing they were dealing with a man who had considerable pull with both the courts and city hall, the cops apologized, saying publicly that they understood gamblers were naturally wary of being robbed and that they should have been clearer about identifying themselves as police.

Rothstein was indicted, but the case was dismissed because the policemen had not seen who had fired the shots, and all of the nineteen men in the room testified before the grand jury that they hadn't either. All but one denied he had even heard shots fired; another testified that he had seen a muzzle flash but didn't know who fired. Any man who can so deftly beat a felonious assault rap is too good to let himself be taken down by murky allegations about fixing some baseball games.

History's best guess as to what it cost to fix the World Series—the cash actually paid to the seven players who took money for agreeing to be a part of the fix—was at most $80,000–$90,000. This was quite literally pocket money to Arnold Rothstein: at the height of his power and celebrity, he would often travel the streets of Manhattan with $100,000 in cash in the pockets of his bespoke suits. Rothstein had in effect financed the biggest sporting scandal in American history with what he had on him.

Arnold Rothstein—A. R. as he was known to associates and newspapermen—remains one of those larger-than-life personalities from the 1920s, someone whose story seems to fit far more comfortably into fiction than biography. F. Scott Fitzgerald modeled Meyer Wolfsheim in *The Great Gatsby* on Rothstein, though Wolfsheim is a far more thuggish and cartoonish figure than the polished, sophisticated, well-connected real-life Rothstein. Damon Runyon, the Hearst writer who mined Broadway for stories and characters the way Rothstein mined it for his pocket money, saw another side of Rothstein when he made him the inspiration for Nathan Detroit, the master of the floating crap game in *Guys and Dolls*. But Runyon, too, portrayed just one dimension of Rothstein—the rakishness and bravura. Nathan Detroit is street-smart and devilishly mischievous, but he's also a bit sentimental, perhaps even a little naïve—thus ultimately far more redeemable than the manipulative, ruthless, vengeful real-life Rothstein.

To the newspapermen, and thus to the American public in the 1910s, Arnold Rothstein was simply a "gambler," which, although making him slightly unsavory, proved no obstacle to admission to the best circles. It gave him cachet.

Rothstein moved comfortably through the worlds of politics, business, Broadway, and Manhattan society. His rumored involvement with the Series fix made him a national figure, but he was already a celebrity in his home city by 1919, his life making wonderful newspaper copy. He married a showgirl and had affairs with at least two others. He owned thoroughbred racehorses and was a visible presence at the horse track. He'd won $300,000 on a single race at Laurel in 1917, a head-turning triumph until he won $850,000 on a single race at Aqueduct in 1921 and another $850,000 on a single race at Saratoga a month later. He ran a Times Square gambling parlor until a reform movement in 1912 landed a lot of New York police officers who had been paid to look the other way in jail. Rothstein responded by starting New York's first and longest-running floating crap and card games, in a different hotel or apartment every night, always one step ahead of whatever police officers he couldn't pay off. After things got too hot in Times Square, he moved his fixed casino out to Long Island, and in the summer of 1919 he opened The Brook, the most elegant of all of Saratoga Spring's wink-at-the-law casinos, where the dress code in season was always evening wear and the clientele came from the demimonde, the Social Register, and all the strata in between—all of them the sort of men who could afford to lose five and six figures a night, and frequently did.

The newspapers almost always treated him kindly, because he was connected in that world too; his friends included Runyon, with whom he regularly shared a table at Lindy's, and Herbert Bayard Swope, editor of the *New York World*, who was a regular at the card and dice games Rothstein sponsored. The newspapers wrote of his friends and sometimes business partners, men like Charles Stoneham, the owner of the Giants and partners with Rothstein in a New York bucket shop, and John McGraw, manager of the Giants and partners with Rothstein in a Midtown pool hall.

Thirty-seven years old in 1919, five foot seven and a fit 160 pounds, abstinent in the matters of smoke and drink, partial to silk shirts and conservative, dark, custom-tailored suits, Rothstein was more than just the raffish gambler from the newspaper stories. He was a gangster, one of New York's most powerful, with tentacles reaching into every corner of gangland commerce. "A. R. fenced millions of dollars in stolen government bonds," wrote his biographer David Pietrusza, "backed New York's biggest bootleggers, imported tons of illegal heroin and morphine, financed shady Wall Street bucket shops, bought and sold cops and politicians."

Any sporting man with brains and guts enough to try to pull off something like a World Series fix would have eventually and inevitably found his way to

Rothstein. He was the gold standard in big-money fixes. "Everyone went to A. R. when they needed something," wrote Pietrusza. "Everyone had to pretend to be his friend. He was the man who made things happen, who put people together." He was the man with whom to have the conversation.

There are conflicting opinions as to whether somebody brought the scheme to Rothstein or whether Rothstein hatched the scheme and passed it to associates who could execute it. Sport Sullivan, former ballplayers Bill Burns and Billy Maharg, St. Louis gambler Carl Zork, and who knows how many others all talked to Rothstein about a fix sometime during the 1919 season, leaving the impression that Rothstein was merely the facilitator. But Chicago gambler Mont Tennes came away from an August conversation with Rothstein in Saratoga believing that he had already put a fix in place. Tennes was so sure he told Cubs owner Charlie Weegham about it.

Carl Zork was part of a cabal of St. Louis gamblers who had long dreamed of fixing a World Series. Between them they knew a fair number of ballplayers who would be willing to tank a game for a few bucks, and they had had some success in influencing the outcome of some regular season games. But to fix a World Series, they needed their contacts to be on a team that was playing in the World Series, and there was never a guarantee of that. The St. Louis men were also rather light in the wallet; it was one thing to make a living as a gambler, quite another to make a good living at it. Thus Zork approached Rothstein—whenever that was—with a proposal that was far more concept than plan. Still, Rothstein no doubt listened with polite interest, as he even then foresaw a role for Zork and his colleagues in this, should it come together in another way.

Bill Burns and Billy Maharg were two former ballplayers who also had a dream and no money. They would prove themselves in over their heads as fix masterminds, though both would be major players in the unraveling. And they, too, would be useful to Arnold Rothstein as he worked toward covering all the angles.

Sleepy Bill Burns had been a major league pitcher for five undistinguished seasons from 1908 to 1912. He played for the White Sox for parts of 1909–10, where for one game in 1910 he had been a teammate of Chick Gandil's. The lefthander compiled a career mark of 30–52, never once posting a winning record. This never seemed to have mattered to Burns, a fact not lost on his teammates, who christened him "Sleepy" for his indifference on and off the field. Burns played in the minors for a time after his big league career was through, and since leaving the game in 1917 he had worked in the oil business in his native Texas, buying and selling oil leases. But working for a living, however lucrative, didn't provide the same rush as gaming the system for a living. Sleepy Bill fancied himself a gambler. He traveled a lot on his job, found himself in a lot of major league cities over the course of a season, and his station as a former big leaguer gave him entrée to active ballplayers whom he would chat up, like all gamblers, looking for information that would give him an edge—who's pitching Saturday, who's got a sore arm, who's hungover, who's having troubles with his wife or girlfriend.

He was in New York on oil-lease business at the end of July and met with Eddie Cicotte. It's unclear whether they discussed a fix, though they might have, for when Burns came back to New York in September and saw Cicotte on the sixteenth, the pitcher told him he had something good for him. Two days later, Burns returned to the Ansonia and met with both Cicotte and Gandil. He had his friend Billy Maharg with him.

The origins of Burns's friendship with Billy Maharg have been lost, but by 1919 they were friends of long standing. Maharg, too, was a former major league ballplayer, though his career comes with an asterisk. He played in two games, for two different teams, four years apart, and both were farcical moments in the game's history. In May of 1912, American League president Ban Johnson suspended Ty Cobb for going into the grandstand and beating up a heckler. His teammates refused to take the field, in sympathy with Cobb, and the Tigers fielded a team of replacement players for the next day's game with the Athletics. Maharg, a fair-to-middling professional boxer and a familiar figure around the Philadelphia sporting scene, was the starting third baseman for the replacement Tigers. He grounded out in his only at-bat and handled two chances in the field cleanly before a third ground ball took a bad hop and hit him in the face, knocking out some teeth and taking him out of the game. The Athletics won, 24–2.

Four years later, Maharg was working as the assistant trainer for the Phillies, where his primary duty seemed to be getting his thirsty friend Grover Cleveland Alexander to the ballpark on time. In the waning innings of the final game of the season, Phillies manager Pat Moran cleared his bench, sending in not only the reserves but the civilians on the bench as well. Maharg pinch-hit in the eighth— he grounded out again—and played an uneventful ninth in right field.

Hanging around the Philadelphia fight and baseball worlds for as long as Maharg had meant hanging around the Philadelphia gambling world as well, and when Burns began thinking about a World Series fix, he asked his friend for an introduction. The Philadelphia sporting men told the pair that the only person with the money to finance something on that scale was Rothstein. That was how the two men came to be in New York.

The "something good" that Cicotte had for Bill Burns was an offer to throw the World Series for $100,000—it was actually Gandil that delivered the offer. Burns told Cicotte and Gandil that he would work on getting the money. To get to Rothstein, Burns and Maharg went to Abe Attell, a former featherweight champion and now a Rothstein factotum. Attell had them speak first with Hal Chase and a man he introduced as "Bennett," a Rothstein representative. The first time Burns and Maharg tried to meet with Rothstein, he sent them away. This was at Aqueduct; Rothstein was busy betting. And in any case he knew what they wanted; he even knew what their plan was, for he had heard about it from Abe Attell. The Burns-Maharg plan was very much like the one that Rothstein already had in place with Sport Sullivan.

Of all the supplicants, Sullivan was the one who won Rothstein's trust. The two men met at least twice in September in New York; it's unclear whether the first meeting was before or after Sullivan's Boston meeting with Gandil; the second meeting was very late in the month, just before Rothstein dispatched Sullivan to Chicago to close the deal with the players. Rothstein himself never met with any ballplayers. He never bothered with such pedestrian affairs; he had people for that. Sport Sullivan was the sort of person Rothstein would have used for something like this—a well-connected sporting man with a long record of both success and discretion. But Sullivan was also an independent contractor, an out-of-towner. Rothstein generally had his own people involved in something this big.

Two of his people were Nat Evans and Abe Attell. Evans was a man Rothstein trusted as much as he trusted anyone alive; Abe Attell, not so much. Evans was a charmer. He had an easy way about him and a gift for making friends. He'd been Rothstein's partner on a number of major endeavors, most notably The Brook. He would be the sort of guy who could win a ballplayer's trust.

Attell could be a charmer too, a gregarious storyteller, particularly if the listener wasn't interested in fact-checking those stories. But he could also be abrasive. He was twice the featherweight champion of the world, from 1903 to 1904 and again from 1906 to 1912, and he was still the little guy out to show the bigger men he was just as tough as they were. He first came to know Rothstein back when he was still in the ring, and after his boxing career he had worked for him off and on as a bodyguard. Attell felt that job was rather beneath the dignity of a former champ, and he was always angling for something more, always feeling that Rothstein was underusing his talents. The partnership between Arnold Rothstein and Abe Attell was one of mutual suspicion and distrust.

Evans and Sullivan would meet with the players, make them an offer, and close the deal. Evans was to take their measure and report back to Rothstein: Could these guys be counted on to follow through? Rothstein didn't lay big money on an underdog unless he had full confidence that the favorite had somehow been compromised. If it was at all possible—and with Rothstein it generally was—he didn't take a chance with his bets. Attell's role was less clear; he was involved, but not included. Rothstein may have been setting him up to be the fall guy should he need one somewhere down the road. It was a role Attell would dive right into.

Arnold Rothstein had two nicknames. He was known as "the Big Bankroll," which was why so many hopeful fixers had found their way to him with their hands out. He was also known as "the Brain," not only for his ability to conceive and execute a deal, but for his ability to see and think through every angle of the deal, eliminating down-the-road surprises that might queer a deal or worse.

"The Big Bankroll" had sent Bill Burns and Billy Maharg packing when they first came to see him. A few days later, "the Brain" invited them to dinner. On Friday, September 26, the same night, at almost the very hour that Sport Sullivan and Nat Evans were meeting with the Black Sox players in Chicago, Rothstein— knowing full well what they wanted to talk to him about—asked Burns and Maharg to join him at the Astor Hotel in Times Square, probably the biggest and the busiest dining room in all of New York. They were shown to a table in the center of the room. In addition to Rothstein, Burns, and Maharg, there were three others at the table, there for no apparent reason except to have dinner. At least one of the men was later reported to be a New York City police detective. Either unaware they were proposing a criminal enterprise in front of a police officer or knowing any police officer sitting with Rothstein at a meeting like this was already in Rothstein's pocket, Burns and Maharg plunged ahead. For $100,000, a core of White Sox players would agree to throw the World Series. If Rothstein financed the fix, the two ex-ballplayers told him, he could make back several times his investment with sure-thing bets. Rothstein listened quietly, and then exploded in carefully planned, and probably practiced, indignation. He fairly shouted at Burns and Maharg, saying he wanted nothing to do with their scheme or with them, not now or ever again. It looked for a time to witnesses that Rothstein and Burns would come to blows. And Rothstein not only scolded, he threatened—if they knew what was good for them, Burns and Maharg would never come near Rothstein ever again. For anything.

It was a performance that would have won him a standing ovation at any of Broadway's nearby theaters. Rothstein wasn't angry; he was a dozen moves ahead in a chess game nobody else even realized had begun, laying the grounds for his defense in the event that someone *might* try to pin this on him somewhere down the line. Anyone in the dining room could have accurately testified that Rothstein was angrily refusing whatever it was his two guests were proposing. The witnesses at the table could testify to specifics. It was perhaps the clearest evidence in the whole case of Arnold Rothstein's criminal genius.

Twelve months later, when everyone *was* pointing the finger at him, Rothstein was able to take the offensive. Never mind rumors, he said, here was fact: When someone did ask me to get involved in a plan to fix the Series, I turned them down flat. Yelled at them to get away my table. I have witnesses.

The Chicago White Sox clinched the pennant on Wednesday, September 24, beating the Browns 6–5, while the second place Indians were losing to Detroit. Two days later, the conspirators were summoned to Eddie Cicotte's room at the Warner Hotel, at the corner of 33rd and Cottage Grove Avenue, a dozen blocks east of Comiskey Park. Felsch, who also lived at the hotel, was there, as were Chick Gandil, Lefty Williams, and Buck Weaver. Some of the players in the room—perhaps Felsch, certainly Williams, and possibly Weaver—came still needing to be convinced. Gandil and Cicotte, as well as two strangers, were there to do the convincing. Gandil introduced the visitors as Messrs. Sullivan and Brown from New York. Sullivan, of course, was Sport Sullivan of Boston. Aside from the little subterfuge about his hometown, Sullivan could travel under his own name, because he had no obvious link with Rothstein. Nat Evans was too closely allied with Rothstein to travel under his own name; Rothstein would be easily implicated if the whole thing started coming apart. So it had been determined that Evans would use the alias Rachael Brown. It proved a most convincing ruse. The nonexistent Mr. Brown would be indicted by a grand jury one year hence, while the very real Mr. Evans never even saw his name in the newspaper.

None of the players in the room, save for perhaps Gandil, knew that Brown and Sullivan were there as proxies for Rothstein. Nor did the players know for sure—again, save for perhaps Gandil—that the two gamblers had brought the cash with them. They hadn't brought much, but it would prove enough to get the fix locked up. The money was the reason everyone was there, and it permeated the room like a cloud of cigar smoke. The two guests told the players that they were the guys who were going to "try to put over this deal," and then offered the players $5,000 each. If Rothstein's men expected this would placate the players, they were disappointed. If it was a first offer, a ploy to bring the fix in cheaply, it worked. Lefty Williams said bluntly it wasn't enough. "For $5,000 I wouldn't throw no world's series," he said. "That isn't enough for an ordinary man to do a dirty trick."

How much would it take? the gamblers calmly asked. "In my estimation, I wouldn't consider nothing under $10,000." Williams replied.

And Mr. Jackson? Sullivan and "Brown" asked, either knowing or sensing that Williams was the key to Jackson's participation. "Whatever [we] do is all right with Mr. Jackson," Williams answered.

"We will start figuring on the difference," one of the gamblers said in reply.

There was more conversation, much of it led by Eddie Cicotte. He talked about how easy it would be to pull it off. "He said that it would be easy for us to pull the wool over the eyes of the public, that we were expert ballplayers, and that we could throw the game scientifically," remembered Felsch. "It looked easy to me too." But Cicotte had a message for Sullivan, "Brown," and Gandil too. He wasn't going any further down this road unless he got his share up front. He said he wouldn't take part unless he had his money before the team left for Cincinnati the following Monday.

Now it was Gandil's turn to talk. He told Cicotte he'd have his money prior to the Series start. He told the others that the fix was going to happen with them or without them, and they may as well get in on the money.

And so it was done. Williams and Felsch came to the meeting not committed to the fix, and left at least believing Gandil when he told them it was a done deal and they could either go along or lose out. Both opted to go along. Buck Weaver's presence at the meeting and his feelings about what was being discussed remains more of a mystery. It may have been at this meeting where Weaver determined that he wouldn't be party to any plot to throw the series. But his presence at this critical meeting was sworn to by both Cicotte and Williams, who testified to his presence before the grand jury a year later. That testimony probably guaranteed Buck Weaver's indictment and fixed his place as one of the fixers.

The conversation had started, according to the memory of those who were there, sometime well after nine o'clock, and lasted for maybe forty-five minutes to an hour. When the meeting broke, the fix effectively now in place, the players suddenly grew very cautious. Felsch and Cicotte were not the only White Sox players to live at the Warner; Eddie Collins and Red Faber lived there too, and the conspirators didn't want to have to explain to their teammates why they had gathered together so late on a Friday night. So when the conversation was ended, Eddie Cicotte went down to distract Collins and Faber while the others left, one or two at a time.

Happy Felsch walked Buck Weaver and Lefty Williams home. As the three men walked south on Cottage Grove Avenue through the late September night, they talked about how they might actually follow through with what they had just committed themselves to doing. There had certainly been times in their long baseball lives where they had lost a game and not cared, or put forth a half-assed effort that they knew would likely result in an error or a strikeout, and thought nothing of it. Lefty Williams must have certainly grooved a pitch or two, for whatever reason, sometime in his life. But to guarantee timely miscues that would ensure they would lose five games in a best-of-nine series against a team they and everyone else believed was their competitive inferior was another matter. It seemed simple at first blush. Errors, strikeouts, and bad pitches were a surefire formula for losing baseball. The hard part was how and when to make those bad pitches, errors, and swings-and-misses. Cartoonish ineptitude would be a red flag to teammates, fans, and writers. Do this badly enough, often enough, and early enough and they might just find themselves all yanked from the games and watching the series from the bench. How do you play to lose without anyone suspecting?

They weren't apparently very concerned about their ability to do it. "It's just as easy for a good player to miss a ball as it is to catch it," said Happy Felsch later, "just a slow start or a stumble at the time or a slow throw and the job is done." It was doable. They were, after all, as Cicotte had said, "expert ballplayers." They would need to be. Losing, it would seem, was going to take even more focus and concentration, an even greater measure of their skills, than winning.

When Eddie Cicotte returned to his room somewhere around 11:30, he found $10,000 in an envelope under his pillow, two or three $1,000 bills, and a thick wad of hundreds. In a few weeks he would use the money to pay off a $4,000 mortgage on his farm and invest the other $6,000 in stock, feed, equipment, and repairs to the farm. He never knew who put the money under his pillow. He remembered thinking for the first time, however, about why it was being done. "I suppose some gamblers [will make] some money," he thought; "the ordinary man would not give up money to throw a series just to have us beaten."

SIX

Losing the Series...

The one thing Arnold Rothstein, "the Brain," did not plan for perfectly was how to keep a lid on the whole thing. Sport Sullivan and Nat Evans got a little chatty in Chicago, and then in Cincinnati. Abe Attell got chatty too, particularly when he came to believe Rothstein was shutting him out of the deal. In fact, soon enough all of Cincinnati was awash in rumors—sporting men, writers, baseball officials, even ordinary fans were hearing things about dropping odds, and how maybe the White Sox weren't the sure bet everyone had thought they were. So many gamblers were talking about a fix being in that Rothstein's agents had some trouble getting money down on the Reds.

The center of the buzz was the Hotel Sinton, Cincinnati's finest, a 750-room behemoth at the corner of Fourth and Vine in the heart of the city's central business district. On the night the calendar turned from September to October 1919, it was bulging at the seams. The entire baseball world was crowded into the guest rooms, restaurants, and lobby of the Sinton, The hotel was Series headquarters for the White Sox; as well as for a large portion of the 275 members of the Woodland Bards who had made the train ride south; for league presidents Ban Johnson and John Heydler; and lastly for most of the nation's elite baseball press, a group that year that included Grantland Rice, Ring Lardner, Damon Runyon, Hugh Fullerton, Charley Dryden, J. G. Taylor Spink, and Fred Leib. Also in the press box were a couple of Cooperstown-bound ex-players, testing their skills as neophyte journalists this week. Former Cubs second baseman Johnny Evers was writing a column for an ad hoc newspaper syndicate, and Christy Mathewson was writing a Series column for the *New York Times*.

The Sinton was also headquarters for the nation's sporting men, who were always part of the periphery at a World Series game or big prizefight. They anticipated that proximity to the action would yield information that would take some of the chance out of their wagers. As usual, they were front and center in public places, calling out if they had money to get down on either the Reds or the Sox, and how much. If some of the numbers being called out—single wagers of $2,000–$3,000 or more—might make the average bleacher sitter blanch, it was nothing the high-rolling crowd at the Sinton hadn't heard. Meanwhile, elsewhere in the city, the bleacher sitters were getting down their dollar or two wherever they could.

Both ball clubs worked out at Redland Field on Tuesday morning, and afterward they took a little field trip, together with their managers, to the Latonia Race Track, across the river in Covington, Kentucky. There they engaged in a sporting wager to see which team could pick the most winners. The *Chicago Tribune* reported the White Sox proved themselves the better gamblers, and reported it with no irony whatsoever, perhaps because there was other, bigger gambling news demanding space in the papers. On the eve of game one, the newspapers began to take note of the "sudden appearance of thousands of dollars of Cincinnati money," attributed, it was said, to rumors of an Eddie Cicotte sore arm, and dropping the odds on the White Sox to win from 7–10 to 5–6. There were even reports of some large bets on the Reds laid off at even money.

At about the same time that the *New York Times* correspondent was typing up his story about the sudden appearance of Cincinnati money, the players committed to the fix were meeting with a second group of would-be fixers in room 708 in the Hotel Sinton. After getting publicly rebuffed by Rothstein at the Astor Hotel dinner in New York, Bill Burns and Billy Maharg had linked up with Abe Attell and were making a presentation to the fix players. Burns and Maharg could not have known about the deal the players had already made with Sport Sullivan and Nat Evans, for had they known the fix was already in, they would likely have just bet instead of double-paying the players. They may have taken Rothstein at his loud and very public word, believing that he wasn't going to get involved, and could have thought they were the orchestrators of the whole thing. But it seems most likely that Burns and Maharg thought they were working for Rothstein— despite what he'd told them in Manhattan—because with them in Cincinnati was David Zelcer, whom they knew as "Bennett." When Abe Attell had introduced

"Bennett" to Burns and Maharg back in New York, he told them that "Bennett" was representing Rothstein. And Attell was constantly invoking Rothstein's name in conversations with anyone who would listen. Whether Attell and Zelcer were actually representing Rothstein's interests in some way is not clear. It's also unclear how much they knew about Rothstein's actual involvement, and about the Sullivan-Evans deal. The lines between conspiracy and comedy sometimes blur.

Nonetheless, it continued to play out. Burns, the ex-ballplayer, had made the contact with Gandil, and met alone with the players first. Chick Gandil was there, as was his roommate Swede Risberg, and Eddie Cicotte, Lefty Williams, Happy Felsch, Fred McMullin, and Buck Weaver. Only Joe Jackson was absent. Burns told the players he had $100,000 lined up if they would agree to throw the Series. The men with the money, he told them, were waiting downstairs. Gandil told him to show them up. Attell, Maharg, and "Bennett" came up to the room. Attell told the players he would pay them in installments, $20,000 after each loss. The men bolstered their story by dropping Arnold Rothstein's name. They told the players that the money was Rothstein's; "Bennett" was acting as his agent. The players, who did not know the deal they had in place with Sullivan and "Brown" was backed by Rothstein, asked: Could this Rothstein be trusted? "Don't worry about Rothstein," Attell assured them; "he's a walking bank."

The players then began talking about sequence. Cicotte, Gandil, and Williams said the first two games should be fixed, probably because they believed Attell's promise that they would be paid after each game, and throwing the first two would put $40,000 in their collective pocket before they got back to Chicago. Cicotte said he wanted to win his second game, because it would help with next year's contract negotiations. The players murmured in assent, saying they wanted to win a game for Cicotte. It wouldn't be game one though. Cicotte promised he would lose game one "if," he said, "I have to throw the ball clear out of the Cincinnati park." It was agreed that Burns and Gandil would be the go-betweens for the two sides, Burns getting the money to Gandil, and Gandil distributing it to the players. Burns, for his work, was to get an equal share of the player's take.

In the hotel lobbies and in speakeasies,* along the streets and behind closed doors, people in Cincinnati were talking about the wild fluctuation in the odds. The surge of Cincinnati money and the drop in odds could have had a very simple explanation. There was always a lot of exuberance when it came to a big event like this, a lot of amateur, emotional money, coming from home team fans

* Ohio had gone dry in May 1919, nearly eight months before the Eighteenth Amendment took effect nationwide.

carrying their hearts in the wallets. That alone could shift the odds in unpredict-able ways. There were fix rumors. too, but there were always fix rumors around a World Series. Conspiratorial whispers were as much a part of postseason base-ball as red-white-and-blue bunting, brass bands, and politicians in the box seats. Those versed in Series rumors, though, noted a subtle difference between the 1919 rumors and ordinary Series scuttlebutt. More than just sporting men and insiders were talking about these rumors. Everyone had heard them, and unlike in normal years, where there was generally a rumor to support any theory, these were both persistent and consistent: the White Sox were in the tank.

The writers were better versed in World Series hearsay than maybe anyone else, and Hugh Fullerton, for one, was particularly bothered by what he was hearing. Early on the day before the first game, he went into a speakeasy, "to get an eye-opener," in the company of a Detroit writer, who happened to be named Joe Jackson (no connection). When they ran into a Chicago gambler Fullerton knew, and Fullerton provided introductions, the gambler, thinking he was talking to Joe Jackson the ballplayer, asked if it was going to be Cincinnati in five straight. Later that night, Fullerton ran into Bill Burns, fresh off his meeting with the players in the Sinton, who told him to "get wise and get yourself some money" by betting on the Reds. Fullerton then sought out a White Sox player, probably Eddie Cicotte, because he later described his source as "one of the principals in the plot." The player assured him he had heard nothing; Fullerton innocently asked him to keep his ears open and let him know of anything he did hear. The player promised he would. In a bar that night, across the river in Kentucky, everybody Fullerton encountered was saying that they had heard the Series was fixed.

Fullerton was rooming with Christy Mathewson, and when he got back to his room he told Mathewson about the rumors; Mathewson grew immediately ani-mated. "Damn them!" he said, meaning not the players but the owners. "They have it coming to them. I caught two crooks and they whitewashed them." Fullerton asked Mathewson how he had come to suspect Hal Chase the season before, and how a player might purposefully lose a game. They were eventually joined by a handful of other writers, and Mathewson provided a tutorial in how to lose a game, adding the caveat that it was very difficult to know for sure. Fullerton determined that he would keep a record of plays he felt were suspicious—he would circle them on his scorecard—and asked Mathewson to provide counsel in the matter.

Sometime that evening, Fullerton sent an addendum to his syndicated column for that day. His instructions said it was to run as a "black-face precede to story," meaning it was to stand out like a headline. It read: ADVISE ALL NOT TO BET ON THIS SERIES. UGLY RUMORS AFLOAT. Only two of the forty newspapers running his column printed the precede. His home paper, the *Herald and Examiner*, was not one of them.

October 1 dawned unseasonably warm and humid; game-time temperatures would be in the mid-eighties, oppressive and uncomfortable for the players but perfect for the citizens, who were in a summer-holiday mood. It had been some time since Cincinnati baseball fans had had much to cheer, and they made the opening of the 1919 World Series a broad-based civic baseball festival. Bunting adorned not only the ballpark but the city streets as well. Banners exhorting the Reds to victory hung from houses all across the city. Streets around the ballpark were closed to traffic, and virtually every business declared a holiday so that their workers might have a chance to attend the ball game, though tickets had all been sold, and the scalpers' prices, as much as $150 a pair, were beyond the purse of most Cincinnati working men. Private homes opened up their guest rooms to out-of-towners shut out of the overbooked hotels.

It happened that this was also the fiftieth anniversary of the first great Cincinnati baseball moment, the birth of the original Red Stockings, the first fully professional ball club, who went undefeated in fifty-seven games as they barnstormed America in 1869. Since those original Red Stockings disbanded after the 1870 season, however, the teams representing Cincinnati in the National League and the American Association had been perennial also-rans, a second-division team most of the time, and never once finishing higher than third until now. Back to witness Cincinnati's return to baseball glory were George Wright and Cal McVey from the 1869 Red Stockings. Much of the Ohio congressional delegation was there, and as many as six Midwestern governors. John Phillip Sousa was in the house; he led his band in "The Stars and Stripes Forever" before the game (the tradition of playing the national anthem before baseball games would not begin until World War II). There were two other bands performing as well. While the White Sox took the infield, one of the bands serenaded them with "I'm Forever Blowing Bubbles," a song topping the sheet-music sales charts.

> I'm forever blowing bubbles,
> Pretty bubbles in the air,
> They fly so high,
> Nearly reach the sky,
> Then like my dreams,
> They fade and die.

At breakfast that morning, Hugh Fullerton bumped into two more Chicago gamblers, who told him in no uncertain terms that the Series was fixed for the Reds. Troubled by all that he had heard, before setting off for Redland Park Fullerton sought out Charles Comiskey. Comiskey said that he had heard the same things, but refused to go to Ban Johnson because he knew that Johnson wouldn't act. "I urged him to forget his feud with the league president and to call on him to act," wrote Fullerton later. "He refused angrily." So Fullerton himself went to Johnson. "He scoffed and said it was just Comiskey squealing," Fullerton wrote of his meeting.

Frustrated, Fullerton tried yet another of the game's power brokers, Barney Dreyfuss of the Pirates, perhaps the most respected and politically savvy owner in the game. Dreyfuss rebuked Fullerton for presuming to accuse ballplayers of a plot to fix the Series. "I lost my temper and raised Cain with him and the entire baseball set-up," wrote Fullerton many years later, "calling them a bunch of whitewashing bastards who were letting a bunch of crooks get away with it because they were afraid of losing money." Fullerton told Dreyfuss five players were involved, and named names. "I told him a lot of things as facts that I couldn't prove," admitted Fullerton, "and he only got madder and more indignant."

A couple of hours later, with his second pitch of the ball game, Eddie Cicotte plunked Reds shortstop Morris Rath right in the center of the back. Over the decades, this has made for a nice dramatic beginning to the Black Sox narrative. In the simply wrought, neatly packaged, cinematic morality play that America carries in its subconscious, it was the first sign of perfidy. In a dramatic scene in *Eight Men Out*, Arnold Rothstein, learning the news of the hit batsman in the telegraph room at the Ansonia Hotel, leaves and places another $100,000 on the Reds. The implication was this was a prearranged signal ordered by the gamblers, but the source for the anecdote is not a very solid one; it was Abe Attell, in an interview he gave to *New York World-Telegram* columnist Joe Williams in 1934. Williams never identified Attell by name in his story, describing him as "the little middle-aged man" who'd "had a lot to do with framing that 1919 World Series," and dropping so many other clues that nobody who had read a single newspaper story back during the indictments and trial would have had any doubt about the identity of Williams's source. Yet the writer's coyness left a nice air of smoke-filled mystery about that identity for any reader coming late to the story—these are all dangerous men, Williams seemed to be saying, and spilling the beans was something that could still, all these years later, get a guy hurt.

In fact, Attell was a notoriously self-serving and unreliable source; his pronouncements through the years would become the cause of much Black Sox confusion and misinformation, which, in the absence of verifiable fact, quickly and surely became a part of the record. The whole notion of the wild pitch as a signal informing gamblers across the county that the fix was on stretches credulity. "The instant that came over the wire, our agents would go into action," Williams quotes Attell as saying. What agents? Attell had been placing bets publicly for forty-eight hours before that first pitch, and so had a lot of the other Midwestern gamblers whom Rothstein had enlisted. They surely needed no signal. Attell wanted Williams and his readers to believe that there had been a vast web of sporting men in on the fix, waiting for some underground message? It made for great newspaper copy, but it was certainly not Arnold Rothstein's style.

"Can you imagine all those sharpshooters with a lot of dough in their kick, itching to get it down on a sure thing, and waiting for that flash, wondering whether it will be a pass, a hit batsman, or some other turn that would do them no good. Boy, that must have been funny!" It's a story filled with a lot of color and cloak-and-dagger intrigue, but not a lot of logic and common sense.

The only man who really knew whether the hitting of Morris Rath was intended to be a signal was Eddie Cicotte, and he never said anything about it. Cook County judge Charles McDonald would testify in the criminal trial that Cicotte had told him he wanted to walk the opening batter, though McDonald said nothing about Cicotte calling it a signal. At Redland Field, any historical relevance of the hit batsman was lost on its witnesses; while it was not seen as the best beginning for Cicotte and the White Sox, it was hardly the cause of any panic or consternation in the dugouts or in the press box. Fullerton put no circle around the play on his scorecard. Those looking for signs of shakiness in Cicotte in that first inning saw what they wanted to see. Rath would come across to score the game's first run, going to third on a Jake Daubert single and scoring on a Heinie Groh sacrifice fly. Cicotte would surrender another walk and was lucky when Ed Roush was caught stealing; otherwise it might have turned into a first-inning rout, for Cicotte was certainly not anywhere near his best. But Rath's would be the only run of the inning, and others in the ballpark would see that first inning as a testament to Cicotte's grittiness—what baseball people of later generations would come to call "pitchability"—getting the job done as he waited to find his form.

The White Sox tied it with an unearned run in the top of the second. Reds short-stop Larry Kopf threw Joe Jackson's ground ball into the grandstand, and Jackson scored a minute later on a Chick Gandil single. Cicotte retired the Reds in order in the second, but when he walked pitcher Dutch Ruether to lead off the third, Fullerton turned to Christy Mathewson and asked, "Do you think Cicotte is right?" Cicotte had walked only forty-nine batters in 306 innings during the regular season, an average of fewer than one and a half per game. Counting the first-inning hit batsman, he was on pace to give out nine free passes in this game.

"No," replied Mathewson, as Fullerton recorded it, "because if he had his usual stuff, the Reds would be getting more foul tips." This is what the writers and players on the field saw, what they were conditioned to look for: signs of an off day born of human frailty, not signs of a duplicitous plot to defile the game.

An inning later, however, even those who refused to believe that a World Series could be fixed began to doubt their convictions. In the fourth, Eddie Cicotte had nothing, and looked for all the world like a guy who was deliberately trying to lose a ball game. The inning began quietly enough. Ed Roush flied out to Happy Felsch. Pat Duncan singled to right. Larry Kopf was up next and hit an easy tapper right back to Cicotte. The pitcher whirled to start the double play, but hesitated. Risberg may have been slow getting to the base. Or he may have been confused by Cicotte's hesitation. In any event, Cicotte threw low, and Risberg caught the ball awkwardly and stumbled off the bag. Duncan was forced, but there was no chance for the inning-ending double play. Hugh Fullerton circled that one on his scorecard.

Greasy Neale hit a grounder back up the middle that Risberg got a glove on but could not stop. Kopf scored on an Ivey Wingo single to right, and the Reds had a 2–1 lead. Pitcher Dutch Ruether sent all of Cincinnati into delirium when he crashed a two-run triple to left-center, between Joe Jackson and Happy Felsch, scoring Wingo and Neale and putting the Reds ahead 4–1. The burly Ruether was so winded by his unaccustomed sprint to third that he sat down on the bag to rest while the Chicago infielders came in to the mound to try and settle Cicotte.

But Cicotte was not going to be settled on this day. He faced just two more batters. Morris Rath doubled and Jake Daubert singled, and the Reds led 6–1 when manager Kid Gleason came out to the mound to send his ace to an early shower. Cicotte walked slowly to the White Sox bench with his head bowed. The line for 1919's best pitcher was three and two-thirds innings pitched, seven hits, six earned runs, two walks, and one hit batsman. The final score would be 9–1 Cincinnati. Dutch Ruether was everything Cicotte was expected to be. A surprise starter, with a reputation for wildness, he scattered six hits, walked only one, and gave up just the one earned run in the second. At the plate he was three for four; in addition to his big triple in the big fourth, he singled in the sixth and blasted another triple in the eighth. He sat down on the bag to rest after that one too.

Aside from Cicotte's miserable performance and the clumsy Cicotte-Risberg ballet on the fourth-inning double-play ball, the Black Sox didn't figure much in the game, and certainly raised no suspicion. They accounted for half of the team's six hits; Chick Gandil had two and knocked in the Sox's only run; Fred McMullin, pinch-hitting in the eighth, had another.

America's baseball press made no history on this Wednesday afternoon. All the pre-Series buzz, coupled with Cicotte's abysmal performance, begged for an examination of the rumors and innuendo they had been hearing in the hotels, as well as some hard questions to players, managers, and game officials. But it wasn't as simple as the hindsight of history suggests it should have been. To begin with, readers and editors needed to see a baseball story. While some readers may have followed the progress of the game via telegraph on one of the public scoreboards set up around the country, in those days before radio and television most would know only the score when they come to their newspapers that evening or early the next morning. The readers needed and wanted game detail. Moreover, even if some reporters might have wanted to report the rumors of a fix, there were libel laws that made editors skittish about such subjects, as some writers would learn when they tried to write of a possible fix in the coming weeks and months and had their stories killed.

And a baseball game whose outcome surprised happened all the time; it's what made sport so intriguing, as both spectacle and story. The fog created by all the fix talk was blinding and disorienting. But however much some writers may have believed that there was a story in the fix talk, finding the story in the fog would be something very different. Rather than pursue what would have been the most significant story of their careers, most of the men of the press box hunkered down and hoped that, like a fog, the rumors would dissipate as suddenly as they had formed. And they wrote what they knew, what their readers expected in tomorrow's papers—the story of an improbable but intriguing upset. Some did what they could to highlight the plays that hadn't passed their smell test. But the stories hinted at no suspicion of duplicity; the suspect plays were highlighted strictly as turning points in the game.

Ring Lardner, always writing with his tongue firmly in cheek, in the semi-literate vernacular that served equally well as the voice of the dugout, grandstand, and street, had a bit more latitude in his work than his brethren.

As for the game itself, they probably has never been a thriller game in a big serious. The big thrill came in the 4th inning when everybody was wondering if the Sox would ever get the 3rd man out. They finely did and several occupants of the press box was overcome. The White Sox only chance at that pt was to keep the Reds in there hitting until darkness fell and made it an illegal game, but Heinie Groh finely hit a ball that Felsch could not help but catching and gummed up another piece of stratagem.

After the game, Lardner confronted Eddie Cicotte at the Sinton and asked him flat out: "What was wrong? I was betting on you today." Cicotte denied anything was awry, but something about his denial convinced Lardner his old friend was crooked. Cicotte had a punishing headache after the game. He tossed and turned all night, never getting to sleep in the room he shared with Happy Felsch. "Hap," he said, "it will never be done again."

Later that night, in a bar across the river in Kentucky, in the company of three fellow reporters, Lardner took the melody that had been cycling through a lot of heads that day—the pregame "I'm Forever Blowing Bubbles"—and fashioned a new lyric:

> I'm forever blowing ball games,
> Pretty ball games in the air.
> I come from Chi,
> I hardly try
> Just go to bat
> And fade and die.
> Fortune's coming my way,
> That's why I don't care.
> I'm forever blowing ball games,
> And the gamblers treat us fair.

When they returned to the Sinton, Lardner and his companions serenaded the patrons in the lobby with their creation, somewhat unsteady of gait, perhaps, but sure of voice.

Times columnist Christy Mathewson, who had been scrutinizing the game for fishy plays, may have been trying to suggest that something was afoul when, after writing that he thought the White Sox looked sluggish in the heat and befuddled by the lefty offerings of Dutch Ruether, he wrote, "I have never bet on a ball game but if we get another warm day tomorrow and [lefty Slim] Sallee starts for Cincinnati, I think I will get down a little wager on the Reds."

Intriguing as it might be to think that Mathewson was hinting at something, the truth is he was probably only writing what was expected of him.

Actual suspicions of game fixing and bribery went unreported. What was in the next day's papers were the usual sidebar stories about the action on the Series. On the streets and in the gambling parlors of America, the betting odds were now 7–10 on Cincinnati, meaning a $10 bet on the Reds would win the bettor only $7 (plus the return of the $10 bet). At the start of betting the week before, with the odds 7–10 in favor of the White Sox, the same $10 bet on the Reds would have won the bettor close to $15.

After the game, Bill Burns went looking for Abe Attell, to get the $20,000 that Chick Gandil, back in his room, was waiting for. He found Attell in the Haviland Hotel. The ex-fighter told him that there was no money for the players. "It's all out on bets," he explained. The players would have to wait until tomorrow morning. After making arrangements to meet Attell in the morning to collect the money, Burns returned to the Sinton and talked to Gandil, Cicotte, Williams, and Risberg. Though it defies credulity, he later testified that he told them he would pay them, *on the field*, the next morning before the game, signaling to them from the railing that he had the money. He later sought out Williams on the street outside the hotel, to reaffirm the game two starter's commitment to the plot. Williams, unlike Cicotte, had not received a penny up front. He assured Burns and Maharg he would still throw the game on credit.

Fans of both teams were buoyant on the morning of game two. Reds fans and the sporting men who were sure they knew something had a lot of Cincinnati money ready, and Sox loyalists were covering it, confident that game one had been an aberration. It seemed impossible that their boys would show poorly two days in a row. Bill Burns again went looking for Abe Attell, expecting him to have collected on his bets overnight and to have the $20,000 for Burns to give to the players. Attell had no money for Burns, instead showing him a telegram. The telegram read "AM WIRING TWENTY GRAND" and was signed "A. R." Burns was beginning to suspect the champ was playing him. Attell could easily have sent that telegram to himself, he thought. He went to the Western Union office, where he was unable to locate a record of the telegram Attell had shown him.

Lefty Williams was known as "the biggest and the littlest man in baseball." Although he stood just five-nine and weighed but 160, Williams had the shoulders, chest, and biceps of a much bigger man, which gave him the strength and endurance to become a staff workhorse; his 297 innings pitched were second in the league to Cicotte's 306. Unlikely to overpower any lineup, he was the quintessential junk-ball pitcher. He lived on his curve ball and his ability to put it anywhere in the strike zone he wanted. He had been a consistent winner as a middle-of-the-rotation pitcher since joining the White Sox in 1916, but had really come into his own in 1919, going 23–11.

Williams was a man of few words and few friends. He had grown close to Joe Jackson; they roomed together on the road, and their wives had become close to the point where the couples socialized together. Mostly, however, Williams was a loner. He may not have been a natural fit with the Gandil-Risberg clique on the Sox, but he was even more distant from the Collins-Schalk clique, which had made him approachable in putting the fix together. So, too, did the fact that Williams had started the season in Charles Comiskey's doghouse, having fled the Sox to play in a shipyard league in 1918, and at twenty-six years old and in his sixth season in the big leagues, he was also notably underpaid at $2,800 for the season. While many of his compromised teammates proved themselves rather inept fixers—either unwilling to lie down or never getting a chance in a key moment—Lefty Williams would prove a natural. When he took the mound at Redland Field in the first inning of game two, he was about to establish a record for World Series futility that stands until this day. Several pitchers have won three games in a Series, both before and since 1919. But no starting pitcher other than Lefty Williams has ever lost three games in the same World Series.*

It started out well enough; Williams held the Reds hitless through three. But he fell apart in the fourth, just as Cicotte had the day before. He walked Morrie Rath. After Daubert sacrificed, Williams walked Heinie Groh. Ed Roush singled in Groh and Williams then walked Pat Duncan, his third walk of the inning. Larry Kopf completed the damage with a triple. Ray Schalk was steaming. The White Sox catcher kept calling for Williams to throw his curve, and he kept getting his flat, middling-speed fastball. He had an animated exchange with Williams on the mound. That night Schalk would have a talk with Kid Gleason.

Williams settled down after the fourth, giving up just two more singles the rest of the way, though another walk would lead to the Reds' fourth run in the sixth. Those three fourth-inning runs would be all the Reds would need, because for the second day in a row the White Sox hitters were frustrated by the left-handed offerings of a Cincinnati starter. Slim Sallee, a thirty-four-year-old, twelve-year veteran who'd won twenty-one games during the regular season, was nowhere near as puzzling as Ruether had been on Wednesday. He gave up

---

* In 1981, Yankees reliever George Frazier also lost three games, but did so out of the bullpen, coming into three games that were either tied or saw the Yankees holding a one-run lead. He pitched only three and two-thirds inning in his three appearances, but surrendered the winning run in all.

ten hits. Still, he never pitched himself into any real trouble. He walked only one, never had more than two runners on in an inning, and might have had the shutout but for a spectacularly bad error by Reds right fielder Greasy Neale in the seventh that led to the only Sox runs. With Swede Risberg on first, Ray Schalk singled to right. In throwing the ball into second, Neale uncorked a throw that not only sailed over second base, but rolled all the way into the left-field corner. Risberg and Schalk both scored. Had Hugh Fullerton suspected the Reds of being on the take, Neale's throw would have likely been a circle on his scorebook.

Depending on how witnesses saw Williams's performance—and many in the press box felt he had outpitched Sallee, giving up only four hits in the complete-game loss—there was little suspicious in the play of the suspect players. Black Sox got eight of the White Sox ten hits; Buck Weaver and Joe Jackson were a combined five for eight, and Gandil, Risberg and Williams all added singles. Happy Felsch was hitless, but mostly luckless, twice robbed of base hits in key situations. Felsch was denied what might have been inside-the-park home run in the sixth when Ed Roush seemingly outran a line drive that was hit over his head, catching the ball at the centerfield wall. Then in the eighth Heinie Groh was nearly knocked down by a Felsch line drive, but hung on. Both hits would have scored at least one run. In the only other clutch situation at-bat for any of the compromised players, Chick Gandil—batting with runners on second and third and one out in the fourth of a then-scoreless game—grounded into a fielder's choice. After two games, Jackson, Weaver, and Gandil shared the team lead in hitting at .375. Eddie Collins, meanwhile, was hitting just .143.

Schalk had more animated words for Lefty Williams after the game. He may have even thrown a few punches, though the source for a fistfight is Eliot Asinof's *Eight Men Out*, and his source is not clear. Schalk was more than frustrated; he was raging. He went to Kid Gleason after the game and told the manager that Cicotte and Williams had both crossed him on pitches multiple times during the first two games. "How many times did that happen during the season?" asked Gleason. "Not once," replied Schalk. Gleason, maybe for the first time, maybe not, had to admit that he too had not liked what he had seen from the Sox thus far. It was time to talk with his boss.

There are three or four different versions of the sequence of events from this point forward. Gleason went to Comiskey, and Comiskey went to John Heydler, the president of the National League, to share the concerns that his catcher, his manager, and now he himself had regarding the integrity of his team. For Comiskey, Heydler was the only approachable member of the National Commission; his antipathy for Ban Johnson prevented him from going to his own league president,

The 1919 American League Champion White Sox. The players who would betray their teammates and become the "Black Sox" are: Back row: Chick Gandil (6th from left), Fred McMullin (5th from right), Ed "Knuckles" Cicotte (3rd from right), and Charles "Swede" Risberg (2nd from right). Front row: Claude "Lefty" Williams (6th from right), Oscar "Hap" Felsch (3rd from right), and Shoeless Joe Jackson (2nd from right). George "Buck" Weaver (front row, 4th from right) was aware of the plot and failed to report it, which earned him the same fate as the seven conspirators. Courtesy of the National Baseball Hall of Fame Library, Cooperstown, NY.

All of America paused to follow the first postwar World Series. Here, crowds in Pittsburgh (above), and Times Square in New York (below) "watch" the Series via play-by-play telegraph dispatches from the ballpark. Pittsburgh photo: Pittsburgh City Photographer Collection, 1901–2002, AIS.1971.05, Archives Service Center, University of Pittsburgh. Times Square photo: The New York Times/Redux.

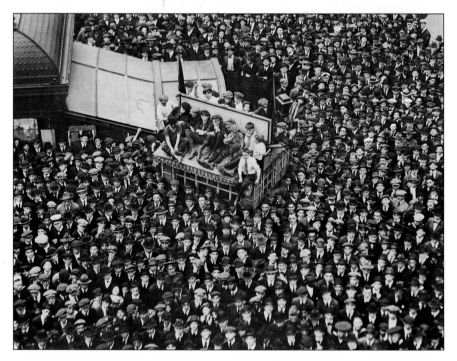

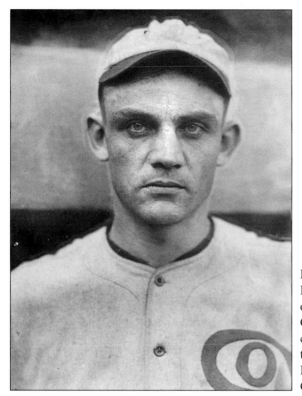

Recountings of the Black Sox story agree on few facts but one: Chick Gandil was at the center of it. Courtesy of the National Baseball Hall of Fame Library, Cooperstown, NY.

Eddie Cicotte was 29–8, with 35 complete games and a 1.82 ERA during the 1919 season. The fix plot would not have been possible without his participation. Courtesy of the National Baseball Hall of Fame Library, Cooperstown, NY.

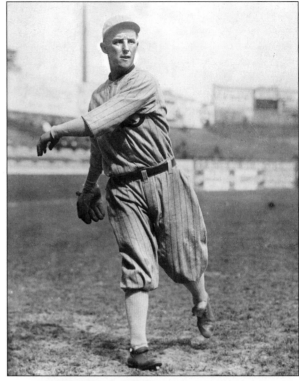

Lefty Williams established a record for World Series futility that has never been eclipsed. He started three games and went 0–3, surrendering 12 runs in 16 innings for an earned run average of 6.61. Courtesy of the National Baseball Hall of Fame Library, Cooperstown, NY.

Happy Felsch batted .192 and committed two errors in the Series, though he would later insist he had tried his best. Courtesy of the National Baseball Hall of Fame Library, Cooperstown, NY.

Swede Risberg reportedly threatened Joe Jackson during the Series when Jackson talked of confessing the plot to owner Charles Comiskey. Courtesy of the National Baseball Hall of Fame Library, Cooperstown, NY.

Utility man Fred McMullin batted only twice in the Series and went 1-for-2. Courtesy of the National Baseball Hall of Fame Library, Cooperstown, NY.

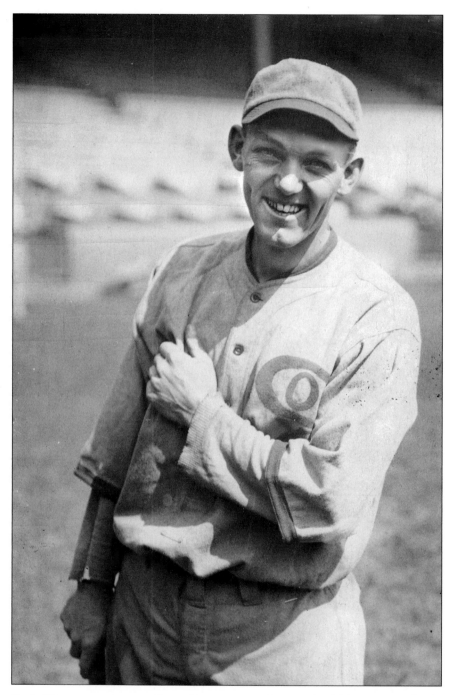

Buck Weaver spent more than thirty years trying to clear his name and win reinstatement to the game. Courtesy of the National Baseball Hall of Fame Library, Cooperstown, NY.

Victim or criminal? The debate over Shoeless Joe Jackson's complicity in the 1919 Series fix has kept the story alive for nearly a century and turned Jackson into an American cultural icon of mythic dimensions. Courtesy of the National Baseball Hall of Fame Library, Cooperstown, NY.

The Clean Sox

Rookie pitcher Dickie Kerr became a hero to White Sox fans for his gutsy wins in games three and six, but two years later he would find himself also banned from Organized Baseball. Courtesy of the National Baseball Hall of Fame Library, Cooperstown, NY.

Catcher Ray Schalk suspected something was afoul with pitchers Eddie Cicotte and Lefty Williams. Courtesy of the National Baseball Hall of Fame Library, Cooperstown, NY.

Captain and second baseman Eddie Collins batted just .226 and committed two errors in the Series. The players who would become the Black Sox resented Collins for his Columbia education and his $15,000 salary. Courtesy of the National Baseball Hall of Fame Library, Cooperstown, NY.

William "Kid" Gleason was in his first season as manager in 1919 but had been a White Sox coach since 1912. As close as a father to many of his players, he felt their betrayal perhaps more keenly than anyone else. Courtesy of the National Baseball Hall of Fame Library, Cooperstown, NY.

and it would have been tricky going to Commission chairman Garry Herrmann, also president of the Reds. One version of this story has Comiskey waking Heydler in his room in the Sinton in the small hours of the morning after game one. There are other reports that the conversation took place on the train back to Chicago after game two. Comiskey's right-hand man, Harry Grabiner, later claimed that he was the one who approached Heydler, on Comiskey's behalf, but didn't do it until Friday morning, after everyone had arrived in Chicago. Where the stories agree is that Heydler went to Johnson after hearing Comiskey. And Johnson, summoning both the old newspaperman's facility with the language and his long-standing contempt for Charles Comiskey, is said to have replied: "That is the yelp of a beaten cur."

Wherever and whenever the conversation took place, and whatever was said, the one certainty of the entire exchange was its outcome. Nothing was done. Everyone, players and gamblers alike, went back to their rooms at the Sinton after game two, before catching the sleeper back to Chicago. Burns and Maharg found Abe Attell in his room together with David Zelcer ("Bennett") and two or three others, virtually swimming in money. The two would-be fixers saw an open suitcase half filled with currency. The men they didn't recognize were on the floor counting more money. Attell lifted the mattress to reveal half a dozen thick rolls of bills. From one of these rolls he took $10,000 and gave it to Burns to give to the players. That's all they get, Attell told Burns; they would have to wait until the Series was over and Rothstein had collected on some of the $300,000 he had out on bets. Burns protested, saying the players were owed $40,000 now. Zelcer objected as well, telling Attell the players shouldn't get anything at all until the Series was over, and maybe not even then. Before Burns and Maharg left the room, Attell told him to tell the players they should win game three; a White Sox win would be good for the odds, he said. The odds were now so heavily in favor of the Reds that bets on the one-time underdog were not going to pay what they previously could. Burns put the $10,000, wrapped in a package about six inches tall, inside his shirt. As he made his way to Gandil's room, he ran into Kid Gleason in the hallway. "Hello, Kid," he said, his bundle bulging under his shirt.

Gandil, Cicotte, Risberg, and McMullin were all in the room when Burns arrived. Two others may have been there too, probably Felsch and Williams. Burns remembered six players in the room, but remembered only that Joe Jackson was not one of them. Burns threw the money on the bed and told them that was all there was for now. Chick Gandil asked Burns if they were being double-crossed. "Not by me, you're not," Burns replied. The subject of game three came up. Burns told them Attell felt that they should win. The players discussed winning, but told Burns if they were going to win, they were going to do it for one of their own—Cicotte or Williams—and not a "busher" like game-three starter Dickey Kerr. What Burns and Maharg heard was that the fix would be in for game three as well, and they planned to continue betting heavily on the Reds.

SEVEN

The End of the Series

As the White Sox and Reds left the unseasonable heat and humidity of Cincinnati behind and made their way to Chicago for games three, four, and five, they were followed, it seemed, by half the city of Cincinnati. Throughout Thursday night and Friday morning, special trains packed with Reds fans steamed into Chicago's Dearborn and Union stations. The Reds fans, equal numbers of men and women, took over the Congress Hotel, unaware, certainly, that the hotel safe held the cash that Sport Sullivan and Nat Evans were betting on the Series. The women of Cincinnati were attired almost wholly in the color of their team, "red bows, badges, plumes, gowns, pennants and stockings." Reds fans numbered a couple of thousand, which left them a distinct minority of the 29,126 crowded into Comiskey for game three; still, they were responsible for most of the ballpark noise. They had been cheering and singing and screaming on the streets of Chicago since arriving, and the cacophony continued inside the gates and throughout the game, from batting practice through the final out. If the White Sox fans were less boisterous, it was perhaps because "they did not feel that their veteran White Sox needed exhaustive and exhausting vocal support," noted a *New York Times* writer. The Chicago fans may also have been short of voice because of what had happened in Cincinnati, and from a nervous concern about what lie ahead.

After seeing both their aces bested in Cincinnati, White Sox fans now had their anxiety heightened by the fact that an untested rookie would go to the mound for the team in the must-win third game. Twenty-six-year-old Dickey Kerr had kicked around the minors for six years before going 13–7 for the White Sox in 1919. At five foot seven and 155 pounds, Kerr was even smaller than Williams. "Kerr looks like the White Sox batboy," according to one writer. A Cincinnati fan was moved to a similar wisecrack when the White Sox first arrived at the Sinton. "What's that kid going to do, carry the water pail?" But Kerr was once an amateur featherweight boxer, and people had been underestimating him for a long time. He was all pluck and junk as a pitcher, and in game three he was masterful, becoming an instant White Sox folk hero for the way he buoyed a city's spirits and put the Sox right back in the middle of things. Kerr gave up three hits, singles all, only one of them hit with any authority, and walked just one. Only one of the four Cincinnati base runners made it as far as second base. And nobody reached base at all after the first batter in the fifth; Kerr retired the last fifteen hitters he faced. In a game that took just ninety minutes, Dickey Kerr had changed a city's attitude.

On the offensive side of things, meanwhile, the players involved in the fix figured in all the scoring. In the second, Joe Jackson led off with a single. Felsch tried to sacrifice, but Cincinnati pitcher Red Fisher threw Felsch's bunted ball into centerfield trying to get the lead runner, and the Sox had men on second and third. Chick Gandil scored them both with a sharp single to right. Felsch, hustling all the way, barely beat Greasy Neale's strong throw to the plate. In the sixth inning Swede Risberg tripled, then scored the third and final Sox run on a squeeze bunt by Schalk.

Ring Lardner took some credit for the victory, telling his readers that the key to the win was his choosing not to bet on the White Sox. "The very instant I made up what is left of my mind not to lay a bet on Gleason's birds, I knowed they would win," he wrote. "As soon as the boys come out to warm up, I told them I was not wagering, which gave them the added confidents needed to win." Lardner may not have wagered, but Bill Burns and Billy Maharg followed through on their plan to let all their game-one and game-two winnings ride on the Reds in game three, and now found themselves suddenly busted and out of the game. Their careers as Series fixers had come to a quick and inglorious end. A year later, however, they would both have another part to play.

At 10 o'clock that Friday night, White Sox fans begin lining up night for bleacher tickets to Saturday's game, scheduled to go on sale the next morning at nine. Some tried to sleep; others whiled away the overnight hours with crap games. When the ticket windows opened they were three thousand strong. When the gates opened they were notably noisier than they been the previous day, though they still had difficulty out-yelling the Reds fans. All of them may have been yelling just to keep warm. A chill wind coming off the lake had blown the summer out of the air in Chicago. Game four would be played in dark, windy, chilled conditions.

Eddie Cicotte would pitch, despite some newspaper reports that his arm was still sore and that he would be out for the remainder of the Series. Over the one hour and thirty-seven minutes of game four, Cicotte disabused the notion that he was suffering from a sore arm, but fired afresh the suspicions that he was in the tank—or perhaps he allayed them. He pitched brilliantly, scattering four singles and a double and walking nobody. Still, there were two plays, both coming in the fifth inning—plays that would have been seen as everyday baseball circumstance were it not for the cloud over Cicotte—that didn't pass the smell test. With one out in the third, Pat Duncan hit a high bounder right back at the mound. Cicotte leapt and stretched his five-nine frame and got his glove on the ball, but managed only to deflect it to the right of the mound. He got to it with time enough to throw out Duncan, but his hasty throw to first bounced in the dirt, low and wide of Gandil, and Duncan took second. Larry Kopf then singled to left. Joe Jackson, charging the ball, fielded it on one hop and came up throwing to the plate. Duncan stopped at third, Kopf at first. Cicotte decided to cut the throw off. In a modern defense, he would have been backing up the plate, but pitchers more often played the cut-off man in those years. With the runners holding at third and first, it was not a bad baseball decision to cut the ball off. The problem was he was slightly out of position and the ball slightly out of his reach. He grabbed for it but missed; it deflected off his glove, rolling past Schalk all the way to the backstop. Duncan scored and Kopf moved up to second. Another circle on Hugh Fullerton's scorecard.

With Kid Gleason's blessing, Joe Jackson then moved in to play a shallow left field, in the hopes of keeping Kopf from scoring on a base hit. But Greasy Neale lofted a fly ball over Jackson's head, a ball he would almost certainly been in position to catch had he been playing a normal depth. Kopf scored. Cincinnati now had all the runs they would need. Cicotte retired fourteen of the last fifteen batters he faced.

Meanwhile, Jimmy Ring, a twenty-four-year-old right-hander who'd gone 10–9 during the regular season, continued the string of brilliant Cincinnati pitching, surrendering just three singles. The only thing resembling a White Sox threat came in the second, when they loaded the bases with two out. But the next batter was Cicotte, a career .186 hitter, who grounded meekly to second. Only once more, in the third, would the Sox have more than one man on base or get a runner as far as third. Black Sox accounted for all three of the team's hits, one each from Jackson, Felsch, and Gandil. Nobody really came up in a critical offensive moment. There weren't any crucial moments for the White Sox offense. As Jack Lait noted in his "In the Wake of the News" column in the *Tribune*: "Ring hit two Sox batters and that's almost as many Sox batters as hit Ring."

In 1919 the practice of journalists visiting the locker room after the game, talking to players about key plays, and incorporating those quotes into the game stories was still a generation in the future. If any of the baseball writers asked Cicotte about his fifth-inning errors, they did so later, and whatever he said in response didn't make the newspapers. Baseball writers of the time wrote what they saw and then put their own spin on things. If any writer saw Cicotte's errors as deliberate, he shared no such suspicions with readers. Syndicated columnist Grantland Rice saw them as part of the game. "Strangely enough, the ancient wing held up and it was the ancient bean that went awry," read Rice's story, which appeared in more than one hundred papers nationwide. "Today, three mistakes in one inning, two misplays and one error of judgment, all lumped into a game-losing mass, cost him his second start."

I. E. Sanborn of the *Chicago Tribune* saw them as less of a factor in the Sox loss than the team's woeful lack of offense. "It was unfortunate that Cicotte had to defeat himself, but there was no chance for him to beat the Reds without a run, and goodness knows how many innings it would have taken the Gleasons to [score] on Ring, the way he was baffling them yesterday."

Damon Runyon saw Cicotte's failings as part of a twilight-of-the-gods drama. As Cicotte and Ring left the field—Cicotte alone, forlorn and thirty-five years old; Ring triumphant and just twenty-four, the cynosure of adoring eyes—Runyon was watching Christy Mathewson and Johnny Evers, sitting together down the row in the press box. "Evers glanced at Mathewson and Evers shook his head," Runyon noticed. "No word passed between them, but there was a world of meaning in the gesture. Better than any others in all that great crowd, perhaps, they knew the feelings of Eddie Cicotte...as he left the field, leaving the glory of victory to Jimmy Ring, the newest star.

"They knew something too, of the feelings of young Jimmy Ring, fresh from his triumph over the old pitcher and the White Sox. They, too, once lived the same hours."

That night, Lefty Williams got a call from Chick Gandil, asking the pitcher to meet him in his rooms; he had a package for him. Williams got there and Gandil gave him two envelopes. "There's your dough," he said. "The gamblers has called it off." There's $5,000 for you and $5,000 for Jackson, he told him. That was apparently all there was to the conversation. Whether the $10,000 was the money Burns had given him two days before or some of the money Sullivan and Evans had given him more than a week before is another of the fix's enduring mysteries.

Williams picked up the envelopes and left, taking a taxi up to the Lexington Hotel, where he and Jackson were sharing a suite together with their wives during the Series.*

He walked into Jackson's room and tossed one of the envelopes on the bed. "That's all we have got. We have been crossed in some way," he told him. The two men counted their money, out of sight of their wives; there were a few hundreds and a lot of fifties in each envelope. They speculated on whether it was the gamblers who had double-crossed them or Gandil. Williams had no opinion; Jackson was convinced their teammate was betraying them. He had asked Gandil after games one, two, and three where the money was, and each answer was more evasive and unsatisfying than the one before. Jackson had told Williams after the first game, "The whole thing was a crooked deal all the way through. Gandil [is] not on the square with us."

Williams continued to keep the news of the fix, and his $5,000, from his wife. Jackson, for the first time, told his wife what he had gotten himself involved in. She wept.

On Sunday morning, October 5, it poured rain in Chicago, more than an inch and a half in an hour's time, flooding the sewers in the Loop and leaving the Comiskey field covered in water. The managers and umpires agreed at 10:30 a.m. to call things off.

Monday, October 6, dawned still cloudy but dry, and Cincinnati manager Pat Moran named his fifth starter in as many games. Hod Eller was a sturdy, five foot eleven, 185-pound righty, a native of Muncie, Indiana. He had been a part of the White Sox training-camp roster back in 1916 but hadn't made the team,

---

* A decade after the 1919 World Series, the Lexington would become infamous as the headquarters of Chicago gangster Al Capone; Capone henchman would patrol the lobby with machine guns. In the 1980s, the hotel, now a derelict building, would have another moment in the headlines when a series of tunnels and a vault were discovered in the building's basement, the vault presumably locked since Capone was arrested at the hotel and taken to prison in 1931. Television gadfly Geraldo Rivera created a stir by speculating that the vault contained thousands of dollars in cash and promising a dramatic opening on live TV. The vault contained nothing but a handful of dusty wine bottles. The building was torn down a decade later.

and was picked up by the Reds a year later. He had the best season of his career in 1919, winning nineteen games during the regular season. He almost didn't make it to the mound for his World Series start, though. Slipping on a discarded plug of chewing tobacco in the hotel hallway that morning, he had slammed his pitching elbow against the concrete floor. It stung for a while, but there was no damage, which was bad luck for the White Sox, for they were as befuddled by Eller as they had been by Ruether, Sallee, and Ring. The Sox managed an anemic three hits, two by Buck Weaver and one by Ray Schalk. The tenor of their offensive day was set in the first inning. With runners on first and third with one out and the heart of their order coming up, Eller got Joe Jackson on an infield pop-up and Happy Felsch on a fly to left. He was never challenged again. He struck out nine, including six in a row in the third and fourth innings.

Lefty Williams, meanwhile, continued to be a cipher to Sox fans and management. In an otherwise solid performance, he had one unfortunate inning that gave the Reds the game, though he was probably less at fault for what happened than the Sox defense. Williams had pitched one hit ball over five innings, but Hod Eller became the second Cincinnati pitcher with an extra base hit in the Series when he opened the sixth with a double to center, on a fly ball that Jackson and Felsch did something of an Alphonse and Gaston on. Eller went to third when Felsch's relay into Risberg was off the mark, and then scored on a Rath single. After a walk to Heinie Groh, Ed Roush's lifted a high fly to deep center that Felsch played like a circus clown. He first came in on the ball, then froze, then ran back, desperately but too late; the fingers of his glove grazed the ball, but it fell to the ground and rolled to the fence. Felsch fell to the ground, finally getting to the ball as it stopped rolling. The play cost the Sox two runs and the services of catcher Ray Schalk, who was ejected from the game after a screaming match with umpire Cy Rigler over the safe call of trailing runner Heinie Groh. A sacrifice fly to left from Pat Duncan scored Roush. Joe Jackson's strike to the plate might have had Roush, but backup catcher Byrd Lynn, inserted in the game just minutes before, and "as nervous as a first-timer at the door of a pawnshop," couldn't handle the throw cleanly.

It was an all-around lackluster performance by the White Sox, far and away their worst of the Series. Perhaps with the exception of the volatile Schalk everyone on the field looked like a beaten player; together they made a team that didn't care, and didn't care who knew it. That finally set off manager Kid Gleason. James Crusinberry of the *Tribune* had been talking to Gleason after the games and writing up his comments in the paper. On that Monday afternoon, he waited for Gleason outside the clubhouse and accompanied him in a cab to his rooms in a downtown hotel. Crusinberry reported that Gleason was silent in the cab, but opened up once he got to the hotel. To this point, for the newspaper readers at least, Gleason had staunchly defended his team, attributing every bad moment to bad luck or good play by the Reds. He asserted his confidence and his belief in his players at every turn. But today that belief and confidence were gone. He made no specific allegations, but his disappointment, anger, and frustration had led him to the conviction that "something is wrong with my gang."

> The bunch I had fighting in August for the pennant would have trimmed this Cincinnati bunch without a struggle. The bunch I have now couldn't beat a high school team....
>
> I am convinced that I have best ball club that ever was put together. I certainly have been disappointed in it in this series. It hasn't played baseball in a single game. There's only a bare chance they can win now. The gang I had in August might do it. The gang that has played for me in the five games of the world's series will have to have luck to win another ball game.

"He clearly indicated he was mad enough to lick a lot of people and go to jail for it," Crusinberry wrote. "He clearly indicated there was something wrong and that he intended to find out about it."

Gleason confronted his players, probably several different times, in several different ways, during the Series. The first time was after the second game, after he had talked to Ray Schalk and before he went to Comiskey, when he gathered the players and told them he had heard stories that gamblers had reached some of the White Sox players. "I hear a hundred thousand dollars is going to change hands if we lose," he told them. He then challenged any player who knew anything to step forward. None did. Outfielder Shano Collins said that the allegations were "a lot of bunk." Gleason felt for a time that he had righted the ship. Kerr's win in game three and Cicotte's strong performance in game four led him to feel that everyone was now playing to win and that the Sox just needed to hit better. Williams's loss in game five changed his mind.

The second confrontation between Gleason and the players came either just after the game five loss, when the Series shifted back to Cincinnati, or just before game seven. Gleason again challenged anyone who was involved with gamblers to admit it or anyone who knew anything to step forward. He promised he would use an "iron"—a pistol—on anyone he could prove had betrayed him.

Gleason again had reason to hope that his tirade in the newspaper and his threats and admonitions to his players had turned things around, for on the train ride back to Cincinnati all the ills and malaise that had plagued the team for a week seemed to suddenly vanished. The Sox took two in Cincinnati, and found themselves coming back home two days later, trailing by only one game and suddenly of a whole new mind.

After the Reds' authoritative win in game five, giving them a 4–1 Series lead, everyone in Cincinnati was expecting to celebrate a World Championship the following afternoon. The record crowd of more than 32,000 at Redland Field was even more like a college football crowd than they had been in games past, with banners and pennants, matching red clothing, coordinated cheers, and rhythmic clapping. The band greeted the arrival of the White Sox on the field with a rendition of "I'm Sorry I Made You Cry." Reds fans bet heavily, giving odds of 7–10, confident that their money was as safe riding on the Reds as it would be in a savings account. And the grandstand fairly quivered with an excitement and anticipation that swelled as the Reds built up a 4–0 lead over Dickey Kerr. But if Kerr was not the same pitcher he had been in game three, he was every bit the fighter. He gave up eleven hits and was in trouble during practically every inning, but continually pitched himself out of it, and allowed no scores after the fourth, giving his team a chance to come back. Which, for the first time in the Series, it did, getting to Dutch Ruether for a run in the fifth and three in the sixth to tie it up, the sixth-inning rally triggered by consecutive hits from Buck Weaver, Joe Jackson, and Hap Felsch. That explosion forced Ruether from the game, but Kerr was still in there in the finish, closing the Reds down one-two-three in the bottom of the tenth after the White Sox had taken a 5–4 lead in the top of the inning on base hits from Buck Weaver and Joe Jackson and an RBI single from Chick Gandil.

Reds fans were denied their party, but still somehow managed to wake up with a hangover. In another of the mysteries of the 1919 World Series, only 13,923 fans made their way to Redland Field for game seven, less than half the number that had comprised the sellout crowds of the three previous games. They wouldn't have had much to cheer. White Sox hitters did not find Slim Sallee the puzzle they had in game two. Joe Jackson drove in one run with a single in the first and another with a single in the third. Happy Felsch drove in two with a double in the fifth. And Eddie Cicotte, finally coming as advertised, scattered ten hits and three walks, which made for a lot of base runners but not a lot of scoring threats. The Sox won 4–1, and suddenly baseball had a Series, good news to Sox fans and those who bet on them, and a very nervous moment for Reds fans and those who bet on them.

In Eliot Asinof's papers at the Chicago History Museum—the notes, letters, and clippings from which he fashioned *Eight Men Out*—there is a copy of a 1959 *New Yorker* article by J. M. Flagler entitled "Requiem for a Southpaw." In it, Flagler tells the story of his 1930s boyhood friendship with Lefty Williams, when Williams lived in the apartment downstairs from Flagler's family's in Chicago. One anecdote in the article has Williams's wife Lyria sharing the player's scrapbooks with Flagler, and then trying to explain why he had done what he had done more than a decade earlier. "All those others were doing it," Flagler quotes her as saying, "and he didn't understand what it really meant, and besides, he was threatened."

He was threatened. No explanation of who threatened him, or what he was threatened with, or when it happened. Just *he was threatened*, a sort of oh-by-the-way afterthought to what was a pretty desperate argument to begin with, made more than a decade after the fact. It isn't clear whether Williams's wife even had firsthand knowledge of a threat against her husband. Williams never said anything about a threat in his testimony before the grand jury, and that was only other known reference to a threat against Williams. That came in a 1920 newspaper story in which Bill Maharg told Jimmy Isaminger of the *Philadelphia North American* that he had heard Williams had been threatened before the last game. But Maharg was hardly a credible corroborating witness on something like this. By the last game of the 1919 Series, he was broke, out of the fix loop, and back in Philadelphia.

Yet from those slender reeds of evidence, Asinof wove a scene in *Eight Men Out* in which he has Sport Sullivan, under instructions from Arnold Rothstein, calling a Chicago thug known only as Harry F. to persuade Lefty Williams that it would be in everyone's best interests, particularly Williams's, if the Reds clinched the Series the following day. At 7:30 on the eve of game eight, Asinof has Williams walking home from a dinner with his wife—a bit odd, given that at 7:30 Lefty Williams would not have been in Chicago but still on the Sox train returning from Cincinnati, which arrived near midnight. In the Asinof telling, as Williams approaches his building, a man in a bowler hat steps from the doorway, and says that he wants a word, in private.

> The man went right to the point. He bluntly told Williams he was to lose the next game. Lefty had shaken his head violently and started to turn away. But the man stopped him, restraining him with a vice-like grip on his arm. No, it wasn't a question of money any more. Williams

was not going to get paid another dime! He was going to lose that ball game or something was going to happen to him. Maybe something might happen to his wife, too.…

There was more to the threat. It had to be done in the first inning. The man eyed him, seeking confirmation of this in Williams's eyes. That's right, the man repeated: Williams was not to last even one inning!

Asinof would later admit that he had invented the character of Harry F., because he had wanted to plant something in his book that would protect him against its being plagiarized. Why he had this fear, or felt the need to fictionalize history, he did not say. Nor did he ever admit to imagining the scene in which Williams is so dramatically threatened. But there is nothing in the record that suggests any such thuggish threat. Asinof's creative history goes to the central problem of trying to tell the story of the Black Sox. There are so many holes, and so many tantalizing ways to fill them.

Whether Williams was threatened or not, there was a buzz of foreboding around the ballpark on the morning of game eight. In a story written two months after the Series ended, Fullerton reported that minutes before game eight he had bumped into a Chicago sporting man outside the press box at Comiskey, who told him to get a bet down on the Reds. "What do you know about today?" Fullerton demanded. "It'll be the biggest first inning you ever saw," the gambler reportedly replied, and then walked away.

Fullerton did not mention the big-first-inning warning in his story on the day after the final game, in an article in which he did note that seven members of the Sox had played their final game for the team. He instead saved it for December, including it in an explosive, accusatory story that helped keep the sense of this-Series-might-have-been-crooked in the public consciousness at a time when it was starting to fade.

Fullerton's reputation has had to survive suspicions of fabrication through the years. Bill Hanna, a New York sportswriter, once told him, "Hughie, you would sacrifice accuracy for the sake of a good story," to which Fullerton replied, "Bill, you would sacrifice a good story for the sake of accuracy." Fullerton's reporting went a long way toward eventually bringing the Black Sox story out into the open. But like everything else in the Black Sox story, Fullerton's story is tangled and complicated. The gambler's warning is an explosive and insightful detail, and it raises the question: Why didn't Fullerton report it right away?

In any case, on October 9 a brisk and gusty wind blew morning clouds from the South Side sky, and the start of game eight was sunny. But the wind remained and would swirl throughout the game, stirring up little cyclones of dust on the infield dirt, causing a good many pauses in play as the infielders closed their eyes and turned their heads. It would take two hours and twenty-seven minutes to play game eight, forty-five minutes longer than the average of games one through seven.

Yet it took fewer than fifteen minutes to decide it. Lefty Williams got two strikes on leadoff hitter Morrie Rath, and then got him to pop to shortstop. It would be the only out he would record. After singles by Jake Daubert and Heinie Groh, Kid Gleason sent Bill James down to the Sox bullpen to warm up. It was clear his patience with Williams was going to be very short. Ray Schalk went out to talk to his pitcher; it could not have been a pleasant conversation. Eddie Roush then doubled to right, scoring Daubert, and Pat Duncan followed with a double to left, scoring Groh and Roush. With the score 3–0, Gleason had seen enough. He came out to get his beleaguered starter, and took Williams with him back to the bench. It was one of the most inglorious pitching lines in World Series history. Williams had thrown just sixteen pitches, lasted just one-third of an inning, faced five batters, and given up four hits. When Duncan would later come around to score, Williams was charged with four runs.

The Comiskey fans nonetheless cheered lustily when the Sox finally came to bat in the bottom of the first. Four runs was hardly an insurmountable deficit. Their spirits were raised when leadoff hitter Nemo Leibold cracked a sharp single to left. Cincinnati manager Pat Moran showed he would be even less patient with starter Hod Eller than Gleason had been with Williams when he sent Jimmy Ring down to warm up after Leibold's single. The cheers of the Comiskey fans grew even more frenzied when Eddie Collins—having a miserable Series, both at the plate and in the field—followed with a double to left center, and the Sox had runners on second and third with nobody out. But Weaver, Jackson, and Felsch all went down quietly, and the White Sox rally died. It was the last real chance they had. When next they mounted a rally in the eighth, they were already trailing 10–1. The final score was 10–4; Hod Eller went the distance for Cincinnati for his second win of the Series.

All of the eight players accused of fixing would later claim that, despite their promise to play crooked, they had played every game to win. There are good reasons to believe them. But the Reds were a pennant-winning team themselves, and baseball is a fickle game, where the best hitters who have ever played failed nearly 70 percent of the time, and pitchers who succeed no more than two times out of three are generally locks for Cooperstown. The White Sox, playing to win or playing to lose, were only partially in control of their own destiny.

The case for Joe Jackson and Buck Weaver playing the Series cleanly is a fairly unassailable one. Both men claimed from the moment of the scandal's exposure until their dying days that they had given nothing less than their best, and the record supports their assertions. Jackson led both teams' regulars in hitting at .375. He had a Series-record twelve hits and the Series' only home run. Weaver had eleven hits, and was second on the team in hitting at .323. Both were in the center of the few rallies the White Sox had; both played errorless baseball. Neither did anything either at bat in in the field to earn one of those circles in Hugh Fullerton's scorebook.

Chick Gandil would not have aroused any suspicions with his play, though, in truth, the fix's supposed mastermind didn't figure into a lot of key plays. He hit .233, more than fifty points below his regular season average, but a couple of his hits—particularly the two-run single in game three that propelled the Sox to their first win and his game-winner in the tenth inning of game six—were big ones. His one suspect moment, a possible circle on Hugh Fullerton's scorecard, came in game two, in the fourth inning of a still scoreless game. With runners on second and third and one out, Gandil came up and "acted like his was afraid he might hit the ball safely," according to Fullerton, and then "jabbed at the ball for an easy out." Gandil had one inconsequential error.

Hap Felsch was both miserable and luckless. He hit only .192, five hits in twenty-six at-bats. But he hit the ball hard on at least five other occasions, and was victimized by some heroic Cincinnati fielding. In the field he had two errors, including the very awkward play on Ed Roush's fly ball in game five. He later said that even some of his crooked teammates had chastised him for that one, telling him he had to be more discreet. He insisted he'd been trying to catch it, and had just been fooled.

Swede Risberg either had one of the worst World Series of all time or had worked hard to earn his money from the gamblers. He had just two hits in twenty-five at-bats, a .080 average. He led both teams with four errors, some harmless, some critical. In the fourth inning of game six, an eventual White Sox victory, with Dutch Ruether running at second, he tried for the out at third and threw it past Buck Weaver, allowing Ruether to score the third Reds run and giving them a 3–0 lead. Scattered throughout the Series, he had another three or four occasions when he came close but couldn't quite get to the ball, or batted it away or made some less-than-perfect throws. We have no idea whether he was trying to make those plays or trying to botch them. Swede Risberg never talked. Neither did substitute Fred McMullin, who had just two at-bats, one hit, and no chances in the field.

The Black Sox committed nine of the White Sox' twelve errors. On the other hand, they batted a collective .255, forty points higher than the collective .215 compiled by the so-called Clean Sox. Of the untainted White Sox, only Ray Schalk had anything approaching a good Series. Schalk hit .304. Eddie Collins hit just .226, nearly a hundred points below his regular season average of .319, and committed two key errors. Nemo Leibold and Shano Collins, who shared the right field duties, were just five for thirty-four between them, a combined .147.

This leaves Eddie Cicotte and Lefty Williams. We have Ray Schalk's allegation that both pitchers were grooving pitches in their first starts. Neither admitted to that in their confessions before the grand jury a year later; both maintained that they had pitched every game to win. Yet Cicotte's paralyzing headache after his game-one loss, his cry that night to Felsch—"Hap, it will never be done again"— suggests a man burdened by great guilt. His starts in games four and seven would seem to bolster his argument about pitching to win. In the two complete games, he was charged with just a single earned run. Yet he also committed those two fifth-inning errors in game four, leading to two unearned runs and a Cincinnati victory. Cicotte seems a man in the throes of a battle between his better and lesser angels. Did he pitch his heart out but for those fleeting fifth-inning moments when he was overcome by his obligation to the men who had paid off the mortgage on his farm? There is a tantalizing line in Lefty Williams's confession to Comiskey attorney Alfred Austrian, shortly before he confessed to the grand jury. Williams was talking about a conversation he and Cicotte had had on the train going from Chicago to Cincinnati after game five. "I told him we were double crossed, and I was going out to win, if any possible chance," Williams said. "Cicotte said he was the same." The question of course is what Williams meant, and what he thought Cicotte meant—that they had been playing to win since the start, or would be playing to win from then on, with the double-cross now clear to them and the Reds up four games to one?

Any experienced baseball observer who had watched Lefty Williams in the 1919 World Series, absent any rumors of a fix and with no reason to suspect anything was wrong, would have concluded that Williams looked dazed and out of his element on the mound, that he was a man who was pitching nervous. The word "choked" would have come up before the word "crooked" did. Some of those who had heard the fix rumors might have also have leaned toward the former.

Lefty Williams seemed more frightened than inept. He told the grand jury that he had been nervous, carrying the burden of the fix to the mound. And though he had been trying to win that first game, nervousness led to wildness, which led to a Cincinnati rally that led to their win. Nonetheless, he did also admit that it might have been more than nerves that failed him in that first start. Asked whether he could have pitched harder in game two, he allowed, "Well, I might have pitched harder if I wanted to." He did not feel that way about his starts in games five and eight. Asked if he could have pitched harder in game five, he replied, "No sir, I pitched as hard in that game as I ever pitched a ball game in my life." When asked about the final game and whether he had played as hard as he could, he replied, "I did." In Williams's mind, there was a distinction between his loss in game two and his losses in games five and eight.

He also freely admitted to being beset by nerves throughout the Series. "Yes, it made me worry. I wished I was out of it, and hadn't been mixed up in it all." If we take Williams at his word, and add it to the evidence of his performance, we might conclude that the gamblers didn't need him to try to lose. They had guaranteed it by getting so deeply inside his head. At this remove of nearly a century, a Black Sox student might also choose the word "choked" over "crooked" in assessing Williams's 1919 Series.

And let us also not overlook the role played by the Cincinnati Reds in the White Sox' 1919 miseries. They will forever remain the most maligned World Series champions in baseball history, yet their pitchers turned in one of the most stellar team performances in Series history. Dutch Ruether, Slim Sallee, Jimmy Ring, and Hod Eller (twice) all had complete-game victories in the Reds' five wins. Ring and Eller had shutouts, and Ruether and Sallee surrendered one and two runs, respectively, in their wins. Only twice did the White Sox score more than two runs in an inning, and one of those times was in the eighth inning of the eighth game, with the Reds leading 10–1 and the Series already securely lost. The Reds' team ERA was 1.63. And this against a White Sox lineup that included four Hall of Famers: the two that are there, Ray Schalk and Eddie Collins, and the two that would have been, Joe Jackson and Buck Weaver. Surely these Reds are men deserving of a better historical fate than their station as accidental champions.

And what of the money and its part in the 1919 World Series? Testimony in the 1921 criminal trial has $10,000, and only $10,000, passing between gamblers and players—the money Abe Attell gave to Bill Burns to give to Chick Gandil after game two. But that was clearly not all the money paid to the ballplayers.

Arnold Rothstein students believe he sent Evans and Sullivan to Chicago with $80,000 to pay the players. Some histories claim they paid out only $10,000, using the rest to bet on their own behalf, meaning only $20,000 of a promised $180,000–$200,000 ever made it to the players. Those numbers don't compute. Evans and Sullivan may not have given the players all of Arnold Rothstein's $80,000, but they almost certainly gave them more than $10,000.

Eddie Cicotte testified that he got $10,000 before the Series began. Joe Jackson and Lefty Williams both testified that they received $5,000 each after game four. Swede Risberg's mistress suggested to one of Charles Comiskey's private investigators that he had gotten $10,000. Happy Felsch admitted to receiving $5,000. Buck Weaver insisted he never took a penny, and no one has ever disputed his claim. That's a payout total of $35,000, which leaves a potential $55,000 unaccounted for. Chick Gandil, the instigator and the banker, probably got most of it. He would in all likelihood have cut in Fred McMullin, who, despite his benchwarmer status, was one of Gandil's lieutenants in putting this together, already in the loop when the others were drafted, already in the room whenever there was a meeting of any consequence. The players' best conjecture was that he must have gotten $5000 too. His silence means it will remain forever conjecture.

In a fact-challenged *Sports Illustrated* tell-all in 1956, Chick Gandil maintained that he never received a dime. Nobody believed that, then or now, or at any time leading up to that. In their grand jury confessions, Cicotte, Williams, and Jackson all claimed they thought throughout the process that Gandil was betraying them. So Gandil had a reason to lie in the *Sports Illustrated* article, even in 1956. Four of the seven players he had probably betrayed were still alive.

But Chick Gandil was far too conniving to have walked away from this with nothing but regrets, as he so disingenuously claimed in the *Sports Illustrated* article. In the spring of 1920, at the age of thirty-three, he was financially secure enough to wave goodbye to his baseball career, refusing the contract Comiskey sent him and instead playing semipro ball in Southern California, where, his old teammates were quick to note, he had just bought a new house.

It has been estimated that $2 million changed hands during the Series in New York alone, and many times that number was no doubt bet across the land. Two million dollars is not a particularly imposing number by contemporary standards, until one considers that the combined value of the entire White Sox and the Reds franchises at that time probably fell quite a bit short of $2 million. The White Sox, one of the more valuable franchises in the game, were probably worth a million dollars; the Reds would have been valued at quite a bit less.

The gamblers, as a class, broke even on the 1919 Series. Every dollar won is somebody else's dollar lost. Every story written after the scandal broke, every bit of gambler testimony told mostly of money lost—it was a loser's way of exacting some revenge. Of the major players in the story, Bill Burns and Billy Maharg ended up broke, losing whatever their original stake was, plus whatever they won on games one and two. Not coincidentally, they were important state's witnesses in the 1921 criminal trial against the players. There is no record of how much money Sport Sullivan and Nat Evans may have won. Neither ever had to tell his story. But we can presume it was considerable, in line with, or even more than, the $30,000 Abe Attell claimed he made on a $9,000 investment.

Publicly, Arnold Rothstein maintained that he had lost $6,000 betting on the White Sox. He is believed to have bet more than $300,000 on Cincinnati, most of it early, when the odds were still in favor of the White Sox.

EIGHT

The Cover-Up Begins

With the Series over, Joe Jackson determined that he would unburden himself of the weight of his shame and the $5,000 in fifties and hundreds that he was still carrying around in the envelope in which he had received it. Set to leave for Savannah that evening—having cleaned out his locker the morning after the final Series game—he went to the White Sox offices and asked to see Charles Comiskey. Harry Grabiner turned him away. Grabiner and Comiskey suspected what Jackson wanted to tell them, and they weren't ready to hear it. With the Series lost and the damage already done, the only way this was now going to turn out well for the White Sox was if it stayed in the shadows, at least until Comiskey could determine what he wanted to do. Jackson's need for catharsis was not welcome at this early moment. At this point, keeping things in the shadows had a fifty-fifty chance of success. Usually these sorts of rumors vanished as quickly as they had formed, and particularly so after the event in question was concluded. But these White Sox rumors were going to prove stubbornly durable.

Comiskey himself—if inadvertently—lent the rumors credibility on the day the Series ended. Kid Gleason was in the White Sox offices after the end of the final game. So, too, was the *Herald*'s Hugh Fullerton. Fullerton and Comiskey went back to the Cincinnati days; he had come less as a reporter that afternoon than as someone looking to comfort an old friend.

Gleason was seething—and quite vocal. He had no doubt that his players had tanked the Series, and he took their actions as a personal betrayal. Comiskey shared his anger and, in the passion of the moment, let slip a statement he would soon come to regret. "There are seven boys who will never play ball on this team again," he told Fullerton.

Fullerton went back to the *Herald and Examiner* offices and reported it. He alleged no fix in his immediate post-Series article and indeed did his best to argue that the rumors of a fix were bunk. "The fact is, this Series was...lost through overconfidence. Forget the suspicions and evil-minded yarns that might be circulated," he wrote. But he also brought all of those suspicions to the fore when he added, "Yesterday's, in all probability, is the last game that will be played in any World Series. If the club owners, and those who have the interest of the game at heart, have listened during the Series, they will call off the annual interleague contest." Readers were surely perplexed. The 1919 Series had been wildly popular, the most followed and best-attended World Series ever. If Fullerton was right that the "evil-minded yarns" were groundless, why would he suggest baseball call off its most visible, popular, and lucrative event? Adding to the mystery, he then passed along Comiskey's threat. "Yesterday's game also means the disruption of the Chicago White Sox ball club. There are seven men on the team who will not be there when the gong sounds next spring." Again, readers had to have been left scratching their heads. If the White Sox were guilty of nothing more than overconfidence during the Series, why would Comiskey remake a championship team so radically?

Comiskey, meanwhile, immediately understood that the rumors of crookedness on the part of his ball club threatened to bring more than scandal and shame; they threatened the very survival of his business. If the story came out of the shadows uncontrolled, it was quite likely that Comiskey and his franchise would be stained right along with the crooked players. If the courts—whether of law or of public opinion—drove the investigation, Comiskey and his life's work could be swept away together with the guilty players. To reduce the chances of ruin, he needed to get out in front of this story, whatever it was, and quickly, for it was already showing signs of galloping away from anybody's control. The Series had ended on Wednesday, October 8. On Thursday Kid Gleason received a telephone call from Max Ascher and Clyde Elliot, two White Sox fans who had lost heavily in betting the Sox in the Series. They had "something of great importance" to share with Gleason and arranged to meet with him and Harry Grabiner at Comiskey Park on Friday, October 10.

As Grabiner recounted the meeting in his diary, their "something of great importance" boiled down to a threat.

> Ascher said that Elliot was a great friend of [gambler and theater owner Harry] Redmon of E. St. Louis, who (Redmon) was crossed in the betting would tell everything if he (Elliot) would so advise and that Redmon was very sore at having lost $5500 and if that was not made good that he would spill the beans 100% and even go so far as to sit in a room and let some of the implicated ballplayers get a flash at him. Elliot said that Redmon was in the room with the ballplayers at the time the fixing was done and while he would not implicate a single gambler he would go all the way regarding the ballplayers.

So less than forty-eight hours after the final out of the World Series, Comiskey and the White Sox had to face something far stronger than rumors and suspicion. They had to face an explicit allegation and a connection to a man allegedly present when the fix was born. Kid Gleason, Clyde Elliot, and Grabiner's deputy Tip O'Neill left the next day for Saint Louis and met with Redmon on Sunday October 12. Again, Grabiner offered an account in his diary of what Harry Redmon told the White Sox men:

> The players were supposed to have received $15,000 per game from the gamblers. The go-between for the players was supposed to be [St. Louis Browns second baseman Joe] Gedeon and Bill Burns while Abe Attell was to handle the betting. The gamblers who paid for the fix were Zork, Redmon, Franklin, a St. Louis mule buyer, and the 2 Levi brothers from Des Moines. The name of Rothstein was also mentioned. The players on the White Sox mentioned as being implicated being: Williams, Jackson, Felsch, McMullin, Risberg, Gandil, Cicotte and Weaver, the last two both being crooked in the first game and then turning. The meeting at which the plans to fix the Series was supposed to have been held was at the Sherman House the Friday before the Series opened, and was attended by all the above players in addition to Attell, Zork and Gedeon.*

---

* Either the Friday, September 26, date or Joe Gedeon's presence at the meeting is likely incorrect. Gedeon and the Browns had left Chicago on Thursday, September 25.

Now Comiskey, Gleason, and Grabiner had names—confirmation of the very players whom Gleason had suspected all along. And they had additional credible allegations. When Gleason returned from Saint Louis, Comiskey brought the whole matter to Alfred S. Austrian, his longtime attorney.

Though he had been the third baseman on his "class nine" at Harvard thirty years before, Austrian was not a baseball man; he had not attended a single game of the recent Series, having been busy with a battery of other clients across the spectrum of Chicago civil and criminal law. But though he seldom went to a game and didn't follow the box scores, Austrian was nonetheless a central figure in Chicago baseball, the lead attorney for both the Cubs and the White Sox, and the personal attorney to both Comiskey and Cubs president William Wrigley. He had been with Comiskey and the White Sox since the very beginning in 1901. Now, in this first meeting, less than a week after the Series ended, Comiskey brought Austrian up to date on what he knew, what he suspected, and what he feared. From that point forward, as the Black Sox story unfolded over the coming months, nothing happened beyond Austrian's awareness. And much of what happened during that time happened because Austrian and his client wanted it to. The nearly year-long cover-up; the confessions of Eddie Cicotte, Joe Jackson, and Lefty Williams; the disappearance of those confessions from the district attorney's office before the trial—all these bear Austrian's mark. No figure in the Black Sox story made fewer headlines yet was more central to the way it unfolded. Moreover, during this period he would also be the architect of the Lasker Plan, the 1920 insurrection on the part of eleven team owners that overthrew the National Commission and brought Judge Landis into the game.

Austrian was forty-nine years old, a tall, slight man with a high forehead and thinning black hair. He had been born in Chicago, the son of immigrants, and attended Chicago public schools before moving to Cleveland with his family and graduating from high school there. While his family returned to Chicago, he moved on to Harvard, graduating in 1891. He then returned to Chicago, and took a job as an office boy to the Chicago attorney Levy Mayer. He was admitted to the bar two years later, and by 1905 he was a named partner in Mayer's firm. A smart, tenacious, careful, and well-connected lawyer, he was a virtuoso in closed-door negotiation and deal making, and was described as a "brilliant pleader" in the courtroom. "He liked the smoke of battle," said one colleague. Austrian could be flamboyant when flamboyance best served his client, as well as discreet when occasion demanded, as it would in the Black Sox case.

Austrian's cases and his clients had a knack for making headlines. He represented the owners of the Iroquois Theater in a spate of trials that resulted from a 1903 fire that claimed more than six hundred lives. He was the attorney for millionaire lumberman James Stanley Joyce in Joyce's divorce case against Peggy Hopkins Joyce, the sybaritic Jazz Age siren, serial bride of wealthy men, and tabloid darling. He represented the *Chicago Tribune* when the United States Senate investigated the paper regarding a 1910 story that charged Illinois senator George Lorimer had won his seat via bribery and corruption, charges that were eventually borne out and resulted in Lorimer's removal from office. He argued before the Illinois Supreme Court on behalf of a woman's right to serve on a jury. Austrian and his firm represented several companies in the liquor industry, and he was widely and prominently quoted in opposition to the Eighteenth Amendment. He successfully defended the Amour Company in its acquisition of another Chicago meatpacking plant amid charges of violating antitrust regulations. And in addition to representing Bill Wrigley's baseball team and other far-reaching business interests, he would represent the Cubs owner in a 1923 libel suit against a magazine that had called the gum magnate a member of the Ku Klux Klan.

Austrian was active in Democratic Party politics, and, recruited by party leaders as a possible mayoral candidate in 1918, his rectitude and seriousness of purpose were seen as a potentially effective counterpoint to Big Bill Thompson, the populist and ethically challenged Republican incumbent. Austrian declined the invitation to run.

Away from the bar and the headlines of his cases, Austrian was an intensely private man. He played golf at the elegant Lake Shore Country Club, and his brethren in the club said he was as competitive and as tenacious on the golf course as he was in the courtroom; he once admitted to spending $10,000 on lessons to ensure that he would win a five-dollar bet. But he spent much of his personal time quietly at his elegant East Division Street townhouse, a block from the lake, with his wife and daughter, tending to an extensive collection of literary manuscripts and first editions—he owned a page from a Gutenberg Bible and manuscripts from Joseph Conrad and Charles Dickens—and a private art collection that included portraits by eighteenth-century English masters Sir Thomas Lawrence and Sir Joshua Reynolds and original sketches from nineteenth-century English caricaturist George Cruikshank.

When Charles Comiskey brought the expanding mess to Austrian's attention, he was interested in three things. In order of importance they were preserving his business; preserving his reputation, which was part and parcel of preserving his business; and preserving his championship baseball team, which of course was also a big part of the success of his business. The trick was in not letting his greed to keep all three imperil his control of the team. The clear-headed Austrian was unlikely to allow that to happen. Neither man had any real moral aversion to having the suspect players back—provided there was plausible deniability as to their guilt. Both on the field and off, what was best for the White Sox business, however, was to have a team free of taint. And if the whole sordid story was to come out, it had to seem as though Comiskey was the principal cleanser. Austrian first launched a plan for a reward offer. As he did for many of the statements Comiskey made during the unfolding of the scandal, Austrian had a hand in writing it.

"There is always a scandal of some kind following a big sporting event like the World Series," read Comiskey's statement, released to the press on October 15, six days after the end of the Series. "These yarns are manufactured out of whole cloth and grow out of bitterness due to losing wagers. I believe my boys fought the battles of the recent World Series on the level, as they have always done. And I would be the first to want information to the contrary—if there be any. I would give $20,000 to anyone unearthing any information to that effect."

The reward offer was genius. Comiskey's statement made headlines from coast to coast, and it gave the owner a righteous tinge—nobody wanted the truth, whatever it may be, more than he did. It also insured that any gambler, ballplayer, or wife or girlfriend of same with information real or imagined would now be bringing that information to the White Sox—and presumably only to the White Sox, for they would know that Comiskey was unlikely to pay a reward for information that had already been in the newspapers or was otherwise in the common conversation. By dangling a $20,000 carrot in front of inherently greedy people, the White Sox would become the repository for all things scandal, and the information thus gathered could be evaluated and used in ways that would best serve Charles A. Comiskey: burying it if they could, revealing it only if had to; and judging the bulk of it to be "not credible" and thus not deserving of the reward.

The first two people shaken from the eaves by Comiskey's offer were Harry Redmon, who reprised the story he had told Kid Gleason in East St. Louis, and Joe Gedeon, the Browns second baseman, friend of Fred McMullin, and reported go-between in the deal. When Gedeon arrived, Comiskey may have told him that his friends had already given him up as part of the fix. His grab at the reward may have instead earned him a lifetime ban from the game. Though he escaped indictment a year later, he was swept out of baseball by Judge Landis in 1921, together with the eight White Sox.

The Redmon and Gedeon visits were widely reported in the press; Comiskey publicly dismissed their information as "not credible" and said he had not paid the reward. In fact the judgment of the press at the time, and history thereafter, is that Comiskey never paid a penny of the reward to anyone. But Bill Veeck, who would buy the White Sox from the Comiskey heirs twenty-five years after the Old Roman's death, felt otherwise. In Harry Grabiner's diary, Veeck notes Austrian hand-delivering a bill for $10,000 to Grabiner on October 19, 1919, and Grabiner paying the same, also in person, one day later. This was a very odd way for a lawyer and his longtime client to be doing business, Veeck notes, and he theorizes that it may have been reward money—or more precisely blackmail money—finding its way ultimately to Joe Gedeon.

Comiskey and Austrian's proactive approach did not stop at the reward. On November 3, three and a half weeks after the last game of the Series and two and a half weeks after Comiskey offered the reward, the two men hired a private detective agency. Again, this was not necessarily to prove the players' guilt or innocence, but to find out what information was out there for the gathering. For there were of course some people in this—the players in particular—with so much at stake that they wouldn't be tempted by $20,000.

The private detective was John R. Hunter, who ran Hunter's Secret Service of Illinois and was an investigator that Austrian used regularly. The targets were some of the players under suspicion—for some reason the investigators stayed away from Jackson, Cicotte, and Williams—and the St. Louis gambling connection of which they had already been made aware. The plan was for Hunter and his operatives to use whatever ruse was necessary to win the friendship and confidence of the subjects—to become their friends and ultimately their confidantes over a period of weeks. Hunter and two additional operatives spent the better part of two months pursing leads full time on four different fronts; one investigation continued into May of 1920. The detectives were remarkably successful at weaving themselves into the lives of their subjects. They were much less successful at turning up any hard information. But, for Comiskey's purposes at this moment, knowing that there was an absence of hard information was quite useful information.

The St. Louis piece of the investigation centered on three St. Louis gamblers: Harry Redmon; Carl Zork, a shirtwaist manufacturer named by Redmon in his conversation with Kid Gleason; and a bookie and pool-hall owner named Joe Pesch. Though he was not mentioned in Grabiner's diary, the White Sox no doubt got Pesch's name from Redmon in the meetings they had had; before the grand jury a year later, Redmon would testify that he had spent the Series in Pesch's company. At this point, the White Sox and their investigator also thought that Abe Attell might be a St. Louis guy, but quickly learned he was not. Since the White Sox had already heard Redmon's story, the investigation there was limited to confirming that he was who he claimed to be—an East St. Louis theater operator.

An operative identified in reports as "E. W. M." was sent down to St. Louis, and he became a daily fixture in Pesch's pool hall for the better part of a month. He made friends quickly, confirmed with Pesch's right hand man that the pool hall was indeed a front for a book, and even got some figures. He was told the pool business lost between three and five dollars a day on average, while the book had handled between $17,000 and $18,000 during the last baseball season, but ended the year with a $1,000 loss, owing—according to the poolroom employee—to a $2,000 loss Pesch had suffered betting the White Sox in the World Series. They were the sort of numbers that, if true, made it quite impossible to imagine the pool hall playing any role in a World Series fix.

But the Hunter man hung around anyway, overheard a customer telling Pesch, "I want to make a bet on the baseball for next year. I want to bet on the Black Sox, as they can't call themselves White Sox any longer. They do not play white baseball. With them a man does not get a good chance for his money." E. W. M. pursued the bettor, but learned the man knew nothing that had not been in the newspapers. Such was the case with most of the poolroom regulars. The gamblers were all remarkably well informed, but only on those matters that had been reported in the press. They all had opinions, but no real information. Nobody there believed that Pesch was involved in any way. "There is no doubt in my mind that the games were tossed by Cicotte and Williams," said the Pesch deputy who had become the Hunter man's confidante. "I do not believe Joe Pesch was in on the deal. If there had been anything doing here I would have known about it. You know well that if I knew anything about the fixing I would have sure tried to get some of…Comiskey's offer of $20,000 for positive information."

The detective's confidante was an old-time St. Louis sporting man by the name of Al Rosenberger; the detective had gotten Rosenberger to loosen up by telling him he was friends with a writer working on a story on the Series fix, who was willing to pay for information. Rosenberger became positively loquacious, and while he knew little, at one point in their conversations he did give voice to the gambler's lament in all of this. The out-of-the-loop gamblers felt as wronged by what had happened as the pure fans. "No, I don't even have any suspicion as to who was in on the deal, as baseball is getting to be like the races, and is one big gambling proposition. You can rest assured that if I knew anything about the deal being pulled off before the series, I would have bet some of my own money and made some big change. Then again, if I knew positively the deal was pulled off, and knew how it was handled, I would go in on some of Comiskey's $20,000. As it is, I am clean out of luck."

Carl Zork, the shirtwaist manufacturer, proved a far tougher nut to crack. E. W. M. moved into the Washington Hotel in St. Louis, where Zork lived. In his time there he saw Zork but a few times, and Zork was always simply passing through the lobby—on the way to his motorcar or back to the room. "I find him to be a man who does not hang about the lobby," E. W. M. reported back to Austrian. After two weeks, he gave up and moved to a hotel that was cheaper and more conveniently located to the downtown pool hall. He never did talk to Mr. Zork.

Hunter himself went out to Los Angeles, where Buck Weaver, Chick Gandil, and Fred McMullin were wintering. He also planned to continue on to San Francisco, where Swede Risberg was living. Grabiner had told the detective that Gandil was the likely ringleader of any conspiracy. Hunter located the first baseman in a brand new, recently purchased bungalow on Chester Street in Los Angeles. The house, which had cost $6,500, was in a new development, and Hunter reached out to a real-estate-agent friend "familiar with our business." Hunter was thus able to pass himself off as a salesman for the firm and in this way become a familiar presence in Gandil's neighborhood. "This afforded an opportunity to meet Gundel [sic] as often as I considered it prudent," he reported, "and my visits to that section attracted no attention other than that of an ordinary salesman." He found Gandil friendly, expansive, philosophical, and positively sphinxlike. "If [Gandil's] statements were connected up," he wrote to Austrian, "they would read as follows":

I have been with Mr. Comiskey for several years and certainly feel keenly the stories that appeared in different papers and magazines regarding our team being bribed to throw the World Series to Cincinnati. But you can take it from me that I neither got any money nor was approached by anyone to make it possible to have Cincinnati defeat our team. I tell you frankly that this whole story originated from those gamblers who bet on our team to win each game or at least three-fourths of them, and when we made such a poor showing as to lose the first two, they began to squeal, and this started rumors of bribery, for which there was absolutely no foundation. I feel certain that no man on that team got a dollar to lend himself to any crooked deal. It is true that possibly the showing our team made in the finals was not creditable to us, as there is no mistake that we had the better team of the two. But baseball is like any other game where conditions figure in decisions. We made some bad plays that rather demoralized our team, and we simply could not recover ourselves. . . . It all goes to illustrate that there are times when the battle is not for the strong, or the race for the swift. We should have defeated Cincinnati this year, but we were defeated not as a result of bribery but as a matter of poor luck for us and the reverse for Cincinnati. . . .

I have a nice little home here and an automobile—any man of ordinary means could support both. I have a mortgage of $3300 on the house. I tell everybody that as they may think it is clear of encumbrance, and consequently may think that I got some of the money claimed by reports to have been paid the White Sox boys to allow themselves to be defeated by Cincinnati.

It was the same story that Gandil was telling everyone that winter. "I fully appreciate the fact that I am having a hard luck in landing anything tangible, but I am putting forth my best efforts," Hunter assured Austrian.

Hunter found Fred McMullin working an off-season job as a blacksmith at the Southern Pacific rail yards. Before talking to McMullin Hunter had learned that the utility man had been talking freely about the Series to his friends all fall, but only to lament the fact that the rumors of a fix were casting aspersions on him and his teammates. Hunter gained access to McMullin "under a pretext"— what that was was never explained more fully than that in his reports back to Austrian. But whatever the pretext, it was convincing enough to McMullin, because while he clearly knew that Hunter wanted to talk about the fix rumors, he may have even known that Hunter was working for Comiskey. "He is very much worried that anything should leak out which would uncover him," Hunter reported. "I assured him that there was no fear of any exposure." He spoke to him in late November.

McMullin not only spoke frankly with the detective; he agreed to help him talk with Gandil and Weaver. "I am going to take a chance with you," he told Hunter. McMullin generally echoed what every other player had been saying, both during the Series and after: he knew nothing of any fix, and questioned whether it could have even been done. "I would do anything to develop the true facts, as baseball would be a dead issue if anything of that kind could be put over." He went on at some length about how difficult it was for any one player to fix a game, but then pointed the finger directly at three men who might have done so. While he stopped short of outright accusation, and he certainly implied no inside knowledge, McMullin nonetheless did make what would be, until the confessions of Cicotte, Williams and Jackson some ten months later, the most direct accusation of one conspirator by another.

> While I do not want to accuse anyone, I am perfectly frank to say there were two men particularly—one man whose playing was absolutely a disappointment—they were Cicotte and Williams, the former especially so. We boys all looked upon Cicotte as the important man in the game. He pitched us to victory in many of the games during the season and to make such a poor showing during the final games was, to say the least, a disappointment, and subject to suspicion. Williams's pitching was also disappointing, but not so marked. Gandil, the first baseman, showed up very poorly, and I could hardly figure him out. As I said before, the whole thing looks bad, and is open to suspicion, and on a general summing up our team as a whole did not make a proper showing. That result would occur if anyone, who was entrusted to an important position in the game, was dishonest. He could in turn throw the entire organization out of line.

Buck Weaver took Hunter for a reporter when Hunter located him in Venice in early December, an assumption the detective "did not affirm or deny." Hunter thought Weaver's sincerity was a little less practiced and a little more genuine than Gandil's had seemed. "I found Mr. Weaver a rather frank outspoken fellow and from what I could gather around the places at Venice where he and all baseball fans hang out, I am inclined to believe that he is honest, and as he says, knows nothing about the matter of crookedness in the final games of the season." Weaver did provide another lead in the case. A Hunter confederate—probably the same real-estate man who'd gotten Hunter entrée to Gandil—learned from Weaver of the existence of two South Side women, one of whom was Swede Risberg's lover. Both women knew and socialized regularly with many of the White Sox players. "If any outsiders knew anything about [any crookedness]," Hunter reported Weaver telling his colleague, "it would be the two women."

Detective E. W. M. was called back from St. Louis in mid-December to look for the two mystery women in Chicago. He found them sharing a room at the Drexel Arms Hotel, a mile or so from Comiskey Park; E. W. M. took a room there too. Their names were Marie Purcell—she was the married Risberg's girlfriend—and Florence Brown, and they proved maybe the most interesting, and revealing, of the investigation subjects pursued by the Hunter agency. The detective stayed with them from late December until early May, seeing them daily, even renting a room from them in a flat they took for three months beginning in February.

Purcell and Brown liked a good time, swiftly welcomed E. W. M. into their social swirl, and spent many a post-midnight hour dancing and drinking with him in the neighborhood speakeasies or just talking in their room, promising him if he stayed around until spring when the ballplayers returned to Chicago, they would "have some fine times together" then. There was a certain primness in the detective's relationship with the young women. The women's parents were frequently about—Florence Brown's mother was also a roomer in the flat the two women shared with the detective. And in his reports back to the office, E. W. M. commonly referred to the women as "Miss Purcell" and "Miss Brown." But despite the courtliness of his reports, these women were clearly not young innocents. There were too many furtive glances between the two, and oblique answers to questions about Risberg and the World Series. "From what I have seen of Miss B. and subject to date and the remarks they have made, I am satisfied that they know all the ins and outs of the subject under investigation," he reported back to Austrian. Gradually, what they knew began to come out.

Marie Purcell kept a framed photograph of Swede Risberg on the mantle of her hotel room. One night she picked it up and began swinging it. "Well old kid," she said, "you may swing worse than that, if you are not careful—if 'they' know what I know."

On January 9, a Friday, a story appeared in a Chicago paper that suggested that Risberg might be quitting baseball to open a restaurant in California. E. W. M. brought up the article that night. Florence Brown's mother said, "Well, I suppose he is going to take his $10,000, which he is supposed to have gotten in the Series, and open a restaurant." Purcell pooh-poohed the restaurant possibility, saying the story was nothing more than a ploy by Risberg to get more money out of Comiskey. But she said nothing about the $10,000, so E. W. M. boldly asked her what she had gotten out of it. She had recently opened a manicure shop; he suspected the $500 buy-in had come from Risberg. When he had asked her about it earlier, she had defensively replied that her father had given her the money. The detective's question now caught her a little off balance.

"Oh he—I got a shop out of it," she told him.

Later he asked what else she'd gotten. Her guard was up this time.

"Say Ed, what are you trying to do, get something on me?" She then laughed and said, "Well, let's change the conversation." They went out to the bars after that, and stayed out until two in the morning, according to the detective, who determined that patience was his best strategy for exacting information from Purcell. "It is just a matter of letting them talk themselves," he reported. "Whenever questions are put to them on the subject, they change the topic of conversation."

Snooping one day after the group had moved into the apartment, E. W. M. found a drawer full of mail and a checkbook among Purcell's things. He had high hopes of discovering something incriminating on Risberg among them, but found nothing.

E. M. W. was also unable to confirm his suspicion that Florence Brown was the "striking blonde" mentioned in a *Collier's* magazine article who had tried to place a $2,000 bet on Cincinnati on behalf of Lefty Williams. Brown clearly knew Williams, mentioning him several times throughout the winter, but said nothing to suggest she had tried to place a bet on his behalf. A year later, in Williams's confession before the grand jury, he was asked directly if he had bet money on the Series, and he denied it. He was then asked again whether he had bet indirectly through anybody. "I didn't, I didn't bet a penny with anybody in my life," he said. Who the "striking blonde" is or was, or whether there ever was such a person, remains another of the many Black Sox riddles.

E. M. W's surveillance of the two women ended in May when they surrendered the flat the Hunter detective was sharing with them. By then he had remained on the job long enough to meet Risberg and some of the other players when they returned to Chicago for the start of the 1920 season. And though he learned that Risberg regularly broke his 11:30 p.m. curfew to spend time in Miss Purcell's company, the Hunter man learned nothing more about the Series.

Finally, there was the Inspector Clouseau–like pursuit of Happy Felsch in Milwaukee by a detective identified in the communications between Hunter and Austrian as "Operative 11." His reports are filled with mentions of stakeouts, oil leases, ice fishing, union suits, Christmas trees, and a great deal of time spent bellied up to the bar in a variety of neighborhood taverns. Now, Comiskey and Austrian were not by nature jocular men, and this was not a moment in their lives when they would likely be given to mirth. Nonetheless, from the remove of nearly a century, it seems possible that the reports from Milwaukee might have produced at least a rueful smile or two in an otherwise very nervous moment.

Operative 11 was quite clearly a Milwaukee resident, but at first he had a difficult time even finding Felsch, who was hiding in plain sight. The detective spent a couple of days staking out the wrong house, until he learned that Felsch had recently moved from the Teutonia Avenue house under surveillance to another home on the same street. Finally, beginning on Friday, November 7, Operative 11 turned his attentions to the correct home, but his timing was off. He seemed generally to arrive at Felsch's house after the outfielder had left for the day; he was getting up early to go hunting most of these off-season days. While Felsch was in the woods, Operative 11 repaired to Rehberg's Saloon, a neighborhood watering hole that Felsch was known to patronize, and spent a lot of time with his foot on the rail there, trying to steer the conversation to Felsch and whether or not his friends had seen him demonstrate any recent profligate ways. He did learn that Felsch had just bought a five-passenger $1,850 Hupmobile car. But little else of any use came from these conversations.

The home office began to grow a little restless at the lack of progress, and sent another detective up from Chicago to help. This operative tried to force the issue. He knocked on the door of Felsch's home and spoke with his mother-in-law. His story was that he was an oil-lease salesman and wished to speak to family members with money to invest. Why an oil-lease salesmen would be going door to door in this working-class neighborhood was apparently never questioned; it was hardly a neighborhood in which one was likely to find the sort of disposable income necessary for the investing in oil leases, or anything else other than the rent and grocery bills. Felsch's Teutonia Avenue home was a $22-a-month, eight-room flat with no bathroom, and he was sharing it with his wife, her parents, her sister, and her sister's two children. The ruse yielded nothing; the second operative returned to Chicago. Operative 11 went back to working the saloons.

It was Christmas trees that finally gave the Hunter man entrée to the White Sox centerfielder. Felsch was selling Christmas trees; the front yard of his home was filled with the evergreens. Operative 11 knocked on the door—again Felsch was not home—and told Felsch's father-in-law that he, too, wished to get into the Christmas tree business and asked if the man would be interested in making a bulk sale. For that, replied Felsch's father-in-law, you must speak with my son-in-law. Eureka. The Hunter man had been on the case for more than a month, and finally he was going to meet the target of his inquiry. They met on Monday, December 15, and Operative 11 arranged to buy twenty-five Christmas trees from Felsch, the negotiations conducted and completed in Rehberg's, where Operative 11 had become almost as familiar a figure as Happy Felsch.

The Christmas tree deal was the beginning of the friendship the detective had hoped for. Felsch was an accommodating sort, particularly when plied by drink—Felsch and a man with a bottle in search of information would become a recurring scene as the Black Sox story unraveled over the years—and soon he was in easy relaxed conversation with a man who was decidedly not his friend.

Over the next three days Hap welcomed this new friend and business associate into his home, and the Hunter man somehow grew to genuinely enjoy the ballplayer's company. Hap showed off and proudly played the new player piano he'd just bought for $560. He told him his tale of woe about the Hupmobile, saying that it had frozen up in his barn in Milwaukee's early-December cold, and it was now up on blocks in a local garage. In response to the operative's queries about what else was new in his life, Felsch told him about the dozen union suits—six summer and six winter—he just received for free from an underwear maker contemplating an endorsement deal. Two days after his first Christmas tree purchase the detective agreed to buy another 190 trees from Felsch. (The Hunter man was apparently selling off his trees to another dealer.) This cemented the friendship.

Nonetheless, Operative 11 had trouble steering the conversation around to baseball. In the bar that first night after consummating the Christmas tree deal, Felsch and his tavern companions wanted to talk only of bowling, despite the Hunter man's repeated requests for stories about Hap's baseball life. In the days following, Felsch would talk of hunting, fishing, and bowling, but not baseball. "I find that it will be necessary for me to get him alone, and in the proper mood, before he will begin to talk about baseball," Operative 11 wrote in his report to Austrian. Hap had promised to take his new friend on an ice-fishing trip, but the weather wasn't cooperating. The intense cold had cracked the ice, Felsch told the detective, and the lake water had washed out, melting the snow, making the conditions inhospitable for fishing; the trip would have to wait until the next snowfall. Nonetheless, Happy Felsch and the private detective working for his employer were now boon companions, practically inseparable over the final two weeks of December and the first weeks of January. The men's wives even become chummy, and from this friendship, Operative 11 reported back to Austrian, he had learned that Felsch believed the team's pitching had let them down, particularly Lefty Williams, who had gotten himself roaring drunk the night before the decisive game. Felsch's wife said that that was the reason, Felsch had told her, for Williams's final-game ineptitude.

The detective got his fishing trip—two of them in fact. The first, which ended on Christmas Eve, had others along, and provided no chance for individual conversation. Still, the talk did come around to baseball. Felsch, mentioning no one by name, said players felt that team executives and employees throughout the game were on the take, accepting graft from team suppliers, encouraging the use of some brands of equipment and prohibiting the use of others. The men also talked about sports in general, and whether or not a game could be fixed. Hap talked in broad generalities about how no sport, baseball particularly, was immune from manipulation. But he put some of the onus for this hypothetical manipulation on the owners, who could bend an outcome to their will by asking players to do their nefarious bidding. Reading between the lines of Operative 11's reports on Happy Felsch, it is easy to see a man who sees everyone else bending the rules and taking something for themselves, and probably justifying his own decision in that way.

Shortly after New Year's Day 1920, Operative 11 got Happy Felsch alone on a three-day fishing trip to Okauchee Lake, some forty miles northwest of Milwaukee. Here, the two men fished and drove about the countryside by day and sat in the cottage smoking and talking at night. Operative 11, knowing that this was probably going to be the end of his professional pursuit of Felsch, finally broached the matter of the Series fix rumors. He did so indirectly, asking Felsch if he'd seen a late December story in the *Milwaukee Journal* about the status of Comiskey's reward offer. Felsch had, and told him that he could not "imagine that any player would stoop so low," and he offered up the observation "that some hard loser has probably caused such a rumor to be spread." Felsch was also clearly uncomfortable talking about this, the detective sensed, and quickly changed the subject whenever it came up.

Like E. W. M. in St. Louis and Chicago and Hunter in Los Angeles, Operative 11 had no smoking gun from his two months in pursuit of Happy Felsch. But he did have a conclusion. "My observations to date: I believe that 'F' is innocent, but at the same time I believe he knows more than he cares to tell," he wrote in his final report back to Austrian and Comiskey.

Such was essentially the case for the entire investigation. In Hunter's final report to Charles Comiskey, dated May 11, 1920, he said his findings "gave some color of credibility to the surmises of bribery extending to the World Series player," but conceded, "We were not able to make any specific connection between the players and the gambling combination." He then told Comiskey the bill for the six months of work and expenses came to $3,820.31.

So what did Charles Comiskey learn for his $3,820.31? He learned that Chick Gandil had a new house, Happy Felsch a new car, and Swede Risberg's mistress a new manicure salon. He learned that there was consensus throughout the gambling world on the players involved. He learned that those players' solidarity was showing signs of cracking, with Weaver, McMullin, and Felsch all quick to point a finger at Eddie Cicotte and Lefty Williams. He learned that knowledge of the fix had spread beyond the closed circle of players and gamblers, and that there were wild cards out there, such as the two women in Chicago and the circle of friends with whom they had apparently shared some information. And he learned that there were double-crossed gamblers like Harry Redmon, angry and looking to get square, however they might.

But from the investigation Comiskey had also learned that there were no loose cannons out there, about to explode in untoward and uncontrollable ways. He learned that the universe of people with firsthand knowledge of anything was a finite one, and that most of them had considerable disincentive to talk. And the information that Hunter had gathered was murky and inconclusive. To an outsider looking at it, it might suggest a conspiracy, but it could also be dismissed as coincidence and circumstance. It was like a photograph that was just beginning to show itself in a tray of chemicals. Parts were almost recognizable, but only if you knew what you were looking for. The picture was still faint, cloudy, uneven, and proved nothing. What Charles Comiskey had learned in three months of discreet but aggressive investigation was that he might be able keep a lid on this after all.

And after the press furor had finally quieted down, Comiskey got a huge Christmas gift from his friend Harry Frazee, the owner of the Red Sox. On the day after Christmas, Frazee reached a deal to sell Babe Ruth to the Yankees for $125,000, more than twice the highest price paid for any professional baseball player to that point. The deal was announced on January 6. Here was a baseball story that would carry the writers all the way to spring training, as the Black Sox rumors had carried them through the fall. Would Ruth pitch or play every day in the outfield? Why had Frazee let his best player and biggest draw leave without getting anything to help his team in return? Were the "two colonels," Yankee owners Colonel Jacob Ruppert and Colonel Tillinghast Huston, crazy to pay that kind of money for one player, even though it might thrust the traditionally moribund Yankees into the American League pennant picture? Would the Yankees finally rival McGraw's Giants in the affections of the New York fans? Babe Ruth was today's news and likely tomorrow's as well. The 1919 World Series was over. The baseball press had moved on.

Charles Comiskey had determined that he could also do the same.

NINE

The Newspapers Try to Figure It Out

Everything about the 1919 World Series rankled Hugh Fullerton. The crooked-ness of the players, of which he was "morally certain," was heartbreaking; the unwillingness of Comiskey, Johnson, Dreyfuss, and his syndicate newspapers to take his warnings seriously was frustrating. And, on a vain and strictly personal level, the whole sordid mess had robbed him of his status as the game's premier prognosticator.

Fullerton was baseball's first sabermetrician. Nine decades before Bill James, Fullerton had developed an elaborate system of formulas and weighted values that only he understood. Nonetheless, he had applied them to the study of the game, particularly the World Series, with a pretty steady success over the years. He did it first with the Series of 1906, picking the White Sox, the "Hitless Wonders," over the mighty 116-win Cubs, in six games, predicting the pitching matchups and scores in each game. His editors at the *Tribune* thought his pre-diction ridiculous and refused to print the story, until it proved exactly right in nearly every detail. They printed the story after the Series was over, together with an apology and affidavit from the editor testifying that the story had been written before the Series began. Fullerton was suddenly the most famous base-ball writer in the land. At World Series time, newspapers lined up to print his predictions; by 1919 he was syndicated in over forty newspapers.

As he continued to write stories "doping" the World Series, assigning position-by-position point values to players, weighting those players differently game by game depending on the starting pitching, he had been accurate enough to have earned a reputation as "the game's greatest dopester." When asked how he did it, Fullerton explained, "I take a large Faber lead pencil, nine sheets of white glazed copy paper, and figure it out." What he had figured out prior to the 1919 Series was that the White Sox would take it, five games to two. Proving there was something amiss with the White Sox would also prove there was nothing wrong with him and his predictions.

Slight of build and professorial in appearance, with round-rimmed, owlish reading glasses and a high, high forehead, Hugh Fullerton was forty-six years old in 1919, and had seemingly been covering baseball for every one of those forty-six years. He started as a teenager, writing for the *Press-Gazette* in his hometown of Hillsboro, Ohio, and left Ohio State, where he had played on the college team, to write baseball for the *Cincinnati Enquirer* in the early 1890s, when Ban Johnson was one of his newspaper colleagues and Charles Comiskey was managing the Reds. After two years in Cincinnati, Fullerton moved to Chicago, working first for the *Record*, shifting to the *Tribune*, and finally writing for the *Herald and Examiner*.

He had already left his mark on the sportswriting game in ways that few of his peers ever would. Arriving at the Polo Grounds in New York for the pennant-deciding makeup game between the Cubs and Giants in 1908, he found each seat in the press box filled with either an actor or a politician, and covered the game while sharing a seat with the theater actor Louis Mann. When the season was over, Fullerton became the catalyst behind the formation of the Baseball Writers' Association of America, organizing his newspaper colleagues in major league cities, and winning the right for the association to control access to press boxes throughout Major League Baseball. He was a great discoverer of young newspaper talent. He took a shine to a twenty-two-year-old Ring Lardner in 1907, and found Lardner his first Chicago job on the *Inter-Ocean*. He became the patron of many other young writers, including Cy Sanborn and C. E. Van Loan, for decades staples of the *Tribune* sports page.

He relaxed happily and frequently over a tableful of drinks, and players and colleagues alike looked upon him with great esteem and even greater affection. Lardner call him "the Old Master," and Grantland Rice once wrote that he was "one of the few baseball writers who can 'pan' a ball player in picturesque detail and still hold his friendship; for the player knows that Fullerton is fair and will be quick enough to change when there is cause for praise."

While his day-after story about seven members of the White Sox not returning in 1920 was as close as any writer had come to that point to suggesting there had been something awry about the recent Series, Fullerton wanted to go much further. When he finally did write something tough, it was not for his longtime Chicago home, the *Herald and Examiner*. In November, Fullerton left the *Herald and Examiner*, and the city where he had been a baseball writer for twenty-five years, and took a job at the *New York World*. We don't know whether he had quarreled with the editors at the *Herald and Examiner* over what he wanted to do, or whether the job at the *World* was simply a career opportunity he had finally determined to grab.

His first story for the *World*, appearing in the Monday, December 15 edition, shortly after the American and National League winter meetings, was perhaps the most important newspaper story of the whole Black Sox scandal. This was not necessarily for what it revealed; it was rather tepid, naming no names, and making broad and unspecified charges. But it nevertheless had a thunderous impact, because for the first time a major newspaper had announced in clear and unambiguous words that the 1919 World Series might have been fixed. The article ensured that the fix rumors would remain fresh in everyone's mind, even if it didn't result in the immediate action Fullerton called for. The story also showed just how toxic this whole subject was for organized baseball, for it made Hugh Fullerton the proverbial turd in the punchbowl, not only throughout baseball but in the journalism world as well.

Fullerton's story led the *World* sports page, and carried the wordy, old-school headline that signified a big story: IS BIG LEAGUE BASEBALL BEING RUN FOR GAMBLERS WITH PLAYERS IN THE DEAL? HUGH FULLERTON REPORTS THAT THE WORLD'S SERIES WAS TAMPERED WITH TO ENRICH GAMBLING CLIQUE IN MANY CITIES—"TIPS" ON BETTING PROVED CORRECT. "Professional baseball has reached a crisis," it began. "Charges that gamblers have succeeded in bribing ballplayers, that games have been bought and sold, that players are in the pay of professional gamblers, and that even the World's Series was tampered with are made without attempt at refutation by the men who have their fortunes invested in baseball."

Fullerton told his readers that he had been alarmed about the influence of gambling on the game for more than two years, ever since "a gambler from Boston, a man I have known by sight for many years, told me that the gamblers 'had men' on every important club in the country." Since receiving that intelligence, said Fullerton—while persisting in his belief that a baseball game would be well nigh impossible to fix without being discovered—he had seen the gambling influence grow. "The extent to which the evil has grown made it certain that sooner or later some player would fall. Many of the players have not avoided the appearance of evil. A number of them have associated and even chummed with gamblers."

A principal point of the story, the justification for writing it now, as he implied, was that the rumors that percolated throughout the Series had not gone away when the Series ended, the way they generally did. "The most serious assaults on the game have been made during and since the World's Series between the Reds and the White Sox. In Chicago, St. Louis and other cities the stories have been discussed, names used, alleged facts stated until half the people believe there was something wrong with the Series."

Fullerton went through the litany of his experiences during the World Series, his encounters with gamblers from almost the moment he arrived in Cincinnati, all of whom told him the fix in. He went much farther than he had in his post-Series stories about seven members of the White Sox "not returning," giving readers the reason he had omitted in his earlier story. "The charge was made that seven members of the Chicago White Sox team entered into a conspiracy with certain gamblers to throw the Series." Perhaps clinging to a personal hope that it all really wasn't true, he also wrote that he still refused to believe it was possible, particularly not by at the hands of people he knew and liked. "Some of the men whose names are used are my friends and men I would trust anywhere, yet the story is told openly with so much circumstantial evidence that one is bewildered."

Fullerton told of how he and Christy Mathewson had watched the World Series games for signs of malfeasance in light of the rumors, and revealed that over the eight games there were seven plays that he had circled on his scorecard as "suspicious." He then offered some of the most insightful observations about the story to that point, arguing that by the time the Series was underway, the rumors themselves were enough to have rendered the White Sox impotent.

"By that time the White Sox team was in turmoil—suspicions and bad feeling had arisen. There was no further need of any 'fixing,' if such a thing was possible. The players were so far in the air they could not have played properly anyhow."

The piece's most explosive and damning revelation was his recounting for the first time the story of being approached by a Chicago gambler twenty minutes before the start of the final game and being told, "It will be the biggest first inning you ever saw."

As critical as he was of the players, however, Fullerton saved his angriest words for the men who ran the game. They could trace their troubles to their refusal dismiss Hal Chase from the game when they had the chance in 1918, he said. The magnates' timidity with Chase, he argued, was consistent with their greed and their see-no-evil, hear-no-evil approach to their troubles:

> The fault for this condition lies primarily with the owners. Their commercialism is directly responsible for the same spirit among the athletes and their failure to punish even the appearance of evil has led to the present situation....
>
> The American League, smirched with scandal, held a meeting, wrangled, fought and blackguarded each other and separated without an effort to clear the good name of the sport.
>
> Some of the club owners are for a thorough and open investigation of the charges and the most drastic punishment of anyone found guilty. Some are for keeping silent and "allowing it to blow over." The time has come for straight talk. How can club owners expect writers, editors and fans to have any faith in them or their game if they take no effort to clean up the scandal?

Prominent among the owners he thought was one of the good guys, however, was the owner of the team at the center of whole scandal, his old friend Charles Comiskey, who, Fullerton said, knew the whole story. "Comiskey is an honest man, a baseball man who has spent his entire life in the game and who is known for sportsmanship and squareness," he wrote, saying the only thing keeping Comiskey from firing the players he suspected was the knowledge that some other owner would immediately sign them and play them against him.

When the story of the 1919 World Series broke ten months later with the confessions of Eddie Cicotte and Joe Jackson, the newspaper coverage of the indicted players would be vitriolic. But it was no worse than the abuse Hugh Fullerton took in the months immediately following the Series for daring to suggest the game of baseball was less than pure. While some of his brothers in the sports departments of the big city newspapers expressed some disappointment in Fullerton, it was the baseball press—specifically Charles Spink's St. Louis–based *Sporting News* and F. C. Lane's New York–based *Baseball Magazine*—that suggested Fullerton was a far worse pox upon the game than any of the gamblers who had sought to corrupt it or the players they were alleged to have tempted.

The *Sporting News*, the "Bible of Baseball," had a national readership and counted amongst its contributors many of the writers—Fullerton included—who covered the game for the newspapers in the big league cities. The *Sporting*

News criticism of Fullerton was measured and paternalistic, the scolding of a child who has misbehaved. Baseball was not ignoring gambling and the Series fix rumors, as Mr. Fullerton had alleged, the *Sporting News* editorial said; it was merely proceeding cautiously and carefully, as it should, and the impetuous Fullerton would be well served to understand that. "Instead of implications that the baseball authorities are attempting to cover up what he terms a scandal," it read, "and wasting words in denunciation of this alleged attitude, he might devote his time and talents—since he is so concerned about the welfare of the game—to producing some evidence that the authorities can work on.

"If he has given that angle of it any thought and attention he must know that such evidence cannot be plucked off every bush. There may be circumstantial evidence—and men have been hanged on such evidence—but there must be facts. If Mr. Fullerton has facts that will stand the test doubtless production of them will be welcome."

If the *Sporting News* wanted Fullerton to better direct his energies, *Baseball Magazine* wanted him publicly drawn and quartered. A popular monthly, and a big booster of the game and its people, *Baseball* was less newsy than the *Sporting News*, featuring interview-based personality profiles and explanatory and analytical pieces on the game's strategies and nuances. It brooked no one who would shame or damage the game, and in the offseason of 1919–20 it saw Fullerton as one of those people, attacking him in virtually every hot-stove issue. Its December editorial took a general swipe at all writers who dared to address the fix rumors, however obliquely, during or after the Series. "If a man knows so little about baseball that he believes the game is or can be fixed, he should keep his mouth shut in the presence of intelligent people." By the February 1920 issue, after Fullerton's *New York World* article, *Baseball* had aimed its editorial battery directly at Fullerton, devoting the whole of its lead editorial to discrediting virtually his whole career.

> The sports world was recently greeted with a giddy screed from the facile pen of Hugh Fullerton.
>
> The screed began with the sensational statement: "Baseball has reached a crisis. The major leagues, both owners and players, are on trial." To this we reply, very interesting, if true. Who is to try them? Presumably Mr. Fullerton. If so, we tremble at the result, for we know of no one less competent by clear reasoning and fairness of vision to pass judgment on so broad a question. Mr. Fullerton goes on to say that certain gamblers, whom he claims to know, have made repeated

assertions that players on the White Sox team were in their pay. Can anything be more vague or unsubstantial than this?...

Referring to these players, Fullerton says, "if these men are guilty, they should be expelled. If they are innocent they should be allowed to prove it and the persons who are responsible for the charges should be driven out of the sport forever."

We agree with Mr. Fullerton. If he were driven out of the sport forever, it would be a consummation devotedly to be wished....

Who is Hugh Fullerton anyway? A visionary and erratic writer noted for two things: First, his celebrated system of doping plays and players whereby he modestly attempts to foretell (erroneously) not only which team will win a series but exactly how many runs and hits will be made game by game. Second for his proclivity in writing sensational stories, usually with the vaguest foundation....

It has proved...impossible to prevent Mr. Fullerton from making a public nuisance of himself, but we hope the National Commission or the Baseball Writers' Association or the Society for the Prevention of Armenian Outrages will be able to do something for him. He needs it.

We realize, with sorrow, that we have given Mr. Fullerton a lot of free advertising in this editorial, but our sincere grief at this is tempered by the hope that we may never have occasion to mention his name again.

Fullerton had never been a favorite of the magazine, possibly because F. C. Lane was himself something of an early sabermetrician and was perhaps jealous of Fullerton's prowess and reputation. Whatever the reason, Fullerton and his predictions—especially when they were inaccurate—had been commonly ridiculed in the pages of *Baseball Magazine* through the years. But never had he been attacked with the edge of the 1919–20 articles, the magazine calling his writing "spiteful and senseless." A month after hoping to never again mention his name, the editors managed to hold to that hope, yet still find a way to pile on, devoting considerable space to Fullerton in the lead-in to a flattering profile of *Chicago Tribune* baseball writer I. E. Sanborn, ironically a Fullerton protégé. The unnamed writer of the piece—probably Lane himself—took note that a baseball writer was either the "best friend" or the "worst enemy" the game had. The article then devoted half a sentence to how a writer was sometimes the game's friend, and half a column to those who hurt the game. "He becomes a peril when his judgment grows warped by personal feeling or when his love of the theatre and sensational leads him to exaggerate and thus intensify the minor evils which afflict the game," the assault began.

> And this merely emphasizes the fact that fairness and common sense are as essential to the successful baseball writers as they are anywhere else. For the writer who possesses them, along with the ability to write, is in a position to render the community a substantial service. Without them he becomes an inevitable danger, for the pernicious ideas which warp his own brain reach, daily, thousands of readers who absorb and to some extent believe what they see in print.
> We have had sufficient evidence of this type of writer in the groundless charges recently made against the integrity of the late World's Series. Such writers are a pest and a real evil. But after all in the long run they hurt themselves much more than they damage baseball.

The abuse of Hugh Fullerton may not have been limited to the verbal during these months. Writing in *Liberty* magazine eight years after the events of that fall of 1919, Fullerton claimed that he had been the target of an assassination attempt not long after the Series had ended. The attempt came on the eve his leaving Chicago to go to New York and his job at the *World*. Walking about the South Side visiting friends, he noticed a man, he said, "whose face I knew" following him. As he walked through a tunnel under a viaduct of the Illinois Central, another man approached him and asked if he were Fullerton. "No, Crane," Fullerton replied, a name he thought up on the spot, and the man hustled away. "As I stepped into the light another voice cried: 'That's the ——' and two shots were fired. I started to run, fell, and the men fled. I got up unhurt and fled in the other direction, into a garage. Fearing I would be held as a witness and our trip East spoiled, I made no complaint, not even telling my family until we had left the city."

It was not unheard-of for newspapermen to be the targets of assaults and assassination attempts in big cities in the 1910s and 1920s, though baseball writers were never popular targets. It was, however, most unusual for a newspaperman and his paper not to turn any such attempt into a big, page-one story.

Whatever flaws or embellishments there may have been in his reporting, Fullerton has won the plaudits of history for his persistence in pursuing the Black Sox story. He was correct in his central charges, and thus stands almost alone among the sad litany of Black Sox–story characters. Fullerton's involvement with the Black Sox story has distinguished rather than embarrassed his legacy.

But Fullerton was not alone in alleging that something had been amiss in the Series, and in calling for Major League Baseball to pursue the story, wherever it might lead. A long-forgotten reporter by the name of Frank O. Klein was right there with Fullerton in the weeks following the Series, even going him one better. Klein named names before anyone else did. Yet Klein has been all but lost to history. Hugh Fullerton was baseball royalty, one of the privileged elite in American baseball journalism. Some of his brethren may have come to see him as something of a wastrel son, yet he was still a peer of the realm. Frank Klein was not. He was easy to ignore because he did not write for the *Sporting News* or cover a major league team for a big city daily. He wrote for *Collyer's Eye*, then a fairly new eight-page weekly published out of Chicago. It was a newspaper devoted to all facets of gambling, written for and read by the men who partook.

Because of its subject matter and its readership, it was easy for those who saw gambling as a scourge—and that included much of the mainstream baseball press—to discredit the sheet as Beelzebub's work, and to give it no more station than the modern world gives to supermarket tabloids. The truth is that, while its focus was narrow, and that focus was regarded in many quarters as an unsavory piece of American daily life, *Collyer's Eye* offered sound, relevant news judgment and stories that were rooted in solid reporting.

Its publisher was a forty-three-year-old Canadian who had come up through journalism's ranks. Bert Collyer got his reporting start covering the Yukon gold rush during the 1890s. He caught on with the Hearst's *San Francisco Examiner*, and moved from there to Hearst's *Chicago American* early in the new century and started writing the paper's racing column. He was himself a horse owner and rider, and horse racing would be at the heart of his own newspaper. But *Collyer's Eye* wasn't a standard tout sheet. It covered the stock market as thoroughly as it covered the horse tracks; that was gambling too. Its two main weekly features, trumpeted on the front page, were "Stocks Worth Watching, Page 2" and "Horses Worth Watching, Page 3." *Collyer's Eye* only covered baseball, college football, boxing, wrestling, and bicycle racing secondarily.

Klein was identified in *Collyer's Eye* as the paper's "chief investigator." What that meant, or what his background may have been, we don't know; indeed, we don't know much of anything about him beyond his byline. His early stories suggest he was well sourced in the gambling world and not badly sourced in the baseball world. He was close enough to Eddie Collins to call him a friend, though if Collins was one of Klein's sources, he left no fingerprints on the stories. Whoever his sources may have been, Klein's reporting in the weeks following the 1919 Series, while not without its flaws, captured the outlines of the story as the world would come to know it in the months and years ahead.

Collyer's first reporting on the story came in the issue of October 18, and either picked up on Fullerton's story about seven White Sox not coming back or secured the information independently. The headline read INVOLVE 7 SOX IN WORLD'S SERIES SCANDAL, and the story was pegged to the news hook of Comiskey's offer of a $10,000 reward.*

Klein said only that there was some "inferential noise" regarding the Series and that "no less than seven members of the Sox team are named as 'under suspicion.'" His article gave no player's name; a sidebar story in the same issue by Reid J. Murdock suggested Chick Gandil wouldn't be back with the Sox in 1920, but the only suggestion that he was one of seven suspects was the placement of Murdock's story next to Klein's lead story. Klein's article was short and concentrated on the gambling, naming Abe Attell and the Levy brothers of St. Louis and suggesting that "the trail seems to wind slowly but surely to New York, where a well-known bookmaker is given the credit of being the 'brains' of the affair." He promised that there was more was to come. "Next week I will endeavor to give readers of this publication a bit more details of my findings, which I promise will be prosecuted to the very limit of my resources."

A week later, in the issue dated October 25, Klein reported that there was "sufficient data to warrant investigation of the various playing 'angles' of Eddie Cicotte," and relayed that Ray Schalk had charged Lefty Williams with "throwing the series" and that Williams, Felsch, and Risberg "were in collusion." The naming of names got Charles Comiskey's attention. According to Klein, Comiskey reached out to the paper after their articles started appearing. "To a subordinate of mine he wished it made plain that he had much rather that this publication had come and 'seen him' prior to my first article, intimating that the widespread publicity might give the culprits time to 'cover up,'" Klein wrote, while the White Sox official statement implied that the *Collyer's Eye* stories were at their core a play for the reward money. Klein responded to that by saying it was his "privilege to announce that the publishers of this paper will not accept one dollar of the reward money."

---

* When Comiskey first announced the reward, he'd announced it as $20,000. As soon as people started coming forward bent on claiming it, Comiskey began referring to the award as a $10,000 offer. The newspapers thus began reporting it as $10,000, without pressing Comiskey on why the number had been cut in half.

The October 25 article named no other suspects directly, but added Joe Jackson by way of publicly exonerating the players Klein judged innocent. "It is important to say my investigations show that Capt. Eddie Collins, 'Buck' Weaver, Dick Kerr, John Collins, Nemo Leibold and Ray Schalk came out of the Series 'clean as a hound's tooth,'" wrote Klein, pointedly leaving out Jackson as the only White Sox regular not mentioned in either of the first two stories, though Gandil had also not been explicitly connected to the fix. Klein was less than subtle in his hints to the reader as to where he felt the two men belonged. After listing the innocent, he closed his story by telling any reader wondering about Jackson and Gandil: "You may write the other two lines yourself."

The *Collyer's* stories were consistent on the matter of Buck Weaver. In three different stories mentioning the names of those "under investigation"—*Collyer's* never came out and called anyone guilty—Weaver was never mentioned, and indeed his only appearance in the *Collyer's* articles included him in the group that was "clean as a hound's tooth." Some parts of the *Collyer's* stories never proved out; in November the paper reported that a South Side poolroom was the site of the payoff between gamblers and players—nothing else in Black Sox fact or myth suggests that. Another element of one of the *Collyer's* stories may have been the genesis for what has become a colorful part of the legend, however much its principal figure tried to deny it over the years. *Collyer's* was the first to report Eddie Cicotte had been upset with Charles Comiskey for denying him a $10,000 bonus in 1917 by holding him out of the lineup and preventing him from winning thirty games. *Eight Men Out* would make this the linchpin of Cicotte's involvement. There is, however, no mention of a bonus on Cicotte's contract card in the archives of the National Baseball Library at the Hall of Fame, and Cicotte himself never mentioned any disaffection over a missing bonus in his confession a year later. *Collyer's* also originated the story that Ray Schalk had called out and fought with Lefty Williams and Swede Risberg after the second game; Schalk spent the rest of his life denying there had been any fight.

But every newspaper reporting on the Black Sox in those early days served up portions of rumor, speculation, and invention and presented them as fact. The *Collyer's* stories are far more disciplined than those of nearly all of the so-called mainstream papers. The central message in the *Collyer's Eye* reporting in the fall of 1919 is unmistakable: the Series had been fixed, and the players responsible were the ones who would be indicted a year later. Still, their reports were either discounted or ignored. It was only a newspaper for gamblers, after all.

As to most of the rest of the press during the fall of 1919, it was either docile or disinterested in chasing down the Black Sox story. There's no evidence that any reporter or newspaper pursued the story from a gambling or law-enforcement angle. The city desk generally left the story to the sports page, and for the most part the sports page was interested only in reporting what was easy to find, and that was generally pronouncements on the part of the baseball establishment that they were treating the fix rumors with the utmost concern, and were they to discover any foundation to them, they would move swiftly and surely to deal with any of-fenders. Their statements were self-important platitudes; the newspaper stories about them empty journalism. "The [National] Commission is thoroughly cogni-zant as to its duty with reference to the alleged charges of gambling on baseball," reported the *Sporting News* in a typical baseball-press news story on the subject, "and the entire proposition will be followed up in a thorough and emphatic manner which will be satisfactory to the baseball public." Frank Klein thought he knew the real reason for the mainstream press's timidity on this story. "It is notice-able...that various scribes—baseball writers—generally accredited with being on the team payroll, are moving heaven and earth for the *suppression bureau*."

All that got reported was what was easy to report and impossible to ignore, like the story of Lee Magee. The Cubs had released Magee after the 1919 season, though he had hit .292 for them in part-time utility duty in the infield and outfield. The Cubs gave no reason for the release, but the newspapers reported it was because of Magee's ties to Hal Chase; he was one of Chase's suspected confederates on the 1918 Reds, when Christy Mathewson unsuccessfully tried to bring Chase to justice. That would have probably been the end of the story, but Magee didn't take his dismissal and go away, as Hal Chase had in late 1919. Instead, he filed suit for breach of con-tract, telling William Phelon of the *Cincinnati Times-Star*: "If I am barred from baseball, I'll take some others with me, players whose reputations are supposed to be pure and unsullied....I'll produce a few cancelled checks, interesting letters and data to sum it up. If I fall, I won't fall alone, but in a considerable crowd."

The case made it all the way to trial, at which Magee was hoist by his own petard. The Cubs' trump card in their defense was the confession Magee had made to Cubs president William Veeck and National League president John Heydler at the Congress Hotel in February of 1920. Magee, trying to save his career, told the two men that he *had* been guilty of conspiring with Chase to throw a Reds game in Boston in June of 1918. His motives for the confession remain unclear. Perhaps he felt he was blackmailing Heydler, threating to reveal to the press what he was telling them, knowing that Heydler was the one who had exonerated Chase after a hearing. Apparently, Magee believed that because he had scored the winning run in that game (he had reached base on an error and scored on a home run) and because he had stopped payment on the check he had bet with a Boston bookie for the Reds to lose, Heydler and Veeck would somehow overlook or forgive his transgression. Magee's thorough discrediting ensured that any charges he made—he never did follow through on his promise to produce "cancelled checks, interesting letters and data"—gained no traction. Nobody tried to link the Magee story to the 1919 World Series. But throughout the 1920 season, 1919 simmered under the surface.

On a rainy day in late July, with the White Sox–Yankees game rained out in New York, Kid Gleason ran into Abe Attell at the bar at Dinty Moore's, a midtown saloon-turned-speakeasy favored by ballplayers and Broadway types. Ring Lardner and James Crusinberry were in the bar as well, and Gleason motioned them over to listen in on the conversation he was having with Attell.

"So it was Arnold Rothstein who put up the dough for the fix?" Crusinberry reported hearing Gleason say to Attell, who was apparently in his cups. "That was it Kid," replied Attell. "You know Kid, I hated to do that to you, but I thought I was going to make a lot of money and I needed it, and then the big guy double-crossed me, and I never got but a small part of what he promised."

Nothing of Attell's drunken admission made it into either Lardner's syndicated column or Crusinberry's space in the *Chicago Tribune* (Crusinberry would finally write about it in 1956). Crusinberry had covered Kid Gleason during the 1919 Series, and knew early on what Gleason suspected, but hadn't been able to write much about it because of his editors' caution. It was the same here; he filed a story that got spiked. His bosses at the *Tribune* were worried about libel suits. Lardner for his part didn't even try to write anything about the story. He became so thoroughly disenchanted with baseball after 1919 that no longer wrote about it with his former verve. "My interest in the national game died a sudden death in the fall of 1919," he wrote years later, "when Kid Gleason saw his powerhouse White Sox lose a world's series to a club that was surprised to win even one game."

The White Sox 1920 season, meanwhile, rolled blithely along, with the Sox either in first place or a game or two out. The writers following the team showed greater than usual interest in the behavior of the players whose names they had heard so often and reported on so seldom. They took note that they were a taciturn group, almost sullen.

The seven remaining Black Sox hung together, and were largely shunned by the Eddie Collins–Ray Schalk faction of the team. Among themselves, they rarely talked about what had happened in October. It was as though they were still unsure what had gone down, and most of what little conversation they had on the subject was not about errors they may have made, or who got how much, but whether they had been double-crossed and by whom. None of it had any effect on their performance. Eddie Cicotte won twenty-one games, Lefty Williams twenty-two. Joe Jackson batted .382, and Hap Felsch and Buck Weaver were both above .330. On August 31, despite having lost three in a row, the Sox still held a half-game lead over Cleveland in their chase for a second consecutive American League pennant.

A bit past lunchtime on August 31, 1920, a couple of hours before the fifth-place Cubs were set to play the last-place Phillies—a midweek, play-out-the-string contest between two also-rans that should have been of interest to practically nobody—the telephone in Cubs president William Veeck's office suddenly began ringing with long-distance calls, and Western Union messengers started arriving one after another with telegrams, a half dozen in all. The telegrams and telephone calls all contained a variation of the same thing: Watch out. Your team is set to throw this afternoon's game to the Phillies. Gamblers in Chicago, Boston, Cincinnati, and Detroit know about it and have bet more than $50,000 on the Phillies.

It would later be reported that Claude Hendrix, that day's scheduled starter for the Cubs, had placed a bet on the Phillies through a Kansas City gambler named Frog Thompson. Veeck didn't know this, and nothing was ever proven against Hendrix, a ten-year veteran whose best days were behind him. But, moments before game time, Veeck ordered manager Fred Mitchell to pull Hendrix and replace him with the Cubs ace, Grover Cleveland Alexander. Veeck offered Alexander a $500 bonus if he won the game, which he could not do; the Phillies prevailed, 3–0.

Veeck was sufficiently alarmed by the telegrams and phone calls that he hired private investigators to look into the matter. The investigators turned up little, determining only that the people who signed their names to the telegrams apparently didn't exist in the cities the telegrams were sent from. Veeck next took his story to the newspapers, asking the Baseball Writers' Association of America to investigate the charges. The reporters did little in the way of investigating, but did yeoman's work in publicizing the charges, suggesting that this was really a matter for the Cook County grand jury. Among the interested readers following the story was the new presiding justice of that grand jury.

Charles McDonald was a familiar figure in both Chicago courtrooms and Chicago ballparks. First elected to the bench in 1910, in July of 1920 he was elected chief justice of the Cook County criminal courts, which made him the presiding justice of the grand jury. His duties as chief justice were slated to begin on September 7, the day after Labor Day, seven days after the suspect Cubs-Phillies game.

During the week before he took office, McDonald met in his rooms at the Edgewater Beach Hotel with his old friend Ban Johnson. The two men went back to the early days of the Woodland Bards. Moreover, McDonald was Johnson's publicly endorsed choice to replace Garry Herrmann, who had resigned as chairman of the National Commission the previous January. It was a position McDonald badly wanted, and this meeting with Johnson was at least partially to determine whether his involving the grand jury in the Cubs-Phillies matter would help or harm his chances of winning the post. Johnson, ever looking for ways to compromise or embarrass the National League, encouraged McDonald to go ahead. On McDonald's first day in office the following Tuesday, he lived every politician's dream by making headlines in every paper in town. In his address to the grand jury, he announced that baseball, "our national sport," the source of "healthful, wholesome exercise" for young boys, was now under assault by a "coterie of unscrupulous gamblers." He called it a matter of public importance that the grand jury investigate the reports surrounding the Cubs and Phillies, "so that everyone implicated in the infamous conspiracy to bring the national game of baseball into disrepute…should be brought to speedy justice and exposed to public scorn." The news was well received by the public and press, save for the *Sporting News*, still clinging to the position that the game was beyond reproach and corruption, and apparently believing if they said it enough it would be so.

Quickly, some in the press began to suggest that since the grand jury was looking into baseball and gambling anyway, it may as well look into all those persistent rumors about 1919. On September 19, the *Tribune* published an open letter calling for just such as expansion. It was signed by a prominent baseball fan, Fred Loomis, but actually written by the *Tribune*'s James Crusinberry.

Judge McDonald, again after apparently checking with Ban Johnson, quickly expanded the grand jury's charge. "A stain has been placed on the great American game, and you and the public will want to know all about it," he told the jury in instructing them to "consider baseball gambling in all its ramifications." The parade of witnesses began on September 22. The supposedly secret grand jury testimony was not terribly secret; there were leaks enough to doom a Lake Michigan freighter. Many of the leaks led to outright invention in the newspapers, particularly when it came to the confessions of the ballplayers a week later.

The first day's witnesses included Charles Comiskey and Ban Johnson and a crowd of Chicago sportswriters. The writers averred only that they believed there were few, if any, crooked players in the game. Comiskey told the jury he had suspected something was afoul during the Series, and so had withheld the Series checks of seven men—Weaver got his—while he instructed Alfred Austrian's detectives see what they could find, a clear acknowledgment that for almost a year he had been dissembling in his public remarks on the Series. Ban Johnson made some news before he went into the courtroom, telling sportswriters that he would be asking Congress to pass legislation that would make fixing a base-ball game a federal crime punishable by prison time. Inside the courtroom, he said he knew of no games during the 1920 season had been compromised by gamblers; but a day later he sprinkled some gasoline on the fire of his relation-ship with Comiskey, telling newspapermen that he had information that the White Sox wouldn't dare win the 1920 pennant, because the gamblers who con-trolled many on the team had forbidden it.

The first day's headlines, however, went to Hartley Replogle, the assistant state's attorney in charge of the investigation. "The last world's series between the Chicago White Sox and the Cincinnati Reds was not on the square," he said flatly at day's end. "From five to seven players on the White Sox are involved."

The second day saw the first ballplayer take the stand, not one of the suspect White Sox but Giants pitcher Rube Benton. Benton was a part of the Cubs-Phillies piece of the grand jury charge, expected to testify that Cubs infielder Buck Herzog, in concert with Hal Chase, had approached him during the 1919 season and offered him $800 to throw a game to the Cubs. But on the Thursday morning Benton was set to take the stand, Herzog beat him to the punch, having his say in a newspaper article, ensuring that the grand jury investigation would pivot from anything Cubs-Phillies to all things 1919 World Series.

Herzog told James Crusinberry of the *Tribune* that Benton's charge was a fabrication, apparently the result of some leftover ill will from a time some years before when Herzog had been player-manager of Cincinnati and Benton one of his problem children. Herzog told Crusinberry that when he had first learned of Benton's allegations earlier in the 1920 season, he demanded a hearing in front of National League president John Heydler. He had come out of that hearing with a letter from Heydler dismissing Benton's allegations and absolving Herzog of involvement in any bribe plot. Moreover, Herzog came away with affidavits from two former teammates—the men who had first tipped Herzog to Benton's bribery charges—that Benton had boasted to them of having bet and won $3,800 on the 1919 World Series, after being told by Hal Chase that the fix was in. Herzog showed the affidavits to Crusinberry; they became a focus of his morning story, as well as the focus of the grand jury questions put to Benton later that day.

Benton's testimony was short; the longer session on that second day of the grand jury hearings belonged to Chicago businessman Samuel Pass, described as an ardent White Sox fan who had lost big on the Series and who was "declared to be closer to the White Sox players than any person aside from Manager Gleason." Pass was in the jury room for an hour and a half, and reporters lurking outside heard his testimony being interrupted by applause. He told reporters afterward that he had offered no direct testimony, only hearsay. He must have then shared the same hearsay with reporters, or maybe it was grand jury foreman Henry Brigham, who also spoke to reporters at day's end. No sources were given, and no byline was attached to the story, but the Friday editions of the *Chicago Tribune* and the *New York Times* both contained the same lengthy story about "the gambler's inside story of the baseball bribe offer by which the last world's series is alleged to have been 'thrown.'" The article named Abe Attell, Arnold Rothstein, and the eight players, whose names every baseball fan in America could now rattle off like the days of the week.

Such were the early days of the grand jury story—scraps and fragments, misdirection and speculation. They were the penultimate link in a chain of mostly small, apparently unrelated events that eventually brought the scandal to light and to trial—each of them critical and essential. Had Hugh Fullerton, *Collyer's Eye*, and a handful of others not kept the rumors alive in the weeks after the Series, the Lee Magee case might not have been news. Were it not for Magee, the warning William Veeck got on the August 31 Cubs-Phillies games might have been brushed aside. Had the chief justice of the Cook County grand jury been someone who was less of a believer in baseball as a force of moral good than Charles McDonald, the grand jury might not have gotten involved in the Cubs-Phillies rumors. And no grand jury inquiry into baseball gambling, of course, would have meant that no expansion of the charge to include 1919.

And yet the final link of the chain was perhaps the most unlikely of all.

It was not in the grand jury room where the fix and the subsequent cover-up finally came to light. Nor was it even in the city of Chicago. It wasn't the state's attorney, or one of Austrian's private investigators, or any of the game's executives, or even a player looking to unburden his soul. The whole thing might have remained forever in the fog had not one of the burned gamblers—following the grand jury from afar—gotten the urge to tell his story.

A lifelong Philadelphian, Billy Maharg knew the sports editor of the *North American*, a man named Walter Schlichter, who had managed Maharg for a time back during his fighting days. Spurred perhaps by thoughts of revenge, pangs of conscience, a yearning to get back into the spotlight, a hope that he might qualify for some of Comiskey's still unpaid reward, or maybe something else altogether, Maharg summoned Schlichter to the Haymarket Hotel, a hangout for both home-team and visiting ball players in Philly, and there told the editor his story.

The *North American* had not been doing much with the Chicago grand jury story. There was a short piece on its sports page when the jury was convened, along with stories when Comiskey, Johnson, and Rube Benton testified, most of them wire-service stories, and all of them subordinated to the stories about another Phillies or Athletics loss. The story that was coming out of the grand jury was becoming a lot more interesting, but in the estimation of Billy Maharg, it was wrong on many counts and incomplete on many others. Maharg's story would become instantly significant because it marked the first time the fix claims were not just hearsay. The charges were now being made by someone who also claimed to have played a direct role.

Schlichter wanted it checked out before it ran, though the *North American* was likely going to run the story anyway. It was not the practice of 1920s newspapers to report themselves out of a story. If someone credible told them something sensational, newspaper instinct was to publish the story first and ask hard questions later, if at all. Determining Maharg's credibility was likely a matter of determining solely whether to play the story big or small. Schlichter gave the task of talking to Maharg to his principal baseball writer, forty-year-old Jimmy Isaminger.

Like Hugh Fullerton, Ban Johnson, and Charles Comiskey, Isaminger had come out of the baseball incubator in Cincinnati. As a preteen clerk in a Cincinnati drugstore, he had sold ten-cent cigars—the most expensive in the case—to Ban Johnson. Isaminger figured any guy who spent ten cents on a cigar was a guy who must know his stuff, and he thereafter became a lifelong Ban Johnson fan. And the respect Johnson had earned as a cigar customer three decades before would serve him well when he tried to help assemble witnesses for the prosecution in the Black Sox criminal trial a few months after.

Short and round, Isaminger had been at the *North American* since 1905. He covered both the Athletics and the Phillies, was in tight with Connie Mack, and was well sourced throughout the game. Maharg showed him a telegram he had received from Bill Burns the year before. It was ambiguous enough—WHAT HAVE YOU DONE ABOUT BALL GAMES—but it gave enough weight to Maharg's story to warrant big page-one play. The telegram was reproduced under the banner headline GAMBLERS PROMISED WHITE SOX $100,000 TO LOSE: PHILADELPHIA

GAMBLER TELLS OF DEAL WITH CHICAGO PLAYERS TO LOSE WORLD SERIES. Isaminger, writing with a keener feel for the urgent drama of the moment than for the judicious use of language, opened the story: "In Philadelphia yesterday, the complete story of the most gigantic swindle in the history of America was unfolded."

Isaminger called Maharg a "former boxer and well-known sporting figure of this city," and reported that Maharg "admitted last night that he and Bill Burns, the former Washington, White Sox, and Phillie southpaw were the pioneers in the conspiracy that resulted in eight members of the Chicago American League team 'throwing' games to Cincinnati in last year's world's series."

Maharg named only one of the eight, Eddie Cicotte, saying that it was Cicotte who initiated the fix when he told Burns and Maharg in a New York hotel that for $100,000 a core of White Sox players would be willing to throw the Series. Isaminger had not pressed Maharg on the identity of the other seven players, and didn't explain to his readers why he hadn't. He summarized the main points of Maharg's story: eight players were involved; the first, second, and final games were the ones fixed; the White Sox were promised $100,000 but got only $10,000; Abe Attell was the one who'd done the double-crossing; Burns and Maharg had lost everything betting on the Reds in game three.

The rest of the story was one long quote from Maharg. In it the would-be fixer told for the first time the story that would become famous when he and Burns told it on the witness stand at the players' criminal trial a year later. He described how they had met with Cicotte at the Ansonia and been told the Series could be had for $100,000; how they had taken the deal to Arnold Rothstein at the Astor Hotel and been turned down; how Abe Attell later came to Burns and said he had fixed it with Rothstein; how Attell and a dozen or more confederates had been betting brazenly before the Series opened in Cincinnati; how he and Burns had repeatedly asked Attell for money for the players and that Attell had refused, then finally surrendered only $10,000 of the promised $100,000; how Burns had offered to sell off some oil leases and pay off the players himself and Maharg talked him out of it; how he and Burns had lost everything betting on the Reds in game three, after the players had told them that if they hadn't won for Cicotte and Williams, they weren't going to win for a "busher" like Kerr.

Maharg used the story to demonstrate his loyalty to Bill Burns, going on at length about what a stand-up guy and great friend he was, and he used it to settle the score with Attell, upon whose featherweight shoulders he put all the blame. "Attell is the man the Chicago grand jury wants. He made the bets, gave the $10,000 to Burns for the Sox players and double-crossed them out of $90,000.

"We were all double-crossed by Attell,"—a claim Isaminger classified as a "naïve assertion," the writer's only attempt at analysis in the story—"and I want everyone who is reading about this investigation to know the truth." Maharg went so far as to absolve Arnold Rothstein of any guilt, saying Rothstein's supposed involvement was just another Abe Attell lie.

The Isaminger-Maharg story of September 28 caused the whole dam to burst. Within twenty-four hours, four players had confessed and eight were indicted. The *North American* dutifully reported the events of the next day and, in typical 1920 newspaper fashion, took credit for making them happen.

TEN

"It Ain't True, Is It Joe?"

On Tuesday morning, September 29, the day after the Jimmy Isaminger/Billy Maharg story had been published, and the first of three off days for the White Sox, Charles Comiskey, Harry Grabiner, and Kid Gleason went early to Alfred Austrian's office. It was clear now that the cover-up was finished, the story had blown up, and it was going to be up to the men in Austrian's office to make sure the White Sox franchise didn't blow up along with it. Comiskey had decided to end the players' White Sox careers that day, and Austrian had drafted a letter terminating their contracts.

But this meeting was about more than simply handing the accused players their releases. The grand jury would be announcing indictments against the eight players later that day; it would be much better for Comiskey if it looked to the public like he was not only cooperating in the investigation but out front, leading the posse. There had been some talk about having Gleason testify before the grand jury, or at least talk with Hartley Replogle, the assistant state's attorney in charge of the investigation, about what he knew. But Gleason had no real evidence, only the same suspicions and hearsay everyone else had. If Comiskey was going to be identified in the public eye as the victim, and not as the overseer of a corrupt and rotten-to-the-core enterprise, he needed to deliver one of the guilty players to the authorities.

"Who" among the suspected players, asked Austrian, "is most likely to tell the truth?"

"Cicotte," came the reply. Testifying to the conversation in the players' civil trial in 1924, Austrian could not remember which man answered the question. Still, it seems as certain as any conjecture can be that the man who best knew that Cicotte was the most likely to bare his soul was Sox manager Kid Gleason.

If one of the great frustrations to students of the Black Sox story is the silence of the participants over the years, another is the silence of the so-called Clean Sox. The men who were above suspicion lived their post-1919 lives as mutely as the guilty and went to their graves without sharing what they knew or suspected, or, most particularly, how they felt about their teammates and what they had done. Nobody's silence leaves a bigger hole in the story than Kid Gleason's.

Gleason was the sort of guy who would have been known as a "player's manager" in a later period. Such was his relationship with his players that he bore the weight of their betrayal particularly heavily; friends claimed he was never quite the same man after 1919. Still, he would be the strongest witness in their defense at their criminal trial in 1921.

William Gleason was fifty-three years old in the fall of 1920, and had been in baseball since he was nineteen. He was short, only five feet seven inches, and small of frame, which as a young man had earned him the nickname he never outgrew. Both a pitcher and a position player in his minor league days, he broke into the big leagues as a pitcher with the Phillies in 1888. He won thirty-eight games, second in the league, in 1890, and twenty or more on three other occasions. He still found some playing time in the field on the days he wasn't pitching, and by 1895 had fully transitioned to second base, spending the last dozen years of his career as an infielder. He kicked around the majors for twenty-one seasons with the Browns, Giants, and Tigers before ending his career in 1912 back where it began, with the Phillies.

Gleason had grown up in the Pocono Mountains coal country, and out of that hardscrabble culture honed a baseball personality to match. As a pitcher, after surrendering a hit, he would sometimes run to the base lines to impede the runner; as an infielder he would kick a sliding runner's foot from the base while holding the tag on him. He was known to stare at opponents, looking for any signs of any extralegal behavior, which he would then instantly bring to the attention of the umpires. "He was, without doubt, the gamest and most spirited ball player I ever saw and that doesn't except Ty Cobb," said Giants manager

John McGraw of Gleason. "He was a great influence for good on any ball club, making up for his lack of stature by his spirit and fight. He could lick his weight in wildcats and would prove it at the drop of a hat."

Gleason joined the White Sox in 1912 as a coach, and he was in many ways the emotional core of the team, a bridge between players and manager, a prankster who liked to sneak into Eddie Collins's room when the team was on the road and tie the sleeping second baseman to the bed frame with a razor strap. Ring Lardner made Gleason a central figure in the Busher stories. He's the guy charged with keeping the talented but self-centered and rather dense protagonist, Jack Keefe, grounded. He does it with a mix of schoolmaster discipline, avuncular love, and locker-room sarcasm; he tries with varying degrees of success to keep Keefe's gluttonous appetites and outsized ego from destroying his considerable talent. He is also the guy Keefe seeks out when even he can see that he's in trouble, and the one guy on the team he invites home to meet his newborn son. That was pretty much the real-life role Gleason had played on the White Sox since arriving eight seasons before. He was named manager prior to the 1919 season, a popular choice with the players. And right up until the very end, 1919 was a lot of fun for the new manager. He later said of the 1919 club, "I think they're the greatest ball club I've ever seen. Period."

Gleason long had little doubt about Cicotte's complicity in the World Series loss, of course, suspecting him from the day he had lost the opening game, those suspicions confirmed by the St. Louis gambler Harry Redmon in the days just after the series ended. And throughout the 1920 season he had watched the previously affable Cicotte grow ever more deeply into himself, shutting out teammates and the outside world, appearing, even to the lay observer, like a man burdened by guilt and shame. It would not take much, Gleason knew, to get Eddie Cicotte to crack.

So Cicotte was summoned to Comiskey Park, where Grabiner met him and brought him in Comiskey's limo to Austrian's office in the Continental and Commercial Bank Building on South LaSalle, where Comiskey and Gleason were waiting. Cicotte arrived right around ten o'clock, and within ten minutes the group was joined by Hartley Replogle, summoned to the meeting by Austrian. Comiskey's lawyer provided the introductions and, according to Cicotte's later trial testimony, Replogle cut right to it.

"We have got the goods on you, and we want you to come clean," he told the pitcher. Austrian said the same thing with a slightly softer edge, and with one big carrot.

"You know, this is going to be a long drawn-out trial," he said to Cicotte, "and you don't want your wife and babies at this trial, do you? If you come clean and tell us the things we want to know, we will save you from going to the penitentiary, or any fine or imprisonment of any kind.

"You need not only believe me, but Mr. Replogle will vouch for what I am saying. Is that right, Mr. Replogle?" he asked, and Cicotte testified the state's attorney confirmed that it was.

At this point, Cicotte may have wept. Replogle would later tell colleagues that Cicotte wept both in Austrian's office and later in the chambers of Judge Charles McDonald—"wept bitterly," according to prosecutors at the criminal trial a year later. Cicotte only acknowledged, "I might have had some tears in my eyes." Whether there were tears in Austrian's office or not, over the next hour Cicotte confessed, in the presence of his manager, his team owner, the state's attorney, and Alfred Austrian, the man he may have believed was serving as his lawyer. Cicotte may have been relieved at having the weight of his guilt finally lifted from his shoulders; he may have been cowed by the threat of jail. From all the later evidence, he had full confidence that Austrian's promise of no jail or fine, and Replogle's assent, was a good-faith and rock-solid guarantee that Austrian was acting in his—Cicotte's—best interests, and that the state's attorney's office wished him only as a witness in this case, not a defendant.

In hearing what he wanted to hear on the matter of the immunity, however, Cicotte was ignoring unequivocal evidence that, whatever Austrian and Replogle may have said, the promise of immunity existed only in Eddie Cicotte's mind. He was sworn in before a notary and his words in Austrian's office taken as a deposition. Austrian's secretary typed up his words, and Cicotte signed the document before leaving to go before the grand jury. The second paragraph of the 250-word document read: "I am making this statement of my own free will and accord without any promise of award of any kind or description." The rest of the statement contained Cicotte's story of how the plot had begun to come together on an early September train ride east, and how he had found $10,000, his promised share, in his room at the Warner Hotel on the Friday night before the Series began. He did not know who else got paid, or how much. He named the seven players who would shortly be indicted along with him.

If Kid Gleason said anything at all to his pitcher during the meeting, it was not recorded. Before the chastened player left for the Cook County Criminal Court Building, it was Gleason's sad duty to give to him the letter that would end his baseball career. It was addressed to all of the seven players still with the team and signed by Charles Comiskey:

You and each of you are hereby notified of your indefinite suspensions as a member of the Chicago American League Baseball Club (the White Sox).

Your suspension is brought about by information which has just come to me directly involving you and each of you in the base-ball scandal (now being investigated by the present Grand Jury of Cook County) resulting from the World Series of 1919.

If you are innocent of any wrong doing you and each of you will be reinstated; if you are guilty you will be retired from organized base-ball for the rest of your lives, if I can accomplish it.

Until there is a finality to this investigation it is due the public that I take this action even though it costs Chicago the pennant.

The taxi ride from Austrian's office to the Criminal Court Building on West Hubbard Street took no more than five minutes. Austrian accompanied Cicotte and Replogle. His presence may have comforted Cicotte, who believed that Austrian was looking out for his interests. Austrian's reason for going along may have been to convey that very impression.

In Judge Charles McDonald's chambers, Austrian provided an introduction and left immediately. Replogle told McDonald that Cicotte was there to confess. Cicotte told the judge what he had told Replogle, Austrian and Comiskey a short time before: He got $10,000; he didn't know who else got what. The eight by now familiar names were the ones involved.

"Well, you know, you know more than you have told," said the judge when Cicotte was finished.

"No, I don't," replied Cicotte.

"Isn't there something about these gamblers that you know?"

Cicotte didn't answer.

"Go ahead, Mr. Replogle and indict him," said McDonald.

Cicotte immediately grew alarmed and agitated.

"Just a minute, Judge," he said, "Mr. Austrian and Mr. Replogle told me that if I would tell what I knew, that they would take care of me."

"Well, what are you trying to do: bull me?" asked McDonald.

"No. No, I just have the word and honor of Mr. Austrian and Mr. Replogle."

At this point Replogle stepped in and asked Cicotte to wait in the judge's bathroom. From behind the closed door, Cicotte heard the sound of voices, but could not make out the words. When he was summoned from the wash-room, Replogle was ready to take him to the grand jury room. As there were more reporters than lawyers in the Criminal Court Building that morning, the two men went in the back way. Cicotte was becoming more than a little anxious about how this was all starting to go down.

"What's the matter, don't this go, what you and Mr. Austrian told me?" he asked Replogle.

"Sure it does," the state's attorney assured him, "anything that I say, it will be all right," and inside the grand jury room, Replogle did begin by telling the grand jury members that it was the wish of Mr. Comiskey that Cicotte be sent home after his testimony. That may have been the one promise made to Cicotte that day that was actually kept.

Alone now before the grand jury, Cicotte was read an immunity waiver: "I testify... with full knowledge of all the facts and of my legal rights, knowing full well that any testimony I may give might incriminate me, and might be used against me..., and now, having been fully advised as to my legal right, I hereby, with said full knowledge, waive all immunity that I might claim by reason of my appearing before the grand jury and giving testimony concerning certain crimes of which I have knowledge." After the waiver was read into the record, Cicotte signed a copy of the document. He then expanded on most of the points he had made in Austrian's office. He told the jury that after the meeting at the Warner in which the fix came together, he went down to distract Red Faber and Eddie Collins, who also lived in the hotel, so that the conspirators in the room could disperse. He testified to finding his $10,000 in his room when he returned. In what would become a pattern over the next two days, he insisted to the grand jury that while he had taken the money and agreed to throw the series, he had played to win in each of the two games he was suspected of throwing.

When Cicotte left Austrian's office, Comiskey and Kid Gleason returned to the ballpark, Comiskey to announce the suspensions to the press, Gleason to pick up Joe Jackson and bring him back to Austrian's office. After having been told by Gleason earlier that morning that Comiskey wished to see him in his lawyer's office, Jackson had spent the morning drinking. Comiskey's chauffer drove Gleason and Jackson up to Austrian's office, where Gleason brought him in and provided introductions, and then left the outfielder and the lawyer alone. It was now a bit after noon.

According to Jackson's later testimony in court, Austrian told the outfielder that he was about to be indicted, "in the next fifteen to twenty minutes." He also told Jackson that he, Comiskey, and officials over in the courthouse "had the goods on all the boys," then rattled off the names of the eight players. He urged Jackson to tell him what he knew, promising they would take care of him, "just like Cicotte," and would let him go home after his testimony, the urbane lawyer telling Jackson that Cicotte was "done gone."

At some point in the conversation, Joe Jackson—the man whom history would come to frame as the illiterate, guileless victim swept up in a maelstrom beyond the comprehension of his limited faculties, who by his own admission might have been "half" drunk at that moment—was shrewd enough to tell Alfred Austrian that he wanted a lawyer of his own. Austrian had no obligation beyond human decency to help Joe Jackson get a lawyer; and he felt no compunction about putting the interests of his client ahead of the civil rights of Joe Jackson.

"We can do you more good than a lawyer," Jackson remembered Austrian telling him, saying he was working together with state's attorney Replogle and Judge McDonald, and that if Jackson told them what he knew, they would take care of him and let him go home.

Jackson insisted that he wanted a lawyer, if only to handle the matter of his bond if he was about to be indicted. "I will go out and get one and come back up here," he told Austrian. "No lawyer will come to my office," Austrian replied.

"Then I will talk to one of your own firm then," Jackson said.

"We can do you more good than any lawyer you can get," repeated Austrian, and the lawyer either stated outright, or inferred, that if Jackson cooperated he wouldn't be indicted; he would testify only as a witness against the gamblers. He finally wore Jackson down on the matter of getting his own lawyer, and Jackson then agreed to tell what he knew to the grand jury. As he had done with Cicotte, Austrian called McDonald from his office and put the ballplayer on the phone. After a short, awkward exchange with the judge, Austrian and Kid Gleason, who had been waiting outside the office, took Jackson up to West Hubbard Street.

Again, as with Cicotte, Austrian first took Jackson to Judge McDonald's chambers. According to Jackson, McDonald told him that if he testified to what he knew about the fix, he would not go to jail, would not be fined, and could leave town and go wherever he wanted; he "could even go to the Portuguese Islands" if he wished. He then asked for a preview of what Jackson would be telling the grand jury. In a virtual replay of his morning exchange with Cicotte, the judge told Jackson that he was dissatisfied with he had been told, and said that Jackson must know more. "That is all I know," said Jackson; "you can take it or leave it alone." McDonald told Jackson he wouldn't get any sympathy with an attitude like that, and then he and Austrian talked for a couple of minutes over by the office window, out of Jackson's hearing. "I guess I will let you tell that story," McDonald said after his conversation with Austrian, and Jackson left for the grand jury room with Replogle.

Replogle reiterated the promise Austrian had made—that if Jackson told what he knew they would take care of him and see that he got to go home. Replogle then said to Jackson: "You know you are not the smartest man in the world." Jackson replied: "I know it." The exact context of this exchange is lost to history, though, according to Jackson, it happened shortly before they entered the grand jury room.

Inside the grand jury room, after Jackson was sworn in, Replogle began by reading into the record a waiver of immunity. With the promises from Austrian and MacDonald of no jail, no fine, and no indictment foremost in his mind, Jackson half listened as Replogle read, and he signed the document without question or complaint.

In testimony lasting thirty minutes, Jackson then told the grand jury that he had been promised $20,000 by Chick Gandil to participate in a scheme to throw the World Series.

"And you said you would?" asked Replogle.

"Yes, sir," answered Jackson.

He testified to having been paid $5,000 by his roommate Lefty Williams after the fourth game of the series. He denied having been to any meetings where a fix was discussed, but did admit to having been aware of the meeting at the Warner. He admitted to twice asking Chick Gandil during the Series where the rest of the money was. He was told after the first game that everything was set, that he, Gandil, had the money. When there was still no money forthcoming after the third game, however, Jackson testified that Gandil had changed his tune, and that now he was telling Jackson that the players had been double-crossed by Abe Attell and Bill Burns. He then told the grand jury that he believed it was Gandil who was doing the double-crossing. Aside from Cicotte's fielding miscues in games one and four, Williams's wildness in game two, and one play from Swede Risberg—when he took what looked like a double-play ball and played it into just a single out by running to the bag himself instead of relaying the ball to second baseman Collins—Jackson testified that he saw nothing from anyone on the team that he would have construed as a deliberate attempt to botch a play.

The most emphatic part of his testimony was Jackson's insistence that he put forth nothing but his best during the series.

"Did you make any intentional errors yourself that [first] day?"

"No, sir. Not during the whole series."

"Did you bat to win?"

"Yes."

"And run the bases to win?"

"Yes, sir."

"And field the ball [in] the outfield to win?"

"I did...."

"Did you do anything to throw those games?"

"No, sir."

"Any game in the series?"

"Not a one. I didn't have an error or make no misplay...."

"Had you ever played crooked baseball before this?"

"No, sir, I never had."

"Did anybody ever approach you to throw a game before this?"

"No, sir, never did."

"Did anybody approach you to throw a game since that time?"

"No, sir."

When Replogle asked Jackson whether he was "peeved" at having only gotten $5,000 when he had been promised $20,000, Jackson replied: "No, I was ashamed of myself."

Jackson finished his testimony at 3:30 p.m. Word of the indictments, suspensions, and Cicotte's and Jackson's confessions was fluttering about the city, and by now the courthouse was teeming with newspapermen, the steps outside thronged with the curious. Jackson was taken back to Judge McDonald's chambers after this testimony. Everyone, including Jackson, expressed a degree of concern for the ballplayer's safety in leaving the courthouse alone into a large and emotional mob. The concern was well taken. The day after Jackson's testimony, with news of the fix and the confessions all over the newspapers, an unbalanced fan recognized Cubs third baseman Buck Herzog in nearby Joliet. Herzog had been in the papers a few days before, after testifying before the grand jury on the initial allegations involving that Cubs-Phillies game in August. Shouting, "You're one of those crooked Chicago ballplayers!" the fan attacked Herzog and stabbed him three times, none of the wounds life-threatening.

Moreover, the grand jury confessions of Cicotte and Jackson had now brought some dangerous men into the spotlight; criminal-world assassinations were common enough in 1920 Chicago that the possibility of violence came readily to mind in moments like this. Jackson's life had already been threatened by teammate Swede Risberg. Jackson told the judge it was retaliation by his fellow conspirators he most feared. Risberg's threat came back during the 1919 series, when Jackson was talking about confessing the plot to Comiskey. The threat unnerved Jackson at the time, and the worry came back to him now; Risberg was not a guy given to empty bravado. "The Swede," Jackson said to the judge, "is a hard guy."

There was also the far more pedestrian matter of whether one man would even be able to open the door against the crowd massing on the steps. McDonald summoned a pair of courtroom bailiffs and asked them to take Jackson back to Comiskey Park, where he had left his car. The scene on the courthouse steps as Jackson emerged with the bailiffs would provide what has become the signature moment of the whole Black Sox scandal, a poignant, made-for-Hollywood moment where a small boy gives voice to a whole nation's shock, and a shamed ballplayer shatters our last illusions with a contrite admission.

As with so much in the story, the say-it-ain't-so-Joe moment on the court-house steps may or may not have happened as it has passed into history and legend. It will remain forever an unsettled argument.

It began with Hugh Fullerton's story in the *Chicago Herald and Examiner* the next day:

> As Jackson stepped out of the building, one little urchin grabbed him
>   by his coat sleeve.
> "It ain't true, is it Joe?" he said.
> "Yes, kid, I'm afraid it is," Jackson replied.
> "Well, I'd never have thought it," the boy exclaimed.

Fullerton's story was widely syndicated; it was also widely rewritten. It was irresistible as both quote and metaphor. Everybody could identify with a little's boy's heartbreak, even if the boy comes off as more perplexed than heartbroken in Fullerton's telling. Somewhere along the line, "It ain't true, is it Joe?" became "Say it ain't so, Joe," the phrase that has passed into the canon, overwhelming any debate over its right to be there.

The common consensus from this remove of nearly a century is that Fullerton made it up. The case against the story's veracity rests on two pillars. One is that Fullerton was only one of several dozen newspaperman in the court-house that day, yet he was the only one who overheard and reported the boy's plaintive question. It is beyond dispute that most newspaper exclusives in those days were scoops mainly because they were made up. Still, it also does not stretch credulity to believe that in the chaos of the courthouse steps as Jackson emerged, with a lot of simultaneous shouts and conversations, Fullerton just might have been in the right place at the right time and thus the only person beyond the two speakers to hear the exchange.

The stronger argument against the say-it-ain't-so legend is Jackson's denial that it ever happened. In a 1949 *Sport* magazine article, written under his own byline, together with longtime Atlanta sportswriter Furman Bisher, Jackson wrote, "There wasn't a bit of truth in it. It just didn't happen, that's all. [The writer] just made up a good story and wrote it.

"Oh, I would have said it ain't so, all right, just like I'm saying it now."

Sport was a major player in American sports journalism at the time, and the denial of the say-it-ain't-so story was one of the article's big revelations; it was the centerpiece of dozens of newspaper stories about the *Sport* article. Also, coming four years after Fullerton's death, Jackson's assertion was never refuted.

But Jackson's memory of that day in 1920 was itself problematic. To begin with, he misidentified the writer and the newspaper, attributing the quote to Charley Owens of the *Daily News*. He also said the only words he exchanged on the courthouse steps were with a deputy who asked Jackson to give him a ride back to the South Side. A small discrepancy, to be sure, but the sworn testimony of two men in 1921—Judge Charles McDonald and Jackson himself—had the bailiff driving Jackson away, not the other way around, because Jackson had been driven to the courthouse by Charles Comiskey's chauffeur.

Just because a man misremembers secondary details from an event three decades earlier does not mean that he's incorrect in his central point, of course. But on the courthouse steps, when Jackson supposedly had his exchange with Fullerton's "one little urchin," he had just come from telling the grand jury that while he had played his best throughout the Series, he had agreed to participate in a fix prior to the start of the series, and had accepted $5,000 for having made that promise. Inside the building, he had just said it *was so*. How great a stretch is it to believe that he might have repeated the point outside?

By 1949, when he made the denial to Bisher, Jackson had been engaging in some revisionist history vis-à-vis his grand jury testimony for going on thirty years. The premise of his 1924 civil suit against Charles Comiskey to recover back salary because he claimed he had been wrongfully terminated was that he was innocent and had never done *or said* anything to the contrary. Eight years before the Bisher story, as he watched a spring training exhibition game in Greensboro, North Carolina, with *Washington Post* writer Shirley Povich, Jackson denied, not for the first time, that he had ever confessed before the grand jury. "There never was any confession by me," he said. "That was trumped up by the court lawyers. They couldn't produce it in court. They said it was stolen from the vault. Does that sound right?" *

At this point, it really doesn't matter whether the say-it-ain't-so exchange happened or not; it has become the very essence of the Black Sox story, destined to remain in sharp relief after the centuries break down the more nuanced and complicated detail. The exchange will forever be part of the story because it so encapsulates the story, a Shakespearean tragedy in miniature. In three sentences there is confusion, disbelief, hurt, shame, pathos, betrayal, and humiliation, a young boy robbed of his innocence, an American hero stripped of his aura and dignity. Whether he made it up or reported it exactly as it happened, Hugh Fullerton nailed it.

On Wednesday morning, the next day, with the newspapers full of stories on the Cicotte and Jackson confessions and Comiskey's suspensions of the seven accused players, the telephone wouldn't stop ringing in Lefty Williams's home at the Tyson apartments on 43rd and Grand Boulevard, a dozen or so blocks from Comiskey Park. Williams was scheduled to meet with the grand jury that morning, and was waiting for a visit from Jerome Crowley, a lawyer his wife, Lyria, had retained to represent him. The phone calls were unwelcome; he had Lyria answer. First to call was Joe Jackson. Williams wasn't interested in talking to his old friend at the moment, who, the newspapers informed him, had implicated Williams in his testimony the day before. Lyria Williams took a message for her husband. Jackson wanted to be sure that Williams knew that he and Cicotte had been promised immunity for their testimony and that Austrian, Replogle, and McDonald would make the same promise to him.

Next to call was Alfred Austrian. Again, Lyria Williams answered, but this time Williams took the call. Austrian invited the pitcher down to his office.

"I can't right now," Williams told him. "I have called an attorney, and he is supposed to be here in fifteen minutes."

---

* As we will see in chapter 12, the original copies of the confessions made by the three players before the grand jury in 1920, as well as the immunity waivers they signed, were stolen from the Cook County Courthouse prior to the start of the 1921 criminal trial. Copies of the documents did survive, however, and were introduced as evidence in the criminal trial.

"You don't want any lawyers," Austrian replied, "Come to my office as soon as you can get loose." Austrian was persistent, telling Williams, as he had told Jackson, that he would get along better without a lawyer that he could with one. Austrian was also apparently very persuasive, because Williams left his apartment before Jerome Crowley arrived, and made his way up to Austrian's office. He found Kid Gleason and Joe Jackson waiting for him on the sidewalk outside the building.

Inside, the conversation and the process unfolded very much as it had with Cicotte and Jackson. Williams began by avowing he had no knowledge of any fix. "Well you know, you have been implicated in this thing pretty bad," Austrian told him, and then dangled the carrot. "Well, we have promised to take care of Mr. Jackson and Mr. Cicotte and we will treat you the same way."

"How is that?" Williams remembered asking.

"We will guarantee there is no sentence of any kind and no fine," replied Austrian. "Isn't that right Mr. Jackson?" and Jackson, who had accompanied Williams upstairs, answered: "Yes."

Williams agreed to cooperate. Austrian then took a deposition. As had Jackson and Cicotte, Williams put Gandil at the center of things, saying it was Gandil who first approached him in New York and Gandil who gave him $10,000 after the fourth game of the series—$5,000 for him and $5000 for Jackson.

The deposition finished, Comiskey's chauffeur took Williams, Gleason, and Austrian up to the Criminal Court Building. As it had with Cicotte and Jackson, the process there began with a visit to Charles McDonald's chambers. What happened there remains in dispute; in conflicting testimony at the players' criminal trial in 1921, Williams and McDonald disagreed on what, if anything, was said between the judge and the pitcher. Williams said he was in McDonald's chambers for fifteen or twenty minutes before leaving for the grand jury room, but exchanged no words with the judge. McDonald—whose testimony in 1921 related to the question of who, if anybody, offered the players immunity before their grand jury testimony—testified that the pair had spoken for fifteen or twenty minutes, and not just about Williams's involvement in the 1919 series fix. McDonald was stunned to learn that Williams had made just $2,800 in salary in 1919 and 1920, to the point where he admitted sympathizing with Williams when he said he did it because he was broke and needed the money. This struck something of a chord with McDonald, who admitted going further with Williams than he had with the others, promising to help him with his legal woes if he cooperated.

Inside the grand jury room, Hartley Replogle told the jury members that Judge McDonald had informed Williams, in his presence, "that if he comes in and helps the State clean up this matter that that might be taken into considera-tion and probably would be taken into consideration if he was found guilty and any punishment to be meted out to him." As with Cicotte and Jackson, Replogle read, and Williams signed, an immunity waiver. Williams's testimony largely confirmed what the grand jury had already heard from Cicotte and Jackson. Gandil was the instigator, and the first Williams had heard of the plan was in New York; the whole thing had come together at that pre-Series meeting at the Warner, and Gandil had given him $10,000 after game four.

It was also Williams's sworn testimony that he had done nothing deliberate to throw the Series. The furthest he would go was to admit to a nervousness, born of regret, he said, that probably contributed to his wildness in game two and his subpar performances in games five and eight. Williams was the last of the players to testify before the grand jury. But there was one confession still to come, and, insofar as public perception was concerned, it was maybe the most far-reaching and significant of all.

Happy Felsch initially denied any involvement in the fix, telling reporters on the day the story broke, "It's all bunk. I've always been on the square." But when a reporter from the news side, not sports desk, showed up on his door with a bottle of scotch on the following day, Happy Felsch told a much different tale.

Harry Reutlinger of Hearst's Chicago *American* was just twenty-three years old, but he was already a five-year newspaper veteran and well on his way to fashioning what would become one of Chicago's legendary journalism careers. He came onto the scene maybe slightly too late to have worked with Ben Hecht and Charles MacArthur, but he could be among the models for the press room ne'er-do-wells in their play *The Front Page*, cut as he was from that anything-for-a-story cloth. A short man who wore elevator shoes and garish neckties, Reutlinger would spend forty-seven years with the saucy Hearst *American*, and tales of how he got his big stories became as legendary as the scoops themselves. Reutlinger may have gotten the first interview with the doctor who delivered the Dionne quintuplets in 1934 by claiming to be a medical professional wanting to ship an incubator to the remote Canadian hospital in which they were born. He may have gotten Charles Lindbergh to confirm that his infant son had been kidnapped, and a $50,000 ransom demanded, by claiming to be President Franklin Roosevelt on the phone. He may have gotten the details of a passenger-ship fire direct from the captain aboard the burning vessel after having been patched through on ship-to-shore radio by telling the operator he was the president of the steamship line. He may have kept three different transatlantic telephone lines open to three different Irish airports so he could be certain of being the first to interview Douglas "Wrong Way" Corrigan, after the flyer landed in Dublin on what was supposed to be a flight from New York to Los Angeles. He may have been twice chased away in his attempts to visit a gunshot victim at Columbus Hospital by an elderly, mop-wielding scrubwoman, only to learn later that the patient's protector was Mother Frances Xavier Cabrini, the founder and director of the hospital, and the first American canonized by the Roman Catholic church.

And he may or may not have identified Happy Felsch as his Black Sox interview target after asking a newsroom colleague: "Who's the dumbest one of these guys?"

However he decided on Felsch, however much of the scotch he may have gotten the player to consume, whether the expansiveness and eloquence of Felsch's voice was his alone or aided greatly by Reutlinger's pen, the writer coaxed from Felsch a confession that is, while perhaps less precise in its specific detail, much richer in color and remorse than any of the confessions before the grand jury. Reutlinger reported to his readers that he had found Felsch in his bathrobe, soaking an injured big toe. He then got out of the way and let the centerfielder talk. "Well, the beans are all spilled and I think that I am through with baseball," Felsch began bluntly. "I got my $5,000 and I suppose the others got theirs too.

> If you say anything about me, don't make it appear that I'm trying to put up an alibi. I'm not. I'm as guilty as the rest of them. We were in it alike. I don't know what I'm going to do now. I have been a ballplayer during the best years of my life, and I never got into any other kind of business. I'm going to hell, I guess.
>
> I wish that I hadn't gone into it. I guess we all do. We have more than earned the few dollars they gave us for turning crooked. All this season the memory of the World Series has been hanging over us. The talk that we threw games this year is bunk. We knew we were suspected and we tried to be square. But a guy can't be crooked part of the time and square the rest of the time. We knew that sooner or later somebody was going to turn up the whole deal.
>
> Cicotte's story is true is every detail. I don't blame him for telling. He knew the grand jury had a case against him and there wouldn't have been any object in holding out. He did the best thing to do under the circumstances. I was ready to confess myself yesterday but I didn't have the courage to be the first to tell.

Felsch claimed that he never knew where his $5,000 had come from; it had just showed up in his locker one day. He said he believed Gandil double-crossed his teammates, keeping most of the money for himself. He further claimed that he was a reluctant fixer, but went along because of the inevitability of it. "I didn't want to get in on the deal at first," Reutlinger quotes him as saying.

> I had always received square treatment from Commy and it didn't look quite right to throw him down. But when they let me in on the idea too many men were involved. I didn't like to be a squealer and I knew that if I stayed out of the deal and said nothing about it they would go ahead without me and I'd be that much money out without accomplishing anything. I'm not saying this to pass the buck to the others. I suppose that if I had refused to enter the plot and had stood my ground I might have stopped the whole deal. We all share the blame equally.

One striking similarity Felsch's confession shared with those of the men who confessed to the grand jury was his insistence that he had done nothing but play his best in the eight games of the series.

> I'm not saying that I double crossed the gamblers, but I had nothing to do with the loss of the world's series. The breaks just came so that I was not given a chance to do anything toward throwing the game. The records show that I played a pretty good game. I know I missed one terrible fly but, you can believe me or not, I was trying to catch that ball. I lost it in the sun and made a long run for it, and looked foolish when it fell quite a bit from where it ought to be. The other men in the know thought that I had lost the ball deliberately and that I was putting on a clown exhibition. They warned me after the game to be more careful about the way I muffed flies.
>
> Whether I could actually have gotten up enough nerve to carry out my part in throwing the game I can't say. The gold looked good to all of us.

When Reutlinger asked Felsch what his plans were to defend himself against the charges, he had none at the moment, but wanted to consult with Buck Weaver and Lefty Williams. He did express a desire to go before the grand jury (which never happened). He closed with a statement that bespoke a very keen awareness of just how much he had surrendered for the very little he had gotten. "I got $5,000. I could have got just about that much by being on the level if the Sox had won the series. And now I'm out of baseball—the only profession I know anything about.

"The joke seems to be on us."

Happy Felsch would be the last of the implicated players to publicly admit to any complicity in the fix. Chick Gandil was in a Lufkin, Texas, hospital when the storm broke in Chicago, recovering from appendicitis surgery two days before. "It's the bunk—nothing to it," he said at the hospital. "The other players are trying to make a goat out of somebody, and I am telling the world that somebody won't be me." His doctor then told reporters he was too weak to say any more.

Reporters found Buck Weaver on Tuesday, just after he had received the letter from Comiskey suspending him from the White Sox. He emphatically denied receiving any money or having any knowledge of a deal to throw the Series. He said his play in the Series was a pretty good alibi. "Any man who bats .333 is bound to make trouble for the other team in a ball game," he told reporters. "The best team cannot win a world's championship without getting the breaks. The Athletics were the best team in the country in 1914, but they lost four straight to the Boston Nationals because the breaks were against them. And nobody ever accused them of laying down."

Weaver next went to Comiskey Park in the hopes of convincing Charles Comiskey of his innocence. He was allowed in to see the boss, but after the meeting, *Tribune* baseball writer I. E. Sanborn reported, he "left the ballpark with his head down and declined all requests for a statement as to the results of his conference."

Swede Risberg and Fred McMullin said nothing.

The other White Sox celebrated. The "Loyal Sox," "Square Sox" or "Clean Sox," as the newspapers had taken to calling them, had a party on Tuesday night at Eddie Collins's house to celebrate the suspensions. Collins, Amos Strunk, Mike Murphy, and Nemo Leibold had been together when they heard the news of the suspensions, and the newspapers reported them greeting the announcement with hugs, backslaps, and smiles. That evening at Collins's house, Ray Schalk, Red Faber, Dickie Kerr, and John Collins joined the group, and they sent out for "cheese and cold chicken and pickles and other things"—*other things* no doubt one of the early Prohibition euphemisms then beginning to find their way into newspaper stories. "No one will ever know what we put up with all this summer," said one member of the group to a *Tribune* reporter. "I don't know how we ever got along. I know there were many times when things were about the break into a fight but it never got that far. We went along and gritted out teeth and played ball. We had to trail along with those fellows all summer and all the time felt that they had thrown us down. Now the load has been lifted. No wonder we feel like celebrating."

Newspapers in Chicago and baseball people everywhere spoke of the "destruction" or "ruin" of the White Sox, but the remnants of the Sox team were still very much alive in the pennant race. The White Sox had won the last game the Black Sox would ever play, beating the Tigers 2–0 on Monday, September 26, giving Dickie Kerr his twentieth win of the season. The standings on the day that Cicotte and Jackson confessed had the Sox trailing the Indians by half a game with three to play. The Clean Sox had three off days to prepare for the season-ending weekend series in St. Louis. While they waited, the Indians won two, pushing their lead to a game and a half. In their first time on the field without their erstwhile teammates, the White Sox lost to the Browns 8–6; Cleveland split a double-header with the Tigers that day, leaving the White Sox with at least a mathematical chance, two games down with two to play. On Saturday, the Sox won behind Dickie Kerr, but the Indians routed the Tigers 10–1, clinching the pennant and sparing baseball a very awkward World Series.

ELEVEN

The Judge

In the fall of 1919, even as he worked to cover up what might have happened to his team during the World Series, Charles Comiskey was working to neuter Ban Johnson. When the cover-up fell apart in September 1920, the chaos brought about by the ruin of his team gave Comiskey an opening to finish the job. He was not working alone; there were a dozen men—a near-unanimous core of National League owners and a trio of American League malcontents who, like Comiskey, had long wished to see Ban Johnson's influence in baseball diminished and were finally beginning to muster an offensive.

If anything, Red Sox owner Harry Frazee disliked Johnson even more than Comiskey. The feeling was entirely mutual. When the boisterous and brassy theater impresario bought the Red Sox from Joseph Lannin in 1916, he became the first American League owner to have not been first personally vetted and approved by Johnson, and Johnson resented him for it. He indiscreetly told some other owners—including Comiskey—that Frazee was not the sort of man he wanted in baseball and aimed to see him driven out.

Yankees owners Jake Ruppert and Tillinghast Huston, meanwhile, were less visceral than Frazee in their dislike of Johnson but no less committed in their opposition to his rule. Their dislike was born of Johnson's decisions in the Carl Mays case. Mays was a talented submarine right-hander who had won twenty games for the Red Sox in both 1917 and 1918. But in June of 1919, he was 5–11 for the out-of-contention Red Sox, and one day he simply walked out of the ball-park and said he was through playing for the team. Johnson ordered Frazee to discipline Mays. Frazee, more practical than principled, looked to trade him instead. Johnson felt Mays's actions threatened the order and stability of the game; if Mays got away with this, any player unhappy on a second division club could stage a similar strike and get himself traded to a contender. Frazee ignored Johnson and reached a deal with the Yankees in mid-July, whereupon Johnson promptly suspended Mays. Ruppert and Huston went to court and got a restraining order against Johnson, and he relented. But his belligerence had driven Ruppert and Huston permanently into the Comiskey-Frazee camp.

Comiskey, Frazee, and Ruppert coincidentally comprised three-quarters of the American League board of directors that year. Board membership had been a rotating assignment among the American League owners through the years, a largely ceremonial post because Ban Johnson always made all the decisions. Beginning in August 1919, Comiskey, Frazee, and Ruppert—Ban Johnson's biographer dubbed them the "Insurrectos"—began calling board meetings, and their agenda items all concerned Johnson's fitness as president. The board met in September and November; Johnson, an ex officio member of the board, and James Dunn of Cleveland, the board's fourth member and loyal to Johnson, both refused to attend. In September, Comiskey, Ruppert, and Frazee, acting as the majority board, passed a resolution condemning Johnson for damaging the owners' businesses by the "promiscuous making of statements" on gambling, statements he was "either unwilling or unable to substantiate with any evidence."

In November, the Insurrectos questioned the very legality of Johnson's position as president, claiming no written contract or other documentation existed regarding the twenty-year appointment he had received in 1910 and, since league bylaws called for the president to be elected annually, Johnson was not legally president. In a statement released to the press, Comiskey, Ruppert, and Frazee then really took the gloves off, questioning Johnson's fitness for office in light of frequent public drunkenness. They cited the 1918 World Series meeting where, they alleged, "he staggered into the umpires room . . . , expressed unconnected and irrelevant ideas and seemed utterly incapable of understanding the arguments of the players or to make any sensible replies." The trio also told the newspapers that Johnson had failed to show up for a Senators game at which President Wilson was set to throw out the first ball, "because he was so drunk that he could not walk."

At the league's annual meeting in December, the renegade owners fired a broadside at Johnson, calling him, in raised voices, a "dictator," and calling for his ouster as president. It was all for show; they knew their resolutions were doomed to fail. Johnson still held sway over the American League, enjoying the continuing and loyal support of a solid block of five owners—Frank Navin of the Tigers, Phil Ball of Browns, Clark Griffith of the Senators, Ben Shibe and Connie Mack of the Athletics, and James Dunn of the Indians. They defeated the call for Johnson's removal by a 5–3 vote. They next voted in four new directors, all of them Johnson loyalists.

But the Comiskey group's actions had further weakened Johnson, whose grip on power was becoming more tenuous. Comiskey released a statement to the press in December saying that, because of the chaos in the American League brought about by the uncertainty of Johnson's leadership, he was making no plans for the 1920 season. This was only partly posturing. In truth he was proceeding cautiously with plans for 1920, lest the lid blow off the World Series scandal and render those plans useless. The headlines the insurrection made throughout the fall of 1919 helped nudge stories about the propriety of the recent World Series further down the sports page. More significantly, the unrest caused by Comiskey and his allies set the stage for the fall of the National Commission the following year, bringing with its collapse the end of Ban Johnson's long reign as the "czar of baseball."

It began with the so-called Lasker Plan. Albert Lasker was America's first great advertising executive. Starting as a floor sweeper at Hill and Thomas ad agency in Chicago in 1898, the Texas native quickly built a transformative career following the maxim that advertising was "salesmanship in print," making brands like Sunkist, Palmolive, and Lucky Strike the dominant brands in their respective fields by fashioning ads and campaigns that didn't just put the company name out there but gave readers a reason to want the product. By 1912, he owned the Hill and Thomas agency, and by 1919 he owned a piece of the Chicago Cubs as well. His investment in the team was considerable, though he was a behind-the-scenes sort, leaving the running of the club to William Wrigley and William Veeck. Nonetheless Lasker was growing increasingly frustrated—as were all of his National League colleagues—with the autocracy and intransigence of Ban Johnson and the resulting diminished stature of the National Commission, and its increasing ineffectiveness in getting anything done. And he had a plan to replace it. By the fall of 1920, the words Lasker Plan would become as familiar to baseball fans as the words double-play or hit-and-run.

With a businessman's eye and sensibility, Lasker understood that modern baseball had grown too big and too complicated a proposition to be left to the baseball men. Sixteen individual owners, each looking out for his own interests, were never going to equal the best formula for arriving at decisions that would benefit the common interest. So together with Alfred Austrian, and with the full knowledge and blessings of Austrian's clients Bill Wrigley and Charles Comiskey, Lasker drew up a plan early in 1920 that called for a three-man National Commission comprised wholly of men without a financial interest in the game. The new Commission would hold absolute power—"unreviewable authority," the draft document put it—to discipline not only players but the owners as well, possessing even the power to declare a franchise forfeit.

By the time of the Black Sox confessions and indictments, the National Commission had been living on borrowed time for a year. At the 1918–19 winter meetings, National League owners instructed their president John Heydler not to support Garry Herrmann's reappointment as chairman. An impassioned plea from Ban Johnson saved Herrmann's job, but only temporarily; sentiment was starting to run to an independent chairman, someone from outside the game. The league presidents, Heydler and Johnson, were named as a committee of two to find the new chair, but they never came close to agreeing upon a candidate or conducting anything resembling a serious interview. Criticism of Herrmann continued to well up throughout the 1919 season, and in January 1920, following the Comiskey-led coup attempt against Johnson, Herrmann resigned. Heydler and Johnson continued as the search committee for his replacement, but as the 1920 season moved along, it had effectively been taken out of their hands.

There were a number of names bandied about as the possible chairman of Lasker's new, outside-the-game commission. Former president William Howard Taft, World War I generals John "Black Jack" Pershing (Lasker's early favorite) and Leonard Wood, and Senator Hiram Johnson of California were all the subject of newspaper speculation and inside-the-game conversation. But the man they quickly focused on was the man Austrian had suggested and courted, Chicago Federal District Court judge Kenesaw Mountain Landis.

In a largely anonymous profession, Landis was the best-known judge in America. Befitting his colorful name, he cut a memorable figure on the bench. He had character-actor good looks, a craggy, chiseled visage, and a thick mane of white, generally tousled hair; in the words of radical journalist John Reed, he had "the face of Andrew Jackson three years dead." He wore a business suit, never a robe, on the bench, but so imperious was his presence and so authoritative his mien that people were shocked to see him away from the bench and find he stood but five and a half feet tall and weighed scarcely more than 125 pounds.

For a federal judge, Landis had a resume that was as unusual as his name. He was named after the Civil War battle of Kennesaw Mountain, where his father, a surgeon with the 35th Ohio, had been wounded and left crippled. Young Kenesaw—his family called him "Squire" when he was a boy—was born in Millville, Ohio, in 1866 and grew up in Logansport, Indiana. If his childhood was never one of want, neither was it one of privilege. He quit high school at age fifteen, flummoxed by algebra, and worked as a newsboy, store clerk, railroad dispatcher, and courthouse stenographer. This courthouse experience exposed him to politics and the law. He helped a friend win election as Indiana secretary of state, and was rewarded with a position on the man's staff. While there he gained admission to the Indiana bar at the age of twenty-two by the simple process of filling out a form. "All a man needed" to win admission to the bar, he later admitted, "was to prove that he was twenty-one and had good moral character." He hung out a shingle and attracted few clients. The harsh realities of life as an unqualified lawyer convinced him he needed some education. He enrolled in the Cincinnati YMCA Law School, spending a year there before transferring to the Union Law School in Chicago, graduating in 1891.

Before his legal career could gain any traction, however, he detoured back into politics, when an old family friend, Judge Walter Gresham (he had been Landis's father's commanding officer during the Civil War) was named secretary of state by President Grover Cleveland and brought Landis to Washington as his personal secretary. Though Gresham had known his new assistant since Landis was a boy, the bond between the two men had been formed only recently, when Landis was a new lawyer, unable to afford his own law library, and Gresham invited him to use his. The secretary of state designate was impressed with the young man's energy and his mental and legal acuity; he also very much liked the fact that Landis knew shorthand, a useful skill in a personal secretary.

Landis quickly proved himself an indispensible deputy to Gresham in Washington, showing an innate sense for both political nuance and bare-knuckle, quid-pro-quo deal making. He impressed many others, including the reporters who covered the State Department, but not everyone. He abraded many of the old-school diplomats, who still came to work in cutaway coats, with his brusque ways and casual dress. President Cleveland found him somewhat cheeky for one of such humble government station. On at least one occasion Cleveland suggested to Gresham that Landis be fired, but Gresham refused, saying if Landis went, he would go, too. "And some day when you and I are forgotten," Gresham told the president, "he will be known as one of the great men of all time."

Cleveland finally came around to Gresham's view on his young aide, and when Gresham died suddenly in the spring of 1895, the president offered the twenty-nine-year-old Landis a post as minister to Venezuela. But the young Landis wasn't interested in being a diplomat. Even at that early date, he wanted to be a federal judge. He turned down Cleveland's offer and returned to Chicago and the practice of law.

Though he had served a Democratic president, Landis was a lifelong Republican. Back in Chicago he understood that a prospective federal judge needed both a legal and a political profile, and he built a successful law practice with clients that included the Grand Trunk and Calumet railroads, while building up his political chits by working behind the scenes for progressive Republican causes and candidates supported by Theodore Roosevelt, who became president after William McKinley's assassination in 1901. While Landis was coming to prominence in Chicago, two of his brothers were meanwhile being elected to Congress, one from Indiana, one from Ohio. In 1905, Roosevelt, now elected president on his own, rewarded Kenesaw's loyalty, and his connections, by naming him to the federal bench for the newly created Northern District of Illinois. He was thirty-eight years old.

Landis's introduction to the American public came two years later, when he stunned the nation, and made himself a household name overnight, by fining John D. Rockefeller $29 million for collusion to fix prices by Rockefeller's Standard Oil Company. The nation watched, transfixed and amused, as Rockefeller played hide-and-seek with teams of subpoena-bearing federal marshals descending upon his many homes, and then cheered as Landis pronounced sentence. The size of the fine was so staggeringly beyond the common experience in 1907 America that newspapers groped for ways to put it in perspective. It was more than half the money coined annually by the US Mint, noted the *Tribune*. If Rockefeller were to pay the fine with twenty-nine million silver dollars, explained the *Record-Herald*, it would require fifty-eight freight cars to move them.

Landis was hailed as a great trustbuster, a fearless and independent jurist with the courage and power to do what others had feared to even attempt. On editorial pages he was suddenly seen as presidential timber. Rockefeller, meanwhile, received word of the fine and said, "Landis will be dead a long time before this fine is paid." Rockefeller was correct. A Federal Court of Appeals overturned the verdict and threw out the fine, chastising Landis in its decision for overstepping his bounds and abusing his judicial discretion. But in the court of public opinion, it was the appeals court that had made the error, not Landis. He remained a favorite of the newspapers and the subject of great public curiosity.

As he had done with Rockefeller, Landis continued to impose surprising sentences, though he was far from a hanging judge; his surprises were as often merciful as they were harsh. He had a knack for generating headlines, and for coming across as the righteous jurist forever on the side of goodness and right, somebody with his finger on the pulse of the public mood. He was often as much prosecutor as arbiter. He made inquiries about subpoenaing Kaiser Wilhelm II for questioning about his role in the sinking of the *Lusitania* in 1915. In an organized crime case in the early teens he berated and shamed a witness from his seat on the bench. "Have you any children?...Boy or girl?...How old?...Did you ever tell her what your business is?...Do you think it's too bad you're in a business you can't talk to your children about? You wear a Knight Templar charm; did you ever tell a lodge of brother Masons about the business you're in?"

After the Rockefeller case, the most prominent of Landis's trials was the wartime prosecution of 113 members of the Industrial Workers of the World (the Wobblies) charged with conspiracy to hinder the US war effort by fomenting strikes in war plants and encouraging draft resistance. The unwieldy, twenty-week trial made for spectacular theater. Radicals, patriots, celebrities, friends of the judge, throngs of curious citizens, and reporters from across America packed Landis's courtroom. As American doughboys fought their way across France during the spring and summer of 1918, courtroom spectators listened to political speeches masquerading as testimony on both ends of the political spectrum.

Through his speeches and courtroom decisions, Landis—whose son Reed was then serving as an army pilot attached to the Royal Air Force—had built a reputation for having little sympathy for war dissenters, and this had worried the Wobblies and their supporters when the trial began. Nonetheless, Landis earned praise from both sides for the extraordinary solicitude he showed for the defendants, and for the order he brought to a potentially out-of-control courtroom. His solicitude for the defendants, however, did not extend to great mercy. When one hundred of the defendants were found guilty, Landis sentenced the vast majority to prison terms of five to twenty years at Leavenworth.

As far as the baseball men were concerned, it wasn't Rockefeller, or the Wobblies, or any of his newspaper-friendly qualities that had attracted them to Landis. What had put the judge on the baseball owners' Christmas wish list that fall of 1920 was a case he had heard some four and half years before, a case that might have had a much bigger impact on baseball than anything he would do as commissioner. A case in which he chose to do nothing, thus preserving—for another half century as it would turn out—baseball's status quo.

Kenesaw Landis never lost a childhood love for baseball. He had played the game as a boy, and it had remained a constant in his life ever since. Reports from his boyhood and early adulthood described him as a talented athlete despite his small physical frame. He roller-skated in the winters and raced high-wheel bicycles in the summer, in addition to playing a fairly respectable first base and serving as player-manager of one of Logansport's many semipro teams. In Chicago, scarcely a week would pass when he wouldn't leave the bench early and go to the ballpark. Though he could be found most regularly at Cubs games, he was a fan of both the Cubs and the White Sox, and even made his way to a few Chicago Whales games during the Federal League's short life. He made it a point of pride to pay his own way in, and to make sure the newspapers knew that, lest a baseball case someday come before his bench. He loved to talk about the game at any time, in court or out of court, with only the gentlest of prodding, and sometimes with no prodding at all. In the weeks after he had leveled Rockefeller's fine, he used baseball talk as a filibuster to avoid answering reporters' questions. "Now take the attitude of the people of Detroit, for instance," he began once, when reporters asked him for comment on the structure of American corporations, "they positively refuse to discuss the baseball situation upon any basis which contemplates even as remotely possible that the Tigers will fail to land on top of the American League heap. I see that the Detroit club is just a little over a game behind the leaders and that if Detroit wins today and Philadelphia loses, they'll be practically tied for first place."

But what about Standard Oil? the reporters persisted. Landis wouldn't bite. "What is the matter with the Cincinnati club?" he offered in reply. "I understand they are up as batters and are all right in the field. I can't understand why they should be in sixth place. Cincinnati is a great baseball town, I have heard, but you ought to see Detroit. They talk nothing but baseball and what they are going to do after the Tigers have foreclosed their airtight cinch on the pennant and destroyed the Cubs in the world's championship series."

The Federal League of 1914–15 was the last attempt to establish a beachhead against Major League Baseball. Never again would outsiders put a team on the field and call it Major League Baseball.*

* In 1959, Branch Rickey announced plans for the Continental League, a third major league that backers hoped would be accepted into organized baseball. Those discussions never progressed very far, but some of the Continental League's proposed cities, and their financial backers, became major league expansion franchises in the early 1960s.

The Feds signed away a handful of major leaguers stars, including Hal Chase and longtime Cubs stars Joe Tinker and Mordecai "Three Finger" Brown. Most of the Feds major league signings were either past-their-prime stars like Tinker and Brown or bottom-of-the-lineup guys, but the defections were nonetheless of sufficient nuisance to organized ball that they countered by threatening to blacklist those players signing with the Feds, by filing a handful of breach-of-contract lawsuits in court, and by raising the salaries of their biggest stars.

The high-water mark for the Feds came in the winter of 1914–15. The Chicago Whales signed Washington ace Walter Johnson to a three-year contract. Clark Griffith of the Senators would quickly better the offer, and Johnson would break his Fed League contract, but for a few off-season weeks it looked as if the Feds had plucked their first real star from organized ball, and that more might follow. The Feds had also filed a lawsuit in federal court in January of 1915 that held great promise. A successful outcome in front of Judge Landis there—and the Feds had every reason to feel hopeful—would all but solidify the league's long-term future.

The ninety-two-page lawsuit charged organized baseball with violating federal antitrust statutes, claiming organized baseball had been operating as an illegal monopoly and, in so doing, had conspired to injure the business of the Federal League. The Feds' suit asked that the National Agreement and the rules of the National Commission (read: the reserve clause) be declared illegal, and that organized baseball be enjoined from operating under those rules. They further petitioned that the court rule that all contracts signed under the National Agreement be declared "null, void and no effect," effectively declaring every player in Major League baseball a free agent. Baseball countered by arguing that the reserve clause was a necessary protection for the owners who had invested years of time and thousands of dollars in the discovery and development of their players. "[The Federal League's] grievance is not that we prevent them from finding young ballplayers on the 'lot' and developing them through training in the various minor leagues as we do," claimed National League attorney George Wharton Pepper. "They want to attain in one bound the advantages we have gained through ten years of labor; they want to profit from the skill developed by our money."

The Feds were thrilled to get on Landis's docket. After all, he was the great trustbuster, the man who had so boldly tried to give John D. Rockefeller his comeuppance. There were not a lot of legal minds that felt the reserve clause would withstand close scrutiny by a court, least of all scrutiny by a trustbuster like Landis. The Federal League plaintiffs were a hopeful bunch when testimony began on January 20, 1915.

But the Landis judging the matter was Landis the baseball fan, not Landis the Rockefeller foil. It was clear from the moment the case opened that he was bothered by what the Federal League suit might do to the game, a game he liked very much the way it was. He was a romantic in his sense of the game; when a Federal League counsel referred to baseball as "labor," Landis interrupted and interjected: "As a result of thirty years of observation, I am shocked because you call baseball 'labor.'"

Time and again Landis scolded the Feds from the bench for bringing a suit that could force him into a ruling that would harm the game. "Do you realize that a decision in this case may tear down the very foundations of this game, so loved by thousands, and do you realize that the decision must also seriously affect both parties?" He seemed to be asking both sides to come to some sort of resolution, and not force him to make a ruling that everyone—jurist and litigants alike—would come to rue. "The time has come when I should ask you gentlemen just what you want me to do," he said after four days of testimony. "Do you want me to stop the teams from going on training trips? Do you want me to break up the clubs, or what do you want me to do?

"You all understand—both sides—that a blow to the game of baseball will be regarded by this court as a blow to one of our national institutions."

Landis was torn between being a judge and a fan. The law here was fairly clearly on the side of the Feds, but he was hardly inclined to "tear down the very foundations of the game," as he saw it. His heart told him to deny the claim, to support organized baseball and the status quo. Nonetheless, doing that, he understood, would bring with it the strong likelihood of his decision being reversed on appeal, of merely delaying the tearing down of those foundations.

So Landis did nothing. He made no ruling while a few more players jumped to the Feds and the teams all decamped for spring training. He did nothing while the season began; and he issued no ruling as summer followed spring and led into the fall, while the Red Sox and Phillies won their respective pennants and the Saint Louis Terriers took the Federal League title. He made no move toward a ruling when the season was over. Whether it was strategy or paralysis at the conundrum facing him, it worked for Major League Baseball. The Feds' financial situation grew more perilous. Brooklyn Tip Tops owner Robert Ward, who had the deepest pockets in the league and had dug into those pockets often to keep the league solvent, died in October. The remaining owners now began looking for a way out. Organized baseball and the National Commission, meanwhile, were motivated to negotiate by the knowledge that the still-unresolved Fed League lawsuit was a sword hanging over their heads; Landis could issue a ruling at any moment that might change everything. The two sides came together in December. The Federal League would go dark; two Fed League owners would be welcomed into the organized baseball fraternity. Phil Ball of the Saint Louis Terriers would be allowed to buy the Browns; Charles Weegham of the Chicago Whales would take over control of the Cubs.*

Judge Landis was at last ready to render a decision. Immediately after the organized baseball–Fed League settlement, he dismissed the case as moot. He had found a way to let organized baseball win without stepping on the law.

Now, five years later, in looking to make him the commissioner, the owners of organized baseball were looking to Landis to come to their rescue again. He had done well by them before, they reasoned; there was no reason to believe that he wouldn't do the same going forward. But if the eleven owners believed that they were only usurping Ban Johnson's power and not surrendering any of their own, they were misreading Landis as badly as the Federal League owners had a few years before.

The conversations about bringing Judge Landis into the game may have begun as early as January 1920. Alfred Austrian approached Landis then, when the Comiskey-led Insurrectos were still trying to convince Johnson's "loyal five" to visit the issue of the legitimacy of Johnson's presidency. Should the American League owners agree to put the question of the legality of Johnson's presidency before Landis, Austrian asked the judge, would he be willing to hear the arguments and render a decision? Landis indicated he would. But that went nowhere; the insurrection had already failed, and wasn't going to be revisited. Austrian certainly knew that. His real purpose in the January conversation was thus likely to begin the dialogue between Judge Landis and the men who would put him in charge of baseball. The talks were mostly sotto voce through the spring and summer, but would accelerate rapidly when the grand jury began its work on the Black Sox in September.

Both Charles Comiskey and Ban Johnson saw the grand jury investigation as a way to get rid of the other. Johnson felt the hearings would bring about the financial ruin of Comiskey and the White Sox, and force him to sell to a Johnson-picked buyer. Moreover, he believed the grand jury hearings would elevate the

* Weegham brought to the Cubs the contracts of all the Whale players, but the Cubs also got a ballpark out of the deal. The splendid new park Weegham had built for the Whales at the corner of Clark and Addison was called Weegham Field, even after Weegham sold the Cubs to William Wrigley a year later. A decade would pass before Wrigley would get around to naming the park after himself.

public profile of his friend Judge Charles McDonald—a virtual unknown on the national stage at the start of the hearings—to the point where he would now be seen as equal in stature to any of the names being thrown about as the possible next chairman of the National Commission. If all went as it seemed it should—indictments of the guilty players, maybe, but a general sense that baseball had finally exposed and eliminated gambling in its midst, surely—McDonald would be seen as the man who had saved baseball and would thus be a natural choice to lead it. And under the chairmanship of McDonald, Johnson believed, his role as the primus inter pares on the Commission would continue as it ever was.

Comiskey, meanwhile, understood that the grand jury now meant there would be no more keeping a lid on the 1919 World Series, and his losses coming out of this were likely to be profound. The challenge now was not in avoiding those losses but managing them. He also saw opportunity. The gambling scandal, in all its sordidness, would drive home the point that the National Commission had been and continued to be an ineffectual management system. It would thus become imperative that the sixteen owners do something dramatic, and do it fast.

On Wednesday morning, September 22, the day the grand jury was scheduled to begin hearing testimony, its two first witnesses spent the early morning hours in the company of their lawyer. There was nothing odd about this, of course, except Comiskey and William Veeck were not discussing their grand jury testimony with Alfred Austrian. The agenda that morning—William Wrigley and Albert Lasker were also in attendance—was how to go about wresting control of the game from Ban Johnson. It wasn't just about finding a new chairman for the National Commission; it was about taking the decision out of the hands of Johnson and National League president John Heydler. "[Wrigley, Veeck, and Lasker], as we [do], recognize the fact that a chairman of the National Commission satisfactory to Johnson can be such only as he can dominate and control," wrote Austrian in a letter to Yankees owner Jacob Ruppert after the meeting. "They want to terminate, as do we, this noxious position that we are now placed in." The group promised one another they would stand together "to eliminate Johnson from the baseball situation," and were convinced that if they had to go it alone, they had the muscle to do so, according to Austrian. "I might say that if no other than the Chicago National League club joins us, our position, in my opinion, will be impregnable, because you know as well as I do that neither league can get along without Chicago as a member of such league," wrote the lawyer, making it clear he was speaking on behalf of his clients. "They even go so far as to say that if they cannot get a man like Landis, or an equally forceful, honorable and well-standing man, as chairman of the National Commission, they are prepared to notify [their fellow owners] that they will not reopen their gates under existing conditions." As ominous as that sounds, the Chicago owners were never really threatening to go dark; they were merely saying that if they could not get what they wanted within organized baseball as it was now structured, they would remake baseball, with other like-thinking men. That threat was very real, and over the next six weeks would be put into place as a ploy to force the issue.

Wrigley and Veeck's job was to bring the other National League owners into the fold, which they did in short order. On Wednesday, September 29, one day after he had delivered up Eddie Cicotte and Joe Jackson to the grand jury and fired the eight Black Sox, Comiskey was back in Austrian's office, joined this time by his fellow American League Insurrectos Ruppert, Huston, and Frazee, and by Bill Wrigley of the Cubs and Charles Stoneham and John McGraw of the Giants. The three American leaguers were there to throw in with the National League in support of the Lasker Plan. The National League men were there to promise the American League rebels that the National League "would stand by signers of this plan to the extent of refusal to recognize such American League clubs as do not agree on [the] new form of Commission." Wrigley and Veeck had secured the support of six National League owners in a plan that would embrace the Insurrectos and create a new league, if need be, without Ban Johnson's "loyal five." At that early date, Wrigley and Veeck were unsure on Charles Ebbets of Brooklyn and Garry Herrmann of Cincinnati, but both came into the fold soon enough. On October 7 National League owners officially gave their unanimous endorsement to the Lasker Plan in a meeting in New York.

Ban Johnson and his allies reacted to the news with obstinacy. Johnson, speaking to the minor league owners' meeting in Kansas City welcomed a war, telling the minor league men it was "the best cleanser." The loyal five proudly proclaimed themselves as such, and the newspapers added both capital letters and quotation marks. But some of the owners allied with Johnson had to know they were whistling past the graveyard. Organized baseball was about to be remade. All that was left for them to determine was how they were going to fit into this new world.

Their choice became more clearly defined, and a lot more urgent, on October 18. Comiskey, Ruppert, Huston, and Frazee met with Austrian that morning and agreed to throw the American League aside. In the afternoon, the men joined the eight National League owners at the Congress Hotel for a noon-to-midnight session during which they laid out specifics of their new world. The loyal five—who had been invited to the Congress Hotel meeting but had declined on advice from Ban Johnson's counsel—would be invited to join the eleven others. If they persisted in their loyalty to Johnson, the eleven clubs would form a new twelve-team league under the Lasker Plan. The twelfth team would be the first of the five to break from the group. If none did, the men of the new league would award a new franchise to one of the loyal five cities, probably either Cleveland or Detroit.

At the Congress Hotel meeting, the eleven owners authorized a salary of $20,000 for the chairman of the new National Commission and $10,000 each for the two associate commissioners. The owners were still talking exclusively about a three-person commission, as was now in place, with the change that none of the Lasker Plan commissioners would have a financial stake in any team nor a formal role in either the American or National leagues. No official endorsement of Judge Landis was to come out of this meeting, though he was most certainly discussed, because sometime in the next day or two, Austrian and Lasker met with Landis to sound him out. It was extremely unlikely that this was the first such meeting. Both Austrian and Lasker were closely acquainted with the judge—"friends" is perhaps too strong a word—saw him frequently, and had communicated their interest in having him run the game over the past months. Austrian reported to Comiskey and Wrigley that Landis had responded favorably to their informal offer, and promised to talk to his family and get back to Austrian before the end of the month. The talks between the three men were obviously specific enough to include talk about money. The $20,000 figure apparently did not impress Landis, for Austrian reported back to his clients that he thought the salary would not tempt the judge unless it was in the $50,000 range.

Ban Johnson may have played one last card, trying to derail the Landis train and shift the focus back on to his candidate, Charles McDonald. Through his Cincinnati ties and his friendship with Garry Hermann, Johnson had connections to Ohio senator Warren G. Harding, now less than a week away from being elected president of the United States. Johnson, or maybe somebody acting on his behalf, may have contacted Will Hays, chairman of the Republican National Committee and, at that moment particularly, a man closer to Harding than anyone else. Sometime in the final days of the presidential campaign, as Landis's name was being bandied about the newspapers as the frontrunner to become chairman of the new National Commission, Hays reached out to Austrian and tried to put a stop to the draft-Landis movement. According to the diary of Comiskey's deputy Harry Grabiner—the principal primary source for the backroom discussions during these weeks—on November 1 "Austrian stated that

Hays…intimated that he did not feel as though the Federal Bench should be tampered with and he wished to use his good offices on behalf of MacDonald [*sic*]." It proved but a small hiccup in the process. Since the alternative Hays was proposing was also a sitting judge, tampering with the Illinois bench instead of the federal bench rightly struck the baseball men as a distinction without a difference. Moreover, Albert Lasker was much closer to Hays and the Harding campaign than anyone in Johnson's office and could be expected to soothe any hurt feelings there. In fact, Lasker spent Election Day with Harding, and someone—Harding himself? Hays? Some third party?—did pressure him to back McDonald, according to Grabiner's diary. Lasker reaffirmed that he was "for Landis 1, 2, 3," but would not oppose McDonald if Landis could not win the votes, an unlikely eventuality at this late hour.

During the first days of November, negotiations continued between the two factions, but it was beginning to look as though the eleven breakaway owners would be going their way together. Ban Johnson believed that the rules of the National Commission stipulated that individual owners did not vote in matter of the game's organization; instead, each league would cast one vote, and as long as his loyal five held firm he had control of the American League's vote. The resolve of his loyal five, however, was weakening; whether or not Johnson was right on his one-league, one-vote theory, what was happening was happening outside the existing framework of the game. The penultimate meeting came on November 8, also at the Congress Hotel. The loyal five, now being called the "Hungry 5" in Grabiner's diary, were again invited and again declined the invitation. Nonetheless, Clark Griffith of the Senators did come to the hotel on behalf of the loyal five. He asked for a compromise: What if a committee formed of three representatives of the eleven, three from the loyal five, and three representing the minor leagues explored the reorganization and the appointment? He was told that if the five owners wished to join the eleven in their meeting that those sorts of things might be discussed, but if the loyal five did not indicate their willingness to talk by four that afternoon, the eleven owners would move forward with their plans. Griffith carried the message back; he returned in the late afternoon with word the loyal five were not yet willing to talk.

And so, at four o'clock, the eleven owners reconvened their meeting. The White Sox, Yankees, and Red Sox formally resigned from the American League. The National League dissolved itself and immediately formed, together with the three erstwhile American leaguers, a new twelve-team National League, the twelfth team to come from one of the loyal five or a new franchise in one of their cities. This new National League then voted unanimously to offer the chairmanship of its commission to Judge Kenesaw Mountain Landis, at a salary of $50,000 per year for a term of seven years. Austrian, Veeck, Ruppert, Charles Ebbets, and Garry Herrmann were appointed as the delegation to call upon the judge and formally make the offer. They found him receptive, though also unwilling to commit on the spot. A short time later, a reporter found him to be both a little bit circumspect and a little bit eager. "A thing of that kind is something I cannot decide in a hurry," Landis told the reporter. "It is a big thing. It is a big job. I deeply appreciate the honor these gentlemen have conferred upon me in offering me the chairmanship, but I told them I would have to give my answer later."

When the reporter then asked Landis whether he had said anything that might suggest he would be turning the offer down, the judge was no longer circumspect. "By no means! Emphatically no!" Landis then asked the reporter what he thought and was told he was "the right man" for the job. Landis seemed to take great comfort in the reporter's support. "Thank you. I—well, all I can say now is that I am a fan and love the game and admire clean sport, and that I would do everything in my power to help make baseball worthy of the name it has borne all these years as the cleanest sport we have."

All that remained now was to determine whether Landis would be overseeing a new twelve-team league—or the American and National leagues as baseball had known them for the past two decades. The answer wasn't long in coming. After the meeting at the Congress, the owners had all entrained for Kansas City, where the minor league meetings were set to begin the next day. By morning, Johnson's loyal five had caved. In a corridor at the Muehlebach Hotel, Bob Quinn of the Browns, the team's general manager, representing owner Phil Ball at the meetings, told Barney Dreyfuss and Garry Herrmann: "If my two boys wanted to fight over anything so silly, I would spank them both." A short while later, Clark Griffith sought out Charles Ebbets and told him the loyal five would accept all the conditions that had been agreed to during the November 8 meeting in Chicago. A meeting of all sixteen teams was scheduled for November 12, back in Chicago at the Congress. No lawyers, reporters, or league presidents would be welcome.

Somewhere between the meetings in the corridors of the Hotel Muehlebach and the meeting rooms of the Congress, the longstanding idea of a three-man commission was cast aside and Landis left standing as the sole commissioner. Harry Grabiner's diary is frustratingly vague on this, saying only: "It was finally agreed that if acceptable to Landis, no associate members would be selected but Landis to be sole judge." *Baseball Magazine* editor F. C. Lane, in an article written at the time, said the decision to go with Landis as sole commissioner had come together in a series of private conversations that first began in Kansas City.

Garry Herrmann raised the question of whether the November 8 decision to pay Landis $50,000 and the two associates $25,000 each was fair; and shouldn't the associates be paid the same as the chairman? Bob Quinn of the Browns was the first to broach the idea of a single commissioner. "Personally, I see no necessity for having three commissioners," he said during some informal meetings in Kansas City. "In my mind, one man would do as well. A man like Judge Landis who is a federal judge and accustomed to handling large business interests can certainly be trusted to administer any business Organized Baseball may give him." The idea met with some initial resistance, but Garry Herrmann changed his mind, and that started a trend; by the time of the meeting at the Congress, most teams had come around to Quinn's point of view.

Why the owners would suddenly change their minds on something so central remains another of the many pieces of this story forever lost to history. Harry Grabiner's diary, so rich with detail on so much of this drama, is mute on this point, beyond noting that the group had agreed to forego the three-man commission in favor of allowing Landis to rule alone. Bill Veeck Jr. and Ed Linn, his ghostwriter, the only two men to have seen Grabiner's diary, and thus its keenest interpreters, speculate that Ban Johnson's loyal five may have exacted that provision to keep Johnson only one seat removed from the ultimate power. "If so," Veeck and Linn note, "[Johnson] made his final mistake. By the time Landis got through interpreting his powers as Commissioner, there was nothing left over for Johnson or anybody else."

Beyond deciding upon Landis as the single commissioner, the biggest decision made at the November 12 all-comers meeting was the decision that each team would cast an individual vote on interleague matters, with ties to be broken by the commissioner. This was the final defeat for Johnson, who had lobbied hard for each league casting a single vote, believing it to be his last chance to cling to even a vestige of his former power.

The sixteen owners spent four hours in their final meeting. At four o'clock, a joint American-National League delegation of eleven men—a mix of former Johnson loyalists and Insurrectos—left to call upon Landis and to again formally offer him a job. He was still hearing a case when the men—Comiskey, Ruppert, Griffith, Connie Mack, James Dunn of Cleveland, and Bob Quinn of the Browns from the American League and Veeck, Herrmann, Barney Dreyfuss, Charles Ebbets, and the Cardinals' Sam Breadon from the National League arrived, and when Landis did not adjourn his court, the eleven owners stood in the back and started chatting, earning themselves a stern rebuke from the soon-to-be commissioner. "There will be less noise in this courtroom," he warned, "or I will order it cleared." After forty-five minutes, Landis brought them into his chambers; by this point, the delegation had swollen to a virtual committee of the whole, as they had been joined at the courthouse by all owners save Phil Ball of the Browns. Comiskey and Veeck, who had been working toward this day for well over a year, spoke for the group and told Landis: "It will make us very happy if you will accept and serve us." Landis had spent four days mulling the offer he had received on November 8. He had been eager to accept, yet also suddenly reluctant to abandon the bench. "I love my work here as judge," he had told the earlier delegation. "And I am doing important work in the community and the nation." This was almost certainly something that had been broached in previous conversations among the owners, for when Landis brought it up in the group meeting, the group did not hesitate. "Why not keep your position on the bench and accept our offer, too?" suggested one owner. "The [baseball] work will not call for much time," said another.

That was all Landis needed to hear. "Gentlemen, we need go no further with this thing," he told them. "I accept. But if I am to remain on the bench, I desire to deduct my federal salary from the original amount you offer me."*

Landis's judicial salary was $7,500 a year, and a contract would be duly drawn up paying him $42,500 as commissioner. In reality he was leaving no money on the table, for he asked for and received a $7,500 expense account from the baseball men. Nonetheless he had won some PR points for his actions, and he had actually negotiated himself a slightly better deal. His $7,500 in expenses would come tax-free.

The collected owners let out a whoop of delight when Landis agreed to join them. They then opened the doors to the judge's chambers to the newspapermen gathered outside. Photographers snapped dozens of images of the new commissioner signing his contract with the owners standing behind and looking down approvingly.

And so the last major player in the Black Sox story was now in place, and the drama awaited only its final piece—the players' day in court.

---

* Landis would keep both jobs for just over a year, resigning from the bench on March 1, 1922.

TWELVE

Judgment

To most baseball fans, the guilt of the eight White Sox players had been swiftly determined by the allegations and the confessions. In the Cook County Criminal Court, however, it was another matter entirely. The case against the players was frightfully thin and about to get thinner.

The grand jury sat in session for another month after the indictments of the ballplayers in late September, generating little by way of evidence or clarity into what had happened, and even fewer headlines. The original indictments had named the eight players, Sport Sullivan, and the mysterious Rachael Brown (Nat Evans). Along the way, additional indictments were handed up for Hal Chase, Abe Attell, and Sleepy Bill Burns. The only matter the newspapers seemed to care about as the hearings went on, however, was the witnesses who alleged Arnold Rothstein's involvement, and the speculation as to whether or not Rothstein would be indicted. The same question was bothering Arnold Rothstein in New York. His confederates Abe Attell and Sport Sullivan had taken to talking to the newspapers after their indictments, implying that if they went down, they would not go alone (Sullivan named no names, but Attell pointed at Rothstein). Not a day went by when Rothstein's name wasn't in the newspaper in connection with the fix.

Not inclined to let circumstances run their course, Rothstein began moving to preempt his indictment. He took to the newspapers himself, playing the role of the aggrieved citizen, denying to the *New York Tribune* that he had had anything to do with the fix and, when his name kept coming up in Chicago, telling the *New York World* he had quit gambling months before, taking well-rehearsed umbrage at "the unwarranted use of my name in this unfortunate scandal.

"It is not pleasant to be what some may call a 'social outcast,' and for the sake of my family and friends I am glad that the chapter is closed." But it wouldn't be closed, despite Rothstein's persistent attempts. He summoned Sullivan and Attell to his home, and then sent them away—Attell to Mexico, Sullivan to Montreal. The latter's exile didn't last long, however; he was back making book in Boston before the grand jury in Chicago was done hearing testimony. In the meantime, stories and testimony out of Chicago were connecting Rothstein to the 1919 World Series. So Rothstein went to Chicago to face them head-on. He not only agreed to testify before the grand jury; he insisted.

He did so on the advice of his attorney, a scene-stealer of a supporting actor in the Black Sox drama by the name of William Fallon. It was said that the old joke—"Is he a criminal lawyer?" "Yes, very"—was first made about William Fallon, barrister to New York's white-collar demimonde in the 1920s. Fallon was the consummate trial attorney, whip-smart, handsome, and theatrical. With the legal acuity of a Supreme Court justice and the courtroom timing of a born actor, Fallon was brilliant at both framing and phrasing an argument. And if he couldn't win acquittal, his techniques could almost always get his client a hung jury, for Fallon was also the consummate jury fixer. He defended 120 men in murder cases over the years; not a single one was ever convicted. Hung jury after hung jury also cheated the jailer of hundreds of bucket-shop swindlers, speakeasy proprietors, and Tammany pols. When he found himself on trial for jury tampering in 1924, Fallon fixed that jury too.

"Go to Chicago," Fallon told Rothstein. "Go to Chicago and begin brow-beating everyone. Find fault with everything. Be temperamental.... I've got a great scheme."

Fallon's "great scheme" was for Rothstein to step up the feigned umbrage he had been showing about being connected to the fix. Rothstein would go to Chicago; Fallon would alert the newspapers. Fewer photographers than Fallon might have wished for actually showed when Rothstein's train arrived in Chicago, but they did their best to capture the New Yorker's image. In a quieter moment, this allowed Rothstein to exercise his outrage. "What kind of country is this?" he asked reporters. "I came here voluntarily and what happens? A gang of thugs bars my path with cameras as though I was a notorious person—a criminal even! I'm intended to an apology. I demand one! Such a thing couldn't happen in New York. I'm surprised at you."

While Rothstein was talking to reporters, Fallon was talking to people who could make a difference in quashing any indictment. Alfred Austrian was one of those people. Austrian met with Rothstein following his arrival, and after Rothstein's grand jury testimony told reporters: "Rothstein in his testimony today proved himself to be guiltless." State's Attorney Maclay Hoyne was another who likely received a call from Fallon. "I don't think Rothstein was involved in it," Hoyne told reporters. And somebody almost surely talked to someone on the grand jury, for two members of that panel suddenly became good personal friends with Arnold Rothstein, visiting him in New York almost annually over the coming years, enjoying his generosity in the form of baseball tickets and dinners. Not surprisingly, the grand jury voted no bill of indictment against Arnold Rothstein. Rothstein and Fallon had to make sure it stayed that way. Abe Attell was one problem. Rothstein had thrown Attell to the sharks in Chicago, telling the grand jury and reporters afterward that "Attell did the fixing." The ex-champ was an ornery cuss who was already saying things to newspaper reporters. Rothstein needed to make sure Attell never said those things to a jury. The case eventually coming to trial was another worry for Rothstein. All of the gamblers already indicted, as well as all the gamblers who would be indicted over the coming months—Carl Zork, Ben Franklin, David Zelcer, and the Levi brothers—had ties to Rothstein. Nobody knew better than Rothstein how little honor there was among thieves.

Bill Fallon went to work on both problems. He kept Attell out of Cook County's clutches with a courtroom buck-and-wing that swiftly became a part of the Fallon legend. When Attell returned to New York from his Rothstein-ordered vacation in Mexico, New York police arrested him on a Cook County warrant. Fallon quashed the extradition order by arguing that the Abe Attell under indictment in Chicago was an altogether different Abe Attell from his client, the former featherweight champion then standing before the court in the Bronx. Fallon was able to hold sway in this fantastic argument, helped by delays brought on by his numerous motions, and by some perjured testimony from the Chicago man who had implicated Attell before the Cook Country grand jury. Samuel Pass, White Sox fan and confidante to White Sox players, was summoned to New York to testify that he had bet on the World Series with Attell. Fallon was waiting when Pass's train arrived at Grand Central, and offered him $1,000, courtesy of Arnold Rothstein. Later that day in court, Pass testified that he had indeed bet with a man claiming to be Abe Attell, but he had never before seen the Abe Attell now before him in that New York courtroom. Attell walked, and would never set foot in a Chicago courtroom.

The first days of the grand jury hearings on the 1919 World Series also co-incided with the final days of the primary campaign for the Illinois state elections in 1920, and on September 15 Cook County state's attorney, Maclay Hoyne, who had run afoul of the Chicago Democratic Party machine, was beaten in his reelection bid. By the time Eddie Cicotte, Joe Jackson, and Lefty Williams confessed before the grand jury, Maclay Hoyne was a lame-duck state's attorney. He left for New York shortly after his primary defeat, ostensibly on vacation. He stayed several weeks, weighed in innocuously a couple of times early in the proceedings during his vacation, saying he felt there was "no doubt the 1919 World Series was crooked." However, the day after the indictments of the eight players, with Charles McDonald and Harley Replogle getting all the headlines, Hoyne blasted his lieutenants back in Chicago, giving court watchers the first public indication that this was going to be a troubled prosecution.

Hoyne announced that the indictments were not really indictments. They may have been voted, he said, but they did not become official until they were returned in court, and he had doubts as to whether that would ever happen. While the question of voted indictments versus returned indictments may have been a distinction that mattered far more to law students than to newspaper readers, Hoyne went on to say he doubted that any indictable crime had been committed. The only crime, he told a reporter for the *New York Times*, seemed to be gambling, a misdemeanor under Illinois law, and thus outside the purview of the grand jury. He criticized his subordinates for not keeping him abreast of what they were doing, and said he had ordered a halt to the proceedings until he returned to Chicago at the end of the week.

The reaction back in Chicago showed how deep the divisions were in the politically charged state's attorney's office, and just how alone Hoyne now was in the Chicago legal community. Charles McDonald said he believed Hoyne had been misquoted. Austrian, like a law professor chastising an insolent student, laid out a series of criminal laws he believed were applicable to the issue at hand. Grand jury foreman Henry Brigham, developing quite a fondness for newspaper reporters himself, promised "the investigation will not be halted."

Hoyne backed off his statements, though when he returned to the office he ordered that all of the grand jury files related to the World Series case be turned over to his custody. And so it was that the confessions of Eddie Cicotte, Joe Jackson, and Lefty Williams, together with their signed immunity statements, were last seen in the custody of Maclay Hoyne.

Hoyne's grab for the documents incensed Charles McDonald. It also caught the attention of the new baseball commissioner. Judge Landis, still on the federal bench, of course, promised a federal investigation if any anything untoward happened to the documents while they were in Hoyne's possession. Hoyne responded defensively, claiming that the prominence of the baseball case was the very reason he felt compelled to protect the grand jury documents, to ensure they would be intact for his successor as state's attorney.

But they weren't. Though their disappearance would not be announced until the trial was underway the following July, incoming state's attorney Robert Crowe learned on almost his first day in office in December 1920 that the documents were missing. The identity of the person who stole the missing confessions and immunity waivers was never proven, but nobody, then or since, pointed to anyone other than Arnold Rothstein. Cook County prosecutors told newspaper reporters that Rothstein had taken the documents when it was first announced that they were missing during the trial in June. But clearly they had no proof. Rothstein, as the cop-and-courtroom dramas like to put it, had the means, motive, and—as we will see—opportunity, and Fallon's thumbprints are all over this. Rothstein's reason for wanting the documents was his continued self-preservation. While he may have avoided indictment, he was far from out of the woods. When the case came to trial, his name was likely to be brought up by every witness. If he could preempt a trial the way he had preempted his indictment, it might keep his name out of the headlines, and perhaps allow him to remain unindicted.

How directly Maclay Hoyne was involved in the theft is unclear, but two of his most trusted lieutenants were major players. George Boothby, a versatile reporter then working for the *New York Herald*, spent a lot of years covering Rothstein and the people in his orbit. He was able to piece together a story on the theft, though he never wrote it, perhaps out of personal fear of Rothstein, but more likely out of regard for the safety of the man who gave him the story, Fallon's law partner, Eugene McGee. McGee had been a Fordham classmate of Fallon's, and he shared his partner's ethics. He had been the bagman in the stolen confessions caper, taking $10,000 of Rothstein's money to Chicago and giving it to Henry Berger, a former assistant state's attorney now in private practice. Berger had been recruited by Fallon to represent Abe Attell in Chicago, should it ever come to that, and was now assisting in the defense of St. Louis gamblers Carl Zork and Ben Franklin in the World Series trial. Berger had been Hoyne's most trusted aide while in the state's attorney's office, and was still very close to his former boss.

Berger in turn gave the money to George Kenney, Hoyne's personal secretary in the state's attorney's office. Kenney, who had collected the grand jury documents on Hoyne's orders and put them under Hoyne's care, was the apparent thief. Kenney gave the documents to Berger, who gave them to Fallon, whereupon another $10,000 changed hands.

And here's where George Boothby first enters the story. Understanding he was now in possession of something of great value, not just to his client but perhaps to himself as well, Fallon looked to make a little money on the side. After redacting all references to Arnold Rothstein in the purloined documents, he offered them to Boothby for a price. Boothby took them to his editor at the *Herald*, and the paper did attempt to sell them in syndication, offering them up for $25,000. But they were either unsuccessful in their efforts or balked at closing the deal, because no stories emanating from the stolen papers appeared in the newspapers in the winter of 1920–21. Boothby learned the full details of the theft only later, from an embittered McGee, who had been promised $10,000 for delivering the first payment to Chicago and had been stiffed, whether by Rothstein or Fallon he didn't know. Both were fully capable of such betrayal.

In the end, missing or not, the documents actually had very little impact on the prosecution's case; it had troubles of a much deeper nature. In December 1920, a game-fixing case from the Pacific Coast League was dismissed in a California court. The judge ruled that no crime had been committed; there was no statute against game fixing in California, and any of the related charges, specifically breach of contract, were matters for a civil court. Cook County prosecutors faced the same problem—no statute specifically prohibited the fixing of a baseball game. And even if the various conspiracy and intent-to-injure-the-business charges the Black Sox players were being tried on did withstand the inevitable dismissal challenges from the defense, it was still a weak case. All the state had were the confessions, which had since been recanted and were being challenged on the grounds that the players believed they had been granted full immunity from prosecution.

New state's attorney Robert Crowe knew he needed more, and requested a delay of the scheduled early-March start date. When the presiding judge refused the delay, Crowe instead announced that he was dismissing the indictments, with the intention of convening a new grand jury immediately, which he did a day later. The second grand jury, sitting for only a week, reindicted all the original defendants, and added gamblers Carl Zork and Ben Franklin of Saint Louis and Ben Levi, Lou Levi, and David Zelcer of Des Moines. The second indictments may have preempted a defense challenge or two, but what it mostly did was buy the prosecution some time to shore up its case—or, rather, to stand by and let Ban Johnson shore up their case.

Johnson was dismayed by the troubles with the case. Should the prosecution in this case collapse—and during the early months of Crowe's administration that was the way it was looking—Johnson would miss his best chance to get back at Charles Comiskey. The Old Roman's championship team would have been compromised, yes, but his business would still be intact, his position as an influential owner in opposition to Johnson still in place. Johnson burned with a determination to see the indicted players in the dock and to see them ultimately led away in shackles to Joliet, believing their shame would attach itself to Comiskey. Johnson may have seen his ultimate power over the game stripped away with the appointment of Judge Landis, but he remained president of the American League, with power over the American League purse. Beginning in February 1921, he would commit the full resources of the American League to aiding the prosecution of the Black Sox case. The case that came before Judge Hugo Friend in late June was fashioned not by the state's attorney's office but by Ban Johnson's.

In early March, with the newspapers rife with speculation that the case would never come to trial, Johnson hired retired Cook Country judge George Barrett (brother of American League attorney Charles Barrett) to assist the lead prosecutor, Assistant State's Attorney George Gorman. Barrett cost the American League $15,000. "It is a relief to know that someone has taken active charge and a keen interest in the prosecution of the indicted players," wrote Johnson.

In early April, Johnson and Barrett met with Gorman, the American League now acting as a full deputy of the Cook County state's attorney. What the prosecution case needed most, they determined, was testimony from one of more of the conspirators, someone who would roll over, define the scope of the plot and implicate the others. They determined their best witness would be Eddie Cicotte. It was time to "build some fires" around Cicotte, they said, have a private detective "hound" him until he agreed to cooperate. In contrast to the morning on which he had confessed six months before, however, Cicotte was now ably represented by counsel, a Detroit friend named Daniel Cassidy, and while Cassidy had entertained some discussion in the fall about Cicotte testifying, he had swiftly rejected the notion. Cicotte was now keeping a very low profile on his farm outside Detroit. He avoided most old acquaintances and all baseball people. Tigers owner Frank Navin, friendly with both Cicotte and his lawyer, apprised Johnson, "I cannot see how a detective would have a chance to get in touch with Cicotte."

Johnson was simultaneously looking at securing the testimony of failed fixer Sleepy Bill Burns, and he had much better luck there. Burns would ultimately become the state's star witness. Burns was hiding out in south Texas, and when he learned from Billy Maharg that Johnson wanted to talk to him, he skipped across the border to Mexico. But baseball-exec-turned-prosecutor Johnson, together with Billy Maharg and Jimmy Isaminger, boxer and sports-writer–turned–private investigators, hunted him down, at some considerable expense to the American League, and Johnson and prosecutor Crowe eventually turned him with the offer of immunity from prosecution and the chance to get even with the people who had left him busted back during the Series of 1919.

Maharg became Johnson's conduit to Burns. Johnson brought Maharg to Chicago, giving him a first-class railway ticket and $100 walking-around money, plus promising to compensate him for lost wages and make things right with his boss at a Ford plant in Philadelphia, and put him up in a Chicago hotel while they sent a flurry of telegrams and letters to Burns at various addresses in Texas and Mexico. When these yielded no response, it was agreed Maharg would go to Texas. He had hunted and fished with Burns there, knew his haunts, and was convinced he could find him. He had either one hell of an adventure in finding Burns or time and imagination enough to concoct one hell of an adventure. He would later tell his story to a newspaper reporter, describing starting on Burns's ranch in San Saba, then traveling north to a fishing cabin Burns kept on the Colorado. He found no Burns inside, but did find a rattlesnake. Maharg traveled next to a town called Milano, where a group of moonshiners mistook him for a revenue agent and drew their weapons. From Milano he drove his rented flivver down to San Antonio, where he spoke to a Burns brother-in-law, then west to Del Rio, then into Mexico, where he found Burns's brother, who pointed him to a fishing spot on the Devils River. There, as with Stanley and Livingstone in the Congo, he finally found Burns. "Why you old son of a gun," Burns greeted him. "I reckon it's sure a treat to see you again." Burns cooked his friend a dinner of fried bass and biscuits, and then Maharg told him why he had come. The pair talked until midnight while wolves howled in the distance.

Burns finally agreed to a meeting with Johnson in Del Rio, Texas. Johnson and Assistant State's Attorney John Tyrell traveled down, and brought Burns back to Chicago in May to talk to prosecutor Gorman. They found Burns "was not a talkative man, and requires a lot of coaching." But their coaching—and promise of immunity—was apparently successful; by the time Burns returned to Texas a week later, he was an enthusiastic participant.

Nonetheless, the folks in Chicago were still not sure. Burns stopped communicating with Johnson upon his return to Texas. He did stay in touch with his wife in Ohio, however, and she dutifully kept Johnson informed. "Probably his staying in a climate agreeable to health will have him in good shape when you call him," wrote Burns's wife to Johnson in late May. "I am sure he will cause you no anxiety in waiting for his presence. If he has not written, it is not because of his lack of interest or appreciation but simply because he is a poor letter writer." Johnson found his letters from Mrs. Burns—that was how she signed her letters, "Mrs. Wm. Burns"—a great comfort in a nervous time. "She is certainly a fine woman," said Johnson to Maharg. "How Big Bill ever captured her is a mystery to me."

None of this was being reported in the newspapers. When Burns was in Chicago, James Crusinberry of the *Tribune* recognized him on the street and followed him to Judge Barrett's office. When he inquired of Johnson and Barrett, they told him they knew nothing of it. Crowe took the same stance in the state's attorney's office. Jimmy Isaminger, meanwhile, now had the whole story and was frantic to write it; Johnson told him the time was "not opportune," and not likely to be anytime soon. "I do not think it would be wise to publish anything prior to the trial in regard to our hunt for Bill Burns through the state of Texas," he wrote to Isaminger in late May. "It might furnish information to the defense and work to our disadvantage." Isaminger was apparently not placated by Johnson's letter, for a day later Johnson was writing to Isaminger's boss at the *North American*. "In order to keep Burns beyond the reach of the lawyers for the defense we were obliged to 'put him away,' " wrote Johnson to John Eckel. "Just as soon as he is again in our possession I will have no objection to a full write-up of the chase through Texas to the Mexican border."

If Ban Johnson found any irony in being in partnership with the sort of baseball gamblers he had been publicly damning for the better part of two decades, it didn't show. Just eighteen months earlier, Burns and Maharg had been the men trying to fix the World Series. Now in his communications with the two men, Johnson was almost cloying in his flattery for what they were doing to help rid baseball of the gamblers who would corrupt it. "I appreciate immensely the good service you have rendered up to date in the matter of cleansing baseball," wrote Johnson to Maharg in early June. "If all of our witnesses are of your caliber, we would have no difficulty in securing convictions and cleansing the game."

By the time the trial began in late June, 1921, there was at least the façade of a great friendship between Johnson and the two ex-gamblers. Johnson's letters continued to offer warm praise to both men; Burns invited Johnson on a South Texas hunting and fishing trip when everything was over; Maharg invited him to tour the Ford plant where he worked the next time Johnson was in Philadelphia. Johnson enthusiastically accepted both offers, though, not surprisingly, neither trip apparently ever came to pass.

When the trial start date was announced, Johnson brought Burns, his wife, and Maharg back to Chicago, where they spent the better part of a month living the good life at American League expense. Johnson stashed them, under assumed names, first in a vacation lodge in Michigan's Upper Peninsula (where Burns, the ex-big leaguer, apparently played a couple of games for the hotel baseball team) and later, when their testimony was drawing closer, in the elegant Pfister Hotel in Milwaukee.

How much Ban Johnson spent in doing his investigative work for the Cook County state's attorney is anybody's guess, but it was likely more than the state's attorney's office spent on the case. Judge Barrett's retainer; salaries for private investigators following several dozen different threads in Chicago, St. Louis, Boston, and New York; and travel and living expenses for Burns and Maharg and a number of lesser witnesses—Johnson sent at least four witnesses to New York to try to get Abe Attell extradited, only to see their testimony blocked by Fallon's delays—probably easily exceeded $50,000 during the first six months of 1920. While this was unusual, none of it was illegal, and none of it was beyond his mandate as president of the American League. In December 1920, as the limits of the state's case were just beginning to show themselves, American League owners had approved $10,000 to investigate the Series-fixing scandal. Shortly thereafter, when it became evident that that was not going to be nearly enough, the league's board of directors—all Johnson loyalists—authorized "the expenditure by the president of the league of whatever further sum of money may be deemed necessary by him in the employment of counsel, a full and thorough investigation and in every other legitimate and proper manner in which the league may aid the State of Illinois in the investigation of the so-called World Series Scandal of 1919 and in the prosecution of the cases against ball players under indictment in connection with the World Series Scandal."

Doing the work of the state's attorney, Johnson may have also fancied himself as possessing some of the state's attorney's powers as well. As the trial testimony began in early July, he sent a letter to a number of baseball executives, players, writers, and others, advising them all, "Hold yourself in readiness to appear as a witness in the trial of the indicted White Sox players and gamblers in the World's Series of 1919."

The letter raised the ire of White Sox secretary Harry Grabiner, who responded swiftly and tartly. "I am curious to know how you procure the authority to order me to appear at any place or time, particularly in view of the fact that this is a proceeding by the State of Illinois," Grabiner wrote. "I am also curious to know why you evidence so much interest at the present time in view of the fact that you did nothing when you were first notified. Your position never fooled me for a moment, and I want you to understand that I do not need any advice from you as to what my actions should be at any given time."

Grabiner's letter helped Johnson—seldom a man to admit an error—understand that he had perhaps let his enthusiasm get the better of him here. "Possibly it would have been better to have had state's attorney office subpoena him," he admitted in a letter to Judge Barrett.

The criminal trial of seven ballplayers and four gamblers began on June 27, 1921, with Chicago in the midst of its hottest summer since record keeping began fifty years earlier.

While the prosecution's case was stronger than it had been before Johnson and the American League got involved, it still had problems. Eighteen men had been indicted by the two grand juries, but the weeks leading up to the start of trial saw that number shrink by six. There was quite literally no case against some of them, and extradition troubles with others. There was no direct evidence against Sport Sullivan. Only Lefty Williams's confession tied him in any way to the case, and there were questions as to whether any part of that confession would be admitted into evidence. Johnson tried for months, but had no better luck than the authorities in gathering any evidence against Sullivan, so prosecutors made no effort to extradite him for trial. It was the same with Rachael Brown, the defendant who never existed. The case was much better against Abe Attell—Bill Burns's testimony would directly link Attell to the plot—but thanks to the courtroom shenanigans of William Fallon, Attell was a free man, and Cook County prosecutors had simply given up the chase. "It simply means that Attell will not stand trial, and consequently there will be one less in the penitentiary when this case is finished," said George Gorman when a New York judge ruled that Attell would not be extradited. Gorman's statement made it clear that while charges were not dismissed—in a perfect world Sullivan, Attell, and Rachael Brown/Nat Evans would be prosecuted separately at a later time—this pragmatically amounted to a dismissal of the charges against the three men who may have been more directly involved than anyone else.

Hal Chase also escaped prosecution because of a botched extradition process. Chase had been defiant from the beginning. "If they want me, let 'em extradite me," he had said when the second indictments were handed up. He was indeed arrested in California, but Cook County state's attorneys so botched the paperwork—"virtual malpractice by the government"—that a judge set Chase loose, free from prosecution so long as he stayed out Illinois.

With Fred McMullin it was transportation troubles that kept him from standing trial with his teammates. The erstwhile utility man had money troubles, and trouble getting himself to Chicago for the trial. He arrived after the jury had been impaneled and, according to law, could not be tried by that jury. He was sent home, with the understanding that he would be tried at a later date.

Before jury impaneling began, St. Louis gamblers Carl Zork and Ben Franklin both claimed illness would prevent them from sitting through a trial at this time. Prosecutors produced an affidavit from a *Sporting News* writer—secured by Ban Johnson—who testified he had seen Zork walking the streets of St. Louis in recent days, looking hale and hearty. Zork was ordered to stand trial, but Johnson was unable to produce similar evidence on Franklin, and he was excused for trial at a later date.

Bill Burns had been present for jury impaneling, listening attentively, knowing the men chosen would not be determining his guilt or innocence. When testimony began, George Gorman announced that all charges against Burns had been dismissed and that he would testify for the state.

It had taken the better part of three weeks to impanel the jury; more than six hundred prospective jurors were questioned; one was excused because he was an ardent Cubs fans and defense lawyers felt that might him make too naturally hostile to anyone from the South Side White Sox. The final twelve were all white males, mostly working-class men with a professed indifference to baseball.

Presiding over the trial was Judge Hugo Friend, a Czech immigrant who would celebrate his thirty-ninth birthday during that first week of testimony. He was former track star at the University of Chicago, a hurdler and long jumper who had competed internationally for the United States in a multination "Olympic" meet in Athens back in 1906. Judge Friend had been on the bench for less than a year; he had been appointed by Governor Frank Lowden while the World Series story was before the grand jury the previous September. He would serve until his death at age eighty-three in 1966, and, as was the case with almost anyone who had had anything to do with the Black Sox story, his connection to the trial would lead his obituary.

The lead prosecutor was George Gorman, a former congressman with a quarter century's experience as a prosecutor. Gorman had been working exclusively on the case for nearly six months. He was assisted by Edward Prindiville, a former first assistant state's attorney now in private practice, tasked back to the state's attorney's office for this case.

Defense counsel comprised a virtual who's who of the Chicago bar. Best known were Benedict Short, representing Joe Jackson, Lefty Williams, and Eddie Cicotte, and Thomas Nash, representing Buck Weaver, Swede Risberg, and Happy Felsch. Chick Gandil was represented by James O'Brien and John Prystalski, recently established in private practice after years working as a team in the state's attorney's office, where they had sent more than a dozen murderers to the gallows. The Des Moines and St. Louis gamblers were likewise represented by an array of seasoned defense attorneys and former state's attorneys, including Henry Berger, suspected middleman in the disappearance of the confessions and immunity waivers a few months before.

Testimony began on Monday, July 18, with the temperature on the streets of Chicago at an official 94° and the temperature inside the Criminal Court Building on West Hubbard Street considerably hotter and sweatier. The press-room on the fourth floor—later made famous as the setting of *The Front Page*—was jammed with reporters from newspapers and news syndicates from around the country. The third-floor courtroom was filled with the curious, young men mostly, baseball fans in shirtsleeves and loosened ties, holding their hats—straw boaters and white straw panamas—on their laps throughout the proceedings.

Trials of any sort are always replete with stipulations, agreements between the two sides that information that is commonly understood need not be formally introduced into evidence. In this case, the prosecution asked for stipulation on the fact that the Chicago White Sox were an incorporated entity, owned by Charles Comiskey, which paid its employees—the ballplayers—a monthly or annual salary based upon the terms of mutually agreed-upon contracts. The defense agreed to no stipulations at all. They wanted Charles Comiskey on the witness stand, believing that he would not make a particularly sympathetic victim and that his presence might perhaps provide some theatrics. He was the first witness called.

The defense got their wish. After a placid direct examination in which Comiskey laid out the details of his career as a player, manager, and owner and introduced some dry boilerplate on the White Sox incorporation and business structure, Benedict Short scored points that were perhaps less legal than emotional, which was no doubt the point. Short wanted to show the working men on the jury that Charles Comiskey was a tough boss to work for. He tried to establish Comiskey's parsimony. "Isn't it a fact that you only paid your players $3 a day board?" he asked, a question that was objected to and the objection sustained. He then returned to Comiskey's days as a player, sought to cast him as opportunistic and selfish, and got the rise out of him he had no doubt been hoping for. "It is a fact, is it not," asked Short, "that you jumped from the Brotherhood to the National League in the early nineties?"

"It is not," thundered Comiskey, rising from his chair and shaking his first at Short. "Don't you dare to say that I ever jumped a contract. I never did that in my life. You can't get away with that with me.... You can't belittle me."

"Well, you are trying to belittle the ball players on trial," responded Short, whereupon Judge Friend reproved both men and told them to move on.

The preliminaries out of the way, the second day brought the start of Bill Burns's three days on the stand. Burns was a compelling witness and provided the trial's most dramatic moments. He was rakishly dressed; he had borrowed some money from Ban Johnson and had some clothes made while in Chicago in May, and he wore them to dramatic effect on the witness stand. The first day he sported a green checked suit, lavender shirt, and bow tie. Balding but still possessed of a trim, athlete's build, he sat comfortably in the witness chair. He sweated a bit in the suffocating courtroom, mopping his brow with a handkerchief frequently throughout his testimony. But little was made of this, for judge, jury, defendants, counsel, and reporters were wiping their brows with handkerchiefs too. He answered questions in a soft monotone that was at times barely audible; defense counsel asked Judge Friend repeatedly to request that Burns speak up. But though his voice was soft, the courtroom was quiet, and spectators leaned forward in their seats and strained to hear what the ex-ballplayer, would-be fixer, and reluctant-turned-eager state's witness had to say.

Under the direct examination of Gorman, he told the story that has become the basic narrative of the Black Sox story. Much of what Burns was saying had been reported in one form or another in the newspapers since the fix story had first broken ten months before. But this was the first time America had heard it from start to finish, and from someone who was involved. Burns told of meeting Cicotte and Gandil in New York in September, of approaching Rothstein and being rebuffed, of meeting Abe Attell through Hal Chase and being told Rothstein was now involved. He identified defendant David Zelcer as a man at Attell's side throughout the Series, a man he knew as Bennett.

He told of meeting the players before game one in Cincinnati, seven of them, all but Joe Jackson, and agreeing that Burns would give them $20,000 after each loss. He told of asking Attell after game one for the player's money and being told it was "all out on bets." He described the scene in Attell's room after game two, where a half dozen men were counting piles and suitcases full of cash, of asking again for the money owed the players—now $40,000—and being given $10,000 by Attell and told to take it or leave it.

He gave the $10,000 to Chick Gandil, he said, and was asked by Gandil whether the players were being double-crossed. He then told of how the players had double-crossed him, telling him they would lose game three and then leaving him broke when they won the game and Burns had all his money on the Reds. He told of how, even after he was broke, Attell kept on him to work the players with promises of more money, but that Gandil had told him after the third game that he was through with the fix. Finally, he told of how he came to be there, of how Ban Johnson and John Tyrell had come to Texas and persuaded him to testify.

On cross-examination, defense attorneys seized on Ban Johnson's role in bringing Burns to the stand, getting Burns to detail the scope of Johnson's largesse over the past months, and suggesting that Burns was somehow doing this to harm Johnson's enemy Charles Comiskey, who had also once been Burns's employer back in 1909, and had refused to pay Burns's friend Maharg the reward he had famously offered for information on the 1919 Series, after Maharg's *Philadelphia North American* story got the whole case started. Still, defense lawyers were unable to shake Burns's testimony in any major way. Burns was, if anything, cooler under cross-examination than he had been on direct testimony. Only Benedict Short managed to bruise him, showing him as a witness interested in more than simple justice.

"The players double-crossed you, didn't they?" Short asked.

"Yes."

"Well, you double-crossed them?"

"Not until they double-crossed me."

"Is that the reason for your testifying?"

"One of them."

"Then it is not for the purity of baseball?"

"Well, they double-crossed me, and I would have been the fall guy for the whole outfit."

"Do you think you are even with the boys now?"

"I am liable to be before I leave here."

Perhaps panicked by the effectiveness of the Burns testimony, the defense also now repeated a somewhat fabulous canard they had thrown out prior to trial—that Burns's confederate Billy Maharg was not actually Billy Maharg but George "Peaches" Graham, one-time catcher for the Braves, Cubs, and Phillies. Maharg, they claimed in support of their assertion, actually being "Graham" spelled backwards. Of all the bizarre claims surrounding the Black Sox story through the years, this is perhaps one of the most far-fetched. It was apparently just a defense sleight-of-hand, taken from the William Fallon (My client Abe Attell is not the indicted Abe Attell) playbook. There was a certain mad logic to it; if they could attach such clearly fantastic little pieces to Burns's story, perhaps jurors would also come to mistrust the central points of his story as well.

"I know Peaches Graham, but I am not he," said Billy Maharg on the stand a week later. Maharg was the prosecution's final witness, called on Wednesday, July 27. He echoed his friend's story of how the fix went down and their role in it. This allowed the prosecution to end their case on high note, with colorful, detailed testimony from another accomplice, after a period of dry testimony following Burns's headline-making turn on the stand. Much of the dryness concerned the admissibility of the stolen confessions of Cicotte, Jackson, and Williams. What might have been the trial's most dramatic moment—and the biggest triumph for the prosecution when they were ruled admissible—turned instead into a tedious slog through legal minutia that left jurors bored and distracted, according to newspaper reporters watching from the press row.

The central argument over the confessions' admissibility was whether or not they had been made willingly or with the understanding that the players would not be prosecuted if they came clean. Cicotte, Jackson, and Williams all took the stand, the only time any of the accused players testified at the trial. They testified with the jury excused, and their testimony was very narrow; it did not include any discussion of what they had actually confessed to. Instead it was limited to what Alfred Austrian, Judge Charles McDonald, and Assistant State's Attorney Hartley Replogle had told them prior to their entering the grand jury room. Judge Friend also heard from McDonald and Austrian before ruling the confessions were admissible, but only insofar as they pertained to the confessing men themselves. They could not be used to implicate any of the others, and had to be redacted before being read into the record. When they were read into the record by Edward Prindiville and John Tyrell, they were read as redacted. Thus the recitation of Cicotte's confession included the line "A few weeks before the World Series, I had a conversation with seven other ballplayers at the Ansonia Hotel, their names being Mr. Blank, Mr. Blank, Mr. Blank, Mr. Blank, Mr. Blank, Mr. Blank and Mr. Blank." The oppressive heat and stifling humidity in the courtroom only worsened the stupefying, disjointed flow of the redacted transcripts.

Outside the courtroom, Ban Johnson saved the day from being a total bore when, again speaking like a state's attorney, he leveled his guns at the New York gambler whose name had come up at trial more than anyone's in the courtroom. "I charge that Arnold Rothstein, New York gambler, paid $10,000 for the grand jury confessions of Edward Cicotte, Claude Williams and Joseph Jackson," he announced. "I charge that this money, brought to Chicago last fall by a representative of Rothstein, went to an attaché of the state's attorney's office under the Hoyne administration." Back in New York, Rothstein puffed and sputtered and threatened a libel suit he was never going to file.

When the prosecution rested its case, the defense made its requisite motions to have charges dismissed for lack of evidence. The state's attorneys agreed to the dismissal of the charges against the Levi brothers, against whom no evidence had been introduced. Judge Friend then all but acquitted Buck Weaver, Happy Felsch, and Carl Zork. "There has been so little evidence presented against these men that I doubt if I would allow a verdict of guilty to stand if it were brought in," he told the court, but, at the insistence of the prosecution, and since there had been some evidence introduced, he allowed the case against them to proceed.

Now, with the defense case ready, reporters and courtroom hangers-on expected great theatrics in the days ahead. Attorneys for the players had indicated throughout that all would take the stand in their own defense. But first, several of their 1919 teammates had been called as defense witnesses. Kid Gleason, Eddie Collins, Ray Schalk, Dickie Kerr, Shano Collins, Nemo Leibold, and relief pitcher Roy Wilkinson all took the stand, and all exchanged pleasant smiles and warm acknowledgments with their former mates as they made their way to and from the witness chair. Defense attorneys wanted them primarily as expert witnesses, manager and players apparently prepared to testify that nothing they saw during the 1919 Series would have led them to believe the accused had been playing anything less than their best. The prosecution objected to this line of questioning, and Judge Friend sustained the objections.

A second defense strategy was to use the players to discredit the testimony of Bill Burns. Gleason, Eddie Collins, Schalk, Kerr, and Wilkinson all testified that on the morning of the first game in Cincinnati, at roughly the hour Burns had testified he had been meeting with the players at the Sinton discussing the fix, the White Sox team, accused players included, were all at a pregame practice at Redland Field. The players thus couldn't have been meeting with Burns, the lawyers emphasized. "Then if Bill Burns said he saw these defendants in a room at the Sinton Hotel in the forenoon, he is not telling the truth?" Weaver attorney Thomas Nash asked Kid Gleason. The question was objected to and the objection sustained, but the point was made.

And then, with that, the defense rested. Two and a half days—twenty courtroom hours—were set aside for closing arguments. Edward Prindiville closed for the state. The crux of his argument was that three players had confessed, and the jury needed no more than that. The jury, he argued, need not convict the players; they had convicted themselves. Those confessions had led to the indictment of Bill Burns, and Burns's testimony in court had completed the circle. Prindiville spent most of his statement—which was split over two days, Saturday and Monday—reviewing the testimony and appealing to the jurors' sense of logic. As he closed, however, he very clearly was targeting their emotions.

"I say gentlemen that the evidence shows that a swindle and con game has been worked on the American people. The crime in this case warrants the most severe punishment of the law. The crime strikes at the heart of every red-blooded citizen and every kid who plays on a sand lot. This country is for sending criminals to the penitentiary, whether they are idols of the baseball diamond or gangsters guilty of robbery with a gun."

To listen to the defense summation was to be allowed a moment's confusion; for the defense attorneys all sounded like prosecutors, and the man they had on trial was Ban Johnson. One after another, they lambasted Johnson and dismissed the trial of their clients as being controlled not by the Cook County state's attorney but by a manipulative and vindictive Johnson for the purpose of destroying his enemy Charles Comiskey. "The state's attorneys have no more control over the prosecution than a bat boy over the direction of play at a World Series game," said Michael Ahern, associate counsel for Weaver, Felsch, and Risberg.

If O'Brien spelled out the what of the defense allegations regarding Johnson, Henry Berger, deputy counsel for Zork, delivered the why. "Byron Bancroft Johnson," he said sneeringly, "whose machinations of years finally have been successful. Johnson has had his revenge on Charles A. Comiskey and it has been sweet. [He] has tried for years to get that gray-haired owner of the Chicago club and he finally had got him. Posing as a hero who would clean up baseball, Ban Johnson has pulled the strings, the puppets have thrown the mud and an old score against Comiskey has been paid."

Thomas Nash addressed the how. "Johnson, with more power over baseball than the Russian Czar had over his subjects, sneaked into the grand jury room and gave his testimony in the dark, which he thought would ruin the players and Comiskey, but he was not man enough to come here in the daylight and testify. He hasn't enough red blood under his skin to do that."

A. Morgan Frumberg, counsel for Carl Zork, charged that Johnson had protected Rothstein, and by extension Sullivan, Attell, and Brown as well. "Why were these underpaid ballplayers, these penny-ante gamblers from Des Moines and St. Louis who bet a few nickels perhaps on the World Series, brought here to be the goats in the case? Ask the powers of baseball. Ask Ban Johnson."

Gandil attorney James O'Brien echoed Frumberg's allegation that Johnson was protecting Rothstein, because he wanted the world to believe that the 1919 World Series was a one-off aberration, and not part of a corrupt operation that he had been helpless to change.

Finally, Benedict Short, speaking last, called the players "galley slaves of a modern Rome, whose work brought wealth and fame to Johnson, the man who now was using them as a means of obtaining revenge on his enemy Comiskey." Short infuriated the prosecution, and brought futile objections, when he then told the jury that "it, the judge, and the defense counsel were the only factors in this case not under Ban Johnson's thumb."

State's attorney George Gorman's rebuttal summary made no attempt to address the fusillade the defense had fired at Johnson. He instead returned to the players' confessions, and tried to evoke sympathy for fans who had come to watch the White Sox in the 1919 Series. "They came to see a ball game," said Gorman. "But all they saw was a con game."

Closing arguments concluded at three o'clock on Tuesday, August 2. Later that evening, in his charge to the jury, Judge Friend explained that because the defendants had been charged with conspiracy to defraud Comiskey, the public, and others, a guilty verdict required that jurors must believe that the nine defendants had entered into a conspiracy where the intent was *specifically to defraud*, and not simply to throw baseball games. The charge was a good sign for the defense, and was vehemently objected to by the state. However effective Bill Burns may have been in convincing the jury of the players' complicity in game fixing, the complex notion of "conspiracy to defraud" never once came up in his, or anyone else's, testimony.

The jurors left just before eight o'clock in the evening to begin deliberations.

Two hours and forty-seven minutes later came three loud knocks on the back of the jury-room door, the signal that a verdict had been reached. It had taken just one ballot. The knocks startled, then electrified the people still in the courtroom, and the room's nervous anticipation heightened as everyone was forced to wait for Judge Friend, who had gone to the Cooper-Carlton Hotel, some ten miles from the courthouse. His trip back took an agonizing forty minutes.

Just past 11:30 p.m., Judge Friend returned to the bench, and the jury returned to the courtroom. The white noise of whispers, chair scraping, and paper shuffling fell silent as clerk Edward Myers read the first verdict: "We, the jury, find the defendant, Claude Williams, not guilty."

The courtroom erupted in noise, quieted enough for Myers to read the remaining eight not-guilty verdicts, and then erupted again, as though the White Sox had just scored in the winning runs in the bottom of the ninth in a come-from-behind victory. Despite the late hour, few had left the courthouse. So several hundred people were still gathered inside the courtroom and in the hallways outside when the verdicts were read. They whistled, shouted, and cheered and threw their hats and newspapers into the air. Somebody shouted, "Hooray for the Clean Sox!" The acquitted players slapped the backs of their lawyers and each other. Eddie Cicotte fought his way to the jury box and shook the foreman's hand. "Thanks," he shouted. "I knew you'd do it." Buck Weaver and Swede Risberg grabbed each other's arms and shouted their joy. The jurors were cheering as loudly as anyone else. Bailiffs shouted for order, but stopped when they noticed the broad smile on the face of Hugo Friend, who in the last seconds of quiet had thanked the jury and told them he believed it was a just verdict. Flashbulbs flashed. Reporters shouted out for comments, but the players mostly demurred. "Talk, did you say?" said Cicotte. "I talked in this building once before. Never again."

As the players left the courtroom, the shouting fans lifted them to their shoulders and carried them out into the warm Chicago midnight. On the courthouse steps, players, lawyers, and jurors posed for a photo. From the courthouse both jurors and players repaired to a nearby Italian restaurant, where they celebrated deep into the morning.

It would be the final time the players would hear the cheers and feel the love of the public. The morning after the jury's verdict, before some of the celebrating players had probably even slept it off, certainly before most of America had fully absorbed the news of the acquittal, baseball's new commissioner, who had followed the trial without comment, spoke now with certitude and a simple but chilling eloquence.

"Regardless of the verdict of juries," said Landis, "no player that throws a ball game; no player that undertakes or promises to throw a ball game; no player that sits in conference with a bunch of crooked players and gamblers where the ways and means of throwing games are planned and discussed and does not promptly tell his club about it, will ever play professional baseball."

The saga of the Black Sox and their sordid 1919 World Series, it seemed, was finally over. In reality, it was just beginning.

THIRTEEN

Timeless Joe

The Black Sox scandal has made Joe Jackson an American folk hero in a way a quiet conclusion to his career never would have. Had he played out his career without incident, he would have been a very early inductee into the Hall of Fame, likely one of the first twenty men elected, perhaps a member of the very first class in 1936, and certainly a member of the second or third, voted in no later than 1937 or 1938. And he would stand in history together with his peers: contemporaries like Walter Johnson, Rogers Hornsby, George Sisler, Tris Speaker, Nap Lajoie, and his White Sox teammate Eddie Collins—Cooperstown immortals all, and men remembered today by only the keenest of baseball historians.

Instead, Shoeless Joe has woven himself into the fabric of American culture as few ever do. Who, from Joe Jackson's time in history, survives in the American psyche with quite the same persistence? Politicians? Only Teddy Roosevelt. Scientists? Einstein and Edison, maybe. Music? Irving Berlin. Captains of industry? Rockefeller, Morgan, Carnegie, and Vanderbilt are still resonant names, but they stand clearly defined only on the pages of schoolbooks; in the popular imagination they've blended together like the layers of a parfait. Literature? Mark Twain was earlier, and Hemingway came later. People still read Dreiser and Edith Wharton, but does anybody still talk about them? Soldiers? We've pretty much forgotten Black Jack Pershing and Sergeant York. Criminals? Well, there's Al Capone.

Copyright.
BURKE+ATWELL.

Ban Johnson early in his career, when he and Charles Comiskey were the best of friends. By 1919, they were the bitterest of foes, and their enmity for one another would influence the unraveling of the Series fix and cover-up. Courtesy of the National Baseball Hall of Fame Library, Cooperstown, NY.

Charles Comiskey, at the players' criminal trial in 1921. He tried for nearly a year to cover-up what he had learned of the Series fix, but when the story came out in September 1920, he and his attorney hand-delivered Eddie Cicotte and Joe Jackson, and their confessions, to the Cook County grand jury. Courtesy of the National Baseball Hall of Fame Library, Cooperstown, NY.

Harry Grabiner, Charles Comiskey's trusted team secretary, whose diary told of his boss's efforts to make Judge Landis commissioner. Their actions were motivated less by a desire to clean up the game than a wish to wrest power from Comiskey's rival Ban Johnson. Courtesy of the National Baseball Hall of Fame Library, Cooperstown, NY.

Charles Comiskey's attorney, Alfred Austrian. A politically well connected and skilled back-channel lawyer, no one was more central to the cover-up, or to the way the case against the players would eventually unfold before the grand jury. Photo courtesy of the Chicago History Museum.

Consummate game-fixer Hal Chase, early in his career with the New York Highlanders. He might have become one of the greatest who ever lived, but he became
instead the poster child for crooked baseball in the years leading up to 1919. Courtesy
of the National Baseball Hall of Fame Library, Cooperstown, NY.

New York gambler and gangster Arnold Rothstein financed the fix with less than $100,000 and reportedly won more than $300,000 betting on the Reds. The players never knew Rothstein was behind the plot, and he was never indicted. Photo by Jack Benton/Getty Images.

Boston gambler Sport Sullivan was Arnold Rothstein's go-between with the players. Courtesy of Bruce Allardice.

Rothstein factotum Abe Attell when he was featherweight champion of the world, 1906–1912. Courtesy of the National Baseball Hall of Fame Library, Cooperstown, NY.

The defendants are all smiles at their criminal trial in 1921, perhaps sensing that things were going their way. Seated (L to R), Chick Gandil, Lefty Williams, Swede Risberg, Eddie Cicotte, Buck Weaver, Joe Jackson, and Weaver's attorney, Thomas Nash. Standing are James O'Brien, attorney for Chick Gandil (2nd from left), Max Luster, attorney for gamblers David Zelcer and Ben and Lou Levi (2nd from right), and two unidentified men. Chicago Daily News negatives collection, Chicago History Museum.

Following the Black Sox players' acquittal on criminal charges, "regardless of the verdicts of juries," new commissioner Judge Kenesaw Mountain Landis banned them from baseball for life. Courtesy of the National Baseball Hall of Fame Library, Cooperstown, NY.

That's a pretty singular collection of American celebrity. But for name recognition, and the ability to start a conversation, Shoeless Joe is right there with them.

What baseball player transcends the game more than Joe Jackson? Babe Ruth and Jackie Robinson, of course. But Ty Cobb? Joe DiMaggio? Probably not. And nobody else even enters the conversation.

But Babe Ruth was the athletic hero incarnate, the man-child delivered unto a nation thirsting for a hero of not only other-worldly skills—*sixty home runs?*— but also that outsized, insouciant personality—*Why shouldn't I make more money than the president? I had a better year!* After the Black Sox scandal, Babe Ruth made it all right for Americans to cheer a baseball player again. He returned some of the innocence that was lost in 1919. And if reality is a little more complicated than that, Babe Ruth was still baseball's first transcendent figure, and he has never been eclipsed.

Jackie Robinson, meanwhile, did nothing less than nudge a nation into finally showing that black and white America not only could but would live as one, a man whose success on the baseball field made inevitable the coming of *Brown v. Board of Education* and the sea-change civil rights gains of the fifties and sixties.

Jackson's place in this greater pantheon is more problematic, and far more visceral. He fires the emotions in different ways for different people. Some feel profound sympathy for a man they believe has been cruelly damned for all eternity for a pardonable venial sin. Others hold no sympathy at all for a man who betrayed a public that worshipped him and felt remorse only when he was caught and punished.

Yet Americans—consciously and subconsciously—identify with Jackson's story. While few possess the skills that can earn a stadium's applause, and will never know the exhilarations, and burdens, of hearing the crowd's applause, like Jackson we are all human, with virtues and flaws existing side by side and sometimes in conflict. And we wonder: How might I be judged if scrutinized and dissected like Jackson?

Jackson, the great player brought low, is perhaps the most human of all baseball heroes. His story is a cautionary tale, revealing just how capricious the judgment of justice, perception, and history.

There is no question that Joe Jackson is guilty of the charges that got him thrown out of baseball. By his own admission, he took the gamblers' money, and he kept the guilty knowledge of the fix to himself. And while there is legitimate doubt about whether he ever agreed to participate, or whether he just stopped refusing to participate, he was certainly aware that he was involved. After the Series began, he inquired daily about the missing payoff money.

There has been, of course, an enormous amount of debate as to whether or not this guilt should have forced him out of baseball. He did nothing to cause the White Sox to lose the 1919 World Series. He took part in no group conversations on the fix; Lefty Williams acted as his surrogate there, possibly without his knowledge or approval. There is convincing evidence and compelling argument that at the very least Jackson was less guilty than the rest. Also, he had wanted to come clean, and Comiskey had stopped him, because a confession at that particular moment would not have served the ball club's needs. Which carries the greater weight here, initial intent or final act? His legacy is deeply paradoxical.

Jackson's story has kept the Black Sox story alive for nearly a century. Had it involved merely the other seven, it would have made headlines during its moment, surely, but it would have held limited fascination for history, no more compelling than the nineteenth-century game-fixing scandals of the Player's Association and the Louisville Grays. Jackson gives the Black Sox staying power and greater—indeed timeless—resonance. He is a figure of both mystery and sympathy, forever a symbol of human frailty and temptation and being caught in a dilemma only partially of one's own making, from which there is no easy way out, maybe no way out at all.

His story as it lives today is biblical in a way. We sit in judgment; do we loose this man's sins or hold them bound?

Joe Jackson was a simple man, but hardly the ignorant rube portrayed in the sports-page caricatures of his day. He never played barefoot because he couldn't afford shoes, or because he was unused to shoes, having grown up without them, as many newspaper fantasies had it through the years. He did once play a couple of innings of one game without shoes, because a new pair had left his feet blistered. This happened while playing in Greenville, South Carolina, either in the city's Textile League or for the Greenville Spinners during his first year of organized ball in 1908. He took at least one at-bat in his stocking feet, either tripled or homered, depending upon the account being rendered, and when he arrived at, or passed, third base, a fan was alleged to have shouted: "You shoeless son of a gun, you!" Carter "Scoop" Latimer of the *Greenville News*, himself then just a teenage reporter, overheard (or invented) the shout, and Joe Jackson was forever after "Shoeless Joe." It was a nickname befitting humble rural roots and an uncomplicated personality.

By that point in his young career, Jackson was already fashioning a baseball reputation deserving of a memorable nickname. Baseball had been his deliverance from an otherwise Dickensian boyhood. He was born in Brandon, a mill town just outside Greenville, in July 1889.*

The oldest of eight children, he had not a day's schooling his entire life. By six, when he might have been in the first grade, he was sweeping floors in a mill in Brandon. By thirteen he was working twelve-hour days in the mill alongside his father. What daylight hours were not spent on the cotton-mill floor were spent on the ball field. He was a big kid; by sixteen he was six foot two and gangly, not yet anywhere near his major league weight of 185 pounds. Still, he already had those Popeye forearms and hands the size of skillets, and, gangly teenager or not, he could hit a baseball half again as far as anybody else in town and throw it like it had been shot from a cannon.

He was playing for the Brandon Mills baseball team by the time he was thirteen. There were thirteen mills ringing Greenville, and Saturday afternoon games in the Textile League would attract crowds of several hundred to a couple thousand or more, and the players became objects of great affection and celebrity in their local mill communities. And nobody was more celebrated than the marvelously gifted teenager from Brandon. "Joe's Saturday specials"—line drive home runs that were still rising when they sailed over the outfielders' heads—became the talk of Brandon, and every time he hit one, his younger brothers would scramble up into the stands to pass the hat so that the Brandon fans might show their gratitude. There were times the fans showed their gratitude to the tune of $10 or so, as much as a full week's wages at the mill. Such a phenomenon was Jackson that he was recruited away from Brandon Mills by the rival Victor Mills team, with the promise of a softer job in the mill and time off to practice.

Greenville got its own team in organized baseball in 1908, and Jackson was one of the first players signed, to a contract paying him a princely $75 a month. Pros or semipros, it was all the same to Jackson; he had a great year, batting over .350 to lead the Carolina Association in hitting. On an off day in July he married his Greenville sweetheart, Katie Wynn—he was nineteen, she fifteen. And in August, he got the news that the Philadelphia Athletics had bought his contract. He was going to the big leagues, as soon as the Carolina Association season was over.

---

* Jackson's birth year has been variously reported as 1887, 1888, and 1889. *The Baseball Encyclopedia* uses 1889. His age in newspaper reports early in his career is also consistent with an 1889 birth date.

The problem was that he didn't want to. He was terrified of leaving home, of being away from his parents and his new bride, and he only got on the train after his Greenville manager, Tommy Stouch, was hired by Athletics manager Connie Mack to make sure the reluctant rookie made it to Philadelphia. Stouch and Jackson got as far as Charlotte, a hundred miles from Greenville, when Jackson's panic got the better of him. When the train stopped at the Charlotte station, Jackson got off, without telling Stouch, and caught the next train back to South Carolina. Back home, he exhibited no interest in going to Philadelphia. Mack sent injured outfielder Socks Seybold, who had formed a bond with Jackson when he had scouted him earlier in the year. Seybold succeeded where Stouch had failed in getting Jackson to Philadelphia. But neither Seybold nor Mack could make Jackson comfortable in the big, strange, northern city.

The newspapers had made him a celebrity of the first order well in advance of his arrival. He came bearing an outsized reputation, as well as his personal bat, handcrafted by a Greenville woodsmith, stained black by rubbed-in tobacco juice, wrapped carefully and lovingly in cloth for the trip, and nicknamed "Black Betsy." In his first big league game against Cleveland, Jackson and Black Betsy singled in his first at-bat to drive in a run. He had no more hits, but hit the ball hard twice more that day, made an over-the-shoulder catch back by the center-field flagpole, uncorked a couple of strong throws from the outfield, and altogether impressed the writers, who made him the focal point of their stories. "Jackson looked extremely good in his first game, and as if he didn't possess a single weakness: good at bat, good on fly balls, good on the bases and fast on his feet," wrote one.

Cleveland left town after that game, and Ty Cobb and the Tigers came in. Newspaper stories were full of anticipation, as Jackson would now be matched against the player to whom he was most often being compared. Two days of rain made the hyperbole particularly heavy, as the writers had nothing else to write. Two days of rain meant that Jackson had two days away from the ballpark, the only place he might possibly have felt comfortable in the large, unwelcoming city.

Major league clubhouses could be cruel places in the early years of the game. Every rookie was a threat to a veteran's job, and they were hazed and bullied unmercifully; every rookie who cracked and went back to the bushes was another who wouldn't be taking somebody's job. Never mind what that rookie might bring to the lineup; self-preservation nearly always trumped team chemistry in this hardscrabble world. When the rookie was particularly naïve and vulnerable, or particularly celebrated—and Jackson was all of these—the abuse could be unrelenting and brutal. Years after the fact, Jackson confided to a friend that in those first days in Philadelphia his Athletics teammates had made him feel as bad as he had ever felt in his life. They mocked his illiteracy and his country-bumpkin ignorance. In their most famous prank, they convinced him to drink the water from the dining-table finger bowl, then laughed loudly and derisively as he left the hotel dining room in shame.

Before the rains had cleared and Jackson could square off against Ty Cobb, he was back on a train for Greenville. This time he stayed ten days, as newspapers reported that he had left because he was afraid of life in the big city—true—and afraid of facing Ty Cobb on the ball field—certainly not true. The newspapers flat-out called him a coward, an unfair pejorative that would dog him for years. Under threat of suspension from Connie Mack, and at the urging of his mother, Jackson returned to the Athletics on September 7. He stayed less than a week, his vulnerability exacerbating his teammates' insensitivity. After going 0 for 9 in a double-header against Washington, he was once again back on the train to Greenville. And this time he wouldn't budge. Mack reluctantly suspended him. The local paper reported, "JOE JACKSON HAS BEEN SUSPENDED BY MACK: BRANDON BOY CAN NEVER PLAY ORGANIZED BALL AGAIN."

Like so many newspaper headlines of the day, that overstated the situation. Jackson reported to spring training in 1909 and showed well, playing together with a team of rookies that included Eddie Collins, Frank Baker, Stuffy McInnis, and Jack Barry, players that would form the corps of the Athletics' championship teams of the next half decade. But while Jackson had shown as well as any of them, and at nineteen going on twenty was probably physically ready for the big leagues, it would take two more years of playing in the South before he was emotionally ready for his big league career to take root. Mack tried to nurture the young, insecure prodigy. He offered to hire an off-season tutor to teach Jackson to read and write. Jackson declined. "It don't take no school stuff to help a fella play ball," he said.

What did help a fella play ball—at least a deer-in-the-headlights player like Jackson—was to play it among friends, and for Jackson that meant playing in the South. According to the Jackson legend, the Athletics were paused at a Reading, Pennsylvania, train station at the end of spring training when Jackson caught sight of a line of milk cans on the platform, their southern-city destination labels in plain view. "I wish you'd put a red tag on me and ship me along with the milk cans down South," Jackson supposedly told Mack, which is how he ended up playing the 1909 season with Savannah of the South Atlantic League. That story was first told by Fred Lieb, as much a legend in the newspaper game as Jackson was in his game. It made for wonderful newspaper copy when Jackson became a star, and a wonderful historical insight later still when Jackson became the subject of histories and biographies. Neither Lieb nor apparently anyone else ever once questioned how the illiterate Jackson was able to read the milk labels to know they were headed south. As a movie newspaperman once noted: "When the legend becomes fact, print the legend."

Jackson led the Sally League in hitting in 1909 with a .358 average, and had five hits in seventeen at-bats when called up to Philadelphia in September. Though Katie Jackson came with him to Philadelphia this time, her support could not penetrate the dugout; the taunts of his teammates continued, and Jackson continued to be uncomfortable in their presence. "My players didn't seem to like him," Mack admitted years later. In 1910, still hoping to buy some time to find a way to make Jackson comfortable in Philadelphia, Mack assigned Jackson's contract to the New Orleans Pelicans of the Southern League, where Jackson again flourished, batting .354 and winning his third batting title in as many minor league seasons. The Pelicans had a close working relationship with the Cleveland Indians—still known then as the Naps, after their captain Napoleon Lajoie—and played a number of spring training games against the big league club. Cleveland management came away very impressed with the young outfielder on loan from Philadelphia, and team owner Charles Somers began asking Connie Mack what he would take to trade Jackson to Cleveland. In midsummer Mack relented, trading Jackson for outfielder Briscoe Lord, a player forgotten to history, to be sure, but a steady major leaguer at the time, who would hit .278 for the Athletics that summer and help them win the 1910 pennant.

Whether it was because Jackson was now two years older or because Cleveland had a wholly different zeitgeist than Philadelphia, Jackson came to Cleveland and immediately became one of the game's biggest stars. He batted .387 in twenty games in 1910 and hit .408 in his first full season in the big leagues in 1911, then .395 and .373, before falling to .338 in 1914. He never won a major league batting title; it was his misfortune to play in the time of Ty Cobb. The year Jackson hit .408, Cobb posted a career-best .420 to win the fifth of his eventual twelve batting titles. Jackson's lifetime average of .356 is third all-time, trailing only Cobb's .367 and Rogers Hornsby's .358. Jackson was the original five-tool player. In the dead-ball era, his career slugging average was .518; he was a speedy and intuitive base runner, and a gazelle in the outfield with that cannon for an arm.

He was happy and comfortable in Cleveland. Home, and frequently away as well, Katie Jackson was a regular at the ballpark, always sitting in the last row of the grandstand, directly behind home plate. The newspapers took notice. At home, however the game might be unfolding, she would always leave at the end of the seventh inning, so that supper would be on the table when Joe walked home to the apartment they shared in the shadow of League Park.

Charles Somers treated his players well, and unlike in Philadelphia, Jackson was accepted and well liked by his teammates. He was never as happy in his major league life as he was during his four and a half years in Cleveland. Nevertheless, the most gifted of ballplayers cannot make a team a winner if he is surrounded by clods, and so it was with Jackson in Cleveland. After a third-place finish in 1913, the Indians tumbled into the American League cellar in 1914, losing 102 games. They would lose ninety-five more in 1915, and by midseason the Cleveland fans had lost interest, and the Indians' balance sheet was as troubled as its won-loss record. The team's finances were placed in the hands of receivers, and owner Charles Somers was forced to sell his liquid assets to save his business. His most valuable liquid asset was Jackson's contract, which went to the White Sox in August. Technically it was a trade; the Indians received three forgettable players in return. But the key to the deal was the large check that Comiskey sent Somers's way, the amount never revealed but reported at the time to be somewhere between $15,000 and $31,500.

Happy though he had been in Cleveland, Jackson was glad to be going to Chicago. To begin with, the White Sox were a wealthy franchise, and Jackson had every reason to hope his salary might improve in Chicago, a misreading of Charles Comiskey, who could be generous when it suited him and earned him headlines, and cheap when no one was looking, which was most of the time. Comiskey had made headlines when he spent $50,000 to acquire Eddie Collins from the Athletics prior to the start of the 1915 season and signed him to a five-year contract at $15,000 per year. He was just as proud of his acquisition of Joe Jackson, calling him "the best straightaway hitter in the game," and boasting to the newspapers that he was paying his new outfielder a $10,000 salary, a bald-faced lie; Jackson's salary was $6,000 per year from 1915 to 1919.

Beyond the hope for more money, Jackson had sound baseball reasons to welcome the move to the White Sox, a team on the cusp of moving into the ranks of the American League elite. In addition to Collins and Jackson, Comiskey had bought the minor league contracts of Happy Felsch, Buck Weaver, and Lefty Williams. The newspapers were saying throughout 1915 that Comiskey was in the midst of assembling the best team money could buy. It would take a couple of seasons for the Sox to prove the prophecy correct, but they ultimately would, and Jackson was one of the main reasons why. His stats slipped a bit from his Cleveland years, but not so much that anyone noticed. He remained among the league leaders every year in batting average, hits, runs batted in, and runs scored.

Chicago marked a transition in Jackson's life. He was no longer the country bumpkin; quite the opposite, he had turned into a big-city dandy. He had his teeth fixed. He developed an affinity for bespoke suits and thirty-dollar pink silk shirts, which he often wore with patent-leather shoes from an extensive collection of showy, expensive footwear. It was almost as if he was saying to the world: "Shoeless? Hardly." He could be seen behind the wheel of a new Oldsmobile, both on the streets of the South Side and in the ads in newspapers and magazines, where Jackson endorsed the Olds. He did not, however, become completely citified. When he traveled, he always brought along a jug of corn liquor.

He was a magnet for kids. The young boys of the South Side would seek him out, and he them. Boys would gather as he left Comiskey Park and scramble to carry his bats. Or he would stop by a sandlot with a baseball he'd taken from the clubhouse and offer to have a catch, and sometimes take a swing or two with the young boys.

But among the older lads, his teammates on the White Sox, Jackson remained very much a loner. He roomed with Lefty Williams on the road, and sometimes the two players would socialize together with their wives in Chicago. But in a clubhouse filled with cliques, jealousies, and mistrust, Jackson coped with the interpersonal dysfunction by withdrawing. His clique was, as always, a clique of two, himself and his wife, Katie.

During his time in Chicago, Jackson admitted to his wife and a few close friends that some of the fun had gone out of the game. He and Katie began to save and invest their money. They bought a home for Joe's parents in Greenville, and after the 1916 season they bought an elegant waterfront home for themselves in Savannah. The city had charmed the couple ever since Joe's minor league season there in 1909, and it would remain their home for more than fifteen years.

Joe's first business venture had been a vaudeville show called *Joe Jackson's Baseball Girls*, with which he toured in the offseason. The show made him some money but almost cost him his marriage. There were rumors in the winter of 1915 that Jackson was involved with one of the girls from the show, rumors with enough credibility to cause Katie Jackson to consult a divorce attorney. The marriage—from all accounts a forty-three-year love story—survived that single rough patch, and Jackson's subsequent investments were more suited to domestic tranquility. He invested in pool halls in Chicago and Greenville, as well as a farm, and later a liquor store, in Greenville. Most lucratively, and most enduringly, he opened a dry-cleaning and valet business in Savannah after he and Katie had bought their home there. Jackson gave his wife credit for his investments. "I've been blessed with a good banker," he said in 1949, "my wife. Handing the money to her was just like putting it in the bank."

But it was Jackson who worked the businesses, managed a dozen or so people in Savannah, dealt with the public, and saw the business through to profitability. Newspaper stories in the later years of his life—always given to exaggeration when it came to Jackson—reported that his investments and business had made him a millionaire. That was far from true. Nonetheless, by the end of his playing career, he was making at least as much money from his business investments as he was from his baseball salary. And when the end of that baseball career came so suddenly in the fall of 1920, the unschooled, unlettered, so often ridiculed Joe Jackson was far better positioned than any of his Black Sox brothers to make a living in the life that would come after.

After the trial verdict, Jackson returned to Savannah and the dry-cleaning and valet businesses. During baseball season, however, the businesses were mostly Katie Jackson's responsibilities, for Joe continued the peripatetic life of a baseball player. He played ball until he was in his late forties, all over the country, for a game or two here and there, maybe for a full season. He often played under assumed names in the early years, right after the banishment, yet word would get around Joe Jackson was scheduled to play, and grandstands and foul lines would be packed with fans. By the 1930s he was playing and coaching under his own name, mostly in semipro leagues in Georgia and South Carolina, where the crowds had ebbed and he was playing for the joy and the memories.

In 1933, he sold his business in Savannah, and he and Katie moved back to Greenville. They built a pleasant brick bungalow in West Greenville, and Joe opened a liquor store. There he lived out his years among his people, buying ice cream cones for the young boys who would stop by his home for some stories and some tips on hitting, enjoying a wide and loyal circle of friends who never asked about Chicago and 1919.

Now and again, others would ask. And Jackson's story as always the same— he was an innocent man. Recovering from a heart attack in the summer of 1942, Jackson gave a lengthy interview to the *Sporting News*. The writer was Scoop Latimer of the *Greenville News*, Jackson's original Boswell, the man who had given him the "Shoeless Joe" moniker back when only Greenville had heard of either of them. The result was a flattering page-one story that was said to have earned *Sporting News* editor Taylor Spink an upbraiding from Commissioner Landis, who was upset that one of baseball's outcasts was being celebrated so by the "Bible of Baseball." The story was heavy on atmosphere; Latimer describes trophies, mementos, and scrapbooks from a long career; shows Jackson surrounded by those neighborhood boys seeking advice on hitting; and lets Jackson summon memories of a certain home run off Walter Johnson and talk of his admiration for players like Eddie Collins and Ty Cobb. It is short on any detail on 1919. In a 3,500-word story, Jackson and Latimer spend fewer than three hundred words talking about the Black Sox, and all of that is given over to Jackson's second newspaper denial of the say-it-ain't-so exchange, and another assertion of his innocence. "I think my record in the 1919 World's Series will stand up against that of any man in that Series or any other World's Series in all history," he said, pointing to his acquittal in the criminal trial as further evidence of his innocence.

"If I had been guilty of 'laying down' in the Series, I wouldn't be so successful today," he continued. "For I'm a great believer in retribution. I have made a lot more money since being out of baseball than when I was in it. And I have this consolation—the Good Lord knows I am innocent of any wrong-doing."

Latimer didn't press Jackson with any hard questions. Neither did Atlanta writer Furman Bisher, who ghosted a *Sport* magazine article that appeared under Jackson's name in October 1949, the thirtieth anniversary of the Black Sox Series. It is unclear how many of the facts in the stories in the *Sport* article were Jackson's memories and how many were stories Bisher had unearthed, but what is clear is that the article was never fact-checked the way a modern magazine article would be. There are facts presented for the first time—Jackson's claim that he went to Comiskey the night before the Series began and begged him to keep him out of the lineup—that have since become a part of the Black Sox legend but have been neither verified nor recorded anywhere else in the voluminous Black Sox history. Jackson and Bisher get some facts wrong, such as the name of the judge in the criminal trial, and there are smaller inconsistencies with history, too. But overall the voice that emerges from the piece is one of dignity and pride, bereft of bitterness, rancor, or the wish to blame others for what had befallen him. Joe Jackson came across as a sympathetic figure, deserving to have his life judged on more than simply the events of 1919.

And people were starting to do that. One springtime in the late 1940s, Ty Cobb and sportswriter Grantland Rice went up to Greenville just after the Masters Tournament in Augusta, about a hundred miles away. The two men arrived unannounced at Jackson's liquor store and found him behind the counter. A flicker of recognition crossed Jackson's face, quickly suppressed when it wasn't returned. Cobb rummaged about the store and finally approached the counter with a bottle of whiskey. No one had said a word.

"Don't you know me, Joe?" Cobb finally blurted.

"I know you," Jackson replied, "but I wasn't sure you wanted to speak to me. A lot of them don't."

The three men talked of old times after that, the subject of 1919 apparently not coming up. Before he left, Cobb told Jackson: "Joe, you had the most natural ability, the greatest swing I ever saw." Of course the vainglorious Cobb couldn't leave it at that. Following Jackson's death in 1951, he backhanded the compliment, telling Arthur Daley of the *New York Times*, "I used my brain to become a great hitter. I studied the art scientifically. Jackson just swung. If he had had my knowledge, his average would have been phenomenal."

Rice, the syndicated columnist with an enormous national influence, had been one of the Black Sox players' shrillest critics back when the scandal first broke. Perhaps still unsure of his feelings on Jackson and his legacy, he didn't write about the visit until much later, when he was composing his memoirs in 1954. Rice's reticence is telling of the overall attitude toward Jackson and the other Black Sox at this point in the story. A quarter century was sufficient time to begin reflecting and reconsidering what had happened; it was not sufficient time for some to begin forgiving. It was a cautious dance that the press and the public did in those last years of Jackson's life. The unbridled scorn had softened, surely, but the public affection was not yet there.

Still, there were efforts to rehabilitate Jackson's reputation in the last years of his life. In February 1951, the South Carolina legislature passed a resolution calling upon the commissioner of baseball to "reinstate Shoeless Joe Jackson as a member in good standing in professional baseball." The petition made its way to the desk of Commissioner Albert "Happy" Chandler, where he ignored it, thus establishing a precedent for Jackson petitions coming before the commissioner of baseball.

In the summer of 1951, the Cleveland Indians, celebrating their fiftieth anniversary and the fiftieth anniversary of the American League, reached out to their fans for votes to name the best players at each position over the team's first half century. The winners would be the first inductees into the Cleveland Indians Hall of Fame. The first ballot was missing Jackson's name, and though Jackson had left Cleveland thirty-five years before, the fans immediately noticed its absence. After a number of complaints and write-in votes for Jackson, the team reprinted the ballot, this time with Jackson's name; he was an overwhelming winner. But while his support was broad and deep-seated, it was not universal. At the induction ceremony in Cleveland in September, which Jackson could not attend because of illness, a handful of newspaper articles and letters to the editor decried the team for honoring a man of "impugned baseball integrity."

If the honor comforted Jackson, the residual criticism that came with it wounded him even more. When the Indians arranged an alternate tribute for Jackson—they would present him with the gold clock representative of his place in the Cleveland Hall of Fame during an appearance on the Ed Sullivan show in New York in December of 1951—Jackson refused to go. It would give his critics another news hook for again bringing up his past, he felt, and he lacked the strength and will to face that again. But Katie Jackson and Joe's brothers, sisters, and friends all pressured him to accept. It would be a chance to state his case and clear his name before a national television audience, they argued. Jackson finally relented and agreed to do the show. His health still frail from his recent heart attack, he would travel in the company of his doctor and, of course, Katie. The appearance was set for Sunday December 16. But on Wednesday, December 5, at ten in the evening, Joe Jackson, in failing health since his first heart attack seven years before, suffered another heart attack and died in the bedroom of his West Greenville home. He was sixty-two. He was the first of the Black Sox players to die.

His legacy upon his death, at least as seen through the prism of the newspaper obits, was uncomplicated. Though most stories acknowledged Jackson's lifelong claim of innocence, the headlines all trumpeted that he was one of the eight White Sox players banished from the game for throwing the 1919 World Series. The ensuring decades have proven it's not that simple.

Jackson's death marked the beginning of a slow but sure transition from man to myth. A portion of the credit for his extraordinary afterlife goes to a pair of gifted novelists, but by and large there have been no powerful and influential voices leading the charge, no baseball officials, no congressmen or senators, no Jackson family members. It has been a grass-roots campaign, carried out mostly by ordinary people, with no tangible connection to Jackson—a gas station owner from Pennsylvania whose petition drive to get Joe Jackson into the Hall of Fame gathered tens of thousands of signatures and found its way to Bud Selig's desk; a college IT guy who started the Shoeless Joe Jackson Virtual Hall of Fame, a comprehensive, engaging, many-layered and ever-growing website on all things Joe Jackson; a Greenville, South Carolina, city employee, who answered the question "What have you got in Greenville about Shoeless Joe Jackson?" enough times to finally want to do something about it and worked to bring about the permanent memorials now scattered about Joe Jackson's hometown, including the Shoeless Joe Jackson Museum, housed in Jackson's final home.

All these people, and thousands more, born generations after Jackson played, who never came closer to the man than the pages of a biography, feel an abiding and genuine kinship with Jackson and his story, and an affection bordering on love. They also feel an almost filial obligation to continue the fight to clear his name. People come to Jackson's museum, stand in the bedroom where he died, and weep; they visit his grave and leave mementos—baseball shoes, baseballs, notes proclaiming belief in his innocence.

The Internet has been a boon to bringing these like-minded people together, of course, but long before there was an Internet to parse every morsel of past and present, Joe Jackson had settled into the American psyche. It started, oddly enough, given that Jackson could neither read nor write, in the pages of literature.

Jackson's obituaries, blended with some other baseball headlines of the era, sparked the imagination of a thirty-seven-year-old Brooklyn native then teaching writing courses at Oregon State University. Searching to find his own voice as a writer, Bernard Malamud had published a small handful of short stories in mostly obscure magazines at the time of Jackson's death, and had written and burned the manuscript for one novel. Malamud would find his voice in *The Natural*, one of the most acclaimed midcentury American novels, and Joe Jackson would be at the protagonist's core. The anecdote that triggers the narrative in *The Natural* is taken from a bizarre episode involving Phillies first baseman Eddie Waitkus, who was shot in the stomach in a Chicago hotel room by an obsessed nineteen-year-old fan named Ruth Ann Steinhagen in the summer of 1949. But in Joe Jackson and Black Betsy, Malamud found the inspiration for Roy Hobbs and Wonderboy. At the start of the book, Hobbs, a nineteen-year-old phenom pitcher on his way to a tryout with the Cubs, gets shot in the stomach in a Chicago hotel room by a crazed woman. He returns fifteen years later, an outfielder now, carrying Wonderboy, the bat he has made from the wood of a tree that had been struck by lightning. Roy and Wonderboy then proceed to take the New York Knights from hapless also-rans to the cusp of a pennant.

Whether Malamud presciently anticipated the way America would come to see Jackson, or whether Roy Hobb's character in some subconscious way helped shape the popular legend of Shoeless Joe, the similarities between Joe Jackson and Roy Hobbs have kept thesis and dissertation writers busy for more than sixty years.

The biographical similarities are undeniable. Offered a bribe to throw a game, Roy first agrees and then reneges. Gus the Bookie is a caricature of Arnold Rothstein, and Judge Banner, the Knights' owner, is an exaggerated amalgam of Charles Comiskey, Ban Johnson, and Judge Landis. Beyond Black Betsy and Wonderboy, there are small things linking Roy and Joe. Roy is hazed and ridiculed when he first joins the Knights. At one point in the story, Roy finds a hairpin on the carpet and puts it in his wallet for luck; collecting hairpins for good luck was a lifelong habit of Jackson's.

Like Jackson, Roy Hobbs is an athlete of transcendent gifts, and a human being of mystery and conflict. He is far from a fully sympathetic character. He behaves badly at many points during the story; he is stubborn, self-centered, and shallow in matters of the heart. And yet Malamud also lets the reader understand that Roy has been forced to bear much in his thirty-four years, and his very presence in the big leagues at the age of thirty-four is a triumph beyond the limits of most men. Roy has publicly stated ambitions of being "the greatest there ever was in the game." He has both the confidence to believe it should happen and the intelligence and fatalism to understand that it probably will not.

Most powerfully, Malamud leaves the story of Roy Hobbs unresolved. Roy's story ends as Joe Jackson's career and life ended: in disgrace not wholly deserved, and in confusion left for the reader to sort out. Readers take whatever Roy Hobbs they want from the story, noble or ignoble, a character of sympathy or scorn, just as they do with the man on whom this fiction was modeled.

Another early popular-culture casting of this mythical, iconic Jackson came from novelist and playwright Douglass Wallop in the 1955 Tony Award–winning Broadway musical *Damn Yankees*, taken from Wallop's 1954 novel, *The Year the Yankees Lost the Pennant*. Wallop's story is a Faustian tale of a middle-aged real-estate salesman named Joe Boyd, transformed into Joe Hardy, an only-in-fantasy-fiction amalgam of Frank Merriwell, Adonis, and Jimmy Stewart's George Bailey. Hardy transforms his hometown Washington Senators from hapless cellar dwellers to American League pennant winners, all while regretting, seemingly with every breath, his bargain with the devil. There was little to overtly connect Joe Hardy to Jackson in the 1954 novel, but in the 1955 play and the film that followed, Hardy—whose made-up past placed his origins in Hannibal, Missouri—became "Shoeless Joe from Hannibal Mo." There was no allegory, no connection to the real Shoeless Joe. Still, it helped to keep Jackson, his eponymous nickname, and the vague sense that he had been the victim of circumstances beyond his control, rattling about in the public consciousness.

Joe Jackson's real comeback came in the 1980s, and began and ended with Canadian novelist W. P. Kinsella. *Shoeless Joe* is a story of family, redemption, love, and the soothing, healing, mythic powers of baseball. Iowa farmer Ray Kinsella hears a voice while standing on his porch one spring evening—"If you build it, he will come"—and knows instantly that he will plow under a part of his cornfield and build a ball field where the ghosts of Jackson and his seven banished mates can return to play the game. Jackson comes, but he is really a minor character in the novel. But he is the linchpin for the story of Ray Kinsella's struggles to keep his farm, and his travels with a surprisingly gregarious J. D. Salinger, one-inning major leaguer Moonlight Graham, and Eddie Scissons, "the oldest living Chicago Cub." All the characters are living with unrealized dreams or unfinished obligations, Ray Kinsella foremost among them. When Ray Kinsella was a boy, Shoeless Joe Jackson was his connection to his father. " 'Twelve hits in an eight-game series. And they suspended him,' Father would cry. Shoeless Joe became a symbol of the powerful over the powerless." Now, the ball field, and Jackson, will connect Kinsella to his father once again. While the plotline may be fantasy, the reader's reaction to the character at the center of all this fantasy is quite real. Just as he provoked powerful feelings in W. P. Kinsella's characters, Shoeless Joe did the same to Kinsella's readers, readers who now took up Ray Kinsella's cause of speaking up for Shoeless Joe.

History, literature, even Broadway, are no match for Hollywood when it comes to seizing America's imagination. Jackson's passage from complicated baseball immortal to American icon was completed in a five-year span during the 1980s, when a trio of films took the Shoeless Joe story from literature classes and Society for American Baseball Research symposia to the water cooler, the front porch, and back onto the front page.

The big-screen version of *The Natural* was first, coming out in 1984 and starting Robert Redford as Roy Hobbs. It was a popular, albeit very ill-reviewed film that eviscerates the power of Malamud's story by delivering up a happy ending. It would seem to be relevant to the evolution of the Jackson story only insofar as it brought a new generation of readers to the book. Or maybe, in making good Hollywood theater, director Barry Levinson also delivered a telling interpretation of an updated American attitude on Joe Jackson. A generation after the complicated-legacy Jackson of the obituaries and the novel, perhaps filmgoers now found Joe Jackson in Roy Hobbs triumphant.

John Sayles's 1988 adaptation of Eliot Asinof's *Eight Men Out* was next. Asinof's 1963 book remains the single most influential telling of the Black Sox story, for it has shaped every telling that has followed. It has also made subsequent retellings of the Black Sox story difficult, for while *Eight Men Out* is confidently presented and highly readable, it is also questionably sourced, and as much a work of imagination as history. Indeed, Asinof made no apologies for seeing and telling the story in dramatic terms, and had originally conceived the project as a screenplay. Sayles's film captures all of the book's charms and flaws. It does take a number of dramatic liberties with the facts, but delivers memorable, true-to-history characters in most roles, and makes a strong case for the innocence—or at least the lack of guilt—of Joe Jackson, and an even stronger case for the innocence of Buck Weaver.

Field of Dreams completes the Joe Jackson saga. Phil Alden Robinson's screen adaptation of Kinsella's novel is a throwback to the Hollywood of yore. It was not crafted with the Oscar voters in mind; it was made for that still considerable segment of the movie-going public that likes a story that makes them smile and their eyes well up at one and the same time. Few modern films play to the emotions as shamelessly and successfully as *Field of Dreams*; it is still making watchers well up twenty-five years after its release. And more than any other work of fiction or nonfiction, it has shaped the contemporary attitude toward Shoeless Joe Jackson.

Never mind that American literature and cinema has not given the American language a phrase as resonant, universal, and enduring as "If you build it, he will come" since "Frankly, my dear, I don't give a damn." How many movie-going Americans take their full understanding of Joe Jackson's life and career from the scene where Kevin Costner, as Ray Kinsella, sits on the tractor with his young daughter on his lap and tells her the story of Shoeless Joe as he plows under his cornfield to build a ball field so that Joe Jackson might again to find the peace he knew only while playing baseball? "Now, he did take their money, but nobody could ever prove he did a single thing to lose those games. I mean, if he's supposed to be throwing it, how do you explain the fact that he hit .375 for the Series and didn't commit one error?" Many came to see Joe Jackson, on field and off, as the film portrayed him—a ballplayer of poise, confidence, and self-satisfaction, but an incomplete human being away from the field, someone whose essence disappears when the subject veers off baseball, just as the ethereal off-field, cinema Joe vanished as he left the field through the corn stalks in center-field. And what did it matter that Ray Liotta's confident, introspective Joe bore little resemblance to the historical Joe? By now, Jackson was anything America wanted him to be.

Field of Dreams made the rehabilitation of Joe Jackson's reputation trendy and chic. And with it came a crusade to win him a place in Cooperstown. At the time of *Field of Dreams*, there was nothing in the Hall of Fame guidelines that would have prevented Joe Jackson from winning election. More immediately, there was nothing in the guidelines that would have prevented Pete Rose from winning election. The time of *Field of Dreams* was also the time of the Pete Rose gambling scandal, the revelations that he had bet on games while managing the Cincinnati Reds in the late eighties. In early 1991, a year and a half after Rose was banished from the game for life by Commissioner A. Bartlett Giamatti, the Hall of Fame adopted a provision stipulating that no one on baseball's permanently ineligible list could be eligible for the Hall of Fame. That meant that now Jackson was not simply excluded from Hall membership; he was prohibited from membership. Until then, his inclusion was technically a matter of simply convincing the right people on the right Veteran's Committee that Jackson belonged. That somehow seemed possible, inevitable even. Now it was more complicated.

A half dozen or more petition drives to have Jackson reinstated began making the rounds in the 1990s. The United States Senate passed three different resolutions calling for Jackson's reinstatement. The petition started by the Philadelphia gas station owner had more than sixty thousand signatures by the time it reached Bud Selig's desk. And somewhere along the line, Ted Williams got involved. Williams once claimed that one of the greatest compliments he'd ever received was when Eddie Collins, Jackson's White Sox teammate and Williams's Red Sox general manager, compared him to Jackson. Williams, of course, had some serious bona fides on matters of righting what he perceived as historical wrongs. He famously used his Hall of Fame induction speech in 1966 to advance the still-evolving civil rights conversation by telling a surprised baseball world that he hoped that one day he would be joined in the Hall by some of the great players from the Negro Leagues. His call became the catalyst for getting the Hall of Fame Veterans Committee to examine, and eventually induct, deserving black players who had been excluded from organized baseball during its long period of segregation.

Now, together with Indians Hall of Famer Bob Feller, Williams endorsed a petition prepared by a Chicago lawyer on behalf of Joe Jackson. "I keep hearing more," Williams said of his support for Jackson's inclusion in the Hall of Fame. "I'm reading books, and there is never once any indication [of Jackson's wrongdoing]. I don't know what you have to do."

The thrust of the argument was that Judge Landis had imposed a sentence of a lifetime ban, and that sentence thus ended at Jackson's death. "Shoeless Joe has fully satisfied the requirements set down by Commissioner Landis," the Williams-endorsed petition read, "and having fully paid his debt, the national game has no further jurisdiction over a deceased player, and makes no further call on Shoeless Joe Jackson."

Major League Baseball has been very cool to the idea of removing Jackson's name from the permanently ineligible list. "I do not wish to play God with history," said Bart Giamatti in response to one of the very early reinstatement petitions. "The Jackson case is now best given to historical analysis and debate as opposed to a present-day review with an eye towards reinstatement."

Bud Selig, who was on the receiving end of most of the pleadings on Jackson's behalf, agreed to review the Jackson case in 1999. "It is a very tragic story and I certainly will try to be objective, as well as fair, in reviewing the entire file," said Selig at the time. Jerome Holtzman was given the task of reviewing the file and preparing a report. Holtzman was a longtime Chicago sportswriter whom Selig had just named official historian for Major League Baseball. He was never a Jackson fan during his newspaper days, and his review of the Jackson file did not change his mind.

And there the matter stalled.

If Joe Jackson does make it to the Hall of Fame one day, he could well owe it to performance-enhancing drugs. At this early moment, the judgment of baseball writers serving as Hall of Fame electors has made it clear that admitted or suspected steroid use will be a bar to Cooperstown. Yet this debate is far from settled. Steroids were not illegal in Major League Baseball until 1991, and nobody was tested for steroids until 2003. So widespread was steroid use during that era that it seems inevitable that when the historical dust settles, some users and suspected users will have gotten in and others will be shut out. Through the years, the various incarnations of the Hall of Fame Veteran's Committee have been very good about going back and scrutinizing overlooked players and eras with the hindsight of history. Should this happen with players from the steroids era, it's not unlikely that baseball will look to the others who were excluded as well—make it something of a Rogues, Rascals, and Rapscallions Committee. There will be the vexing matter of the permanently ineligible list, which the Hall has used as a reason for excluding Pete Rose from its ballot in modern times and for never taking up the matter of Joe Jackson or any of the other Black Sox. But players, owners, and others have been removed from the permanently ineligible list dozens of times through the years—indeed, the only people who seem to be truly permanently on the permanently ineligible list are the Black Sox and Pete Rose. This list is kept at the whim of the commissioner of baseball, so removing Joe Jackson from the list could come one day like a lightning bolt.

Or it could never come at all. And Joe Jackson and the rest of the Black Sox could remain in this peculiar baseball limbo—in the corn stalks, if you will, caught between the baseball fields of our collective memory and the final judgment of history.

Epilogue

Baseball Is Fine

Twice more in the 1920s, the Black Sox found themselves back in the headlines.

In 1922 Buck Weaver, Hap Felsch, Swede Risberg, and Joe Jackson all filed separate suits against the White Sox, claiming their contracts had been wrongfully terminated and that they were owed back pay. The Weaver suit was filed in Chicago; the Felsch, Risberg, and Jackson suits, in Wisconsin, where the White Sox business was incorporated. Only the Jackson case ever came to trial, heard in Milwaukee over two weeks in January and February of 1924. Most of the principals in the Black Sox case either testified or had depositions read into the record, and if the case attracted somewhat less newspaper interest than the criminal trial two and a half years earlier, it was still a front-page story for the length of its run.

Jackson was the trial's most dramatic witness. On direct examination he told the story of having been duped by Harry Grabiner, before the 1920 season, into signing a contract he had been told had excluded the hated ten-day clause, the standard major league provision that allowed a club to terminate a contract for any reason with ten days' notice. Jackson was a persuasive witness, well spoken and sympathetic as he told his story.

On cross-examination, however, the court saw a different witness. For some reason, Jackson denied all that he had said to the Cook County grand jury in September 1920. When White Sox attorney George Hudnall read from the transcript and repeatedly asked: "Were you asked this question and did you give this answer?" Jackson repeatedly answered: "No, Sir, I didn't," or "I didn't make that answer." According to Black Sox–trial historian William Lamb, Jackson denied or repudiated 119 points from his sworn grand jury testimony. It was peculiar, if not bizarre testimony, and it did not sit well with Judge John Gregory, who held his tongue for the moment. However, when the White Sox had completed their case—which included testimony from the Cook County grand jury foreman and stenographer, saying that Jackson had indeed said all that he had just denied—and Gregory had charged and excused the jury, he called Jackson before the bench. "You stand here self-convicted of the crime of perjury," he told him, and ordered bailiffs to arrest him and hold him on $5,000 bail. "When the jury has returned its verdict, I shall have something more to say on this case," Gregory said. While waiting for the verdict the following morning, he told the court: "Either [Jackson's] testimony here or his testimony before the Chicago grand jury was false. I think the false testimony was here."

Jackson was in custody only a few hours before making bail, and was in the courtroom the following morning when the jury returned its verdict. They found for Jackson on all counts, awarding him $16,711.04. Normally, this is the point at which the judge thanks the jury for its service and its verdict. Judge Gregory instead scolded them. "How you could answer some of those questions in the manner you have, the court cannot understand. Jackson stands before this court a convicted perjurer and has been committed to jail. It did not need a court or a jury to determine that. Jackson determined that for himself." Gregory then set aside the jury's verdict on the grounds of fraud and perjury, though Jackson would never stand trial on those perjury charges.

The outcome of the Jackson trial took the starch out of the other three suits. All were plagued by delays and postponements and never came to trial. The Felsch and Risberg suits were eventually settled for pennies on the dollar. The same may have happened with the Weaver case; court records show only that it was terminated in December 1925.

The last Black Sox splash in the headlines came in late 1926, a reverberation of an accusation that might have rivaled the Black Sox Scandal had it unfolded in a different way, or at an earlier time. Ex-Tigers pitcher Dutch Leonard forwarded two letters to Ban Johnson and Judge Landis that seemed to back up Leonard's allegation that back in 1919 Ty Cobb and Tris Speaker had colluded to throw a late-season Tigers-Indians game to Detroit and then made money betting on the Tigers. Particularly damning was a letter from Cobb to Leonard in which he seemingly told of his frustration at the difficulty of getting his bet down before the game. When the Leonard letters were presented to Cobb and Speaker, both men, without admitting guilt, asked if they could resign from their player-manager positions with the Tigers and Indians, without the charges against them being made public. Johnson and Landis acquiesced. But the sudden, unexpected, and unexplained resignations of two of the game's biggest figures set off a predictable newspaper firestorm, and Landis was compelled to provide the backstory to the resignations.

When the story became public, the two men rescinded their resignations and demanded a hearing to clear their names. Speaker denied everything; Cobb admitted to betting on the Tigers but said he played that game and every other game in his entire career to win.

As this story was playing out in the headlines, Swede Risberg decided that this would be a good moment to send Landis a letter detailing the collection the White Sox players had taken back in 1917 in order to reward the Detroit Tigers for dropping a pair of late-season double-headers to the Sox as they battled Boston for the American League pennant. Risberg's letter made clear that a number of the so-called Clean Sox, Eddie Collins and Ray Schalk chief among them, had been eager contributors to the pool. "They pushed Ty Cobb and Tris Speaker out on a piker bet," Risberg said at the time. "I think it's only fair that the 'white lilies' get the same treatment." As soon as the Risberg charges hit the newspapers, Chick Gandil chimed in to affirm the Risberg charges and assert that he could tell of much worse.

Now Landis put the Cobb-Speaker case in abeyance while he dealt once more with Risberg and the Black Sox. He interviewed Risberg in his office on New Year's Day 1927, and five days later had thirty members of the 1917 White Sox and Tigers in his office. By this time both Charles Comiskey and Frank Navin had spoken up, admitting to knowing about the collections but insisting it was not a payoff for the Tigers throwing games but rather a reward for their having beaten the Red Sox late in the season. The players testified to exactly the same thing when they met with Landis, and his ruling supported that argument, calling it a "gift fund" and saying the whole thing was "an act of impropriety, reprehensible and censurable, but not an act of criminality."

Which allowed Landis to return to Cobb and Speaker. Not surprisingly, given his ruling in the Risberg matter, he vindicated the two stars as well. They "have not been, nor are they now, found guilty of fixing a ball game," he said, and they were allowed to rescind their resignations. Neither Detroit nor Cleveland wanted Cobb and Speaker back, however, and they ended up signing with the Athletics and Senators, respectively. By then, for Landis, enough was enough.

"Won't these Goddamn things that happened before I came into baseball ever stop coming up?" he asked a friend, and he then established a five-year statute of limitations on baseball offenses. More than five and a half years after Landis had banned them from the game, the Black Sox had made their final headlines.

Though they would be forever linked in history, the men of the Black Sox scandal lived their lives out separate from one another. They played together in some exhibition baseball games in the years just after their banishment, capitalizing on their infamy. But the 1924 civil trial may have been the last time any of the players were in each other's company. They drifted to every corner of America, made do in a variety of ways, and never stepped out of the shadow of 1919. It was the first line of every obituary.

Arnold Rothstein came to the earliest and surely the most famous end of any of the Black Sox figures. His legend had increased as a result of his presumed involvement in the fix, and the public and skillful way he managed to avoid indictment in the case. Throughout the 1920s he made millions from bootlegging, drug trafficking, and gambling and became one of New York's biggest celebrities, holding court each night from a table at Lindy's, on Broadway just north of Times Square. But it all came to a violent end on a windy, sleet-filled Sunday in November 1928. Rothstein had an early dinner with his mistress and then repaired to Lindy's. Sometime after ten o'clock, he left, alone, for a meeting at the Park Central Hotel on Seventh Avenue, where he was shot in the stomach sometime around 10:30. He lived long enough to talk to police but refused to name his assailant. His killer was probably George "Hump" McManus, a Tammany-connected gambler who was registered in the room where Rothstein was shot, and a man to whom Rothstein owed money that he'd been slow to pay. McManus was charged, but acquitted in a trial that was badly and suspiciously botched by the prosecution. Rothstein was forty-six when he was murdered.

Abe Attell spent his life claiming that Arnold Rothstein pinning the fix rap on him had shamed him and cost him business opportunities and a career as a boxing referee and promoter. But the ex-champ lived a long and comfortable life after the Black Sox. After some lean years in the 1920s and 1930s, he married well in 1939, and, in partnership with his new wife, settled into a career of managing a couple of Manhattan bars, where he told stories and retained much of the glory of a former champ, and little of the infamy of a Black Sox fixer. He was also a regular at the big fight cards at Madison Square Garden. He died in a New Paltz, New York, nursing home in 1970. He was eighty-five.

Nat Evans was never connected to the mysterious "Rachael Brown" of the Black Sox indictment, and he remained an invisible figure throughout the indictments and trial. He worked on as Arnold Rothstein's partner in The Brook, until buying him out in 1925. The Brook, and Saratoga in general, fell upon hard times with the lifting of Prohibition and the onset of the Depression. In November 1934, Evans took out a $117,000 insurance policy on The Brook. When the building burned to the ground less than two months later, the insurance company balked at paying. By that time it mattered little to Evans, who was on his deathbed in a New York City hospital. He died in February 1935.

Joseph "Sport" Sullivan remained as much a mystery after the Black Sox scandal as he was during it. During the 1920s, he lived in the Boston suburb of Sharon and drove his Packard into the city on a daily basis, hanging around Boston newspapers and at Young's Hotel—"Boston's chief center of mild dissipation"—remaining very much in the gambling game. Though he would be an almost daily visitor to different newspapers, he seldom appeared in their pages. Infrequent mentions in Boston papers referred to him as a "well-known betting commissioner" and reported on large wagers on prizefights and World Series games. Ban Johnson spotted him at Yankee Stadium during the seventh game of the 1926 World Series and had him thrown out. By this time, he had been barred from Boston major league parks as well, and by the 1930s he had mostly faded from the public consciousness. He died in Boston in 1949 at the age of seventy-eight.

Sleepy Bill Burns disappeared from public view after the Black Sox trial, and all but disappeared from his family as well. His marriage ended in the late 1920s, and when he died in San Diego in June 1953, at the age of seventy-three, his family had not had contact with him in more than twenty years.

Billy Maharg went back to Philadelphia, where he remained close friends with Grover Cleveland Alexander until Alexander's death in 1930. Maharg worked for twenty-six years as a mechanic at the Ford plant in Chester, Pennsylvania. He never married, and shared a Philadelphia apartment with his younger brother for most of those years. He retired in 1946 to a farm in the then-remote Philadelphia neighborhood of Burholme, where he raised dogs and hunted. He died of a heart attack in Philadelphia in 1953. He was seventy-two and left no survivors.

Hal Chase went home to San Jose after having been cut loose by the Giants in 1919, and played the 1920 season with the hometown Prune Pickers, now a member of the Pacific Coast League. Near the close of the season, at just about the same moment that news of the Series fix was breaking back east, the Pacific

Coast League banned Chase for life for attempting to bribe a pitcher to throw a game. He played and managed in an outlaw league in the Southwest throughout the 1920s, and stayed on in Tucson when he was done playing, working odd jobs and drinking too much. In the mid-1930s he returned to California and lived the last dozen years of his life as a sickly pauper with his sister and brother-in-law, both of whom resented his presence in their lives. He died in 1947 at sixty-four.

Ring Lardner continued as one of America's most prolific and popular short story writers and one of America's most widely read columnists. But he never again wrote a baseball story infused with the joy of the "Busher" tales, and though he continued to cover baseball for the rest of his life, he ceased taking much pleasure in the task. "I had forgotten what terrible things worlds series were so I consented to cover this year's," he wrote in a letter to F. Scott Fitzgerald in 1925. "I got drunk three days before it started in the hope and belief I would be remorseful and sober by the time I had to go to it." His last years plagued by alcoholism and insomnia, he died in 1933 at the age of forty-eight. In 1963 he was named the second winner, after the award's namesake, of the J. G. Taylor Spink Award, baseball journalism's highest honor, which carries with it enshrinement in the writers and broadcasters exhibit in the Baseball Hall of Fame.

Hugh Fullerton never again covered baseball on a daily basis after the Black Sox scandal, partially because, like Lardner and many others in his generation of writers, he felt the game had lost some of its appeal with the advent of the lively ball and the home run in the 1920s. Yet if Fullerton had grown disillusioned with the game, the game had grown disillusioned with him too, and he was made to feel unwelcome by many who believed he had broken some sort of unspoken code by writing his December 1919 stories, that his fealty to the image of the game should have trumped his fealty to his readers and truth. The confessions and indictments in 1920 brought less a vindication than an increase in the discomfort, some who had shunned him in the months after the Series not knowing how to apologize, others feeling he was the person who had brought this all on. He did write of baseball frequently over the next twenty years, for publications such as the *Sporting News* and *Liberty Magazine*, but the writing was far more nostalgia than reporting, and it didn't provide a living. By 1928, he was back in Ohio, where he spent the last seven years of his active career writing general assignment stories for the *Columbus Dispatch*. He died in Florida in 1945 at seventy-two, and was named the third winner of the Spink Award in 1964.

Alfred Austrian was plagued by ulcers through the 1920s and, after surgery in 1930, spent the last year and half of his life a homebound invalid. He died in January 1932, at sixty-one, and even in death he remained in the background.

His passing made the front pages of many of the Chicago newspapers, and his obituary appeared in all of them, but the news was dwarfed by the page-one headlines announcing the death that same day of his longtime client, Cubs owner William Wrigley.

Kenesaw Mountain Landis ruled the game of baseball with the same iron-fisted certitude he showed in his Black Sox ruling until his death at seventy-eight in November 1944. He had been elected to the Hall of Fame earlier that year.

Harry Grabiner stayed with the White Sox for another twenty-five years, effectively serving as the team's chief executive during the final decade of Charles Comiskey's rule and then during the ownership reigns of the Comiskey children, Louis and Grace. He retired after the 1945 season, but soon thereafter went to work for Bill Veeck, Jr., son of the onetime Cubs president, who had just bought the Cleveland Indians. As Indians vice president, Grabiner did for Veeck what he had done so well for the Comiskey family—a little bit of everything. He oversaw the construction of the team that would win the 1948 World Series, but he never got to savor the triumph. He suffered a fainting spell near season's end, which turned out to have been caused by a brain tumor. Grabiner died in a Chicago hospital in late October 1948. He was fifty-seven. While with the Indians, he spoke often of the diary he had kept back in 1919, a diary Veeck would find when he was owner of the White Sox more than a decade later and excerpt at great length in *The Hustler's Handbook* in 1966. To the everlasting frustration of Black Sox students, the diary thereupon once again vanished.

Ban Johnson never accepted Kenesaw Landis's appointment as commissioner. He saw Landis as an interloper from outside baseball, who did not have and would never have his own experience with and sensitivity for the game. He vocally opposed him on every point. If Landis had issued a decree saying baseballs were white, Johnson would have followed with a statement claiming they were black. John Kiernan of the *New York Times*, quoting an unnamed French philosopher, said of Johnson: "All his troubles came because he neglected so many wonderful opportunities to remain silent." Johnson's intransigence began to wear on the American League owners, and when he lambasted Landis for his ruling in the Cobb-Speaker case, they had had their fill. Johnson was forced out as American League president in November 1927. He spent the last years of his life a bitter man, writing as-told-to articles and granting a series of lengthy interviews to friendly writers, resulting in a half-dozen or more multipart articles, all telling his side of the story. In March 1931, he succumbed to diabetes and a host of other afflictions that had been plaguing him for years. He was sixty-seven. Six years after his death, he was part of the second group of men elected to the Hall of Fame.

Charles Comiskey was a sympathetic figure when the scandal broke, and he was loudly applauded when he resolved to rebuild the championship team that had been destroyed. But it never happened. The White Sox were a second division club for the final decade of Comiskey's life, and he swiftly lost interest in running the team, turning over the day-to-day operation of the club to the trusted Grabiner and the ceremonial duties to his son Louis, the team treasurer. The scandal seemed to age him almost overnight. The robust and athletic sixty-year-old from the summer of 1919 was a gaunt, stooped, and frail-looking man at the trial of the players just two summers later. From time to time during the 1920s he would give a newspaper interview, generally to one of the old-time writers who'd enjoyed his largesse and always treated him kindly in turn. Comiskey would talk expansively about the old days with the Browns and the early days of the White Sox, but the interviews are shocking for the absence of even a single mention of 1919. As the decade passed, Comiskey spent more and more of the baseball season at his vacation home in Eagle River, Wisconsin, particularly after the death of his wife in 1922. He died of a heart attack in Eagle River in October 1931; he was seventy-two. He was elected to the Hall of Fame in 1939.

Reds manager Pat Moran and the twenty-four men who played for him in 1919 chafed at being regarded as accidental champions. All went to their graves believing they had won their world championship because they had been the better team on those eight days in October.

Kid Gleason stayed on as manager of the White Sox until the close of the 1923 season, finishing seventh, fifth, and seventh after the team had been torn asunder by the Black Sox. The on-field mediocrity was compounded by off-field mismanagement, owing to the indifference of the broken Comiskey. After he left the White Sox, Gleason stayed away from the game for three years; friends claimed that the Black Sox scandal had broken his spirit too. Connie Mack saw him in 1926, "with the fire gone from his eyes," and persuaded him to come to the Athletics as coach, where he spent the next five seasons as Mack's principal lieutenant. He was slowed by heart disease before the 1932 season and died in January 1933 at age sixty-seven. Following his death, a woman with whom he had eloped forty-seven years earlier, and to whom he had been married for just a year, surfaced and claimed the couple had never been divorced, and that she was therefore entitled to a portion of his modest estate. She demanded a grandfather clock and some jewelry.

Eddie Collins was named player-manager of the White Sox late in the 1924 season, and led them for the next two seasons. He finished above .500 in both 1925 and 1926, but that was good for only fifth place each year, and he was fired as manager and released as a player following the 1926 season. He went back to Philadelphia and spent four seasons as player-coach. In 1933, he told a young Tom Yawkey—Ty Cobb had introduced the two some years before—about an opportunity to buy the Boston Red Sox, and when Yawkey bought the team he brought Collins to Boston as president and general manager. Collins spent the rest of his career with the Red Sox. He was elected to the Hall of Fame together with Charles Comiskey in 1939. He died in Boston in 1951 at sixty-three.

Ray Schalk succeeded Eddie Collins as manager the White Sox in 1927, and lasted a season and a half, never once getting the club out of the second division. He too ran afoul of Charles Comiskey. When he was replaced as manager, Comiskey offered him a job as backup catcher and catching coach, albeit at less than a third of his $25,000 managerial salary. Insulted, Schalk refused. He coached for three seasons with the Giants and Cubs, but never wore a major league uniform after 1931. He managed for a decade in the minors at Buffalo, Indianapolis, and Milwaukee, and then settled into a long career as a part-time college coach, first at Wisconsin, and then for eighteen years at Purdue. He owned a Chicago bowling alley, and served as an active member of Mayor Richard Daley's Youth Commission. He was elected to Hall of Fame in 1955 and died in Chicago in 1970 at seventy-seven.

Dickey Kerr, the most heroic of the Clean Sox, who became something of a folk hero for his two wins in the 1919 World Series, ironically saw his baseball career end with his banishment from the game, not all that long after his teammates had been kicked out. Kerr went 21–9 for the White Sox in 1920, but when he slumped to 19–17 in 1921—the first post–Black Sox year, a season in which the White Sox finished a hapless seventh—Comiskey tried to cut his salary by $500. Kerr refused to sign the contact, declared himself a free agent, and signed with an outlaw league in his native Texas, whereupon Commissioner Landis immediately suspended him permanently from the game. The ban was lifted after three years, and he tried a twelve-game comeback with the White Sox in 1925, going 0–1, with a 5.15 ERA. He then had a long career as a minor league manager and a major league scout, where he had a profound influence on the life of future Hall of Famer Stan Musial. Kerr was managing the Daytona Beach Islanders in 1940 when, one day late in the season, he watched Musial, then his best pitcher, dive for a ball during batting practice and badly damage his pitching shoulder. Kerr told Musial, who had won eighteen games for Daytona that year, that he was a pretty good hitter, and encouraged him to try his hand as a position player if his pitching shoulder didn't heal. A year later, with Musial now the best hitter on the Islanders, Kerr drove Musial and his wife to the hospital on the night their first child was born. The two men remained close friends for the rest of Kerr's life, and when Kerr was out of the game and down on his luck in the late 1950s, Musial bought him a house in Houston. Kerr remained quite bitter toward the game that had turned its back on him, saying, "All baseball ever gave me was the boot." In 1963, he died in the house Musial had bought him. He was sixty-nine.

Joe Jackson was the first of the Black Sox to die, and his passing was in many ways the beginning of a renewed interest in the Black Sox that has continued until this day.

Fred McMullin lived all of his post–White Sox life in Los Angeles. During the 1920s and 1930s, he would religiously show up before local semipro games, in a uniform free of all markings and numbers, and take infield and batting practice. When the games began he would leave, for the LA semipro scene included a good many moonlighting players from organized ball, and the Black Sox were banned from all games involving anyone from organized ball. He worked for a time as a carpenter, and for a time as a film studio handyman. And for the last decade of his life, McMullin, one of baseball's eternal outlaws, worked as a Los Angeles County marshal. He died a day after suffering a stroke in November 1952. He was sixty-one.

Buck Weaver never left Chicago, and never flagged in his efforts to clear his name and get himself reinstated to the game. He first applied for reinstatement just a year after the 1921 criminal trial, hoping, at age thirty-two, to resume his playing career. Twice more he appealed to Judge Landis to no avail. He appealed to new commissioner Happy Chandler following Landis's death, and filed his final appeal thirty-one years after his first, when he was sixty-three and Ford Frick was commissioner, hoping to finally separate himself from the scandal after half a lifetime's worth of effort. In the last years of his life he worked as a clerk in the pari-mutuel section of a couple of different Chicago racetracks. He was on his way to meet his tax preparer in January of 1956 when he suffered a heart attack while walking along 71st Street on Chicago's South Side, some thirty-five blocks from Comiskey Park. He was sixty-five.

Lefty Williams drifted for a time in the 1920s, playing outlaw and semipro ball, sometimes with his brother Black Sox, before returning to Chicago, where he lived for most of the early 1930s in a basement apartment on the North Side, Cubs country. He befriended a young boy who lived in the apartment above his, teaching him to throw a curve. "While his manner was friendly, Lefty never said more than a few words on these occasions," remembered Jack Flagler, who, as J. M. Flagler, would become a correspondent for the *New Yorker* and *Look*.

Sometime after that, Williams and his wife made their way to Laguna Beach, California, where he spent the next twenty-plus years working in the nursery business. He died in November 1959, just a few weeks after the White Sox had played in the World Series for the first time since 1919. He was sixty-six.

Happy Felsch was welcomed back into the bosom of the Milwaukee neighborhood where he lived his whole life. He played semipro ball in Milwaukee and elsewhere in the upper Midwest through the 1920s and early 1930s and supported himself by working in construction and running a neighborhood tavern. He was the only one of the banished players ever to speak to an author working on a Black Sox book, when he spoke to Eliot Asinof in the early 1960s. Taking a cue from Harry Reutlinger, the Chicago reporter who'd plied a confession out of Felsch with the help of a bottle of scotch, Asinof showed up on Felsch's door with a bottle of scotch. But the interview added little to the Black Sox story; Asinof got less from Felsch than Reutlinger had forty years earlier. Felsch died in Milwaukee in August 1964 at seventy-three.

Eddie Cicotte spent twenty-four years working for the Ford Motor Company in Detroit, and, following his retirement from Ford, raised strawberries on the Livonia, Michigan, farm whose mortgage he had paid off with the $10,000 he had received for his part in the fix. He followed baseball for the rest of his life—"it gets in your blood, you know. Nothing can make you forget it." But he kept a very low public profile and, after his grand jury testimony, never again spoke in specifics about what had happened or why. Whenever the occasional sportswriter would find him and manage to coax a few words from him, he never tried to deny or rationalize his part in the fix, and said only that he was trying to live his life with the honor that had abandoned him in 1919. "I admit I did wrong," he said. "I've tried to make up for it by living as clean a life as I could. I'm proud of the way I've lived, and I think my family is too. . . . I've tried to be a good father, a good grandfather, and now—thank God—a good great-grandfather." He lived to see his brother's grandson pitch in the major leagues in the late 1950s and early 1960s. When Al Cicotte broke in with the Yankees in 1957, Eddie said: "I'll do anything I can to help Al. . . . But I'll be cheering for him, not the Yankees. My heart is still in Chicago." When Eliot Asinof reached out to him in 1961, requesting an interview for *Eight Men Out*, Cicotte returned the letter, with his terse handwritten reply across the top: "I'm not interested. Thanks for remembering me. Ed Cicotte." He died in Detroit in May 1969 at eighty-four.

Chick Gandil may have lived the most unburdened life of any of the guilty players. He was the first of the Black Sox to vanish from the public eye, choosing not to sign with the White Sox in 1920, and while he played semipro ball in the years immediately following the fix, he spent most of the next three decades working as a plumber, first in Los Angeles and then in Oakland, California. In 1956 he collaborated with Los Angeles writer Melvin Durslag on a tell-all article for *Sports Illustrated*. It is a wholly unsatisfying piece, heavy on melodrama, self-serving to a fault, written with a dispassionate distance from the events, reading, in fact, like the words of a man who wasn't even there. Gandil retired to a home in Calistoga, California, in the Napa Valley, shortly after the *Sports Illustrated* article appeared, and died there in December 1970 at the age of eighty-two. The obituaries in the local papers listed him only as a retired plumber, which was how his neighbors knew him. It was three months before the baseball press learned that the Napa Valley plumber was the Black Sox mastermind.

Swede Risberg was the last surviving member of the Black Sox. He died on October 13, 1975, his eighty-first birthday. He barnstormed throughout the Midwest, playing ball through the 1920s and early 1930s, but always returned to the family farm in Rochester, Minnesota, during the winter, where he and his father-in-law sold eggs to the Mayo Clinic. He relocated his family to far-northern California in the late 1930s, where he operated a string of roadhouses, eventually owning one called Risberg's in the late 1940s and 1950s. As with many of his fellow banished, the game of baseball remained central to his life. He never talked much to his two sons about his baseball past, but he taught them both the game, and watched his younger son play for Chico State. And he watched and listened to radio and television games every chance he got. "He still loved baseball, you know," said his older son, Bob. "There were a few people in baseball and a few judges around that he didn't like, but he loved the game of baseball. You know, baseball didn't throw him out of baseball. Landis did, and so there was nothing wrong with baseball. Baseball is fine."

Sources and Acknowledgments

Adding to the intrigue and mystery of the Black Sox story is the fact that so much of the historical record is missing. There is no complete transcript from the players' 1921 criminal trial. In the surviving papers of Judge Kenesaw Mountain Landis at the Chicago History Museum, there are few documents relating to his work as baseball commissioner and none at all relating to his work on the Black Sox. There are no Charles Comiskey papers, and those papers that survive from Comiskey's attorney, Alfred Austrian, and from his longtime nemesis, Ban Johnson, are frustratingly incomplete. Harry Grabiner's diary from the weeks immediately following the 1919 World Series and from talks a year later to bring Commissioner Landis into the game—excerpted at great length in Bill Veeck's *The Hustler's Handbook* in 1965—has disappeared. And while the nation's newspapers provided voluminous coverage of every stage of the Black Sox story, those 1919–1921 reporters were far more stenographers than investigators.

But despite those holes, a rich Black Sox record survives. The two most important archives are the collections of Black Sox papers at the Baseball Hall of Fame in Cooperstown and at the Chicago History Museum.

The archive in Cooperstown comes from papers of Ban Johnson. They primarily detail his work in aiding the investigation of the Cook County state's attorney in the months leading up to the 1921 criminal trial of the Black Sox players and the indicted gamblers. Access to these files is controlled by Major League Baseball, and I thank Tom Ostertag of the Major League Baseball legal department for granting permission to consult and quote from them.

The Giamatti Research Center at the Hall of Fame also holds the papers of Garry Herrmann, Cincinnati Reds president and longtime chairman of the National Commission, invaluable for understanding the work of that body in early years of the modern game. The exhaustive clipping and photo files at the Giamatti Research Center are indispensable to the telling of any piece of baseball history, and, as the source notes reveal, I benefitted immeasurably from those as well.

I want to thank Jim Gates, the librarian at the Hall of Fame, for both his professional assistance and his friendship. I am also indebted to Jim's staff, which included Freddy Berowski and Tim Wiles when I began my research and Cassidy Lent and Matt Rothenberg when I concluded it.

The Black Sox archive at the Chicago History Museum is a relatively recent addition to the Black Sox conversation, and a most valuable one. Purchased at auction in 2008 from an anonymous seller, the two cartons of papers were once part of the files of Alfred Austrian, attorney for Charles Comiskey and, as these documents reveal, a central player in the attempts to cover up the suspicions of crookedness in the 1919 World Series. To the archivists and librarians who facilitated my passage through those documents, and to the many others whose names I never knew who helped me at the Chicago, New York, and Boston public libraries, I offer a heartfelt thank you.

The idea for this book first came from Timothy Bent, my editor at Oxford University Press. For his idea, and for his confidence in my ability to execute it, I am deeply grateful. He gave every page of my manuscript careful and thoughtful attention—a rarity in modern publishing—and it is a much-improved story for his clear eye. This is the second book I've had the privilege of writing for Tim, and I am hopeful there will be more to come. Tim's assistant Alyssa O'Connell and production editor Joellyn Ausanka oversaw the transformation of a completed manuscript into a finished book, and I thank them both for their skill and patience in that task. Copy editor Ben Sadock called my attention to countless awkward turns of phrase, misspellings, and mixed metaphors, and tightened and brightened the manuscript with great care and even greater sensitivity. Responding to his edits was like having a sustained and altogether delightful conversation on the challenges, joys, and discipline of writing.

At Northeastern University, I'd like to thank my colleagues for their interest and encouragement in my work, especially Bill Kirtz, Link McKie, and the late

Stephen Burgard. As ever, I want to thank my students, who keep me young and alive and engaged in life, and never realize that they have a greater effect on my life than I do on theirs.

Finally, and most importantly, I want to thank my wife, Cathy, whose presence in my life reminds me every day of what a good life it is.

Charles Fountain
Cambridge, Massachusetts
April 14, 2015

Source Notes

Abbreviations

AAH	August A. Herrmann
BBJ	Bryon Bancroft Johnson
BSP	Black Sox Papers (there are collections at both the Chicago History Museum and the Giamatti Research Center at the Baseball Hall of Fame)
CAC	Charles A. Comiskey
CHM	Chicago History Museum
GRC	Giamatti Research Center, Baseball Hall of Fame
NYT	*New York Times*
Trib	*Chicago Tribune*
TSN	*The Sporting News*

Introduction

1 Hotel Buckminster meeting—Arnold (Chick) Gandil, as told to Melvin Durslag, "This Is My Story of the Black Sox," *Sports Illustrated*, Sept. 17, 1956; Asinof, *Eight Men Out*, 6–9. Gandil's account of the meeting is a simple statement that it occurred. Asinof's, unsourced, is replete with detail, color, and dialogue. It is exactly the sort of passage that makes Asinof's book so compelling as story and so suspect as history.

1 Burns meetings with Gandil and Cicotte—"Burns Reveals Shame; Gives Cicotte Boast," *Trib*, July 20, 1920.

2 Cicotte grand jury testimony—BSP, box 1, folder 2, CHM.

2 Cicotte confession to Comiskey—BSP, box 1, folder 2, CHM.

2 Cicotte approaches Weaver—Veeck, *Hustler's Handbook*, 284.

2 Rothstein, Weegham, Mont Tennes—Pietrusza, *Rothstein*, 154.

3 Nearly went on strike—Asinof, *Eight Men Out*, 16–18.

3 Petitions the National Commission—AAH papers, box 91, folder 7, GRC.

5 Indictment charges—website of the Cook County Clerk of the Circuit Court, http://www.cookcountyclerkofcourt.org/?section=RecArchivePage&RecArchivePage=black_sox.

10 Throwing games in Cubs-White Sox series—Seymour, *Golden Age*, 281–83; Ginsburg, *Fix Is In*, 70–74.

10 "Why should I have won?"—Seymour, *Golden Age*, 281.

10 "I am not a saint."—ibid., 282; Ginsburg, *Fix Is In*, 72.

11 "weakest effort ever"—Seymour, *Golden Age*, 282.

11 Locke letter to Herrmann—Ginsburg, *Fix Is In*, 73.

Chapter 1

12 "honorable Joes"—Arnold (Chick) Gandil, as told to Melvin Durslag, "This Is My Story of the Black Sox," *Sports Illustrated*, Sept. 17, 1956.

12–13 William Wansley/New York Mutual game fixing—Ginsburg, *Fix Is In*, 6–8.

13 "could not throw game all by himself"—ibid., 22.

13 All-rogue team—ibid., 30.

14 "hippodroming has prevailed"—ibid., 19.

14 "respectable, honorable and profitable"—ibid., 40.

14 Louisville Grays scandal—ibid., 37–51; Seymour and Mills, *Early Years*, 86–88.

14 Diamond stickpins—Seymour and Mills, *Early Years*, 87.

15 "hereby declared forfeited"—Ginsburg, *Fix Is In*, 47.

15 Devlin letter—Seymour and Mills, *Early Years*, 87.

15 "damn you, you have sold a game"—ibid., 88.

18 Baseball pools, "gamblers reservation"; "MAKE YOUR BETS"—Seymour and Mills, *Golden Age*, 278–80.

19 1903 World Series fix rumors—Stout and Johnson, *Red Sox Century*, 35–44.

20 McGraw's betting—Deford, *Old Ball Game*, 117.

20 "disgusted at their unwillingness"—ibid.

20 "sousepaw"—Seymour, *Golden Age*, 105.

21 Fogel accused Waddell—ibid., 305.

21 Fogel banished—ibid., 30–31; also see AAH papers, box 123, folder 7, GRC.

21 "Here's $2,500"—Ginsburg, *Fix Is In*, 75.

Chapter 2

23 Throwing games in sagebrush league—S. L. A. Marshall, "An Amoral Man," undated clipping Hal Chase file, GRC. (The columnist in this story, "Slam" Marshal, would later, as Col. S. L. A. Marshal, become one of the leading historians of World War II, first as an officer in the Army's history division during the war, then afterward as the author of books for a general audience.)

24 "completely and congenitally amoral"—ibid.

24 "made all other men appear mechanically imperfect"—ibid.

24 F. C. Lane quote on Chase—"A Half Hour with Hal Chase," *Baseball Magazine*, June 1912, Hal Chase file, GRC.

25 Civil engineering—ibid.

25 Santa Clara has no record—Dewey and Acocella, *Black Prince of Baseball*, 9; Kohout, *Hal Chase*, 13–14.

25 "one of the game's immortals"—Frederick Lieb, "Prince Hal Chase...Dies in California"—*TSN*, May 28, 1947, Chase file, GRC.

25 "might hit one of those dopes"—Frank Graham, "The Greatest First Baseman." *TSN*, May 28, 1947, Chase file, GRC.

25 *Sporting Life* quote—untitled clipping, *Sporting Life*, June 6, 1906, Chase file, GRC.

26 Chase and Lajoie—Frank Graham, "The Greatest First Baseman." *TSN*, May 28, 1947, Chase file, GRC.

26 "at first base, there was only one Chase"—ibid.

26 Clark Griffith quote—Shirley Povich, "This Morning," *Washington Post*, May 20, 1947, Chase file, GRC.

26 Moonlighting with semipros—"Chase in Trouble," publication unknown, Sept. 8, 1906, Chase file, GRC.

26–27 Playing in California State League, 1907—Dewey and Acocella, *Black Prince of Baseball*, 74; Kohout, *Hal Chase*, 60–64.

27 California State League, 1908—Dewey and Acocella, *Black Prince of Baseball*, 93–95.

27 Reinstated—ibid., 101.

27 "How could anyone say that Hal Chase caused trouble"—Kohout, *Hal Chase*, 65.

28 *NYT* suggestion of game fixing—ibid., 50.

28 Joe Vila, "cowardly knockers"—ibid., 60.

28–29 Chase and Stallings—Dewey and Acocella, *Black Prince of Baseball*, 137–40.

29 Johnson's hatred of Stallings—ibid., 102.

30 "CHASE TO THE FRONT"; "CHASE BLAZES"—ibid, 136.

30 "wouldn't trade for Ty Cobb"—ibid., 178.

31 "throwing games on me"—Lieb, *Baseball as I Have Known It*, 98.

32 Jennings on Hal Chase—"Jennings Gives Hal Chase a Grilling," publication unknown, Mar. 23, 1916, Chase file, GRC.

32 Harry Sinclair paying Chase contract—"Hal Chase Probably Will Remain Idle," undated clipping, Chase file, GRC.

33 "archetype of all crooked ballplayers"—Seymour, *Golden Age*, 288.

33 Groh, Neale, and Magee approach Mathewson—Kohout, *Hal Chase*, 197.

33 twenty-seven games—ibid., 200.

33 "what are the odds"—ibid., 197.

33 Mathewson quote—ibid., 194.

34 "other players…glad he is out of lineup"; "letting easy rollers…go past"— ibid.

34 "if that testimony warrants [Chase's] expulsion"—Garry Herrmann to John Heydler, Oct. 10, 1918, box 68, AAH papers, GRC.

34 "I'm accused of"—Kohout, *Hal Chase*, 196.

34 Pol Perritt—ibid., 197.

35 Evidence against Chase—ibid., 198.

35 Chase leaking details to newspapers—ibid., 206.

36 "Ring made statements differing from…affidavit"—John Heydler to August Herrmann, Feb. 5, 1919, Chase file, GRC.

36 "clique that had it in"—"The Case of Hal Chase," *The Reach Official American League Guide, 1919*, Chase file, GRC.

36 "In justice to Chase"—John Heydler, "Findings in the Matt of Charges against Player Hal Chase," Chase file, GRC.

36–37 "To have found Chase guilty…would have been impossible"—Heydler to Herrmann, John Heydler to August Herrmann, Feb. 5, 1919, Chase file, GRC.

37 McGraw had assurances from Chase and Mathewson—Kohout, *Hal Chase*, 215.

37 Chase and Mathewson not speaking—Robinson, *Matty*, 197.

37–38 Zimmerman implicated Chase—Charles C. Alexander, *John McGraw* (Viking, 1988), cited in Kohout, *Hal Chase*, 224.

38 Heydler gets proof—Lieb, *Baseball as I Have Known It*, 102. Lieb is one of the game's iconic writers, and his reporting has generally held up well under the scrutiny of history. On the same page where he tells of Heydler finally getting proof on Chase, however, he also reports that Chase was then suspended from the Giants. That much, at least, is not correct.

38 Chase was sick—Kohout, *Hal Chase*, 226.

Chapter 3

39 154 of 531 in service—survey of major league teams conducted by National Commission, Sept. 1918, box 113, folder 6, AAH papers, GRC.

40 Pregame military drill—Seymour, *Golden Age*, 247.

41–44 Betting in Boston ballparks—this entire section is taken from detective reports, newspaper clippings, and correspondence between Ban Johnson, GH, John Tener, and Walter Hapgood, July–Sept. 1917, box 113, folder 8, AAH papers, GRC.

44 No more than three or four players left—"National League has Few Players Above Draft Age," *Pittsburgh Post*, undated clipping, box 112, folder 26, AAH papers, GRC.

44 Johnson call for draft exemptions—"Players of Quality are Needed," publication unknown, undated clipping, box 112, folder 26, AAH papers, GRC.

45 John Tener's response—Fred Lieb, "Tener Wants No Draft Favoritism," publication unknown, undated clipping, box 112, folder 26, AAH papers, GRC.

45 Baker and Ruppert quotes—ibid.

45 Lieb criticism—Lieb, "Fans Continue to Criticize Johnson," publication unknown, undated clipping, box 112, folder 26, AAH papers, GRC.

45 Johnson backing off remarks—Lieb, "Tener Wants No Favoritism."

45–46 Baseball's case for work-or-fight exemption—GH to Gen. E. H. Crowder, June 15, 1918, box 112, folder 31, AAH papers, GRC.

46 Harding suggests going directly to president—Warren G. Harding to GH, June 21, 1918, box 113, folder 1, AAH papers, GRC.

46 Angered Johnson—Johnson to GH, July 2, 1918, box 113, folder 1, AAH papers, GRC.

47 Permission to play World Series—E. H. Crowder to GH, Aug. 27, 1918, box 112, folder 27, AAH papers, GRC.

48 Aug. 3 meeting in Cleveland—Harry P. Edwards, "Club Owners let Ban Johnson Know He No Longer Can Rule League as Dictator," publication unknown, undated clipping, box 112, folder 2, AAH papers, GRC.

48 "If the club owners wish to take a chance"—ibid.

48–49 Comiskey et al. statement on Johnson—ibid.

49 Babe Ruth's shipyard contract—Montville, *Big Bam*, 73.

49 Remington Arms recruiting letter—Remington Arms Co. to Cincinnati National League Baseball club, July 30, 1918, box 112, folder 3, AAH papers, GRC.

50 Joe Jackson joining shipyard team—Gropman, *Say It Ain't So, Joe*, 148.

50 *Chicago Tribune* on Jackson—ibid.

50 "fighting blood" of the Jacksons—Frommer, *Shoeless Joe and Ragtime Baseball*, 81.

51 "no room for jumpers"—ibid., 82.

51 "attention has already been called"—National Commission to Newton D. Baker, Aug. 1918, box 112, folder 2, AAH papers, GRC.

52 deposition—BSP, box 1, folder 2, CHM.

52 Grabiner diary on Gene Packard—Veeck, *Hustler's Handbook*, 296.

53 Johnson drunk—Murdock, *Ban Johnson*, 165; Seymour, *Golden Age*, 254; Deveney, *Original Curse*, 189–90.

53 1918 attendance—Seymour, *Golden Age*, 253.

53 1918 Series shares—ibid., 255.

53 Players refusing to play—Deveney, *Original Curse*, 189–90.

53–54 Johnson puts arm around Hooper—"what do you think the public will think"—Murdock, *Ban Johnson*, 165.

54 No World Series medals presented—National Commission to "Members of Contesting Teams in the 1918 World Series," Nov. 4, 1918, box 112, folder 28, AAH papers, GRC.

54 Newspaper discussions about geographical leagues—F. C. Lane to GH, "A Plan to Maintain Professional Baseball in 1919 Upon a Major or Near Major Plane," draft of article for *Baseball Magazine*, Sept. 19, 1918, box 112, folder 27, AAH papers, GRC; untitled, undated clipping, *Brooklyn Standard Union*, box 112, folder 29, AAH papers, GRC.

55 "the AEF takes its own time"—Fountain, *Sportswriter*, 156.

55 "distinguishing...gold from dross"—I. E. Sanborn, "Self Interest Reacting on Club Moguls," *Trib*, undated clipping, box 112, folder 3, AAH papers, GRC.

55 "altogether too much aloofness, suspicion"—"Too Much Suspicion among Owners—Heydler," publication unknown, Nov. 26, 1918, box 112, folder 28, AAH papers, GRC.

56 "wholesome effect of a clean and honest game"—I. E. Sanborn, "Chief of Staff Removes Ban on National Game," *Trib*, undated clipping, box 112, folder 28, AAH papers, GRC.

Chapter 4

57–58 Comiskey and the press—Axelson, *Commy*, 309–10.

58 "best-liked magnate"—*New York Journal*, Feb. 26, 1915, GRC.

58 "great believer"—John Kiernan, "Charles Comiskey, The Old Roman" *NYT*, undated clipping, Comiskey file, GRC.

58 "in every sphere"—"Sam Crane Writes of fifty Greatest Ball Players," undated clipping, Comiskey file, GRC.

58 "baseball genius"—undated clipping, Comiskey file, GRC.

58 "One way or another"—Damon Runyon, "Charles Comiskey Not a Piker," publication unknown, Aug. 21, 1915, Comiskey file, GRC.

58 "King of them all"—*Philadelphia Public Ledger*, Aug. 29, 1915, Comiskey file, GRC.

59 Attendance figures—"1910–19 Ballpark Attendance Figures," http://www .ballparksofbaseball.com/1910-19attendance.htm.

59 Comiskey and his father—G. W. Axelson, *Commy*, 10–16.

60 "der boss president"—"Chris von der Ahe," http://www.baseball-reference .com/bullpen/Chris_von_der_Ahe.

61 "what should I have done?"—Murdock, *Ban Johnson*, 15.

61 "mint, hops and rye"—ibid.

62 "great leaders in baseball"—ibid., 22.

69 World tour—Axelson, *Commy*, 219–62.

Chapter 5

72 Gandil-Speaker fight—Gay, *Tris Speaker*, 280; Ross Tenny, "White Sox Lose Every Game since Tris Trimmed Gandil," *Cleveland Press*, June 3, 1919, Gandil file, GRC.

72 Crusinberry quote—Ed Sherman, "A Start Like No Other," *Trib*, May 13, 2005, available online at http://articles.chicagotribune.com/2005-05-13/sports/0505130263_1_kid-gleason-eddie-cicotte-dickie-kerr.

73 leaving home in boxcar—various clippings, Gandil file, GRC; Daniel Ginsburg, "Chick Gandil," SABR Baseball Biography Project, http://sabr.org/bioproj/person/945ce343.

73 "suited me just fine"—Arnold (Chick) Gandil, as told to Melvin Durslag, "This Is My Story of the Black Sox," *Sports Illustrated*, Sept. 17, 1956.

73 charged with stealing $225—Daniel Ginsburg, "Chick Gandil," SABR Baseball Biography Project, http://sabr.org/bioproj/person/945ce343.

73 quarreled over cigarettes—"Cigarette Was Real Cause of Gandil Coming," *Cleveland News*, Mar. 12, 1916, Gandil file, GRC.

73 "Get Your Seats for '17 Series"—Daniel Ginsburg, "Chick Gandil," SABR Baseball Biography Project, http://sabr.org/bioproj/person/945ce343.

74 collecting money to pay the Tigers—various clippings, Gandil file, GRC.

74 "pretty soft games"—ibid.

74–75 Collins and Gandil not speaking—Collins quoted by Joe Williams, "Black Sox Team Was Best, So Claims Eddie Collins," *New York World-Telegram*, June 29, 1936. Black Sox file, GRC.

75 "none too popular"—Ross Tenny, "White Sox Lose Every Game since Tris Trimmed Gandil," *Cleveland Press*, June 3, 1919, Gandil file, GRC.

75 "He was the whole works of it"—Joe Jackson grand jury testimony, Sept. 28, 1920CHM, box 1, folder 2, BSP, CHM.

75 Sport Sullivan background—"Not Enough Evidence," *Boston Globe*, July 24, 1907.

75 Gandil-Sullivan meeting in Boston—Arnold (Chick) Gandil, as told to Melvin Durslag, "This Is My Story of the Black Sox," *Sports Illustrated*, Sept. 17, 1956.

77 "talking with his priest"—Carney, *Burying the Black Sox*, 118.

77 "They ain't a smarter pitcher"—Yardley, *Ring*, 38.

77 "clear from these final four Jack Keefe stories"—Ring Lardner Jr., "Foul Ball," *American Film*, July–Aug. 1988, Black Sox file, GRC.

78 "we were not getting a devil of a lot of money"—synopsis of testimony given by Edward W. Cicotte before the grand jury of Cook County on Sept. 28, 1920, box 1, folder 2, BSP, CHM.

79 Gandil recruiting Williams—Claude Williams grand jury testimony, Sept. 29, 1920, box 1, folder 2, BSP, CHM.

79 Gandil recruiting Jackson—Jackson grand jury testimony, http://www .baseball-almanac.com/articles/joejackson.shtml

79 "When they let me in"—*Chicago American*, Sept. 30, 1920.

80 "meet one or two at time"; "throw the Series"—Jackson grand jury testimony.

80–83 Information on Arnold Rothstein not otherwise cited comes from David Pietrusza, *Rothstein*.

80–81 shooting three cops—Pietrusza, *Rothstein*, 140–46.

81 Rothstein carried $100,000—ibid., 4.

82 Betting on horses—ibid., 106–7, 118–21.

82 Rothstein physical description taken from Arnold Rothstein autopsy report, quoted in Nick Tosches, "A Jazz Age Autopsy," *Vanity Fair*, May 2005.

82 "A. R. fenced millions," Pietrusza, *Rothstein*, 4.

83 Carl Zork—ibid., 160.

83 christened him "Sleepy"—"Sleepy Bill Burns Caught Napping in Series Sellout," *TSN*, Oct. 21, 1920. Burns file, GRC.

84 Burns meeting with Cicotte and Gandil—Bill Burns criminal trial testimony, July 19, 1921, reported in *NYT*, July 20, 1921.

84 Maharg background—Bill Lamb, "Billy Maharg," SABR Baseball Biography Project, http://sabr.org/bioproj/person/60bd890e.

85 Cicotte and Gandil offer to throw Series for $100,000—Burns trial testimony, July 19, 1921, *NYT*, July 20, 1921.

85 Rothstein refuses to meet with Burns and Maharg—Pietrusza, *Rothstein*, 153.

85 Evans background—ibid., 95.

86 Rothstein, Burns, Maharg dinner at Hotel Astor—ibid., 153–54.

87 Sullivan and Brown—see William F. Lamb, "A Black Sox Mystery: The Identity of Defendant Rachael Brown," May 26, 2010, Black Sox file, GRC.

87 "try to put over this deal"—Claude Williams grand jury testimony, Sept. 29, 1920, box 1, folder 2, BSP, CHM.

87 Offered $5,000—ibid.

88 "isn't enough...to do a dirty trick"—ibid.

88 "whatever [we] do is all right with Mr. Jackson"—ibid.

89 "just as easy...to miss a ball as...catch it"—*Chicago American*, Sept. 30, 1920.

89 Williams, Felsch, and Weaver talk about how to throw games—Claude Williams grand jury testimony, Sept. 29, 1920, box 1, folder 2, BSP, CHM.

89 Cicotte finds money under pillow—synopsis of grand jury testimony given by Edward Cicotte, box 1, folder 2, BSP, CHM.

Chapter 6

90 Trouble getting money down on Reds—"Tell How Players Made Gamblers Lose," *NYT*, July 21, 1921.

91 Betting odds drop—"Gothamites Dig Up Some Bets on Reds," *NYT*, Oct. 1, 1919.

91 Players at the race track—"Gleasons Back Winning Ponies on Latonia Card," *Trib*, Oct. 1, 1919.

91–92 Meeting in Hotel Sinton Room 708; "clear out of the Cincinnati park"— "Burns Tells of Plot to Throw World Series," *NYT*, July 20, 1921.

92 Hugh Fullerton hearing rumors—Fullerton, "As I Recall," *TSN*, Oct. 17, 1935.

93 "Damn them!...They have it coming"—ibid.

93 Only two newspapers printed warming about rumors—ibid.

94 Bunting and banners, work holiday—"Ruether to Oppose Cicotte in Opener," *NYT*, Oct. 1, 1919.

94 Band played "I'm Forever Blowing Bubbles"—"Red Rout White Sox in Opening Game," *NYT*, Oct. 2, 1919.

95 Fullerton goes to Comiskey, Johnson and Dreyfuss—Hugh Fullerton, "As I Recall," *TSN*, Oct. 17, 1935.

95–96 Attell claiming hit batsman was signal—Joe Williams, "An Echo of 1919 Sell Out, One of the Fixers Speaks," *New York World-Telegram*, Apr. 10, 1934, Black Sox file, GRC.

96–97 "Do you think Cicotte is right?"—"Hitting Power of Reds Will Carry Team to Victory—Matty," *NYT*, Oct. 2, 1919.

98 rumors like a fog—Fountain, *Sportswriter*, 172.

98–99 "keep the Reds in there hitting until darkness fell"—Lardner., *Ring around the Bases*, 590.

99 "What was wrong?"—Yardley, *Ring*, 214.

99 Cicotte's headache after game one—synopsis of testimony of Edward W. Cicotte, box 1, folder 2, BSP, CHM.

99 "I'm forever blowing ballgames"—Yardley, *Ring*, 214–15; Fountain, *Sportswriter*, 174.

99 "get down a little wager on the Reds"—Yardley, *Ring*, 214.

100 Odds now 7–10 on Cincinnati—"Reds Now 7–10 Betting Favorites," *NYT*, Oct. 2, 1919.

100 "biggest and littlest man"—Jonathan Dunkle, "Lefty Williams," SABR Baseball Biography Project, http://sabr.org/bioproj/person/0998b35f.

Chapter 7

105 "red bows, badges, plumes"—"Plenty of Enthusiasm, but Less Noise, While Chicago Scores Its Victory," *NYT*, Oct. 4, 1919.

108 Mathewson and Evers—Damon Runyon, "Jimmy Ring is New Hero of Ball Series," *Chicago Herald and Examiner*, Oct. 5, 1919.

108 Gandil giving Williams $10,000—Claude Williams grand jury testimony, Sept. 29, 1920, box 1, folder 2, BSP, CHM.

109   "that's all we have got"—ibid.

109   "Gandil is not on the square with us"—Jackson grand jury testimony, Sept. 28, 1919.

109   Jackson tells wife—ibid.

113–114   Threat on Lefty Williams—Asinof, *Eight Men Out*, 117.

114   Asinof concedes inventing Harry F.—Carney, *Burying the Black Sox*, p. 205.

114   "the biggest first inning you ever saw"—Hugh Fullerton, "Is Big League Baseball Being Run for Gamblers, with Players In on the Deal?," *New York World*, Dec. 15, 1919.

114   "sacrifice accuracy for sake of a story"—*Dictionary of Literary Biography*, Hugh Fullerton, http://www.bookrags.com/biography/hugh-fullerton-dlb/#gsc.tab=0.

120   Attell won $30,000—Abe Attell, "The Truth behind the World Series Fix," *Cavalier Magazine*, Oct. 1961.

120   Won $300,000—Pietrusza, *Rothstein*, 160.

Chapter 8

122   Gleason seething; "There are seven boys"—Asinof, *Eight Men Out*, 123.

122   "last game that will be played in any World Series"—Hugh Fullerton *Chicago Herald and Examiner*, Oct. 10, 1919.

122–123   Grabiner diary entries—Veeck, *Hustler's Handbook*, 261–62.

124–125   Alfred Austrian background from Austrian obituaries, *Chicago American*, *Trib*, *Chicago Daily News*, *Chicago Herald and Examiner*, *Chicago Evening Post*, *NYT*, Jan. 26–27, 1932.

126   "always a scandal of some kind"—*New York Tribune*, Oct. 16, 1919.

126   Gleason talks to Redmon; Redmon and Gedeon visit Comiskey—Veeck, *Hustler's Handbook*, 261–62.

127   Veeck theory on reward—ibid., 276–77.

127-137 All information regarding the reports of the Hunter detective agency comes from reports written to Alfred Austrian, Harry Grabiner, or Charles Comiskey, Nov. 16, 1919–Jan. 29, 1924, box 1, folder 1, BSP, CHM.

133 "didn't bet a penny with anybody in my life"—Claude Williams, grand jury testimony, Sept. 29, 1920, box 1, folder x, BSP, CHM.

Chapter 9

138 "morally certain"—Hugh Fullerton, "As I Recall," *TSN*, Oct. 17, 1935.

138 Fullerton and 1906 World Series—Yardley, *Ring*, 69.

139 "take a large Faber lead pencil"—Tom Nawrocki, "Hugh Fullerton," *Dictionary of Literary Biography*, http://www.bookrags.com/biography/hugh-fullerton-dlb/.

139 Sharing press box seat with actor—ibid.

139 Finding Ring Lardner Chicago job—Yardley, *Ring*, 70–71.

139 "one of the few baseball writers who can 'pan'"—Tom Nawrocki, "Hugh Fullerton," *Dictionary of Literary Biography*, http://www.bookrags.com/biography/hugh-fullerton-dlb/.

140 *New York World* story—"Is Big League Baseball Being Run for Gamblers, with Players In on the Deal?," *New York World*, Dec. 15, 1919.

143 "Instead of implications that the baseball authorities are attempting to cover up"—"Calling Mr. Fullerton," *TSN*, Nov. 20, 1919.

143 "If a man knows so little about baseball"—"Editorial Comment," *Baseball Magazine*, Dec. 1919.

143 "greeted with a giddy screed from the facile pen of Hugh Fullerton"—"Editorial Comment," *Baseball Magazine*, Feb. 1920.

145 "becomes a peril when his judgment grows warped"—"Irving Sanborn a Baseball Educator," *Baseball Magazine*, Mar. 1920.

145 Assassination attempt—Carney, *Burying the Black Sox*, 84–85.

146 Bert Collyer background—"Death Takes Bert Collyer," *Miami Daily News*, July 29, 1938, available online at http://news.google.com/newspapers?nid=2206&dat=19380729&id=wwYtAAAAIBAJ&sjid=dtQFAAAAIBAJ&pg=5064,6652909.

146 Klein called Eddie Collins a friend—"Collins Charges 1920 Games Fixed," *Collyer's Eye*, Oct. 20, 1920, BSP, GRC.

147 "INVOLVE 7 IN WORLD'S SERIES SCANDAL," *Collyer's Eye*, Oct. 18, 1919, available online at http://www.blackbetsy.com/imagefarm/collyers-eye/collyers_1919_oct18_p1.jpg.

147 "sufficient data to warrant investigation"—*Collyer's Eye*, Oct. 25, 1919.

147 "To a subordinate of mine"—ibid.

148 South Side poolroom site of payoff—*Collyer's Eye*, Nov. 15, 1919.

148 Schalk, Williams, Risberg fight—*Collyer's Eye*, Oct. 25, 1919.

149 "[National] Commission is cognizant as to its duty"—"Promise Action against Gamblers," *TSN*, Jan. 15, 1920.

149 "generally accredited with being on the team payroll"—*Collyer's Eye*, Oct. 18, 1919.

149 Lee Magee case—various correspondence, clippings, and legal documents. Magee file, Aug. Herrmann papers, GRC.

150 Abe Attell confesses to Kid Gleason—James Crusinberry, "A Newsman's Biggest Story," *Sports Illustrated*, Sept. 15, 1956.

150 Crusinberry's editors feared libel suits—Yardley, *Ring*, 215.

150 "My interest in the national game died a sudden death"—ibid., 216.

151 Cubs-Phillies games of Aug. 31—"President Veeck Gives Out Details on Alleged Game," *NYT*, Sept. 5, 1920.

151 Writers asked to look into Cubs-Phillies—"Scribes Will Go into 'Fixed Game' Charges on Request of Cubs," *Trib*, Sept. 6, 1920.

152 McDonald meets with Ban Johnson—Murdock, *Ban Johnson*, 190–91.

152 McDonald quotes re grand jury—"A New Friend on High," *TSN*, Sept. 16, 1920.

152 *Tribune* publishes open letter—*Trib*, Sept. 19, 1920.

153–154 Grand jury stories Sept. 22–29—various Chicago and New York newspapers, Sept. 23–30, 1920; also *TSN*, Sept. 23, 1920.

154–157 Maharg-Isaminger story—*Philadelphia North American*, Sept. 28–Oct. 1, 1920.

Chapter 10

158 Talk of sending Gleason to testify—Hartley Replogle testimony, 1921 criminal trial, box 1 folder 2, BSP, CHM.

159 Austrian remembered the conversation naming Cicotte—Alfred Austrian testimony, 1924 civil trial, box 1, folder 4, BSP, CHM.

159 Kid Gleason background—Dan Lindner, "Kid Gleason," SABR Baseball Biography Project, http://sabr.org/bioproj/person/632ed912.

160–161 Cicotte's meeting in Austrian's office—Cicotte, Replogle testimony, 1921 criminal trial,box 1 folder 4, BSP, CHM.

163–166 Jackson's meeting in Austrian's office—Jackson testimony, 1921 criminal trial, box 1, folder 4, BSP, CHM.

166 Attack on Herzog—Carney, *Burying the Black Sox*, 128.

170 McDonald's surprise at Williams's salary—McDonald testimony, 1921 criminal trial, box 1, folder 2, BSP, CHM.

170–171 "if he comes in and helps the state"—Williams testimony, 1921 criminal trial, box 1, folder 2, BSP, CHM.

171 Reutlinger background—"The Press: War Horse to Pasture," *Time*, May 2, 1960; "Harry F. Reutlinger Dies at 66," *NYT*, Nov. 21, 1962.

172 Mother Frances Cabrini—John R. Schmidt, "The Story of Chicago's Saint," *Chicago History Today*, WBEZ, Nov. 14, 2011, available online at http://www.wbez.org/blog/john-r-schmidt/2011-11-14/story-chicagos-saint-mother-frances-xavier-cabrini-93855.

172 "Who's the dumbest"—"The Press: War Horse to Pasture," *Time*, May 2, 1960.

174 Gandil—"Chick Gandil, in Hospital, Calls Charges 'Bunk,'" *Trib*, Sept. 29, 1920.

174 Weaver—"Weaver, Felsch Deny They Took Part in 'Frame,'" *Trib*, Sept. 29, 1920.

174 "left the ballpark with his head down,"—I. E. Sanborn, "Loyal Sox Idle," *Trib*, Sept. 29, 1920.

174–175 Party at Eddie Collins house—"Shadow Lifted, 'Square Guys' of Sox Celebrate," *Trib*, Sept. 29, 1920.

Chapter 11

176 Frazee not the kind of man he wanted in baseball—minutes of American League board of directors meeting, Dec. 10, 1919, box 2, folder 4, BSP, CHM.

176–177 Carl Mays—Seymour, *Golden Age*, 264–72.

177 "Insurrectos"—Murdock, *Ban Johnson*, 171–77.

177 Comiskey, Ruppert, Frazee Board of Directors' meetings—BSP, box 2, folders 1–4, CHM.

178 Lasker background—Gunther, *Taken at the Flood*; "The Personal Reminiscences of Albert Lasker," undated magazine clipping, box 2, folder, 4, BSP, CHM.

179 Possible commissioner candidates—Seymour, *Golden Age*, 312.

179 "Andrew Jackson three years dead"—Pietrusza, *Judge and Jury*, 122.

179–181 Landis biography—ibid., chapters 1–2.

181 Rockefeller case—ibid., chapter 4.

181 "will be dead a long time"—ibid., 67.

182 "Have you any children?"—ibid., 104.

182 Wobblies trial—ibid., chapter 9.

183 "take the attitude of the people of Detroit"—ibid., 73.

184–185 Federal League trial—ibid., chapter 11.

184 "not that we prevent them from finding young ballplayers"—ibid., 155.

186 Austrian talks to Landis—Austrian to Jacob Ruppert, Jan. 19, 1920, box 2, folder 5, BSP, CHM.

187 "a chairman...satisfactory to Johnson"—Austrian to Ruppert, Sept. 22, 1920, box 2, folder 5, BSP, CHM.

188 Meeting of Sept. 29 "refusal to recognize such American League clubs"— Veeck, *Hustler's Handbook*, 279–80.

188 "best cleanser"—Pietrusza, *Judge and Jury*, 167.

189 Austrian and Lasker speak to Landis—Veeck, *Hustler's Handbook*, 282.

189 Austrian approach by Hays—Veeck, *Hustler's Handbook*, 287.

190 Nov. 8 meeting at Congress Hotel—ibid., 289–90; Pietrusza, *Judge and Jury*, 166.

191 Landis speaks to reporter—Pietrusza, *Judge and Jury*, 166–67.

191 "If my two boys wanted to fight"—ibid., 167.

192 "see no necessity for having three commissioners"—ibid., 168.

192 Grabiner on single commissioner—Veeck, *Hustler's Handbook*, 291–292.

192 "Johnson made his final mistake"—ibid., 292.

Chapter 12

195 "not pleasant to be…a 'social outcast'"—Pietrusza, *Rothstein*, 176–77.

195 William Fallon background—Fowler, *Great Mouthpiece*.

195 "Go to Chicago"—Pietrusza, *Rothstein*, 180.

195 "What kind of country is this?"—ibid., 183.

196 Austrian and Hoyne statements on Rothstein's involvement—ibid., 184.

196 Rothstein's friendship with grand jurors—ibid.

196 Fallon and Abe Attell—ibid., 184–86.

197 "no doubt 1919 World Series was crooked"—Lamb, *Black Sox in the Courtroom*, 41.

197 Hoyne's statements on indictments and whether a crime had been committed—"Not Sure of Crime in Baseball Plot," *NYT*, Sept. 30, 1921.

197 McDonald, Austrian and Bingham reaction to Hoyne—"Baseball Inquiry Will Go to End, Says Judge," *NYT*, Oct. 1, 1921.

197 Hoyne takes possession of grand jury documents—Lamb, *Black Sox in the Courtroom*, 66–67.

198–199 Rothstein and Fallon involvement in stolen grand jury documents—James R. Price to Ban Johnson, undated letter, box 1, folder 14, BSP, GRC. Price was relating a story he had heard from Joe Vila of the *Sun*, who had learned it from Boothby and other sources.

199 Missing documents had little impact—Lamb, *Black Sox in the Courtroom*, 119. Lamb, a former prosecutor and the keenest student of the legal pieces of the Black Sox story, makes clear that from an evidentiary perspective, the missing documents would have been easily and legally reconstructed from the court stenographer's shorthand and from the testimony of grand jury members.

200 Barrett's $15,000 salary—BBJ to Phil Ball, Mar. 7, 1921, box 1, folder 5, BSP, GRC.

200 "someone has taken active charge"—ibid.

200 "build some fires"—BBJ to Frank Navin, Apr. 5, 1921, box 1, folder 6, BSP, GRC.

200 Avoided old acquaintances, "cannot see how a detective"—Navin to BBJ, Apr. 6, 1921, box 1, folder 6, BSP, GRC.

201 Maharg's search for Burns—"Mystery Man in Sox Case Tells of Hunt for Burns," *Chicago Daily News*, July 24, 1921.

201 "not a talkative man"—BBJ to James Price, June 7, 1921, box 1, folder 8, BSP, GRC.

201 "staying in a climate agreeable to health"—Mrs. Bill Burns to BBJ, May 24, 1921, box 1, folder 7, BSP, GRC.

202 "how Big Bill ever captured her"—BBJ to Maharg, May 28, 1921, box 1, folder 7, BSP, GRC.

202 "do not think it would be wise to publish"—BBJ to James Isaminger, May 27, 1921, box 1, folder 7, BSP, GRC.

202 "as soon as he is in our possession I will have no objection"—ibid.

202 "I appreciate immensely the good service you have rendered"—BBJ to Maharg, June 7, 1921, box 1, folder 8, BSP, GRC.

203 Burns and Maharg staying in Michigan and Milwaukee under assumed names—various documents, box 1, folder 10, BSP, GRC.

203 "the expenditure...of whatever further sum of money"—document in BSP, box 1, folder 19, GRC.

203–204 Johnson-Grabiner letters; "would have been better to have had state's attorney office"—BSP, box 1, folder 10, GRC.

204 "one less man in the penitentiary"—Lamb, *Black Sox in the Courtroom*, 98.

204 "let 'em extradite me"—ibid., 82.

205 Johnson secures affidavit on Zork's health—BBJ to J. G. Taylor Spink, June 23, 1921, box 1, folder 9, BSP, GRC.

205 Hugo Friend background—*University of Chicago Magazine* 13–14 (1920), available online at http://books.google.com/books?id=wjrOAAAAMAAJ&pg=PA177&lpg=PA177&dq=judge+hugo+friend&source=bl&ots=m_BibBSWCM&sig=Mcdhvr8FDqDP1jLnsORDZxwty9o&hl=en&sa=X&ei=4x23U6etIo2PyATnwoF4&ved=0CD8Q6AEwCA#v=onepage&q=judge%20hugo%20friend&f=false.

205–206 Background on prosecutors and defense attorneys—Lamb, *Black Sox in the Courtroom*, 102–4.

206 Official temperature at 94 degrees—"Hottest in Years," *Chicago Daily News*, July 19, 1921.

207–208 Comiskey and Short exchange—"Comiskey Rages at Trial of Sox," *Trib*; "Came Near Blows at Baseball Trial," *NYT*, both July 19, 1921.

207 Burns was rakishly dressed—various newspaper accounts, July 19–22, 1921.

207 Borrowed money to have clothes made—BBJ to George Barrett, May 17, 1921, box 1 folder 7, BSP, GRC.

207–208 Burns testimony—*Trib*, *NYT*, *Chicago Daily News*, *Boston Globe*, July 21–23, 1921.

208 "Do you think you are even with the boys now?"—"Burns Says Players Made First Offer," *NYT*, July 22, 1921.

208 Peaches Graham—"Two Men Go Free in Baseball Case," *NYT*, July 28, 1921.

209 Cicotte, Jackson Williams testimony on confessions—criminal trial record, 561–692, BSP, CHM.

209 "Mr. Blank, Mr. Blank, Mr. Blank"—Lamb, *Black Sox in the Courtroom*, 126.

209 "I charge that Arnold Rothstein…paid $10,000"—"Confessions Enter Trial of White Sox," *NYT*, July 26, 1921.

210 "I doubt if I would allow a verdict of guilty"—"Two Men Go Free in Baseball Case," *NYT*, July 28, 1921.

210 Defense case—"Defense Rests Case in Baseball Trial," *NYT*, July 29, 1921.

211 "evidence shows a swindle and a con game has been worked"—ibid.

211 "state's attorneys have no more control...than a bat boy"—Lamb, *Black Sox in the Courtroom*, 140.

211 "whose machinations of years finally have been successful"—"Says State Tried to Make 'Goats' of Penny-Ante Gamblers," *Boston Globe*, Aug. 2, 1921.

211 "More power...than the Russian Czar"—ibid.

211 "these underpaid ballplayers, these penny-ante gamblers"—ibid.

211 O'Brien charges Johnson protecting Rothstein—Lamb, *Black Sox in the Courtroom*, 139.

212 "galley slaves of a modern Rome"—"Players Acquitted at Baseball Trial," *Boston Globe,* Aug. 3, 1921.

212 "all they saw was a con game"—Lamb, *Black Sox in the Courtroom*, 140.

212 Friend charge to jury—"All Black Sox Acquitted in Single Ballot," *Trib*, Aug. 3, 1921.

213 Courtroom scene after verdict—"White Sox Players Acquitted by Chicago Jury," *NYT*, Aug. 3, 1921; "All Black Sox Acquitted in Single Ballot," *Trib*, Aug. 3, 1921.

213 "I knew you'd do it"—"All Black Sox Acquitted in Single Ballot," *Trib*, Aug. 3, 1921.

213 "Talk, did you say?"—ibid.

213 "Regardless of the verdict of juries"—multiple newspapers, Aug. 4, 1921.

Chapter 13

218 "Jackson looked extremely good"—Gropman, *Say It Ain't So, Joe*, 45.

219 Drinking from finger bowl; made him feel as bad as he ever felt—Gropman, *Say It Ain't So, Joe*, 52.

219–220 Milk cans—Frommer, *Shoeless Joe and Ragtime Baseball*, 22; Gropman, *Say It Ain't So, Joe*, 57.

220 "print the legend"—John Ford, dir., *The Man Who Shot Liberty Valence*, Paramount Pictures, 1962.

221 Indians finances in receivership—*NYT*, Aug. 21, 1915.

221 Jackson sold to White Sox—ibid; also Larry Schwartz, "'Shoeless' Joe Jackson Traded to White Sox," ESPN.com, November 19, 2003, http://espn.go.com/classic/s/moment010820-shoeless-joe-dealt.html.

222 Vaudeville show put strain on marriage—Gropman, *Say It Ain't So, Joe*, 130–31.

222 "blessed with a good banker"—Joe Jackson, as told to Furman Bisher, "This is the Truth," *Sport*, Oct. 1949.

225 "used my brain to become great hitter"—Arthur Daley, "The Shoeless One," *NYT*, Dec. 10, 1951.

226 "What have you got in Greenville"—interview, Arlene Marcley, Greenville, SC, June 5, 2014.

227 Stand in his bedroom and weep—ibid.

227 Leaving items at his grave—Marc Fisher, "At the Shoeless Joe Jackson Museum, It Ain't So," *Washington Post*, undated clipping, Jackson file, GRC.

228 "the greatest there ever was"—Malamud, *The Natural*, 114.

231 Ted Williams quote—Rick Regan, "Williams Hits for 'Shoeless Joe,'" CBSNews.com, Jan. 30, 1998, http://www.cbsnews.com/news/williams-hits-for-shoeless-joe/.

231 "Shoeless Joe has fully satisfied"—ibid.

231 Bart Giamatti quote—"Giamatti Says No to Shoeless Joe," undated Associated Press clipping, Jackson file, GRC.

Epilogue

233 Civil Trial—Lamb, *Black Sox in the Courtroom*, 149–89.

234 "No, Sir, I didn't"—ibid., 172.

234 "self-convicted of the crime of perjury"—ibid., 187.

234 "I think the false testimony was here"—ibid.

234 "Jackson stands...a convicted perjurer"—ibid., 190.

234-235 Cobb-Speaker, Risberg stories—Seymour, *Golden Age*, 382–86.

236 "Won't these Goddamn things...ever stop coming up?"—ibid., 385.

236 Arnold Rothstein—Pietrusza, *Rothstein*, 284–315.

236-237 Abe Attell—Abe Attell, "The Truth behind the Fix," *Cavalier Magazine*, Oct. 1961; "Abe Attell Dies, boxing Champion," *NYT*, Feb. 7, 1970.

237 Nat Evans—Pietrusza, *Rothstein*, 135, 362.

237 Sport Sullivan—detective report to BBJ, Apr. 28, 1921, box 1, folder 15, BSP, GRC.

237 Burns—C. B. Burns to Lee Allen, Baseball Hall of Fame, Feb. 20, 1961, Burns file, GRC.

237 Billy Maharg—Bill Lamb, "Billy Maharg," SABR Baseball Biography Project, http://sabr.org/bioproj/person/60bd890e.

237-238 Hal Chase—Lynn Bevell, "Prince Hall and His Arizona Odyssey," undated clipping, Chase file, GRC.

238 Resented his presence—Dewey and Acocella, *Black Prince of Baseball*, 401–8.

238 Ring Lardner—Fountain, *Sportswriter*, 180.

238 Hugh Fullerton—various clippings, Fullerton file, GRC.

238-239 Alfred Austrian—various obituaries, Chicago papers, Jan. 26–27, 1932.

239 Harry Grabiner—"Harry Grabiner, Baseball Executive," *NYT*, Oct. 25, 1948.

239 Ban Johnson saw Landis as interloper—Earl Obenshain, "Landis High Handed Actions Forced War with Ban Johnson," *Marietta Sunday Times*, Jan. 27, 1929, Johnson file, GRC.

239 "neglected...opportunities to remain silent"—John Kieran, "Sports of the Times," undated clipping, Johnson file, GRC; various other clippings, Johnson file, GRC.

240 Charles Comiskey—various clippings, Comiskey file, GRC.

240 Kid Gleason—Dan Lindner, "Kid Gleason," SABR Baseball Biography Project, http://sabr.org/bioproj/person/632ed912; "Many Tributes Paid to Kid Gleason for Courage and Devotion to Game," Gleason file, GRC.

241 Eddie Collins—Paul Mittermeyer, "Eddie Collins," SABR Baseball Biography Project, http://sabr.org/bioproj/person/c480756d; Bob Broeg, "Quick Thinking Eddie Collins, Infielder Who Could Do it All," *TSN*, Aug. 10, 1969; Collins file, GRC.

241 Ray Schalk—various clippings, Schalk file, GRC.

241 Dickie Kerr—various clippings, Kerr file, GRC.

241 Fred McMullin—Shav Glick, "He's a Rose by Another Name," *Los Angeles Times*, Jan. 21. 2004; McMullin file, GRC; "Fred McMullin Dies at 61," *TSN*, Nov. 21, 1952; Jacob Pomrenke, "Fred McMullin," SABR Baseball Biography Project, http://sabr.org/bioproj/person/7d8be958; various other clippings, McMullin file, GRC.

241 Buck Weaver—Stein, *Ginger Kid*; various clippings, Weaver file, GRC.

242–243 Lefty Williams—J. M. Flagler, "Requiem for a Southpaw," *New Yorker*, Dec. 5, 1959; "Claude Williams is Dead at 66," *NYT*, Nov. 7, 1959; Jonathan Dunkle, "Lefty Williams," SABR Baseball Biography Project, http://sabr.org/bioproj/person/0998b35f.

243 Hap Felsch—various clippings, Felsch file, GRC.

243 Cicotte—various clipping, Cicotte file, GRC, particularly Joe Falls, "Cicotte, 46 Years Later," undated 1965 clipping, *Detroit Free Press*.

243 "I'm not interested"—letter in Eliot Asinof papers, CHM.

243–244 Gandil—"Chick Gandil, 82, Threw '19 Series," publication unknown, Feb. 26, 1971; Arnold (Chick) Gandil, as told to Melvin Durslag, "This is My Story of the Black Sox Series," *Sports Illustrated*, Sept. 26, 1956; both stories, Gandil file, GRC.

244 Swede Risberg—ESPN interviews with Gerald and Bob Risberg, transcripts in Risberg file, GRC.

Selected Bibliography

Alexander, Charles C. *Ty Cobb*. Southern Methodist University Press, 1984.

Algren, Nelson. *Chicago: City on the Make*. University of Chicago Press, 1979.

Asinof, Eliot. *Bleeding between the Lines*. Holt, Rinehart & Winston, 1979.

Asinof, Eliot. *Eight Men Out*. Holt, Rinehart & Winston, 1963.

Asinof, Eliot. *1919 America's Loss of Innocence*. Donald I. Fine, 1990.

Axelson, Gustaf W. *Commy: The Life Story of Charles A. Comiskey*. Reilly & Lee, 1919.

Boyd, Brendon. *Blue Ruin: A Novel of the 1919 World Series*. Norton, 1991.

Brown, Warren. *The Chicago White Sox*. Kent State University Press, 2007.

Carney, Gene. *Burying the Black Sox: How Baseball's Cover-Up of the 1919 World Series Fix Almost Succeeded*. Potomac, 2006.

Cook, William. *The 1919 World Series: What Really Happened*. McFarland, 2001.

Deford, Frank. *The Old Ball Game: How John McGraw, Christy Mathewson, and the New York Giants Created Modern Baseball*. Grove, 2005.

Dellinger, Susan. *Red Legs and Black Sox: Edd Roush and the Untold Story of the 1919 World Series*. Clerisy, 2006.

Deveney, Sean. *The Original Curse: Did the Cubs Throw the 1918 World Series to Babe Ruth's Red Sox and Incite the Black Sox Scandal?* McGraw-Hill, 2010.

Dewey, Donal, and Nicholas Acocella. *The Black Prince of Baseball: Hall Chase and the Mythology of the Game*. Sport Classic Books, 2004.

Dickson, Paul. *Bill Veeck: Baseball's Greatest Maverick*. Walker, 2012.

Farrell, James T. *My Baseball Diary*. Southern Illinois University Press, 1998.

Fountain, Charles. *Sportswriter: The Life and Times of Grantland Rice*. Oxford University Press, 1993.

Fowler, Gene. *The Great Mouthpiece: The Life of William J. Fallon*. Blue Ribbon, 1931.

Frommer, Harvey. *Shoeless Joe and Ragtime Baseball*. Taylor, 1992.

Gay, Timothy. *Tris Speaker: The Rough and Tumble Life of a Baseball Legend*. Globe Pequot, 2007.

Ginsburg, Daniel E. *The Fix Is In: A History of Baseball Gambling and Game Fixing Scandals*. McFarland, 1995.

Gropman, Donald. *Say It Ain't So, Joe: The True Story of Shoeless Joe Jackson*. Citadel, 2001.

Gunther, John. *Taken at the Flood: The Story of Albert D. Lasker*. Harper, 1960.

Holtzman, Jerome. *No Cheering in the Press Box*. Holt, Rinehart & Winston, 1973.

Kinsella, W. P. *Shoeless Joe*. Mariner, 1983.

Kohout, Martin Donell. *Hal Chase: The Defiant Life and Turbulent Times of Baseball's Biggest Crook*. McFarland, 2001.

Lamb, William F. *Black Sox in the Courtroom: the Grand Jury, Criminal Trial and Civil Litigation*. McFarland, 2013.

Lardner, Ring. *Lardner on Baseball*, edited by Jeff Silverman. Lyons, 2002.

Lardner, Ring. *Ring around the Bases: The Complete Baseball Stories of Ring Lardner*. Scribner's, 1992.

Lardner, Ring. *You Know Me, Al*. Scribner's, 1960.

Lardner, Ring, Jr. *The Lardners: My Family Remembered*. Harper & Row, 1976.

Lieb, Fred. *Baseball as I Have Known It*. University of Nebraska Press, 1996.

Luhrs, Victor. *The Great Baseball Mystery: The 1919 World Series*. A. S. Barnes, 1966.

Mack, Connie. *My 66 Years in the Big Leagues*. Amereon House, 1960.

Malamud, Bernard. *The Natural*. Farrar, Straus & Giroux, 1952.

Masters, Edgar Lee. *The Tale of Chicago*. G. P. Putnam's Sons, 1933.

Montville, Leigh. *The Big Bam: The Life and Times of Babe Ruth*. Doubleday, 2006.

Murdock, Eugene C. *Ban Johnson, Czar of Baseball*. Greenwood, 1982.

Nathan, Daniel A. *Saying It's So: A Cultural History of the Black Sox Scandal*. University of Illinois Press, 2003.

Pacyga, Dominic A. *Chicago: A Biography*. University of Chicago Press, 2009.

Pietrusza, David. *Judge and Jury: The Life and Times of Judge Kenesaw Mountain Landis*. Diamond, 1998.

Pietrusza, David. *Rothstein: The Life, Times and Murder of the Criminal Genius Who Fixed the 1919 World Series*. Carroll & Graf, 2003.

Rice, Grantland. *The Tumult and the Shouting*. A. S. Barnes, 1954.

Ritter, Lawrence S. *The Glory of Their Times*. Macmillan, 1966.

Robinson, Ray. *Matty: An American Hero*. Oxford University Press, 1993.

Seymour, Harold, and Dorothy Seymour Mills. *Baseball: The Early Years*. Oxford University Press, 1960.

Seymour, Harold, and Dorothy Seymour Mills. *Baseball: The Golden Age*. Oxford University Press, 1971.

Stein, Harry. *Hoopla*. St. Martin's, 1983.

Stein, Irving M. *The Ginger Kid: The Buck Weaver Story*. Brown & Benchmark, 1992.

Stout, Glenn and Richard Johnson. *Red Sox Century*. Houghton Miflin, 2000.

Veeck, Bill. *The Hustler's Handbook*. With Ed Linn. Ivan R. Dee, 1965.

Veeck, Bill. *Veeck as in Wreck*. With Ed Linn. G. P. Putnam's Sons, 1962.

Wallop, Douglass. *The Year the Yankees Lost the Pennant*. Norton, 1954.

Yardley, Jonathan. *Ring: A Biography of Ring Lardner*. Random House, 1977.

Index

Gandil, Chick (*continued*)
  payout following game four and, 108–9
  player relationships with, 74–75
  recruitment for scandal by, 79, 80
  scandal origins and, 1–2, 78
  as scandal's central figure, 75
  Speaker fight with, 72–73
  statistics on, 73–74
  Sullivan and, 75–76
  Warner Hotel meeting and, 87–88
  Williams, Lefty, and, 170, 171
Gedeon, Joe, 123, 126–27
Giamatti, A. Bartlett, 7, 231
Gleason, William "Kid," 123, 150, 210
  anger of, 121–22
  background about, 159–60
  Burns and, 103
  Collins, Eddie, and, 160
  confronting players, 111
  final years of, 240
  meetings in Austrian's office, 158–59, 160,
    161, 163, 164
  1919 World Series, 5th game, and, 110–11
  Schalk and, 102
  silence of, 159
Gorman, George, 200, 212
  on Attell, 204
  background about, 205
Gowdy, Hank, 41
Grabiner, Harry, 52, 122–23, 127
  final years of, 239
  Johnson, Ban, and, 203–4
  sole commissioner and, 192
Graham, George "Peaches," 208–9
Grand Jury of Cook County investigation
  Cicotte and, 163
  Comiskey and, 153, 186–87
  Crowe delay tactics and, 199
  files stolen in, 198–99
  first day of, 152–53
  Hoyne takes files of, 197–98
  indictments and, 197
  indictments handed down by, 194
  Jackson, Joe, and, 165–66

  Johnson, Ban, and, 153, 186–87
  McDonald heading, 152
  Rothstein avoiding, 194–95, 196
  second day of, 153–54
  Williams, Lefty, and, 170–71
The Great Gatsby (Fitzgerald), 81
Gregory, John, 234
Gresham, Walter, 180–81
Griffith, Clark, 73, 190
Guys and Dolls (Runyon), 81

Haldeman, John, 14
Hall, George, 14, 15
Hall of Fame. *See* Cleveland Indians Hall of
    Fame; National Baseball Hall of Fame
Hanna, Bill, 114
Hapgood, Walter, 43
Harding, Warren G., 47, 189–90
Hart, James
  Johnson, Ban, and, 63
  Taylor and, 10–11
Haughton, Percy, 43
Hays, Will, 189–90
Hendrix, Claude, 151
Herrmann, August A. (Garry), 10, 22, 34, 35
  background of, 65
  Johnson, Ban, and, 65–66
  National Commission and, 65–66, 179
  resignation of, 179
  sole commissioner and, 192
  work-or-fight order and, 47
Herzog, Buck, 153
  stabbing of, 166
Heydler, John, 34, 36–37, 38, 55, 153
  Comiskey and, 102–3
  Johnson, Ban, and, 103
  Magee and, 149–50
Highlanders, 27–28
hippodroming, 13–14
Hobbs, Roy (fictional character), 227–28
Holmes, Ducky, 69
Holtzman, Jerome, 232
honorable Joes, 12
Hotel Buckminster, 1